Medici Gardens

PENN STUDIES
IN LANDSCAPE ARCHITECTURE

SERIES EDITOR
John Dixon Hunt

This series is dedicated to the study and promotion
of a wide variety of approaches to landscape
architecture, with special emphasis on connections
between theory and practice. It includes
monographs on key topics in history and theory,
descriptions of projects by both established
and rising designers, translations of major
foreign-language texts, anthologies of theoretical
and historical writings on classic issues, and critical
writing by members of the profession of landscape
architecture.

The series was the recipient of the Award of Honor
in Communications from the American Society of
Landscape Architects, 2006.

Medici Gardens

From Making to Design

Raffaella Fabiani Giannetto

PENN

UNIVERSITY OF PENNSYLVANIA PRESS

PHILADELPHIA

Published with the assistance of the Getty Foundation.

Published by
University of Pennsylvania Press
Philadelphia, Pennsylvania 19104-4112

Printed in the United States of America on acid-free paper
10 9 8 7 6 5 4 3 2 1

Library of Congress Cataloging-in-Publication Data

Giannetto, Raffaella Fabiani.
    Medici gardens : from making to design / Raffaella Fabiani Giannetto.
       p. cm. — (Penn studies in landscape architecture)
    Includes bibliographical references and index.
    ISBN-13: 978-0-8122-4072-6 (hardcover : alk. paper)
    ISBN-10: 0-8122-4072-3 (hardcover : alk. paper)
       1. Gardens—Italy—Florence—History—15th century.   2. Gardens—Italy—
Tuscany—History—15th century.   3. Medici, House of.   4. Gardens in art.
I. Title.
    SB466.I82F5652   2008
    712'.60945511—dc22   2007042566

For my parents

CONTENTS

APPENDIX B
Metric Letter by Alessandro Braccesi 189

PREFACE

This book examines the nature of the early Renaissance Medici gardens on the outskirts of Florence. In particular, it is an inquiry into the human intentions and motivations that guided the construction and cultivation of gardens, orchards, and kitchen gardens within the Medici properties of Trebbio, Cafaggiolo, Careggi, and Fiesole (fig. 1).

Recently it has been argued that the role of these properties within the history of the Florentine villa in the early Renaissance has been much overemphasized, in that this tiny sample is often considered representative of fifteenth-century Florence. (Amanda Rhoda Lillie's *Florentine Villas in the Fifteenth Century: An Architectural and Social History* [2005] is an example of this argument.) This consideration is all the more accurate if one takes into account that among the studies on these villas, the few that address their gardens tend to portray them not only as typical of early Renaissance Florence but also as the prototypes of the *giardino all'italiana*. Writings on the most popular of the Florentine gardens tend to reiterate information that is often taken for granted, and accepted without reservation. Therefore, the history of the Medici gardens deserves to be addressed, although only those that were built and/or renovated in the early Renaissance will be reviewed here.

This book takes as its starting point the understanding that garden history lies as much in the history of the gardens as it does in historiography itself. And the writing of history is the reflection not only of an author's cultural and professional background but also, like the gardens themselves, of the times in which it occurs. It can be influenced, for example, by ideologies and strategic rhetoric. The very definition of the Italian garden style occurred at one of those moments in which history merged with historiography in the service of centralized authority. In fact, the history of the Italian garden that many foreign expatriates wrote during their sojourn in Florence toward the end of the nineteenth century was rewritten in the first half of the following

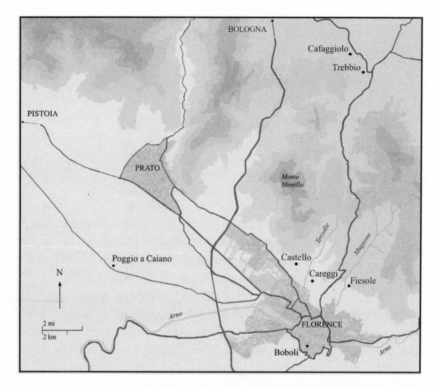

Fig. 1. Medici villas on the outskirts of Florence.

century according to the demands of fascist leaders, and it was inevitably tainted by political propaganda. The Medici villas, in particular, offer an example of the way gardens were reinterpreted to define a shared understanding of a selected past that sustained and privileged an ambiance steeped in Renaissance culture, and that was intended to serve political legitimization and economic development.

Since the beginning of the twentieth century, garden historians and architects have undertaken a reconstruction of the physical configuration and appearance of Medici pleasances, and they have already published many studies that illustrate their hypotheses and speculations. Other works have classified these gardens under specific typological and stylistic headings. This is one of the most common scholarly approaches, though it risks attributing labels to places that do not merit them. In fact, accounts of the Medici villas have often fallen prey to the teleological temptation of setting their gardens, or at least the gardens' assumed physical appearance, in the larger context of the

Italian garden "type" that they are said to anticipate. To make these arguments, two major themes, the relation of practice to theory, on the one hand, and the question of patronage, on the other, are forced into predetermined patterns: that is to say, two notions usually taken for granted are that the practice of garden making follows theory and that every work of garden art is commissioned from a designer. These notions imply the separation and distancing of two activities: the thinking process, which is assumed to precede manual labor, and the transformation of thought into appropriate material form, a form that is usually said to embody lofty concepts, such as philosophical and theological constructs.

While challenging traditionally held assumptions, this book purposely disregards the relationship of the Medici gardens to the idealized paradigm of the Italian garden of the Renaissance, and tries instead to place these pleasances within the context of material culture, which includes the lives of the Medici and the different attitudes of the family members toward the countryside. The evidence is drawn from published and unpublished epistolary exchanges, books of memoirs, tax returns, notarial deeds, and drawings. Using archival data and primary sources, the book traces the evolution of the relationship between man and the natural environment from the implementation of kitchen gardens and orchards to the design of gardens; that is, from the cultivation of grounds set aside for the growing of vegetables, herbs, and fruit trees for household use or for sale, to the design of outdoor verdant places that embody allegorical programs and that become alternative venues for costly private, and often theatrical, events. This objective is accomplished by moving beyond the temporal and spatial framework of the Medici villas, which constitute the focus of the first chapter. The notes to this chapter provide the context for the archival documents invoked in order to clarify the Medici family tree, especially in the fourteenth century, and the ownership history of the properties.

An inquiry into the extent of man's engagement with and manipulation of the natural world in the age of humanism also needs to address the humanists' own representation of such a relationship in their works of literature and philosophy. Thus, the intention of the section on Petrarch and Boccaccio is to analyze the nature of humanist gardens at an epistemological level—the fictional—which is different, yet comparable, to the nature of the actual gardens. In the same way as the *orti* of the fifteenth century reflect the empirical modus operandi of their makers, the rhetorical pleasances of Petrarch and Boccaccio offer clues to understanding the humanists' poietic activity, whether it be the planting of actual laurels or the writing of poetry. In either case, their gardens read as eloquent subjects and, as in the case of the Medici gardens, resist objectification through the ways they materialize the sentiments and disposition of the author, whether imagined or real. While the section on Marsilio Ficino is not an account of Neoplatonic gardens, it is also not an attempt to establish whether the layout of the garden at Careggi—the celebrated seat of Ficino's Academy—reflected Neoplatonic philosophical principles, it addresses, nevertheless, Ficino's interpretation of human creativity as a spontaneous human activity that parallels the extemporaneous creation of gardens at the time.

The final chapter proposes that the origin of garden design may be traced to that moment when a few gardens, such as those of the Medici grand dukes, started to be laid out by means of tools (e.g., drawings and models) previously used in other disciplines. The concluding section shows, moreover, that it is only after those gardens are designed that a theory of garden making starts to be articulated in written form by the writers of the most relevant treatises of the sixteenth and seventeenth centuries.

It is precisely the emphasis on the practice of garden making and its evolution into a theory of design that distinguishes my approach to and interpretation of these historical gardens. In the past, garden historians who addressed the Medici villas rarely questioned the notion that the hand of a single person could have designed those old gardens of Italy. In addition, the interpretation of Renaissance gardens as objects of art has favored the application of methods of art historical analysis to their studies. Thus, while the application of iconography has allowed historians to study the semantic content embodied by the morphology of the garden, and of garden elements, at a symbolic level, this approach has also tended to interpret Renaissance gardens as discrete objects, separated from the context of early modern Italian society. In contrast, the architectural approach has privileged morphological and typological analyses of gardens, and it has led scholars to focus exclusively on the reconstruction of their physical configuration, discussed further from a design point of view. This book, however, describes the Medici gardens as integrated within a larger cultural context, their implementation, design, and fruition influenced not only by aesthetic concerns but also by political, economic, and ultimately social forces.

This book is the product of several years of research, which started at the University of Pennsylvania, indeed one of the most fertile scholarly environments.

At Penn, I benefited from the intellectual generosity and meticulous advice of John Dixon Hunt, whose faith in this project has sometimes surpassed my own. It is thanks to his encouragement and support that my work has now been turned into a book. I should like to express my deep gratitude to David Leatherbarrow, for his guidance during the early stage of research, and to Kevin Brownlee, for encouraging me to cross disciplinary boundaries. Their remarks and criticism were extremely helpful. I am also indebted to Nicholas Mann for reading the section on Petrarch and Boccaccio and offering generous advice. An earlier version of this section was delivered at the sixth international Conference for Word and Image Studies held in Hamburg in 2002, and was published afterward in *Studies in the History of Gardens and Designed Landscapes* 23, no. 3 (2003).

I should like to thank the friends and colleagues who attended the theory colloquia at Penn at which I presented excerpts of my work. Their responses and insights much improved the book. I am especially grateful to Paul Carranza for reading an early draft of the manuscript and for his numerous comments and corrections.

I am also indebted to the following individuals and institutions in Florence for their assistance: Alessandro Alinari and Selvaggia Lensi Orlandi, for sharing with me their research on Cafaggiolo and Trebbio; Mirella Branca and Donata Mazzini, for their insight on Careggi and Fiesole and for inviting me to visit and photograph these villas. I am particularly grateful to the Kunsthistorisches Institut in Florenz, especially to Jörg Stabenow, for allowing me unlimited access to the Institute's library and photo archive, and for inviting me to present my work at the Studienkurs in September 2003. I should also like to thank the former vice-director of the Biblioteca Medicea Laurenziana, Angela Dillon Bussi; the staff of the Archivio Storico Comunale and of the Archivio di Stato, in particular, Susanna Gori, for her precious help in the last stage of research; Edward Goldberg and Patrizia Urbani; and Lucia Monaci Moran at the Gabinetto Disegni e Stampe degli Uffizi.

This book is also indebted to James Hankins, whose scholarship has been for me a major source of inspiration, and I wish to thank him here for always being willing to share his insights the few times I met him at conferences around the world. I should also like to express my gratitude to an anonymous reader for the Press, whose generous advice and specific suggestions for improvement guided my revisions.

This study owes much to the critical comments and intellectual support offered by Michel Conan during my fellowship year at Dumbarton Oaks in

2004–2005; I am also grateful to the staff for their help, and to my fellowship friends, with whom I often engaged in useful and enjoyable discussions. The resources of Dumbarton Oaks allowed me to expand on most of the topics. I should also like to thank the American Philosophical Society in Philadelphia for providing financial support in the last stage of my research. I wish to express my gratitude to Laurel McSherry, for her friendship and support, and Piera Bigi, whose companionship has made my sojourns in Florence less solitary.

Finally, to Gün Akkor goes a special word of thanks for his understanding, patience, and unfailing good humor that has cheered me up in weak moments. To my parents, to whom this book is dedicated, I shall always be grateful for their encouraging me to pursue my dreams, even when these took me far from home. The cheerful memory of a tour of Roman and Tuscan gardens I undertook with my father in the summer of 1998, *quando tutto è cominciato*, will always be with me.

Introduction

A TYPICAL ITALIAN-STYLE garden often seems to be a garden that is enclosed by a wall or surrounded by a hedge of boxwood trimmed closely so as to resemble a wall; with geometric flowerbeds, and stonework channeling rushing waters; with a bosquet of evergreens in the background, and terraces connected by symmetrical staircases and ramps mirroring the architecture of the house. And this style is said to have originated during the Renaissance.

This definition, reiterated in the pages of books on the history of the Italian garden, seems as rigid as the geometry informing the layout of these verdant places. But not only does it ignore the fact that the notion of an Italian-style garden would have been foreign to anyone living in the Renaissance, it also takes the concept of design as self-evident, as if all the gardens of the Italian Renaissance had been conceived as works of art or, more specifically, architecture.

A number of reasons, historical, political, cultural, and methodological, may explain the genesis of this concept and its crystallization over time. For instance, there is the fascination of many foreign intellectuals with an idea of Italy resting solely on its Renaissance past; the effort of the fascist regime to form and corroborate a national garden tradition that disallowed regional differences; the contemporary process of back formation that urges some scholars to use later sources to reconstruct earlier gardens—all contribute to define the Italian garden as a work of art as fixed as a painting, unaffected by the passing of time.

It is probably not surprising that the earliest association of gardens in Italy with Renaissance principles of order and "formal" layout is mostly due to foreign scholars, to whom we owe the first narratives on the history of Italian villas and gardens, produced toward the end of the nineteenth century. In fact, the fascination with Italian culture in general, and Renaissance art in particular, seems to have motivated the travels both of British citizens and of many Americans, who would arrange lengthy sojourns in Italy in an effort to shorten the cultural distance between the Old World and the New.[1] And they were men and women of letters, art historians and critics, collectors of Quattrocento Italian art, and connoisseurs.

When traveling to Italy, most foreigners chose to reside in Florence, which was considered a *ville toute anglaise*, "the only Italian city with a strong British accent."[2] After all, the idea of Italy was inseparable from that of Tuscany, both because of the region's own struggle for independence and because of the Tuscan language, that of the *Divine Comedy*, which many considered the most perfect form of Italian, and on which they predicated the country's linguistic, and therefore political, unity.

After a prolonged stay at a hotel or pension, the foreigners were likely to rent or buy properties in the countryside, and in their new residences they tried to re-create the magic of an atmosphere they associated with an idea of Florence. But it was a timeless Florence, more literary than actual, which the English and the Americans constructed in their minds before the start of their journey. They projected a city crystallized in its medieval or early Renaissance image,[3] to the shaping of which the Pre-Raphaelite aesthetic had contributed. Thus, for instance, Francis Joseph Sloane, who bought the Villa Medici at Careggi in 1848, had it restored until 1857 to what he thought was the villa's fifteenth-century appearance; in 1873 the Pre-Raphaelite associate John Roddam Spencer Stanhope purchased the Villa dello Strozzino (or Villa Nuti) at Bellosguardo, to the south of Florence, for which he painted large wood panels in a neo-Botticelli style and furnished with "rich brocaded hangings, fine needlework, mediaeval treasures in art and furniture."[4] In 1879 Frederick Stibbert started the restoration and extension of his family house, Villa Stibbert at Montughi, for the display of his ever-growing collection of works of art. The most stunning room was decorated in a neomedieval style to house his numerous old weapons and armor. In 1885 John Temple Leader purchased the medieval castle of Vincigliata, at Fiesole, and spent twelve years renovating it in accordance with the then popular "Gothic revival" style.

Things changed slightly toward the end of the century, when a few foreigners no longer limited themselves to investing in properties on the hilly outskirts of Florence, and to transforming them according to an earlier ideal, but started to show an interest in the city, and its suburban villas, as they were then. Their more objective approach produced a number of historical narratives on the subjects that interested them most. Thus, for instance, Janet Duff Gordon, who lived with her husband, Henry Ross, at the villa at Poggio Gherardo, published one of the earliest such studies, *Florentine Villas*, in 1901.[5]

Among the subjects that stimulated the curiosity of this new generation of foreigners were the gardens of the villas in which most of them lived. In order to narrate the origin of their design, a few of them systematically toured and surveyed the most important villas, both in Florence and throughout Italy. Often their objective was not only to write a history of gardens in Italy but also to identify and spell out the gardens' principles of design. Exemplary in this sense are the works of Vernon Lee, Edith Wharton, Charles Adam Platt, and Sir George Sitwell. Although these studies proved very useful, in that most of them were based on the reading of primary sources and thus constituted an invaluable source of information for subsequent scholars, they also contributed to the construction of the Italian garden myth. The typical *giardino all'italiana* was identified with a geometric work of topiary art, whose layout followed the principles of symmetry reflecting the architecture of the house, and whose design was said to date to Renaissance Rome. Such earlier gardens as those of Lorenzo de' Medici in Florence were not yet considered exemplary of the national style, because they lacked those elements of "perspective, architecture, decoration" that characterized the Roman gardens created under the popes, the cardinals, and their nephews during the Renaissance.[6]

In addition to identifying the Italian gardens par excellence with the gardens of Rome, the objective of Platt, Wharton, and Sitwell, in their respective studies, was to teach their readers how to visit the gardens of Italy, and what to appreciate during their visit, so that the "garden lover" would be able "to extract from the Italian gardens . . . principles which may be applied at home."[7] In the years following the publication of their books, numerous gardens, both in Italy and abroad, were restored or re-created according to the ready-made Italian tradition.[8] The phenomenon is all the more evident if we consider that while Sloane, Stibbert, and Temple Leader, to mention but a few, created English-style parks on their Florentine properties in the last quarter of the nineteenth century, the members of the new generation were more intent in re-creating the "magic" of what they thought was an authentic Italian garden. Wharton herself complained that "the English who have colonized in such numbers the slopes above the Arno have contributed not a little to the destruction of the old gardens by introducing into their horticultural plans two features entirely alien to the Tuscan climate and soil, namely, lawns and deciduous shade-trees. Many, indeed, are the parterres and terraces which have disappeared before the Britannic craving for a lawn." She suggested that "there is much to be learned from the old Italian gardens, and the first lesson is that . . . they must be copied."[9] Similarly, Sitwell judged "absolutely unsound" the whole theory of the English natural garden—which "spread like a plague all over Europe."[10] He claimed that the new generation of garden designers was in charge of reviving the gardens of the Italian Renaissance, which "for more than two centuries" had lain "under a cloud, exciting . . . little but contempt and disgust in all who viewed them."[11]

Thus, in 1907 Arthur Acton and his wife, Hortense Mitchell, bought La Pietra, where they tried to re-create a sixteenth-century Italian garden designed as a series of outside "rooms" surrounding the villa, with terraces, parterres, and fountains, linked by hedged paths; Bernard and Mary Berenson bought I Tatti in 1905, and in 1909 started the construction and planting of its architectonic garden; in 1908 Charles Loeser bought the Villa Torri Gattaia and started the restoration of the house and layout of the grounds, which continued until 1910. The gardens were composed of geometric and symmetric hedges, alternating with rose bushes and rows of cypresses and olive trees; Charles Augustus Strong commissioned the construction of a new villa and Italian-style garden, called Le Balze, in 1911; in 1915 Lady Sybil Cutting started the restoration of the Italian-style gardens at the Medici Villa at Fiesole.

Most of the wealthy owners commissioned their new "old Italian gardens"—which responded to the schemata described by Wharton, Sitwell, and the like—from Cecil Pinsent, an English architect who had set up practice in Florence in 1909.[12] By 1912 Pinsent had established a formal partnership with Geoffrey Scott—Mary Berenson's protégé—with whom he had been collaborating on the design of Villa I Tatti. Pinsent and Scott were steeped in the debates on the Italian garden that had attracted the attention of several scholars at the turn of the century; moreover, their acquaintance with Vernon Lee, Reginald Blomfield, Bernard Berenson, Wharton, and Sitwell had contributed not only to each other's ideas but also to shaping their taste and developing their sensibility. In other words, Pinsent and Scott happened to find themselves in the right place at the right time, for they had the cultural background and intellect necessary to satisfy the demands of their patrons.[13] Thus, they are usually regarded as the protagonists of the Italian garden revival, although theirs was not really a revival but rather the interpretation of an ideal.

It is worth noting that the title Pinsent chose for the only article he ever published, "Giardini moderni all'italiana, con i fiori che più vi si adattano," implicitly suggests that the Italian-style garden is, in fact, a modern creation, although it draws inspiration from classical antiquity's principles of order, and their Renaissance elaboration. In his article, Pinsent breaks down the elements constituting the modern *giardino all'italiana* (flowers, bosquets, pergolas, fences), some of which he had observed at the first Mostra del giardino italiano held in Florence at the Palazzo Vecchio in 1931 (fig. 2).[14]

The Italian garden exhibition signaled the awakening of Italian scholarship toward a subject that, since then, had attracted almost exclusively the interest of foreign intellectuals. The study of Renaissance Florence carried out by the foreigners had been part of an elite cultural tradition, but Italian scholarship transformed it into an experience of mass culture. Only a few publications appeared on the Italian garden in the years following the first exhibition, and very few had scholarly ambitions.[15] Those subsidized by the government were intended as descriptive guidebooks. Such was, for instance, Arturo Jahn-Rusconi's *Le ville medicee: Boboli, Castello, Petraia e Poggio a Caiano*. Jahn-Rusconi says that the gardens of the four villas used to be exemplary of the Italian, or better yet, Florentine, garden style, and he identifies the garden at Castello as their prototype.[16] Thus, the Italians contributed to the stiff definition of the national garden style, but their motivations, especially in the 1930s, were altogether different from those of their foreign predecessors in that they aimed at fulfilling a fascist ideal.

The scope of the Mostra was to "revive" the *giardino all'italiana* that had been pronounced dead seven years earlier by Luigi Dami. He had identified the decline of the national garden style with the moment at which, in the eighteenth century, painting replaced architecture as the most important source of inspiration for the design of the garden.[17] Although in the early twenties, when Dami published *Il giardino italiano*,[18] the subject of a national garden would probably not have made much sense to the average working-class Italian, as it was mostly foreign scholars who visited, wrote about, and owned the most beautiful of the "Italian" villas, at least in Florence,[19] ten years later highlighting this very shortcoming became the fascist regime's strategy for a new political and cultural propaganda within the Tuscan region. Acting as a newborn Lorenzo de' Medici, Mussolini sought to protect Florence from the interests of the "foreign expatriates who had for decades served as its unofficial guardians."[20]

Within this climate, the rhetoric of the 1931 Italian garden exhibition catalogue is self-evident: "The goal of this exhibition is to reclaim a place of

Fig. 2. Lithograph printed for the Mostra del Giardino Italiano (1931). ASCF, Cassettiera Fondo Comune, Piano III, Stanza B.

honor for our singular art, which, after having conquered the world, has been obfuscated by other fashions and hidden under foreign names."[21] That is to say, the exhibit sought to reclaim the national garden from the foreigners who had carefully confected its image over the previous century.

However, fascist leaders did more than simply appropriate a concept that had largely been defined by foreign studies. In fact, if the latter had stressed the link between the first Renaissance villas and the city of Rome, the regime went to great lengths to grant the primacy to Florence, in an effort to maximize the existing medieval and Renaissance resources of the city. For the same reason the exhibition catalogue says that the Medici made "the greatest contribution to the art of the garden" and describes Lorenzo's villa at Poggio a Caiano as "the first real grand villa of the Renaissance."[22] Moreover, Roman Renaissance gardens are said to descend from Florentine examples: "And just as the empire of architecture was transferred from Florence to Rome, so also the Florentine garden, designed for level ground, gated and walled, was transformed into the Roman garden, dynamically modeled in response to the rolling ground and sloping-down terraces and open to the horizon."[23]

Rome, on the other hand, did not need its Renaissance villas in order to construct its self-image, for the city's most glorious days dated to the Roman Empire. In fact, of the ten model gardens constructed for the exhibition in order to illustrate the development of the Italian garden style from the time of Pompeii to the nineteenth century, three were dedicated to Florence and Tuscany: the Tuscan garden of the fourteenth century, the Florentine garden of the fifteenth century, and the Florentine garden of the sixteenth century; one model condensed the Roman garden of the sixteenth and seventeenth centuries.[24]

If the regime's objective was to strengthen a recently formed national identity by insisting on the country's shared culture, Italian intellectuals were careful to maintain and even emphasize, although selectively, local resources and traditions. Thus, if the celebration of *romanità* and the rhetoric of antiquity took place in Rome,[25] and served to authorize the regime's empire-building agenda, in Florence fascist leaders had to simply corroborate the medieval and Renaissance image of the city that foreign scholars had already constructed in the nineteenth and early twentieth centuries.[26]

It is worth noting, moreover, that in order to achieve public consensus, and at the same time educate the masses by exposing them to the new ideals, part of the cultural heritage now offered to the people of Italy was reinterpreted, sometimes rewritten, and historical accuracy did not always receive priority. The instructions given to the regional committees in charge of organizing the national garden exhibition, for instance, were driven by a hastened historicism; their goal was to achieve a generalization that would have convinced middle-class Italians of the existence of such a common, national, cultural patrimony. In short, the effort was to offer an image of a shared artistic past with regard to the art of garden design in Italy: always flawless, always consistent.[27]

The promotion of Renaissance garden studies did not, however, produce scholarly publications, due to the fact that the targeted audience was the average working-class Italian. And, in fact, most studies of Italian gardens published after the 1930s were travel guides. Later on, in the aftermath of World War II, the need for solutions to large-scale planning problems, and the particular political and cultural climate of postwar Italy, distracted scholars from the study of gardens. The only notable exception is the work by Giulio Lensi Orlandi Cardini, *Le ville di Firenze*. But even this book is a catalogue—although accurate and comprehensive—of villas that are grouped geographically *di qua* and *di là d'Arno*. The author describes the Medici gardens as typically Florentine, and although he is mostly concerned with the architecture of the villas, he briefly outlines the history of the Florentine garden in the introduction: "The most famous of the remaining classical Florentine gardens are the two very altered works by Tribolo, the garden at Castello and the one at Boboli."[28]

We have to wait until the 1960s to see a return of scholarly interest in the subject of Italian gardens with the publication of *Giardini d'Italia* by Camillo Fiorani and *Italian Gardens* by Georgina Masson.[29] These books, however, reflect the influence of the stiff Italian garden discourse carried over from the previous generation. They not only offer historical accounts that focus exclusively on the genesis and development of the architectonic garden in Italy; they also criticize any alternative form of garden design, which is often condemned for being "without dignity."[30] The influence of the 1930s debates is evident. The catalogue of the 1931 exhibition is among the recommended readings in Masson's *Italian Gardens*. Even the layout of her book resembles that of the exhibition catalogue, where the gardens are grouped geographically by region and time of construction. According to Fiorani and Masson, the English landscape garden was for Italy a disruptive trend that displaced the only "true" garden type worthy of being called Italian: "In attempting the impossible by trying to create an English landscape even in the confined limits of the gardens of many small Tuscan villas, the formal parterres, which were an integral part of the original design, were destroyed and their place was taken by meandering paths and ugly irregular beds that bear no relation to the scale, character or site."[31]

The way Masson describes the extant examples of architectonic gardens clearly shows that by the 1960s the Italian garden tradition established during the fascist regime, when its origin had been identified and its revival endorsed, was consolidated. However, Masson, like others after her, perpetuated a misreading of the primary sources that occurred precisely thirty years earlier, in an effort to validate the idea of a national garden at the Mostra fiorentina. This is particularly evident in the historiography of the Medici gardens, as the ensuing chapters will show.

The fact that Italian gardens from the eighteenth to the twentieth centuries have received scholarly attention only rather recently testifies to the long-lasting influence of the 1931 exhibition on Italian garden studies. The historiography of the Medici gardens seems not yet to have distanced itself from that legacy. Most studies, in fact, still interpret the *orti dei Medici* as the prototypes of the Italian garden style.

One of the goals of this book is, therefore, to provide a historiographical critique of Medici garden writings. My interpretation of Trebbio, Cafaggiolo, Careggi, and Fiesole, rather than portraying them as the canon of early Renaissance gardens, shows that in fifteenth-century Florence the practice of garden making coincided with an empirical knowledge that was handed down from one generation to another. And this tradition, of course, was still alive in the sixteenth century, with the only difference being that in the Quattrocento it was kept alive by those who practiced it, and they were not interested in putting it on paper (perhaps some of them were illiterate), whereas in the following century it was put into writing by those connoisseurs who took over the elements of the garden tradition and transformed them into that which historians now call the Italian garden of the Renaissance. Toward the seventeenth century, the writing down of tradition did produce a theory of garden design, fully two centuries following the making of the early Medici gardens.

CHAPTER ONE

Medici Gardens

Trebbio and Cafaggiolo

The earliest studies on the properties of Trebbio and Cafaggiolo date to the end of the eighteenth century. Then and throughout the nineteenth century the most common tendency in the study of Florentine villas was to describe them from the point of view of a traveler who gives a detailed account of the villas unfolding along his or her path during an imaginary tour across the countryside. Exemplary in this sense are the studies of Domenico Moreni, Guido Carocci, and Giuseppe Baccini, three Tuscan scholars whose archival research has thrown light on the origin and history of many properties of the *contado fiorentino*, and on the vicissitudes of their owners.[1] In these studies, however, the information about the Medici gardens is scanty. In *Il giardino italiano* Luigi Dami explains why: "Cafaggiolo, in spite of Vasari's assertion, probably never had gardens in the strict sense of the word. Even less Trebbio and the others."[2] A few years later, Rose Standish Nichols, drawing from Dami, Inigo Triggs, and Vernon Lee, writes, "After Cosimo's purchase of Careggi, in his rebuilding of the old house and in the additions to the gardens, Renaissance influence becomes clearly apparent as it had *not* been in his castles—Trebbio and Cafaggiuolo—surrounded only by ilex woods and farmlands in the more remote valley in the Mugello" (emphasis added).[3]

Scholars writing during the second half of the twentieth century say something entirely different, namely, that the early Medici residences included designed gardens,[4] which are often regarded as an anticipation of the Italian garden style, identified with the architectonic garden of Renaissance origin. These scholars do not, however, tackle actual Quattrocento gardens. The source used as evidence for the presence of pleasure gardens in the fifteenth century turns out to be a series of lunettes that were, in fact, painted a century later, around 1599, when the grand duke of Tuscany, Ferdinand I, commissioned them from the Flemish Giusto Utens to decorate one of the rooms in the Medici villa of Artimino (fig. 3). The lunettes representing Trebbio and Cafaggiolo (figs. 4 and 5) show the gardens as they appeared in the late sixteenth century, rather than in the Quattrocento. Nevertheless, these lunettes are the earliest visual rendering of the gardens at Trebbio and Cafaggiolo, and the lack of other kinds of documentary sources, such as drawings that would allow for a reconstruction of the original layout, have legitimated an anachronistic reading of the past on the basis of later historical evidence.

Many historians lament that one of the difficulties concerning the study of these two Medici properties is related to scanty sources at the archives. The documentary evidence for the existence of pleasure gardens in the Mugello is indeed negligible, and not a single indication has provided even a hint of the circumstances surrounding their construction, not to mention the professional figure who might have "designed" them. However, a careful analysis of the archival material turns out to be useful. The lack of written and visual information concerning the design of gardens at Trebbio and Cafaggiolo in itself suggests that the implementation of the outdoors was not indebted to a design process but was perhaps more extemporary, and dictated by need rather than purely aesthetic concerns. The absence of fifteenth-century garden drawings, moreover, shows that the layout of the garden, which may be called its "form," was not yet distinguished from its plants and trees, that is, its matter, which demonstrates that the *orti* at Trebbio and Cafaggiolo were not yet conceived as works of art, designed by the hand of a single artist, but were instead the product of on-site implementation. This will become clearer as we take into account, in the following chapters, the sources available for later Medici gardens, which prove that at some point the practice of garden making evolved into a multifaceted process involving a time for thinking and intellectual speculation. This determined the actual layout and design of such later gardens as Castello and Boboli.

Among the Medici properties, Trebbio and Cafaggiolo are the oldest. They are located in the Mugello, an extended valley to the north of Florence, bisected by the river Sieve, which is said to be the region from which the Medici roots stemmed, and to which the members of the family always returned even after having established themselves in Florence as powerful

Fig. 3. Medici Villa at Artimino, Stanza delle Ville, Florence. Photo from Daniela Mignani, *Le ville medicee di Giusto Utens* (Florence: Arnaud, 1993), 103.

Fig. 4. Giusto Utens, *Il Trebbio* (1599). Florence: Museo di Firenze Com'era. By permission of Ministero per i Beni e le Attività Culturali.

Fig. 5. Giusto Utens, *Cafaggiolo* (1599). Florence: Museo di Firenze Com'era. By permission of Ministero per i Beni e le Attività Culturali.

bankers.[5] The amenity of the Val di Sieve earned the region the appellation of Tuscany's earthly paradise.[6] According to Father Chini, who wrote one of the earliest histories of the Mugello, in the Middle Ages this region presented a vast number of castles and towers, possibly built at the time of the Lombard invasion and conquest of Tuscany (A.D. 600).[7] The Lombard family of the Ubaldini ruled the west Mugello until the fourteenth century, but there is no record of them at Trebbio, whose name derives from the property's proximity to the crossing of three roads (*trivium*) that connected Tuscany with Romagna. As for Cafaggiolo, we know that the Lombards used the toponym to indicate fairly extended sections of land, in particular those planted with trees and surrounded, or protected, by hedges, ditches, and other forms of fencing.[8]

In the fourteenth century Trebbio and Cafaggiolo were fortified buildings rather than villas, and this explains why little attention was paid to their surroundings. Documents at the Archivio di Stato di Firenze concerning the early Medici properties reveal that a number of *orti* existed outside the fortresses, usually bordering the main squares in front of the buildings. The word *giardino* appears in few documents, and, as we shall see, it is always used to describe a cultivated piece of land of small proportions, whose products simply served the needs of the family.

The earliest document that, to my knowledge, describes the Medici residences in the valley of the Sieve dates back to 1319.[9] It is a deed in which Cafaggiolo is described as including a *palatium* and an *ortum*, while the description of Trebbio does not make any mention of castles, orchards, or kitchen gardens. It appears, then, that Trebbio was at that time a *podere* of cultivated fields, similar to the other possessions mentioned in the document: Sancti Johannis, Fortuna, Faeto, and Villa Nuova. In contrast, Cafaggiolo had an *ortum* of about six meters by six (430 square feet), and a path of little more than two meters running through it; but no more details are given.

Two other fourteenth-century sources refer to Cafaggiolo: one is a letter from the Signoria to Niccolò della Foresta (1349), the vicar of the Mugello, asking him to make sure that Cafaggiolo is protected and defended by the two nearby towns of Villanuova and Campiano.[10] The second document is a letter written in 1359 to the Signoria by two inspectors who were in charge of gathering *grano e biada* across the province.[11] They report the amount of wheat and fodder they are able to collect: thirty-four hundred bushels at Cafaggiolo against the two hundred and fifty-five they are able to obtain from the rest of the province. The two visitors also write that the Signoria should tell Giovanni de' Medici—probably Giovanni di Conte de' Medici,[12] the owner of Cafaggiolo at that time—how to shore up the building properly or else he would have to vacate it.[13]

A garden at Cafaggiolo is mentioned for the first time in a book of memoirs written in the year 1373 by Filigno di Conte de' Medici, who records the presence of his ancestors in the Mugello as early as the 1260s.[14] The document includes a description of the property.[15] The building was organized around a central court with a loggia, and was surrounded by walls—probably a double loop of walls—with a moat and drawbridge for defense purposes. There is also mention of a kitchen garden outside the walls. A few *casolari* or small outbuildings are said to overlook the square in front of the building: "Also a piece of land with a shed and threshing floor and with many fruit trees and vineyards, located in the abovementioned parish beyond the square of Cafaggiolo, which is called garden, and which is bordered on three sides by the road, and on the fourth side by the children of Biccio di Malatesta de' Medici. It measures about five *staiora* [six-tenths of an acre]."[16] A detailed description of several other fields follows.

Although in this document the word *giardino* appears for the first time, it is unlikely that it can be anything like a prototype of the *giardino all'italiana*. In fact, the garden is described as having fruits and vines, not to mention a shed and a threshing floor possibly used to winnow wheat and fodder. The latter are also listed in the earlier document from 1319, in which the *giardino* is, however, called *ortum*.[17] The presence of fruit trees and grapevines suggests that this *ortum* was similar to other kitchen gardens of the Florentine countryside. The most popular cultivation practice in the *contado fiorentino* in the fourteenth and fifteenth centuries is precisely the *coltura promiscua*, or mixed culture, so called because it included the simultaneous cultivation of herbaceous plants and trees within the same piece of land: there would be olive trees and grapevines, planted in rows or isolated, fruit trees of every kind, and typical Tuscan trees, such as poplars, elms, and willows.[18] This is what the primary sources mean when we read: "Uno peço di terra . . . cho' molti frutti e viti."[19] It seems, therefore, that the words *orto* and *giardino* were used as synonyms.

In her article "Le proprietà medicee nel Mugello" Giovanna Casali writes that the properties of Trebbio and Cafaggiolo are mentioned for the first time in a *lodo divisorio* of 1386: "The two buildings at Trebbio and Cafaggiolo, around which large extensions of land were concentrated, were included in the subdivision of the patrimony that was by then quite plentiful."[20] Although we know that Cafaggiolo is mentioned in earlier documents, cited above, the 1386 *lodo* could be the first written record of a building at Trebbio, and may yield a description of its surroundings. But the document cannot be found.[21]

A garden at Cafaggiolo is mentioned again in a legal document from 1402.[22] The property, which the document describes as a fortified building with a courtyard, loggias, wine cellars, and so forth,[23] includes: "A seeded garden of about five *staiora* located in the abovementioned parish, which is limited by the road on three sides, and on the fourth side it is bordered by Francesco di Bicci. Also a piece of arable land located in the abovementioned parish, called the place on the castle's moats, which is bordered on three sides by Francesco di Bicci, and on the fourth side by the said moat."[24] In this case the term *garden* is used for a field *a seme*, that is, a field cultivated either for grass to feed animals or for vegetables to feed people. By 1425, however, when Averardo di Francesco[25] lists his properties for the *Otto di Guardia*, the word *garden* is no longer mentioned. In this document the description of the property appears more concise: "A fortified building with houses used as stables and a family building, located in Mugello, at a place called Cafaggiolo, in the parish of the parish church of San Giovanni in Petroio, with some *ortali* for the benefit of the household but from which I do not derive any income."[26] By the word *ortali* the author may actually mean gardens, insofar as they do not yield any income—"però non tragho fuori stima"—and they are also considered as being an extension of the house that is used as living space:

"per mio habetare"; on the other hand, these *ortali* could also be kitchen gardens, whose products are not declared for tax purposes for the simple reason that they supply the daily needs of the family.

A number of *ortali* at Cafaggiolo are reported again in a document from 1427 in which Averardo di Francesco de' Medici listed his possessions.[27] The description of the property addresses the fortified building, adjacent to which are two houses surrounded by cultivated fields.[28] We can infer that the *ortali* located beside the building, listed in the same group as vineyards and pastures, are market gardens, which together with the *terre lavorative* yield a *rendita* for Monna Filippa. Again there is mention of a threshing floor and sheds in front of the building. It is possible that cultivated fields were adjacent to the main building on the side of the moat, and also located farther east, closer to the street and more isolated.

One of the earliest records of an *orto* at Trebbio is found in a document from 1427 with which Giovanni di Bicci,[29] Francesco's brother, declared his possessions to the *Catasto*: "A fortified building used as our residence, with many farms for our use, with a kitchen garden, courtyards, meadow, and cistern, and other houses, located in the parish of Santa Maria a Spugnole,[30] at a place called Trebbio, which is limited on the first, second, and third sides by the road, and by the vineyards of the *chancello* and of the *posticcio* on the fourth side. It does not yield any income, since it is added to the properties reported below."[31] We learn from this document that the *orto* was edged by a house called Malborghetto, and also by a small vineyard and a field.[32]

The description of Trebbio was repeated as a formula on the cadastral documents written in the following years as a basis for taxation.[33] We find another description of the property in the year 1433, when Cosimo il Vecchio and his brother Lorenzo di Giovanni de' Medici compiled their tax return.[34] Cultivated fields, vineyards, and woods, producing wheat and fodder, wine, and pork, surrounded the fortified building. In this document the word *prati* appears for the first time next to *orti*. It would be possible to think of these as gardens and meadows, but it is more plausible to interpret them as kitchen gardens and grass for grazing cattle.[35] In fact, grass for pasture was very much needed in the fifteenth century, given the scarcity of land left aside for this purpose after the deforestation and farming of most parts of the Florentine countryside. Moreover, without a *prato*, the cattle would feed on the leaves of the trees to which the grapevines were wedded, and on the hedges protecting the fields.[36] Therefore, as Michelangelo Tanaglia also recommended, it was necessary to set aside some land for the growing of grass, and this was called a *prato*, or meadow: "The meadows should abound with water / So that my herds can maintain themselves."[37]

In the 1430s the description of Cafaggiolo changes little from accounts in earlier documents. For instance, in the *portata al Catasto* written in 1430, we read again that the property included "many kitchen gardens for the use of the household."[38] The information about Cafaggiolo is very concise in the *portata catastale* of 1442 written by Cosimo il Vecchio and Pierfrancesco di Lorenzo de' Medici.[39] The document reports "a fortified building with kitchen gardens for our own use, located in Mugello, at a place called Cafaggiolo."[40] In the *portata al Catasto* of 1446 Cosimo lists Il Trebbio as a property belonging to both him and his nephew.[41] Again the words *prato* and *orto* are mentioned, as in the previous document, but no more information is given about the outdoor areas.[42] These are described in greater detail in the *lodo divisorio* between Cosimo and Pierfrancesco de' Medici,[43] in which Trebbio is listed among the properties assigned to Pierfrancesco.[44]

This document mentions two *pratelli*, one of which is enclosed by a wall and is located in front of the building, while the other seems to be open and located toward Scarperia, that is, to the northeast side of the property. An *orto* of one-third of an acre is enclosed by a wall and contains two pergolas and some fruit trees. It is located on the side of the property toward Spugnole on the southeast side. Woods of oaks and chestnut trees also surround the *habitatione*. In this document, dating from 1456, we find new elements in the description of Trebbio, namely, the two pergolas, the wall surrounding the *orto*, and a *fonte*, or wellspring. Notwithstanding the presence of new elements, we still cannot say that the *orto* at Trebbio was designed according to the principles of "formal" layout that are usually associated with the *giardino all'italiana*. But this does not exclude the possibility that it was a garden of some sort, such as, for example, a kitchen garden.

In the *lodo divisorio* the description of Cafaggiolo, which had been assigned to Cosimo, is not substantially different from reports in earlier documents.[45] Another version of the deed is written in Latin and yields more precise information. Cafaggiolo is: "A fortified building located in the parish of Santa Maria a Campiano of Mugello in the county of Florence, a place called Cafaggiolo, with a landowner's house, with two towers and drawbridge and moats and with a kitchen garden to the back and a meadow or square in front of it and with five small buildings overlooking the said square. And with a church near the Sieve which is called San Jacopo and with many woods, chestnuts and streams and uncultivated fields and pastures belonging and entrusted to the said house."[46] The possessions assigned to Pierfrancesco are also listed: "The part assigned by the said lots to the said Pierfrancesco . . . one fortified building located in the county of Florence and in the parish of Santa Maria or San Nicola a Spugnole of Mugello in the county of Florence; a place called Trebbio, with a landowner's house, with towers and meadow and kitchen garden and stable and other buildings, with an enclosure or en-closed place for wild animals, with a house used to store wheat and similar things, and stable, and with many woods, and with vineyards that we call *a posticci*, with chestnuts . . . near the said building and with a wellspring."[47]

From the previous *lodo divisorio*, written in Italian, we learn that Cafaggi-olo possessed a *piazza*, bordered by five small houses on one side, and a church dedicated to St. Jacob. But these elements were simply listed and the spatial relationship between them was ignored.[48] In the Latin document, on the other hand, we read that the houses and the church were lined up along the river Sieve, and the *piaça* they bordered was also called a *platea*, or open space, and coincided with a *pratello*. As it appears from the document in Latin, the property also included woods, chestnut groves, streams, unculti-vated fields, and pastures. In both documents the *orto* is reported as being lo-cated to the back of the building. In the section regarding Trebbio, however, the description of the property remains unchanged, apart from the fact that the wall surrounding the *orto* and the two pergolas are no longer mentioned. However, an enclosure for wild animals is reported, which suggests that be-sides being a farm, with its wheat fields, pastures, and vineyards, the property also functioned as a hunting lodge.

In 1468, after Piero di Cosimo's death, his sons Lorenzo and Giuliano recorded all their possessions in the Mugello.[49] Despite the similarity with the document examined previously, we learn here that at Cafaggiolo there was a seeded *horto* of about half an acre. In 1480 Lorenzo di Piero de' Medici gave a slightly different description of Cafaggiolo in his *portata al Catasto*.[50] A more detailed document was written on November 15, 1485, when Lorenzo di Piero de' Medici gave up his possession of Cafaggiolo in favor of Lorenzo and Giovanni di Pierfrancesco as a result of a controversy between them. From the inventory we learn that the *orto* at Cafaggiolo was surrounded by a wall on two sides and by a wooden fence on the third side. The fourth side was probably formed by the rear of the building.[51]

As the archival documents record, by the end of the fifteenth century the possessions of Trebbio and Cafaggiolo belonged to the minor branch of the Medici family. On September 15, 1498, an inventory of the possessions belonging to Lorenzo and Giovanni di Pierfrancesco de' Medici was compiled, in which we find a description of the properties. From the description of Cafaggiolo, we learn that the *piazza* was bordered by service houses, used as stables or as *tinaie*, that is, to store the utensils and tubs for the grape harvest. Not many details are given, on the other hand, about the *orto murato*.[52]

In 1506 a new *lodo divisorio* was formulated in order to resolve the dispute over the possessions in Mugello between Pierfrancesco di Lorenzo di Pierfrancesco de' Medici and his cousin Giovanni di Giovanni di Pierfrancesco, who, being a minor at that time, was represented by the *ufficiali dei pupilli*.[53] Here the *orto* at Cafaggiolo is no longer mentioned within the description of the building and its annexes but is now described as part of a *podere*. It is unclear, however, whether the mentioned *orto* corresponds to the one that in previous documents was located to the back of the *palagio*, or if the document is simply listing a *podere* located beyond the *orto*, that is, [*di là*] *da l'orto*. The 1506 *lodo* assigns the property of Trebbio to Giovanni (later called Giovanni dalle Bande Nere),[54] and we read about the *pigioni pertinenti al Trebbio*. Two houses on the square of Trebbio are used as blacksmith shops. One of them also has a kitchen garden. More interestingly, the document mentions another "house with a shop on the ground floor, and with a kitchen garden, located below the kitchen garden at Trebbio, in a place called Malborghetto, rented to the heir of Piergiovanni."[55] Later we read again of "a house with a kitchen garden and shed located at the abovementioned place of Malborghetto below the kitchen garden of Trebbio, rented to the bakers Giovanni and Agnolo di Niccholò together with the said bakery."[56]

Last, it is worth examining one more document: the so-called *Campione de' beni di Cosimo I*, written in 1566. Among the properties listed we find a detailed description of Cafaggiolo, which is presented as a fortified palace with moats, a one-acre kitchen garden, a wood of one and one-third acres for bird hunting, a meadow surrounding the building, and several other houses used by the potters and blacksmiths to which other kitchen gardens are attached.[57] We also read about the presence of "a *vendemmia* [a building used for the grape harvest, often open on its sides] located on the square at Cafaggiolo with a granary ... and a stable on the same square,"[58] which clarifies the kind of activities that used to take place on the *piazza*. The *Campione* also reports a list of the *pezi di terra* included in the property, which is called "*fattoria*—and not villa—*di Cafaggiuolo*." A similar document was written in the year 1568, but here the *orto* appears to be located at the back of the building.[59]

As we have seen by examining the primary sources, the words *orto* and *giardino* were both used, perhaps as synonyms, in cadastral descriptions, books of memoirs, and legal documents from the Middle Ages to the early fifteenth century. The question, though, of what the nature was of these *orti* or *giardini* remains to be answered. The use of these terms is independent of whether they are mentioned in conjunction with a *casa da signore* or *palagio*, that is, with the landowner's house, or with a *casa da lavoratore*, or farmhouse. In Filigno de' Medici's book of memoirs, *giardino* is used for a simple *peço di terra chon chapana e aia*, that is, a piece of land with a shed and threshing floor. In another case we have *uno giardino di staiora cinque o circha a seme*, and we are not told its exact location within the property. On the other hand, some terms seem to acquire a different meaning depending on the context in which they are used. For example, the word *ortale* appears to have been used to mean either market garden or kitchen garden.[60]

The word *orto* is a descendant of the Latin *hortus*. One of the earliest definitions of the Latin word is to be found in the *Etymologiae* written by the Spanish bishop Isidore of Seville in the seventh century A.D. Despite its unreliability, Isidore's encyclopedia was often cited as a reference work throughout the Middle Ages, and maintained its authority even in the Renaissance.[61] The term *hortus* is defined in the section about herbs: "A *hortus* is so called because something always grows [*oriatur*] there. Unlike any other land that produces something only once a year, the *hortus* is never without produce."[62] Tommaseo defines the term *orto* in his historic dictionary of Italian: "A field surrounded by a wall or hedge in which vegetables and fruit trees are cultivated."[63] From both the Latin and Italian definitions we learn that the *hortus/orto* had a functional purpose, namely, that of producing edible herbs and fruits. We deduce, therefore, that the piece of land set apart and enclosed by means of a wall or hedge was similar to what we call orchard and kitchen garden. But this is not all, for one of the quotations cited by Tommaseo to show the usage of the word in the Italian language reads, "Graceful and plentiful kitchen gardens, which cater to the needs of our lives with little physical toil";[64] the example is extracted from the vulgarization of the so-called *Collazioni di Santi Padri*, whose Latin version had been collated by a monk in the fifth century and was also known to the Accademici della Crusca.[65] If the quotation suggests again that *orti* were sorts of kitchen gardens insofar as they were a source of food—appreciated because it did not require great physical exertion—the adjective *graziosi* implies that a useful place could also be admired for its beauty or, even better, for its *grazia*.

In the second half of the thirteenth century, Brunetto Latini complains in his *Livre du Tresor*—a sort of compendium of scientific knowledge—about the merely utilitarian function that informs the buildings of the Italian countryside, whereas the French approach to the country leaves room for a purely enjoyable contemplation of nature: "But the French build large houses, complete in all their parts and painted, and large rooms in order to be joyful and to delight, without annoyance and conflict, although they know better than other people how to make meadows, gardens and orchards in all their properties, since this is something that brings great pleasure to man."[66] Brunetto uses the word *vergier*[67]—a synonym of *giardino*—which in France described a place that is particularly pleasurable. In Italy, on the other hand, as we have seen, a pleasurable place was always linked to usefulness, or to the good.

Giovanni di Pagolo Morelli uses similar vocabulary some time later, between 1393 and 1402, in *Del paese e luogo proprio donde anticamente siamo*.[68] Morelli's language is especially notable for the attributes with which he describes the Florentine countryside. He speaks of his native land, the Mugello, in terms of its three major qualities: beauty, goodness, and greatness. In the first section, dedicated to the beauty of the region, he writes: "Farther off you will see the town, located amid a beautiful plowed plain with beautiful and pleasing fruit trees, thoroughly plowed, yielding all possible goods like a garden. . . . You will see that the fields adjacent to the buildings are all wellplowed, with fruits and beautiful vineyards, and with plenty of wells or springs; people's houses are located in beautiful and pleasing sites, well located, with beautiful sights, overlooking beautiful cultivated fields, with gardens and meadows."[69]

In the second section, dedicated to the goodness of the Mugello, Morelli writes: "In the plain of Mugello you will see the best and most fruitful fields of our county, which yield two or three harvests per year, each of which very plentiful: and anything you would want to ask for is perfectly made here. And farther off, you see perfect fields on the hills, yielding plenty of wheat, fodder, fruits, and oil, and similarly plenty of wine, wood, and chestnuts, and so many cattle that they are said to provide one-third of the needs of Florence."[70]

Morelli also describes the greatness and usefulness of the place: "Third, all there is left is to see the good quality and usefulness of the buildings: and you will see this first in five castles, as mentioned, which are located on the plain. . . . The rest of the country, that is, the hills and everywhere else, has many buildings, as we have said, which are good in addition to being beautiful and

Fig. 6. Benozzo Gozzoli, *Procession of the Magi* (1459–1463), detail. Florence: Palazzo Medici-Riccardi. Scala/Art Resource, New York.

located on a good site with good air, with many dovecotes and wells and anything that is useful and good; and similarly, there are enough fortified buildings that could defend us against the whole world and they are so numerous that they satisfy every need, and could host the whole town with all its belongings: and this is a blessing for the people."[71]

A few years later Benozzo Gozzoli would depict the castles and fields around Florence in the famous fresco commissioned by Cosimo de' Medici for the Chapel of the Magi (fig. 6).[72] In both the painting and Morelli's verbal description, the Florentine landscape appears to be composed of beautiful buildings and tilled lands that are at the same time good and useful. The adjectives *buono* and *utile* that Morelli uses refer both to the positive effect clean air and water have on people's health and to the abundant produce of farmland that is so fertile as to allow for two harvests a year. It is even more telling that the adjective *bellissimo* is used to describe the same land, which yields beautiful fruits and vines that adorn it as if it were a *giardino*. The passage written by Morelli is therefore a confirmation of the fact that the word *giardino* was introduced into the Italian language to signify both the main quality of a *hortus* and that of a *jardin*.

It seems that at some point, following the example of French, Italian had to supply a word that allowed for the description of an *orto* that, besides being appreciated for its produce, could be regarded as pleasurable. Thus followed the use of the word *giardino*, which derived from the Frankish *gardo*, meaning "enclosed place," in the thirteenth century.[73] Moreover, if a kitchen garden could be called a *giardino*, since, like *orto*, it described an enclosed space, the French *jardin*, diminutive of the old French *jart*, supplied the Italian language with a term that implied a pleasurable quality. This is confirmed by the definition of *giardino* that we read in Tommaseo's dictionary: "Place surrounded by a wall or hedge, where flowers, trees, etc., are cultivated for pleasure and not for profit."[74]

The *orti* of Trebbio and Cafaggiolo were so called insofar as they yielded produce for the needs of the Medici family; however, as we have seen, they were occasionally referred to as gardens, perhaps because at times they were used for pleasurable purposes unconnected with cultivation.[75] The element of the *pergola* at Trebbio is an example of how a utilitarian construction used to grow vines could also be considered a pleasurable shaded pathway. In fact, some sources show that Trebbio was possibly used not only as a hunting lodge but also as a venue for social gatherings, which usually involved music and dancing. For example, on August 2, 1443, Pierfrancesco de' Medici wrote a letter to his brother at Careggi, asking him to send a bagpipe to Trebbio "because many women are coming here on Sunday and we cannot find one [bagpipe] in this town."[76] Therefore, the residence—and especially its surroundings when the gatherings took place in summer—must have yielded a delightful atmosphere that would have pleased the guests.

Yet the legal and personal documents considered here do not imply the presence at Trebbio and Cafaggiolo of gardens like those painted by Giusto Utens. The first association of the early Medici properties with Utens's paintings dates to the Mostra del giardino italiano that took place in Florence in 1931. At the Palazzo Vecchio five rooms were dedicated to the Medici villas. Confronted with the lack of primary textual and visual sources regarding the outdoors at Trebbio and Cafaggiolo, the exhibition organizers decided to display for each villa the respective lunette that Utens painted for Ferdinand I.

The organizers claimed the existence of both a Tuscan garden of the fourteenth century—for which they created a model after Giovanni Boccaccio's literary descriptions in the *Decameron*—and a Florentine garden of the fifteenth

Fig. 7. Enrico Lusini, model of the Quattrocento Florentine garden (1931). Alinari Archives, Florence.

and sixteenth centuries, identified with the two later Medici villas of Careggi and Castello.[77] The architect Enrico Lusini created the models representing these gardens: they all presented a regular layout and were surrounded by walls or tall hedges whose symmetry and proportion echoed the sharp geometry of the parterres. The brief descriptions that appear in the exhibition catalogue say that Lusini modeled the Quattrocento garden as a *hortus conclusus* (fig. 7) after Alberto Avogadro's description of the garden at the Palazzo Medici, within the city walls, and also following Alessandro Braccesi's description of the garden at Careggi,[78] literary sources that are somewhat questionable as tools for the reconstruction of the gardens' layout. The fact that sources related to the Medici villas inspired the design of Lusini's models is not surprising, especially if we consider that in the exhibition catalogue the Medici are said to have given "the greatest stimulus to the art of gardens"[79]—beginning with Cosimo il Vecchio, who commissioned from Michelozzo the villas at Cafaggiolo, Trebbio, Careggi, and Fiesole,[80] and ending with the Medici cardinal Francesco Maria, who owned the last eighteenth-century villa of Lappeggi.

Even if the catalogue was not meant to be a detailed study of the Medici villas—for it only served the purpose of recording the exhibition—it nevertheless had an impact on subsequent studies of Medici gardens that is hard to overestimate. The catalogue, in fact, perpetuated the anachronistic association of early fifteenth-century gardens with late sixteenth-century painting, such as the lunettes representing Trebbio and Cafaggiolo. Since then this association put forth by the Mostra del giardino italiano has been taken up by many scholars who consider Utens's lunettes a model from which to extrapolate the elements of fifteenth-century Florentine gardens. And the most important feature that is usually drawn from the lunettes is precisely the formality of the design, which makes scholars point to the fifteenth-century Medici properties as early examples of the Italian garden style, which, they maintain, would flower more vigorously later in the Renaissance: "The high bourgeoisie merchants—writes an author addressing the transformation of both Tuscan landscape and society between the fifteenth and sixteenth centuries—become landowners: the *giardino all'italiana* spreads to all of their villas in imitation of those at the Medici residences."[81]

One of the immediate consequences of this approach is that the gardens of the fifteenth and sixteenth centuries are usually described as works of art that are fixed and immutable—and that have always existed. Georgina Masson, for example, writes, "An interesting picture of what a Medici villa of this period [fifteenth century] looked like is to be seen in one of the fascinating lunettes of the Medici properties. . . . Although this painting representing the villa of Cafaggiolo dates from the end of the sixteenth century, from the very simplicity of the layout it is probable that it had not been changed in the hundred and fifty years since it was first laid out."[82] Similarly, she describes Il Trebbio as a "rare treasure," a fifteenth-century garden that "has retained its simple charm almost untouched through centuries. . . . A lunette . . . painted possibly by Utens or an unknown artist of the early seventeenth century, shows the layout of the house, chapel, farm, and walled garden, just as it probably looked in Cosimo's time and almost exactly as it is today."[83] As we have seen, the archival sources do not support this point of view, especially if we consider the vague rhetoric of the legal documents, and the fact that there are no representations of the early Medici gardens prior to the Flemish lunettes.

There does exist a visual rendering of the Medici villa at Cafaggiolo that supposedly antedates the Utens lunette (fig. 8). André Durand depicted it in the nineteenth century, claiming that his reconstruction was based on a faithful drawing of the villa from 1510.[84] However, as the original is lost, it is not

Fig. 8. André Durand, "Villa Ducale de Caffaggiolo (État ancien, 1510)," in *La Toscane: Album Monumental et Pittoresque exécuté sous la direction de M. le Prince Anatole Démidoff* (Paris: Lemercier, 1863). GDSU 109070, tav. 33. By permission of Ministero per i Beni e le Attività Culturali.

possible to ascertain how accurate Durand's copy is, and, in any case, the lithograph does not show the gardens. Another visual source is a series of plans drawn by Giorgio Vasari the Younger. The plan of Trebbio includes two handwritten notes (fig. 9), one of which says that the building is surrounded by a *prato grandissimo* on three sides; the other note reports: "Here is a garden two-hundred *braccia* in length and thirty *braccia* in width."[85] This drawing is contemporary with the lunette painted by Utens, but Vasari, unlike Utens, chose not to represent the gardens. This is all the more surprising if we consider that the same collection of drawings by Vasari does include garden plans (fig. 10).[86] All we learn from Vasari's second note is that the *giardino* was located to the southeast, which corresponds to the location of the garden in the lunette.[87] The plan of Cafaggiolo also does not represent the garden, but again it is mentioned in a handwritten note at the bottom of the drawing, which shows the rear of the building (fig. 11). It follows that it is not possible to establish the accuracy of Utens's representation of the Medici gardens, as we cannot compare the lunettes to other contemporary sources. Moreover, it

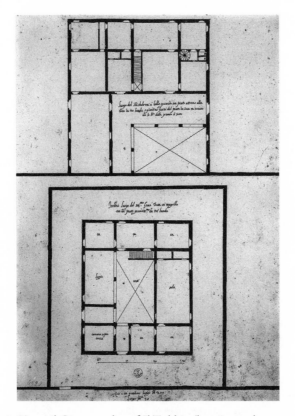

Fig. 9. Giorgio Vasari il Giovane, plan of Il Trebbio (late sixteenth century). GDSU 4920A. By permission of Ministero per i Beni e le Attività Culturali.

is not even possible to say whether the lunettes represented existing sixteenth-century gardens, or whether the gardens were designed after the lunettes.[88] Therefore, the use of these paintings as evidence for the gardens' layout during the fifteenth century is even more questionable.

At any rate, it is significant that there are no representations of potential "Italian garden" prototypes before the end of the sixteenth century. If such prototypes had existed, it would be surprising that they were not painted, considering that fifteenth-century artists were attentive observers of the landscape, which often provided the background for their lofty subjects. On the other hand, we have numerous representations of the Florentine countryside which show that fifteenth-century Tuscan painters were aware of the techniques, old and new, used by farmers to cultivate the land. Saint George and

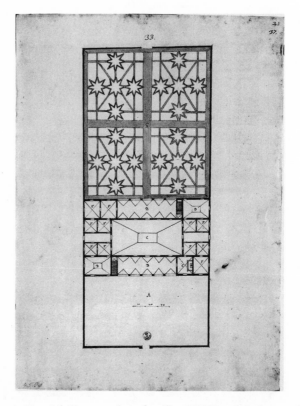

Fig. 10. Giorgio Vasari il Giovane, plan of a villa. GDSU 4561A. By permission of Ministero per i Beni e le Attività Culturali.

the dragon, for instance, in the famous canvas by Paolo Uccello (fig. 12), stand out in a background landscape that is described minutely and accurately. It is composed of geometrically shaped fields, characterized by the so-called *porche* (convex stripes of soil flanked by ditches for water runoff)[89] surrounded by hedges and trees, and alternating with meadows enclosed by "live" elements, which gives an idea of what the *prati* listed in the Medici tax returns may have looked like. Similarly, the fresco of the Magi Chapel shows Gozzoli's familiarity with the techniques of planting trees *a rittochino*, and of creating terraces by means of grassy edges, without the use of retaining walls (see fig. 6).[90]

If the advent of sharecropping contributed to the formal regularization of the land in the early Renaissance, it is possible to imagine the *orti* of the Medici being as geometric as the fields depicted by Paolo Uccello, or by

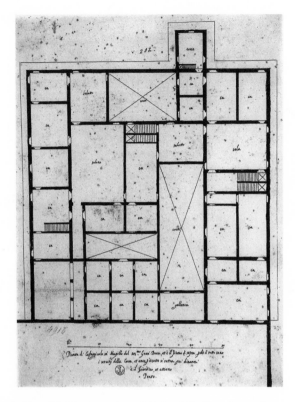

Fig. 11. Giorgio Vasari il Giovane, plan of Cafaggiolo (late sixteenth century). GDSU 4916A. By permission of Ministero per i Beni e le Attività Culturali.

Benozzo Gozzoli. After all, this is what Michelangelo Tanaglia says in the middle of the fifteenth century. He recommends squaring off the shape of *orti* and *prati*, because if these are laid out in straight lines and right angles, they will please the eye and make the soil more fertile.[91] But if the regular layout of the fields was mostly due to agricultural convenience, and to the belief that it would make the soil more productive, we can also imagine someone simply tracing such a layout directly on the ground, without the need for drawing a plan to make sure that it would obey the rules of symmetry and arithmetic proportion. From this perspective, there is good reason to read Utens's representations of the Medici gardens as early examples of the architectonic garden that is usually associated with the Italian type, but, as we have seen, the archival sources do not support the existence of such *giardini all'italiana* in the fifteenth century, nor do they say that the Medici

Fig. 12. Paolo Uccello, *Saint George and the Dragon* (1458–1460). Paris: Musée Jacquemart-André. Scala/Art Resource, New York.

gardens were, in fact, designed according to a certain ideal embodied by their layout.

The *orti* of the Medici, which combined the utilitarian characteristics of kitchen and market gardens with the pleasurable aspect of gardens, were definitely free from theoretical definitions and from the morphological constraints applied to them in the twentieth century.

Careggi

Like the gardens at Trebbio and Cafaggiolo, a Medici garden at Careggi is often charged with the responsibility of having served as the model for subsequent Florentine gardens. Although there are lunettes of the earlier Medici *orti*, however, no lunette was painted for Careggi. And the reason for this may be that by 1599, when Ferdinand I commissioned the fourteen lunettes from Utens depicting his properties, Careggi had lost its importance as a Medici residence.[92] Nevertheless, a garden at Careggi had been praised probably more than any other Medici garden by many humanists, chroniclers, and diarists throughout the centuries.

Giovanni Villani in his *Cronica fiorentina* of 1339 wrote one of the earliest expressions of praise about this portion of the Tuscan countryside, located on the south side of Mount Uccellatoio, four kilometers to the west of Florence. Villani writes that the landscape of Careggi surpasses the rest of the world not only for the amenity of its buildings and gardens but also for the fact that its plenteous beauty is nobly shared among all its people, for their own delight: it is "the most beautiful country of the world with its villas and most noble houses and gardens [created] for the pleasure of its inhabitants."[93] Emanuele Repetti too writes about the *contrada* of Careggi: "The King's Territory . . . competes with Fiesole for the mildness of its climate, for the delicious goods [produced by] its fields, for its beauty, and because it is the most abundant in villas that crown the populous and cheerful outskirts of the queen of the Arno."[94]

In addition to these celebratory writings, the presence of the Medici villa has given Careggi a legendary character, not only because Lorenzo de' Medici is said to have founded a sort of protobotanical garden there, which, among other things, seems to have inspired the famous Botticelli painting *La Primavera*, but also because it appears that the villa was the seat of the Neoplatonic Academy. It was there that on November 7 of every year the Neoplatonists gathered in order to celebrate the anniversary of Plato's birth and death, reading aloud the *Symposium*, as Marsilio Ficino tells us in his commentary on Plato's famous dialogue.

In the absence of detailed visual representations of Careggi, some scholars have suggested that the writings of the academicians, such as those of Ficino, not only disclose the meaning of Careggi's gardens but also yield precious information about their physical configuration. But it is even more problematic to attempt to reconstruct Careggi's garden on the basis of Ficino's Neoplatonic philosophy, in that nowhere in his writings does Ficino discuss the Medici villa,[95] and recent studies in the history of philosophy have even cast doubt on the very existence of a Neoplatonic Academy in fifteenth-century Florence. Two poems written by Alessandro Braccesi and Alberto Avogadro da Vercelli are also used as evidence for reconstructing the gardens.[96] But this evidence is not persuasive.

Rather than dwelling on a morphological reconstruction of Careggi's garden, I shall focus on its changes and transformations, especially functional, that occurred over time and that relate to the use the property was put by the members of the Medici family, from Cosimo il Vecchio to Lorenzo il Magnifico. In the fifteenth century Careggi was used as a farm, and also as a retreat that offered both the peacefulness of the country and the advantage of proximity to the city. As archival sources report, the property also included an *orto*, vines, and

fruit trees, which served the needs of the family. The importance and significance of Careggi, however, changed according to its owners and their personal
culture. If Cosimo, for example, still valued nature as agriculture—so-called
second nature—Lorenzo, as a Renaissance humanist, set out to imitate the
classics by longing for a primeval nature—the first one, still untouched by humans.[97] Moreover, as we shall see, with Lorenzo gardens start to be singled out
from the larger context of agriculture and begin to be considered more as places
of pleasure and luxury. Unlike his grandfather, Lorenzo was in fact never directly involved in the cultivation of the land, such as the pruning of vines.

Cosimo valued the lesson of the old generation of Medici, who, since the
second half of the fourteenth century, had increased their land possessions,
from which they derived most of their revenue. Poliziano reports in his diary
that "the abovementioned Cosimo used to say that he liked their house at
Cafaggiolo in Mugello better than the one at Fiesole, because anything that
he could see at Cafaggiolo belonged to them, whereas this was not the case
at Fiesole."[98] It seems that Cosimo enjoyed the sight of his possessions more
than a beautiful vista.

As Gene Brucker has pointed out, the tendency of spending more time
in the *contado* supervising one's property "had become so widespread that a
contemporary Florentine, Paolo di Messer Pace da Certaldo, wrote in his
'*Libro di buoni costumi*': 'A villa makes good animals and bad men, therefore
use it sparingly: stay in the city and involve yourself in [some sort of] craft or
business and you will be fine.' "[99] Whether or not the Medici followed Paolo's
advice, Careggi offered the benefit of country life and the advantage of easy
access to Florence; therefore it must have been favored by those members of
the family who performed civic duties or took part in the political life of the
city and in the business interests of the family bank. Thus, for instance,
whereas Trebbio and Cafaggiolo were usually the residences where the young
Medici spent most of their childhood and adolescence, together with their
tutors and mothers,[100] Careggi was the place to which Cosimo, his son Piero,
and later Lorenzo used to retire after a day in Florence.[101] There they also
sought refuge whenever plague broke out in the city;[102] and, finally, it is at
Careggi that all of them chose to die.[103]

Considering that Cosimo, his son, and his grandson all suffered from gout,
which made it extremely difficult for them to walk, it is surprising that they did
not spend their last days at the *palazzo* in via Larga, which was the most comfortable and luxurious of all their residences, and also close to the church of San
Lorenzo, which housed the family tomb.[104] An explanation for their preferring

Careggi may be that here they could enjoy the tranquility lacking in the city; but most of all they could find comfort in the intimacy of the place, immersed in that nature they either cultivated or sang of. Moreover, it is at Careggi that they used to discuss with their fellows such reassuring topics as the immortality of the soul. For instance, two years before he died Cosimo wrote from Careggi to Marsilio Ficino: "Yesterday I went to my estate at Careggi, but for the sake of cultivating my mind and not the estate. Come to us, Marsilio, as soon as possible. Bring with you Plato's book on *The Highest Good*, which I suppose you have translated from Greek into Latin as you promised. I want nothing more wholeheartedly than to know which way leads most surely to happiness. Farewell. Come, and bring your Orphic lyre with you."[105]

Indeed, in the preface to his translation of Xenocrates' *Consolation of Death*, Ficino tells how Cosimo, during their last conversation at Careggi on July 10, 1463, asked him about death: "Tell me . . . in Latin, Marsilio, what the Greek Xenocrates says,"[106] and was eager to learn more about the immortality of the soul. If Careggi could bring back such memories, it must have been the most comforting home to the spirit of a dying man. In an atmosphere of privacy and contemplation of the past, the presence of few close friends was probably all that the ceremony of death—*ars moriendi*—required, especially if we oppose it to the celebrations that used to take place in the streets and *piazze* of the city, such as marriage festivities, which were often a public display of abundance and wealth shared among the population of Florence.

The functional transformations of Careggi depended on the personality and temperament of the different members of the Medici family, but they depended also on the cultural demands of a changing society. We learn, for instance, that Cosimo took an active role in the maintenance of his villa, unlike his grandson Lorenzo. In the biography of Cosimo written in the fifteenth century by Vespasiano da Bisticci, we read: "Cosimo was an expert in horticulture, and used to talk about it as if he had never talked about anything else. He commissioned the *orto* at San Marco, and this was a noble gesture. When he commissioned it, the field there was bare, and it belonged to some friars who had lived there before Pope Eugene reformed it. As in all of Cosimo's possessions, there are not many things related to agriculture in which Cosimo would not take an interest, such as the cultivation of fruit trees and grafting."[107]

The legal documents written at the time he was the owner of Careggi show Cosimo's involvement with agriculture. We read, for example, of "a building with walled kitchen garden, meadows, loggia, and chapel, located at

Careggi, with a vineyard called *la vernaccia*[108] that we tend with our own hands and with a farm belonging to the said building, which we bought for 1,200 florins. Construction works went on until the year 1440 for about 1,300 florins, therefore we estimate that the above house with the said farm is worth 2,500 florins. The farm overseer is Domenicho Baroni with his children."[109] This is the *lodo divisorio* between Cosimo and his nephew Pierfrancesco made effective in 1456. Cosimo's attitude toward "second nature"—agriculture—is reminiscent of the teachings in Alberti's opuscule entitled *Villa*: "Buy the villa in order to provide for your family, not for the delight of others . . . furnish the house with that which is and might be necessary. Do not buy any of those goods that your fields produce."[110] Here Alberti advises the paterfamilias to provide for his family with the produce derived from his fields and to consider the villa not as a pleasurable place but rather as an ethical investment. In fact, for Alberti, as for Cosimo, cultivating the land for the sake of one's own family is a matter of virtue and of conducting a honorable way of life that goes both beyond a mere interest in practical domestic economy and beyond recreational activities.

In order to find out to what extent Cosimo was interested in agriculture and how deep his conception of nature was, it is useful to know what books on agriculture the *pater patriae* had in his private library.[111] It is known, for instance, that he possessed a copy of Cato's *De re rustica*, which at that time was quite a rarity.[112] Although the Cato volume was the first book on agriculture that Cosimo owned, the numerous works by Cicero in his library shed more light on the meaning Cosimo might have attributed to second nature.

In particular, in Cicero's *Cato Maior de senectute* Cosimo would have read: "Nothing can be more abounding in usefulness or more attractive in appearance than a well-tilled farm."[113] In this passage the character of Cato cites some illustrious men of the past who had an interest in agriculture, thereby establishing an authoritative precedent for himself, and for the reader— Cosimo—as well. Speaking through Cato, Cicero also says that "no life can be happier than that of the farmer, not merely from the standpoint of the duty performed, which benefits the entire human race, but also because of its charm already mentioned, and the plenty and abundance it gives of everything that tends to the nurture of man. . . . And there is his garden, which the farmers themselves term 'the second flitch.'"[114] From this passage we infer that in *De senectute* the discourse on agriculture covers also the cultivation of gardens. Cato in fact says, "Nor does the farmer find joy only in his cornfields, meadows, vineyards, and woodlands, but also in his garden and orchard, in the rearing of his cattle, in his swarms of bees, and in the infinite variety of flowers. And not only does planting delight him, but grafting also, than which there is nothing in husbandry that is more ingenious."[115]

According to Cicero the ideal farmer ought also to be a man of good judgment. As his Cato says, "The pleasures of agriculture ... [are] in the highest degree suited to the life of the wise man."[116] This is because only wise men can enjoy the labor that comes with agriculture, and appreciate the ordered beauty of a cultivated land; Cato himself tells his interlocutors that he finds joy not only in the utility of the vine but also "in its culture and very nature; in the even-spaced rows of stakes, with strips across the top; in the tying up of the branches; in the propagating of the plants; in the pruning of some branches ... and in the leaving of others to grow at will."[117]

Besides being suited to wise men, agriculture according to Cicero's Cato is also popular among statesmen or senators, "if the story is true that Lucius Quinctius Cincinnatus was at the plough when he was notified of his election [to the dictatorship of Rome]."[118] Moreover, the farmer ought to be a frugal man, as was Manius Curius, a Roman general who, after defeating many armies, retired to his modest country house, where he spent the rest of his life.

In sum, we can see how inspiring the reading of *De senectute* must have been for Cosimo de' Medici, who was taught by his father Giovanni never to appear pretentious to his fellow citizens, in order to deter feelings of envy, and whose way of life, like that of Cicero's Roman general, was characterized by prudence and temperance.[119] If Cosimo agreed with Cicero's view on second nature—as I believe he did—he would have regarded Careggi as a place in which both his garden/kitchen garden and tilled fields contributed to stimulate feelings of joy, their beauty deriving both from the usefulness of produce and from the eye-pleasing order bestowed on the land by the regularly spaced furrows, vines, and fruit trees.

Besides the *De senectute* Cosimo possessed Cicero's *Epistolae ad Atticum*,[120] in which the Roman statesman and orator Atticus speaks of his villas and of the intellectual inspiration he gained from living in the country.[121] The reading of these works exposed Cosimo to the classics' celebration of nature at an early age—he was not yet thirty years old at the time the first inventory of his books was compiled—and offered him a model for the pursuit of an ethical conduct that conformed to the moral principles of his upbringing.

A contemporary compendium written by Maffeo Vegio in 1433, entitled *Laudensis de educatione liberorum et eorum claris moribus*, shows how georgic writers were interpreted in the fifteenth century. Vegio's is a treatise in six books on the education of children and their moral preparation. In the fourth chapter of the final book Vegio offers an encomium on country life, and quoting from several georgic writers he says that the country generates love of righteous living, contempt for sensual pleasures, and hatred of vice. In this chapter Vegio also tells his readers that "though death must be met by all, this will not be difficult for one who has dreaded vice and zealously embraced virtue."[122] He mentions Cato, who said that country life encourages virtue, whereas the city favors vices. Vegio remarks that there is nothing more sacred, sweeter, and loftier than living in the country, and he also quotes from Cicero and Varro, according to whom the country is God-given, whereas the city is created by men. In the country, remarks Vegio, it is useful for reading to follow working, so that the study is more intense and the intellect nourished. Finally, hunting is allowed, mainly because it fortifies the body.[123]

We find similar ideas in a letter that Poggio Bracciolini wrote to Cosimo in about 1442. Here the author praises the country vis-à-vis the city and tells his friend about the importance of engaging in light farming activities as well as in intellectual pursuits. Yet nowhere in the letter, as Philip Foster has pointed out, does Poggio mention "the pleasure of parties and banquets, hunting, fowling or fishing."[124]

We know of a manuscript in Cosimo's collection that according to Albinia de la Mare bears a note handwritten by Cosimo, namely, the *Liber ruralium commodorum* by Petrus de' Crescentiis.[125] The fact that Cosimo owned it shows that he found a place for a handbook on agriculture that was closer than Cato's to his own time. Another book on agriculture that belonged to Cosimo is Palladius's,[126] which he acquired from Coluccio Salutati. This manuscript must have been obtained at a later date, since it does not appear in the inventory of 1417–1418.

Another interesting holding of the library is Saint Gregory the Great's three-volume *Moralia in Job,* which, according to Vespasiano da Bisticci, Cosimo read at Careggi in the short span of six months, alternating the reading with his horticultural activities: "One day, while the plague was in Florence, I was talking with him [Cosimo]. He [told me that when he] was still young they all went to Careggi in February, that is, when the vines are pruned. He would carry out two activities every day: as soon as he got up he would prune his vines, and for two hours he would not do anything else. In this he imitated Pope Boniface IX, who had some vines planted at the foot of his palace so that every morning he could go and prune them with his own hands. . . . Once Cosimo was back from pruning he used to read the Morals of Saint Gregory, a noble work in thirty-seven books, and he claimed to have read them in six months."[127] It seems that Cosimo followed Poggio's advice of engaging in horticultural activities while carrying out intellectual pursuits.

Cosimo's book collection is impressive if one considers the fact that he was not a scholar. His love for books, especially works of moral philosophy, was not a pose but a passion nourished by a deep interest. Cosimo was eager to put his learning into practice; thus, the meaning of agriculture, as he had apprehended it through the words of Cicero, was for him a matter not only of pleasurable reading but also of practical engagement with the cultivation of the land, for this coincided with the cultivation of virtue "in the hope of living and dying well, of achieving salvation and a measure of good fame."[128] Moreover, as Vespasiano tells us, Cosimo had a good relationship with his farmers: "It is amazing that, in spite of the many things he had to take care of, there was no grafting in his possessions that he would not remember; and when his overseers went to Florence, he would ask them about the fruit and place where the grafting had been done, and he enjoyed grafting and pruning with his own hands."[129] Francesco Fracassino, Cosimo's farmer and overseer, frequently wrote to Cosimo to report on the agricultural activities at Careggi:

> Of the ditches you asked us to dig, we completed one, that is, the one
> that reaches the stream Terzolle. Also the other two dug by those of
> Assagiolo are completed: and these run from the road that goes to
> Careggi to the house of Assagiolo; we did not dig any other ditches.
> As for the *melarancie* tree, the small one planted near the corner of the
> dovecote has died, but it did not have many branches and did not pro-
> duce fruit; the other ones are doing fine; it is true that they do not have
> many leaves yet, maybe because it has been so cold and windy that
> Biascio had to keep them covered until the first of January, and had I
> not told him to do so he would have not done it either . . . that pome-
> granate tree that we planted to the left of the second walkway grows fast
> and produces beautiful fruits. We put some of them in the rooms on the
> tenth of February.[130]

Besides being used as a farm, Careggi had an *orto*, and we need now to ask what role this played within the larger agricultural context of the villa. Given the fact that agriculture was associated at the time with ethical values—as it had been in Roman times—and that agricultural discourse involved gardens, at least according to Cicero's teaching, we would expect that an *orto* to reflect the same values as a cultivated field. Therefore, we would probably not be far from the truth if we assumed that the *orto* at Careggi was not, for Cosimo, a leisure place and was not considered an object of artistic appreciation, as is often maintained today by those who apply to fifteenth-century gardens the rules of modern aesthetics.

The earliest known archival document about a walled *orto* is in an act endorsed by Ser Piero Calcagni on June 7, 1417, when Tommaso Lippi sold his property at Careggi to Giovanni di Bicci de' Medici for eight hundred *fiorini*. The document includes a short description of the property: "A farm, that is, a palace with its courtyard, loggia, well, cellar, chapel, stables, dovecote, tower, walled kitchen garden, with two farmhouses, with cultivated fields and vineyards, olive trees, a place called Careggi, located in the parish of Santo Stefano in Pane."[131]

Another description of Careggi can be found in a cadastral document from 1433, which is the tax return of Cosimo and Lorenzo di Giovanni di Bicci.[132] For the first time we are told that in addition to the *orto* the property possessed *frutti*, or fruit trees. This is an example of *coltura promiscua*, the simultaneous presence of olive trees, grapevines, and fruit trees.

As Amanda Lillie has noted, the tax return of Cosimo and Lorenzo shows a shift in the expansion policy of the Medici family. Whereas Giovanni di Bicci had focused his agricultural investments on the enlargement of his properties in the Mugello, the younger generation concentrated on the development of Careggi, "although this was in addition to and not a substitute for continued growth in the Mugello."[133] Moreover, the expansion was a family enterprise, rather than a policy carried out by a single individual, as it had been at the time of Giovanni di Bicci.

Lorenzo inherited Careggi when his father Piero died in 1469, only five years after the death of Cosimo.[134] As I mentioned earlier, Lorenzo spent most of his childhood and adolescence in the Mugello, engaging in such activities as fowling and hunting,[135] but in the late 1470s only his wife and children stayed at Cafaggiolo, in order to flee the plague, whereas Lorenzo stayed in Florence and at Careggi.[136] As several letters written by Lorenzo's overseer, Francesco Fracassini, show, the young Medici managed his property in the Mugello from afar, sending written directions and requests to his overseer. This person, in turn, informed him about the wheat harvest and the selling of produce at the market or simply wrote to ask his advice about specific matters.[137] Lorenzo returned to Cafaggiolo occasionally for bird hunting and fishing. From a letter written by Piero di Lorenzo to Niccolò Michelozzi,

Lorenzo's secretary, we also learn that in 1492 Lorenzo left Florence for Careggi, "in order to flee from boredom and also to avoid the trouble that the visit of the Duke of Ferrara would have caused him. He will probably go also to Poggio, but for no longer than two days, for the air at Careggi is better."[138] Evidently, Lorenzo used Careggi mainly as a retreat. There is no record showing that he ever directly engaged in light farming, such as the pruning of vines, which delighted his grandfather Cosimo. However, as we have seen, the letters written by Fracassini show that in Lorenzo's time Careggi was productive, as it had been when it belonged to Cosimo. Confirmation of this is given by other archival sources.

The earliest document in which Careggi is declared to be among the properties belonging to Lorenzo di Piero de' Medici dates to 1480: "A farm with a landowner's house and a farmhouse located at Careggi in the parish of Santo Stefano in Pane, where we live. With cultivated fields, vineyards, olive trees, with kitchen garden and meadows and its annexes. It is tilled by Marco di Jacopo and his brothers . . . it yields wine . . . oil . . . fodder."[139] This account—unlike the documents that date back to Cosimo's time—includes the names of the people who were in charge of the *orto*, vineyards, and other cultivated fields, whereas there is no mention of Lorenzo being directly involved in any horticultural activity.

An inventory of Lorenzo de' Medici's possessions was also compiled after his death in 1492, in which we come across a description of Careggi: "A building at Careggi with its farms and annexes, etc. A building in the parish of San Pietro, located at a place called Careggi with meadows, kitchen garden, and houses, with its annexes."[140] After reading a description of the interior rooms of the villa, including Lorenzo's *studiolo*,[141] we learn that the Medici owned seven *poderi*, or fields, which yielded wheat, wine, fruit, oil, and fodder, located at Santo Stefano in Pane; they had eight more *poderi* at San Piero a Careggi, yielding the same kinds of produce, especially figs and almonds. The document briefly mentions the so-called Careggi Vecchio, described as "a palace with tower, courtyards and kitchen garden, loggias,"[142] which belonged to Orlando de' Medici, who rented it together with the surrounding *masserizie* from 1491 onward. Later a more thorough description of the Medici villa is given: "A building located in the parish of Santo Stefano in Pane, a place called the building of Careggi, with kitchen garden, courtyard, loggias, stables, and rooms for several families, granaries and bakery, kitchen, and many houses and rooms on the first floor, second and third floors, with cellars, and with a large meadow in front of it and behind it, with a wellspring and channeled water, a loggia and *vendemmia* [building for the grape harvest] in the meadow, that is, a house that was used by a farmer and now it belongs to the said building."[143] From this description we learn that the villa had two meadows, one of which was probably the place were the grape harvest was brought. In fact, the word *vendemmia* that appears in the document refers to a temporary construction, probably a shelter open on its sides, under which the tubs for the grapes were placed. Again, though, the name of Lorenzo is not mentioned.

Even if he did not practice horticulture with his own hands at Careggi, Lorenzo did show an interest in agriculture, but for reasons that are different from those of his predecessors.[144] With him the expansion policy that characterized the rural investments of the Medici family started to change. First, he felt that further acquisition of land in the Mugello was unnecessary, and Careggi was enlarged only slightly: "Two more farms and seven pieces of land were bought in the five years between 1472 and 1477."[145] His expansion moved farther away from Florence, in the direction of Pisa, probably influenced by the entrepreneurial efforts of his mother, Lucrezia Tornabuoni.[146]

Moreover, Lorenzo was not as wise a banker as his predecessors had been, and eventually he led the family toward a financial crisis. As noted by Raymond Adrien De Roover, Alison Brown, and Amanda Lillie, in addition to appropriating the funds of his cousins Giovanni and Lorenzo di Pierfrancesco—which later cost him the confiscation of Cafaggiolo—he drew from the public funds of the Monte Comune.[147] He also showed a certain amount of self-indulgence, spending the most when he could least afford to. Nonetheless, Lorenzo was an innovator when it came to agriculture. He was the first Medici to introduce specialization and diversification of products, and he did so on a commercial scale. For Lorenzo a country estate did not just present the possibility for ethical conduct, as it had for Cosimo, and it did not serve the sole purpose of providing for his own family, as Alberti, belonging to the older generation, had advised. In fact, it is not by chance that Lorenzo turned to agriculture when the Medici bank started to collapse; his interest in the agricultural realm of Cicero's second nature was dictated by the necessity of making profitable investments. Moreover, the fact that he enjoyed and took a personal interest in the breeding of guinea fowl, the importation of Arab racehorses and rabbits, and the production of silk, for which he had mulberry groves planted,[148] shows that his priorities were altogether different from his grandfather's, for they reveal a preference for luxury goods in which Cosimo surely would have had no interest.

Considering Lorenzo's propensity for expensive goods, we could say that the *orto* at Careggi was part of the luxury with which the young Medici loved surrounding himself. "Descriptio horti Laurentii Medicis," a poem in the form of a letter written by Alessandro Braccesi in 1480,[149] addresses precisely the beauty and bounty of nature in Lorenzo's garden. Braccesi lists all the vegetal species at Careggi, which are described in terms of the Olympian gods and goddesses to whom the plants are sacred. He also compares the garden to more famous examples. A poem attributed to Francesco Camerlini seems to confirm that Lorenzo took a great interest in something for which it seems there was not even a specific word yet, namely, the landscape. According to this poem, entitled "Allusio in villam Caregium Laurenti Medicis," Lorenzo added to Careggi groves worthy of Pan and fountains depicting the Nereids decorated in the manner of sylvan deities.[150]

The importance of these poems lies in the fact that they bear witness to a change of attitude toward nature that took place in Lorenzo's day. If for Cosimo, as for Cicero, gardens were still considered part of second nature, in Lorenzo's time they are identified as something different, something that closely recalls the pagan poets' yearning for primeval nature. In fact, if in Lorenzo's time gardens—still called *horti*—are considered elite places and, as the primary sources show, venues of lavish entertainments, stimulating people's curiosity besides their bodily senses, it is surprising that it is not "gardens" per se that the young Medici praises in his own poems. Rather, he expresses a longing for a sort of dreamlike place, reminiscent of the "first" nature Virgil sings of in his *Eclogues*. It is a place inhabited only by shepherds and nymphs, satyrs and fauns:

> Joyful villas, fields, and you, sylvan
> woods, fruit-bearing trees and uncultivated ones,
> grasses, shrubs, and you, rugged and thick heights,
> and you, delightful meadows aroused by my love;
>
> planes, hills, high and shady mountains and alps,
> and rivers where the beautiful springs gather,
> and you, tamed and untamed animals,
> nymphs, satyrs, fauns, and terrestrial gods.[151]

Here Lorenzo evokes the bucolic landscape of pastoral poetry in order to celebrate his love for a woman. These verses may remind us of Petrarch's *Canzoniere*, not only because of the language but also because of the *topos* he deploys: even the wildest and most uncivilized landscape flourishes, and figuratively rejoices, because of the presence of his beloved woman; and when she departs, the landscape is stripped bare and is as cold as it is in wintertime.

Like Braccesi's poem, these verses have a quality of uprootedness, even if both poems seem to draw inspiration from existing places. In fact, the title of Lorenzo's poem, "Sonetto fatto quando una donna che era ita in villa," shows that he too drew inspiration from a contingent episode, and an actual place. In particular, the object of Lorenzo's love has been identified as Lucrezia Donati, and the villa is thought to be her house at San Miniato. However, Lorenzo's goal is to describe his love experience in the only manner he had learned, that is, by turning it into an allegory using and manipulating classical and medieval *topoi*, where the landscape often embodies the poet's feelings.

Considering the abstract quality of the *loci* described by Lorenzo and by Braccesi, it is surprising that contemporary scholarship has read their verses literally, as if they were an objective description of actual places. Two other primary sources, the panegyric on Careggi written by Alberto Avogadro, and Galeazzo Maria Sforza's letter to his father in which he gives an account of a day spent at the Medici villa, are given the same interpretation by garden historians.[152] However, even if Braccesi's verses and Avogadro's were taken literally, a reconstruction of the garden's layout based on these poems would be arbitrary. The same can be said for the Sforza letter, which actually says very little about the gardens in general.

Despite the title Braccesi gives to his poem, which promises a *descriptio* of Lorenzo's *hortum*, he limits his narrative to a list of plants and does not provide the reader with any details about the articulation of space in the villa's grounds.[153] In fact, had Braccesi wanted to describe the structure of the garden, he could have made use of the rhetorical models for a spatial description of a supposedly Olympian place (e.g., Boccaccio's pleasances in the *Decameron cornice*). But this, as we shall see, was not the author's objective. From a biography of Braccesi written at the beginning of the last century we learn that the letter in verse was likely commissioned by the very addressee, Bernardo Bembo, who had asked another Florentine to write a poem on the same subject.[154] In other words, it seems that Bembo initiated a sort of contest with two contenders, Braccesi and Migliore Cresci, both erudite humanists and well versed in the composition of Latin poetry.[155] According to Bice Agnoletti, Braccesi's biographer, Cresci's description of Careggi is to be found in the *Collectiones Cosmianae* assembled by Bartolomeo Scala for Lorenzo de' Medici, which have never been published.[156] As Braccesi himself makes clear, his goal is to carry out a bravura exercise showing his superiority to the other contestant, who, ironically, is called Migliore. Therefore, the whole composition is a calculated display of erudition.

During the transition from the Middle Ages to the Renaissance, that is, during the Quattrocento, erudition meant especially knowledge of the classics, in particular of Latin literature. And, in fact, each vegetal species that Braccesi lists in his poem—about thirty-three species of trees, twelve species of shrubs, thirty-four species of herbs, grasses, and spices, seventeen kinds of vegetables, several varieties of flowers—is discussed in Pliny's *Naturalis historia*, Virgil's *Eclogues*, Columella's *De re rustica*, Cato, and Ovid.[157] In fact, Braccesi's "Descriptio horti Laurentii Medicis" is like a mosaic in which the citations from the georgic writers of antiquity are finely inlaid.[158]

Braccesi's poem on Careggi shares the poetic ecphrasis of conventional eulogies written by the earlier generation of *literati*, such as a panegyric written by Alberto Avogadro da Vercelli, which dates to the 1460s.[159] Avogadro's poem is an encomium on Cosimo's architectural achievements, and it is said to include a description of the Medici villa at Careggi. However, Careggi is not mentioned once throughout the poem, and the supposed description has little basis in actual reality. The following are the only lines that possibly refer to a villa's outdoor space: "What a splendid lookout! If you happen to sit down by the window, you will see the villa and the entire glory of the countryside; and you will see how a jet of water bubbles forth from a clear spring and waters the meadows with its small stream—the meadows, I say, a patchwork of varied colors—and [you will see how] a scent wafts on the varied breezes."[160] In the remainder of the poem Avogadro makes use of the conventional characters of rhetorical *amplificatio*, such as fauns and satyrs, empyrean gods and goddesses, and legendary poets. The only elements that might remind us of Careggi are an arcaded courtyard and the Medici coat of arms: "Your banners stand at the entrance, the balls, which shine in a bright red color stand out against a golden background."[161]

Another source that is quoted very often is the letter written in 1459 by Galeazzo Maria Sforza to his father Francesco, the Duke of Milan.[162] However, this letter, like Braccesi's and Avogadro's poems, does not yield information about the layout of the gardens at Careggi. In fact, all that Galeazzo says is "Neat gardens, which are indeed an even too graceful thing,"[163] which does not attest to the morphological configuration of the garden, let alone the nature of that *giardino*. All we learn from the letter is that the gardens were *polidi*, neat, and even too *ligiadri*, graceful, and that the banquet that was prepared at Careggi in his honor was also an occasion for listening to music and poetry, and for dancing. But we are not even told where in the villa these activities took place. The importance of this letter lies in the fact that it is the only document in which Cosimo's *hortus* is called a *giardino*; but it may be significant that it was written by a Milanese rather than a Florentine.[164]

The encomiums on Careggi, with their mythological references and characters, seem to have contributed to the corroboration of the Medici garden myth. Some historians claim not only that Braccesi's verses describe the layout of Careggi but also that the garden itself, and therefore the poem, served as a model for subsequent fifteenth-century Florentine gardens. For example, in a study on Careggi published in 1992 we read: "Within our collective memory the garden at Careggi is taken as the symbol of fifteenth-century Florentine gardens; in fact, at the exhibition of the Italian garden that took place at Palazzo Vecchio in Florence in 1931, Careggi inspired the architecture of the model representing this typology, and the descriptions written by Avogadro and Braccesi, addressing respectively the gardens at Palazzo Medici and Careggi inspired the layout of the vegetal structure [the garden layout of the model]. . . . From [Braccesi's] description of the vegetal species it is possible to reconstruct the layout of [Careggi's] garden."[165]

As we have seen in the cases of the Medici *orti* of Trebbio and Cafaggiolo, in an effort to reconstruct the appearance of the garden at Careggi contemporary studies rely on the sources of the first Mostra del Giardino Italiano, in this case written sources rather than painted, so that the value of the exhibition as an authoritative study of gardens in Italy is again endorsed. Yet, since Braccesi's verses do not provide a spatial description, it is not possible to establish whether or not Careggi was a physical model for other Florentine gardens, namely, if it initiated a typology. Moreover, the paucity of detailed visual sources makes any attempt to reconstruct the garden's physical appearance a very limited undertaking.[166]

The earliest visual recording of Careggi is a plan of the ground floor drawn by Giorgio Vasari the Younger at the end of the sixteenth century (fig. 13).[167] The plan shows the portion of the villa as it probably appeared after Michelozzo's transformation in the late 1430s. In addition, the rectangular block to the north (on the right-hand side of the drawing), which an elongated courtyard separates from the older building, is a sixteenth-century expansion. Also, the two loggias flanking the herb garden to the west seem to have been added in the late fifteenth or early sixteenth century, but it is unclear whether or not they are attributable to a second intervention by Michelozzo.

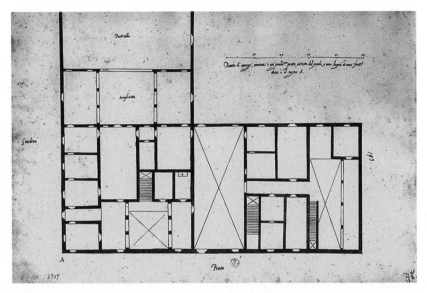

Fig. 13. Giorgio Vasari il Giovane, plan of Careggi (late sixteenth century). GDSU 4907A. By permission of Ministero per i Beni e le Attività Culturali.

In the drawing Vasari distinguished four green areas around the building: the first is located on the east side, and it is called *prato*, or meadow, which is where the main entrance to the villa is located. This side is flanked by the road to Castello; the term *giardino* written on the left-hand side of the drawing indicates the presence of a garden on the side of the building looking toward Florence to the south; another green area, which probably corresponds to the platform sustained by the retaining wall, can be identified on the west side. It is the area that Vasari calls *pratello*, or small meadow, neighboring the two loggias and the *semplicista*. As we can see, even if the artist had located the green areas around the building on the drawing, the plan would be an insufficient tool for the reconstruction of the garden. Had Vasari provided more details about the outdoor space, we would still not be able to use them, as the garden, meadows, and kitchen garden would have been very different a century earlier, that is, in the Quattrocento.

   An idea of what Careggi might have looked like in the fifteenth century is given by a map representing the oldest building, called Careggi Vecchio, prior to Michelozzo's intervention, that is, before the year 1433.[168] The old building is shown in the midst of cultivated fields in which rows of vines seem to alternate with rows of trees (fig. 14). The drawing also shows walled vineyards in which, as the legend indicates, Moscatello grapes were grown. However, this plan was actually drawn in 1696, and it is not known what visual or written source the author used to depict the appearance of Careggi almost three centuries earlier.[169] Yet one cannot fail to note that, whatever his source, the author depicted all the elements cited by early Quattrocento archival sources, such as the courtyard, well, stables, cellars, and tower. The tower is also shown in the northwest elevation of the building overlooking the stream Terzolle, on the right-hand side of the drawing, whereas on the left-hand side is an example of the two *case da lavoratore* mentioned in the primary sources.

Two other plans of Careggi Vecchio were drawn in 1742 and 1769, respectively (figs. 15 and 16), and their similarity to the earlier version leads us to assume that the three draftsmen based their reconstructions on the same evidence, now unfortunately lost, which all of them must have considered trustworthy.[170] The earlier drawings (figs. 14 and 15) are particularly useful in that they show that Cosimo's garden might have been a combination of vineyards, fruit trees, and kitchen gardens, that is, an example of that second nature to whose cultivation he devoted much of his life.[171]

There is no reason to doubt that the gardens at Careggi may have retained their early fifteenth-century appearance even after Michelozzo's intervention. After all, the *lodo divisorio* mentioned above refers to a large sum being spent on *murare*, which very likely refers to the construction of new walls for the house, rather than to the "design" of the garden. Moreover, the amount of twelve hundred florins was spent not on the implementation of the *podere* but on its purchase. And the fact that it yielded a *rendita* shows that it was productive.[172] In short, as the archival documents report and the drawings show, it is more likely that the grounds at Careggi were used to cultivate vines and fruit trees than the ornamental plants suitable for a pleasure garden.

Among other visual sources representing Careggi are a few paintings. One of these dates to the year 1636, when Francesco Furini represented the villa as the background to a group of humanists identified with the members of the Florentine Academy (fig. 17). In the lower margin of the painting we read, "Look here in Careggi's beautiful breezes at Marsilio and Pico and a hundred noble intellects, and say whether Thebes and Athens counted more in the shade of their Elysian myrtles."[173] Another late representation of Careggi is the famous *veduta* engraved by Giuseppe Zocchi in 1744 (fig. 18).[174] Unlike Utens's lunettes, these two paintings are not bird's-eye views of the Medici

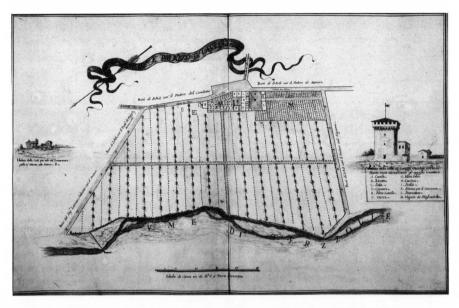

Fig. 14. Plan of Careggi vecchio (1696). ASF, *Piante dello Scrittoio delle Regie Possessioni*, serie tomi, 8–47/48–26. By permission of Ministero per i Beni e le Attività Culturali.

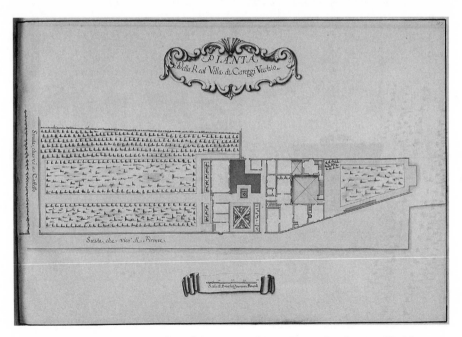

Fig. 15. Giuseppe Ruggieri, plan of Careggi vecchio in *Piante di palazzi e ville del Granduca* (1742). BNCF, ms. Palat. 3.B.1.5, tav. 23. By permission of Ministero per i Beni e le Attività Culturali.

Fig. 16. Plan of Careggi vecchio (1769). ASF, *Scrittoio delle Regie Possessioni*, piante topografiche, fol. 68. By permission of Ministero per i Beni e le Attività Culturali.

Fig. 17. Francesco Furini, *Lorenzo il Magnifico Among the Poets and Philosophers of the Academy at Careggi* (c. 1635), detail. Florence: Palazzo Pitti, Museo degli Argenti. By permission of Ministero per i Beni e le Attività Culturali.

Fig. 18. Giuseppe Zocchi, *La Real Villa di Careggi*. Copper etching, 1744. Archivio del Museo storico-topografico Firenze Com'era. By permission of Servizio Musei Comunali.

property, and even if they show the villa in perspective, the vantage point is too low to allow for a visual rendering of the garden.

Given the scarcity of documentary sources, especially visual, illustrating the Quattrocento garden, some scholars turn to contemporary philosophical writings. One frequent claim is that the layout of the gardens at Careggi was inspired by Neoplatonic philosophy, which was revived in Florence by Marsilio Ficino. And the legitimacy of this claim rests on the belief that the villa was the very seat of the Neoplatonic Academy: "The fame of Careggi's gardens derives from the mythical memories linked to it since the moment of the old Medici residence's construction. The gardens were . . . the meeting place of the Neo-Platonic circle, and have also notably inspired, from a botanical point of view, the naturalistic background of Botticelli's *Primavera*."[175] Thus, it is not uncommon to read that the gardens at Careggi are "the visible embodiment of the Academy's gnosiological theories,"[176] meaning that Neoplatonic speculations must have determined the design of the grounds.[177]

Recent studies in the history of philosophy and hermeneutics have called into question the very existence of the Neoplatonic Academy that is sustained by the historiographical tradition. James Hankins says that "in deciding how to spread the good medicine of Platonism through Florentine society, Ficino naturally turned to the example of Plato's Academy and tried to piece together from fragmentary ancient accounts how it had lived and worked."[178] Ficino learned from Diogenes Laertius that the Academy was Plato's "suburban place" outside Athens where he lived and taught his students.[179] According to Ficino, Plato practiced an ascetic way of life at his Academy, which was located in a deserted swamp—here Ficino drew from Jerome—in order to help him and his disciples mortify the flesh. Moreover, Ficino thought of Plato's Academy in a loose sense "as a collective name for Plato and his disciples."[180] He believed that Plato's disciples would gather at informal meetings where they would engage in improvised conversations on the Socratic model, as in Plato's own dialogues; moreover, these meetings would not always take place at the same location, such as at Plato's Academy outside the city walls; in fact, they could take place within the city, in gymnasia, or at banquets such as that described in the *Symposium*. Hankins argues that Ficino, aiming at the imitation of the Socratic way of teaching, informal and improvised, would never have directed an institution governed by rules and with fixed curricula.

For Hankins the importance of Ficino's own "Academy" has been much exaggerated. It was not the great center of Florentine intellectual life it is often depicted to be; it did not meet regularly at the Medici villa or at the *praedium* that Cosimo had donated to Ficino at Careggi;[181] and "it was not a creation of Medici patronage. . . . Most likely it was a private gymnasium attended by young men under Ficino's tutelage."[182] In "The Myth of the Platonic Academy of Florence" Hankins explains the recurrence of the word *Academy* in Ficino's writings not only as a name to indicate Plato and his disciples but also as a reference to the Platonic dialogues; for Ficino, the dialogues, that is, the Academy, were the means of religious and political reform sent to Christendom by God, and he sought to pass on those means to his pupils.[183]

The word *academia* is used as a synonym for *gymnasium* in some documents, such as the *Declamationes* written by the humanist Benedetto Colucci.[184] This is the only known text that describes "the activities of a group identified as Ficino's academy (not, needless say, his 'Platonic Academy')."[185] In fact, the title of Colucci's text refers to the orations delivered in 1474 by five noble Florentine young men to an audience of older men, among whom were Poliziano, Braccesi, and Niccolò Michelozzi. Ficino is referred to as "*Academiae princeps*" (leader of the Academy), but the scene of action is twice called "*gymnasium*." Thus, Hankins concludes that Ficino's Academy was a *gymnasium* that he kept in Florence for his own students, and that was informally associated with the *Studio fiorentino*.[186]

With regard to Ficino's small *podere* at Careggi or to the Medici villa nearby, there is no sound evidence that either place ever served as the seat of the "Academy." First of all, Ficino's country house was "too small and inconveniently situated to be the center of his academy."[187] Moreover, there are only a few sources in which the association between the Medici villa at Careggi and the Academy is clear, but these sources are not wholly reliable. The first piece of evidence is a letter written by Ficino to Cosimo in 1462, which mentions "Academiam . . . in agro Caregio."[188] According to Hankins these words cannot refer to "Ficino's own house and [it] is very unlikely [that they] refer to a Platonic circle meeting at the Medici villa."[189] The second source is Ficino's preface to his *De amore*, in which the philosopher gives an account of the discussion about Plato's *Symposium* that took place during a banquet held at Careggi. As Sebastiano Gentile has demonstrated, however, "the original text of the *De amore* [for which Ficino had not yet written a preface] made no reference to the symposium at Careggi"; hence, it is possible that Ficino fabricated a fictional event only for "propagandistic purposes."[190] This is plausible, given the fact that the book on love was dedicated to Lorenzo, the supposed host of the banquet; by including him among the Neoplatonists, Ficino, besides celebrating Plato, was praising his potential patron.

If the mythification of the Medici villa cannot be gainsaid, the urge to reconstruct the garden of Careggi, given the lack of reliable sources that would support such an effort, must be questioned. In fact, neither Neoplatonic philosophy nor the often-cited literary sources provide enough details to afford a physical reconstruction. Moreover, there are reasons to believe that Neoplatonic philosophy was not involved in the "design" of the garden. If we consider, with Hankins, that a Neoplatonic Academy was probably never established, and that Plato was not the only philosopher that was read and translated in Florence,[191] and if we also take into account that Michelozzo, the supposed maker of the garden, did not take part in philosophical discussions,[192] then the very attempt to reconstruct the form of the garden on the basis of Neoplatonism is implausible. Moreover, as we shall see in the next chapter, Ficino's remarks on creating a place that most promotes men's good health involve suggestions about the quality of air, the variety of plants and colors, and temperate scents—surely none of which helps us hypothesize the spatial organization of the garden. In short, we would not be able, on the basis only of Neoplatonic writings, to draw a plan of the Medici garden, not to mention a sketch of the garden in perspective, which is what a true reconstruction would yield. In the context of fifteenth-century Medici gardens the writings of Ficino are relevant for other reasons. They express his thoughts about human creativity, which seems to be a spontaneous rather than discursive process. Therefore, Ficino's notion of the anonymous artificer, who creates as a result of habit, though driven by cosmic influences, more closely describes the men who were involved in the extemporary implementation of Quattrocento gardens.

Ultimately, the common belief that the garden at Careggi was the prototype of fifteenth-century Florentine gardens, that is, that the Medici property initiated a typology of gardens, is problematic.[193] I agree with Amanda Lillie when she writes that "Careggi can also very usefully illustrate the pitfalls encountered by architectural historians in their determination to categorize country houses and define distinct types."[194] If it is wrong to identify the architecture of the Medici villa as a type, it is even more problematic to define its garden in the same terms.

As we have seen, whether or not the Florentine Academy was a formal institution, there is sound evidence that both Cosimo and later his grandson

Lorenzo engaged in philosophical discussions at Careggi.[195] Although this place had been a productive farm ever since it was acquired by the Medici family, the relationship of the Medici with it changed over time according to the personalities of the family members, and also as a result of an evolving society and culture, which at first demanded moderation and ethical conduct, and later display of wealth, erudition, and a measure of self-indulgence. It is in this context that the garden at Careggi starts to be praised at length, for its plenty and beauty rather than for its usefulness. However, the language in which the garden is described displays little innovation, showing as yet little or no awareness of the transformation that is taking place, involving humans and therefore their environment.

Fiesole

If Hankins took pains to find evidence of a Neoplatonic Academy, or gymnasium, gathering at Careggi but concluded that such meetings did not occur there, we have plentiful sources bearing witness to the fact that Florentine intellectuals, including the alleged members of the philosophical circle, often met at the Medici villa at Fiesole. In fact, an eighteenth-century historian like Domenico Moreni, and later also Angelo Maria Bandini, thought that the members of the Academy used to meet at both Careggi and Fiesole.[196] Bandini describes the function of Fiesole at the time of Lorenzo:

> [The villa at Fiesole] was used as the retreat of that flourishing age's
> sublime intellects. Poliziano tells us about it . . . in one of the letters
> that he wrote to the mentioned Lorenzo: "But I also, having imitated
> your example, for these days of most recent Lent, as if [I were] a
> fugitive from the city, I was often at Fiesole with my Pico della Miran-
> dola; we both attended that monastery of the Regular Canons, con-
> structed at the expense of your grandfather. Because there [was] the
> Abbot Matteo Bosso from Verona, man of holy morals, and wholesome
> life, but also incredibly knowledgeable in the most refined literature;
> thus he entertained us with his humanity, and the sweetness of his
> speech, when we left him, soon only Pico and I the only ones left
> (which almost never happened before) did not seem we had had enough
> of each other."[197]

Both Moreni and Bandini also cite a letter that the poet Angelo Ambrogini, called Il Poliziano, wrote while he was staying at the Medici villa at Fiesole to Marsilio Ficino at Careggi:

When you are made uncomfortable by the heat of the season in your retreat at Careggi, you will perhaps think the shelter of Fiesole not undeserving of your notice. Seated between the sloping sides of the mount, here we have water in abundance and, being constantly refreshed with moderate winds, find little inconvenience from the glare of the sun. As you approach the house it seems surrounded by trees, but when you reach it, you find it commands a full prospect of the city. Populous as the vicinity is, I can enjoy here that solitude so gratifying to my disposition. But I shall tempt you with other allurements. Wandering beyond the limits of his own property, Pico [della Mirandola] sometimes steals unexpectedly on my retirement, and draws me from the shade to partake of his supper. What kind of supper that is you well know; sparing indeed, but neat, and rendered graceful by the charms of conversation. But be my guest. Your supper shall be as good, and, your wine perhaps better, for in the quality of wine I shall contend for superiority even with Pico himself.[198]

It seems that Poliziano was used to retiring to Fiesole in order to work on his new projects or bring some of them to completion, such as his *Sylvae*, especially the "Nutricia" and the "Rusticus," and his translation of Plutarch's love tales (1478). In the "Rusticus" Poliziano wrote the following lines about Fiesole: "I composed these verses while I was at Fiesole's retreat, the Medici's suburban farm, at the place where the sacred mount looks over the city of Meonia and the current of the twisting Arno, where the benign Lorenzo gives joyful hospitality and placid quietness, Lorenzo is not Phoebus' last glory, Lorenzo is the Muses' trusted anchor [when they are] at the mercy of the storm."[199]

It is at Fiesole, according to Moreni and Bandini, that the meetings of the Neoplatonists used to take place. As Bandini records, "Under this blessed sky, and within the beautiful walks of the surrounding hills, as if the famous Academy of Plato had been resurrected, the deepest sciences were meditated upon, the work of the very Plato, as well as that of Plotinus, of Iamblichus, of Proclus, and of others; and if we [were to] read the first chapter of the commentary on Plato's *Symposium*, [we would see how] his memory was brought back

to life, as it had been in the past, at Lorenzo de' Medici's villa at Careggi . . .
and this was done in order to relieve the soul after the solemn philosophical in-
quiries that were undertaken at this villa of Fiesole."[200] The two authors also
report several encomia written in the fifteenth century by people who often
used to go to the Medici villa as guests, such as Benedetto Varchi,[201] Andrea di
Giovanni Razzi, Cristoforo Landino, Ugolino Verino, and Pier Crinito.[202]

Fiesole occupied in the late eighteenth and early nineteenth centuries the
place that Careggi now holds among most garden historians. In fact, Bandini
merely said that philosophical discussions took place at Fiesole "as if the famous Academy of Plato had been resurrected";[203] it was only later in the
nineteenth century that the Medici villa came to be considered the very seat
of the Neoplatonic Academy founded by Lorenzo the Magnificent, as we
learn from Emanuele Repetti's dictionary, written from 1833 to 1845.[204]

It may be that the importance attributed to Fiesole in the eighteenth
century coincided with the belief that the villa had been commissioned by
Cosimo il Vecchio, who, according to Moreni, used to go to the monastery
of St. Jerome in Fiesole to enjoy the company of Carlo of Montegranelli,
founder of the order of the Girolamini. Bandini seems to believe that the
Medici villa and gardens at Fiesole were commissioned by Cosimo de' Medici.
In fact, Bandini reports the words of Vasari: "For Giovanni, Cosimo de'
Medici's son, [Michelozzo] built another magnificent and honorable building
at Fiesole, which he constructed on the steep part of the hill at a great expense, but not without a good reason, for on the lower part of the building he
could build cellars, stables, storage rooms for the tubs, and other beautiful
and comfortable rooms. On the upper part, in addition to more or less ordi-
nary rooms, he created some rooms for the storage of books, some others for
music."[205]

Some of the earliest sources related to Fiesole show that it was indeed
Giovanni, and not his father Cosimo, who commissioned the villa. This, for
example, is what Filarete writes of Cosimo's younger son in 1464: "On the
hill of Fiesole, by the monastery of Saint Jerome, he commissioned the
construction of a church, which was appropriate according to a sacred building, and also [commissioned] an honorable place nearby, which allowed him
to breathe the fresh air from the fields any time he wanted to. And he also
enjoyed delicate things, books and ancient works, tools, and various things,
and especially the construction of this villa."[206] And Stefano Rosselli, the
Florentine cartographer, wrote toward the end the fifteenth century, "Both
the church and the adjacent convent were restored and enlarged and almost

reconstructed from their foundations together with the beautiful building below it by Giovanni."[207]

Considering how little has been written about the figure of Giovanni de' Medici,[208] we can infer that his villa at Fiesole received a great deal of attention from nineteenth-century scholars only because it was erroneously thought to be Cosimo's enterprise. Moreover, because Guido Carocci emphasized Cosimo's role as a patron of architecture at the turn of the century, the *Pater patriae*'s commission of Fiesole was also widely accepted in the 1900s.[209] We have to wait until the 1980s for Philip Ellis Foster to draw attention to the one Medici who is truly responsible for the construction of the villa, namely, Giovanni.[210] Amanda Lillie too has emphasized Giovanni's role as patron of the arts, providing sources that testify to his involvement with the construction of the Fiesole residence.[211] For example, there are twenty-seven letters written to Giovanni between 1453 and 1459 confirming that Cosimo's son was the client.[212]

Lillie notes that there was no need for a new country house for the Medici: "Apart from Cafaggiolo in the Mugello, where Giovanni frequently stayed, there was already one suburban villa, Careggi, and there were innumerable other properties available for residential conversion. Piero, for example, never felt the need to create his own separate rural estate."[213] She believes the reason for a new villa lies in the desire to gain ownership of a property that was not a result of a division of family estates. And this is also suggested by the timing of Giovanni's purchase of the site, either in 1452, at the time of his engagement to Ginevra degli Alessandri, or 1453, when he married her. It is also likely that Giovanni had wanted to build an entirely new villa. Unlike the earlier Medici properties at Trebbio, Cafaggiolo, and Careggi, the villa at Fiesole was the first to be built from scratch, and not the result of the renovation and expansion of a previously existing building bought by the Medici. This may explain why the architecture of the villa, with its loggias integrated into the mass of the building, instead of being simply superimposed on it as at Careggi, constitutes a point of departure from previous Medici residences, which bear the traces of their medieval past.[214] With regard to the Fiesole gardens, the most innovative aspect is their being layed out as terraces on the steep slope of the hill. The several letters addressing the structural problems encountered during the construction of the terraces not only show Giovanni's determination to bring the *orti* to completion but also suggest that he had a precise idea about the configuration of the grounds. This does not mean that we can already speak of a design process, since there is no record of drawings and models that might have preceded the implementation of the gardens, nor do the archival documents make reference to a designer who may have been responsible for the gardens' layout. The sources do, however, present some elements that suggest a clear separation, possibly taking place in the 1490s, between a kitchen garden for the cultivation of produce and a pleasure garden for the growing of flowers.

According to archival documents, the gardens at Fiesole seem to have been completed by 1457. A letter written by Giovanni di Luca Rossi to Giovanni de' Medici at the Baths of Petriuolo shows that orange, lemon, and pomegranate trees had been ordered from Naples already in 1455.[215] Another letter from 1457 makes reference to a dovecote, and to hedges, cypresses, and fruit trees.[216] The tax return from the same year, the first to list the villa at Fiesole, describes the property as follows: "A house, or rather dwelling with *risedio*, kitchen garden and market gardens located in the parish of the presbytery of Fiesole, a place called at Fiesole, which is limited by the road on the first, 1/2 and 1/3 sides, by the properties of the presbytery of Fiesole on the 1/4 side, the fields having been bought by several people."[217] If we compare this description to the ones of Trebbio and Careggi, we immediately understand that we are dealing with a smaller building, in that it is not called "palagio." Nor is it called "casa da signore"; it is simply "chasa" or "chasamento," that is, a dignified dwelling of smaller proportions. "Orto" and "ortali," on the other hand, refer to a kitchen garden and market gardens. So far the archival documents have not, however, indicated the exact number of gardens, nor have they given a clear sense of their spatial relationship. Equally disappointing is Giovanni di Cosimo's inventory of 1460, in which the only reference to gardens is in the phrase "room above the kitchen garden,"[218] while the presence of hedges seems confirmed by the mention of a tool used to prune them.[219]

A tax return compiled by Lorenzo de' Medici in 1480 also yield slim results: "A house, or rather a dwelling with *risedio*, kitchen garden and market garden, all belong to the same property, in the parish of the presbytery of Fiesole in a place called at Fiesole."[220] The following year the description changes slightly to add "meadows" and "a farmhouse with oil mill and with a number of tilled fields, vineyards, unfarmed land, and quarries with all its belongings."[221] The inventory compiled after the death of Lorenzo in 1492 is much more helpful, in that it allows us to make a first hypothesis about the location of the gardens.[222] There seem to have been two gardens, located on two separate terraces that were put to different uses. At folio 86v we read: "A garden behind the said palace with many curbed flowerbeds surrounded by curbs and a field in the said garden with cypresses, firs, etc., used as a bosquet

Fig. 19. Domenico Ghirlandaio, *Dormitio Virginis* (1486–1490), detail. Florence: Santa Maria Novella. Courtesy of Kunsthistorisches Institut in Florenz.

and a kitchen garden at the foot of the said building, surrounded by a fence, all the abovementioned things are about six *staiora* [3,150 square meters; nearly one hectare]."[223] The 1492 inventory is the first document in which one of the *orti* is called a *giardino*. This seems to be the garden on the higher terrace, located "behind" the palace, which means that it was situated on the side opposite to, or at least "other" than, the main façade and entrance of the building. The kitchen garden, on the other hand, was on the lower level.

The presence of two terraces is visible in contemporary paintings representing the Medici villa. The earliest one is the *Dormitio Virginis* frescoed by Domenico Ghirlandaio (1486–1490) in the upper right-hand portion of one of the lunettes in the Tornabuoni chapel, which corresponds to the choir of Santa Maria Novella in Florence (fig. 19). The second painting is the *Annunciazione* attributed to Biagio d'Antonio Tucci, which today is at the Accademia di San Luca in Rome (fig. 20).[224] In the *Annunciazione* we notice how the plane of the southern façade of the building coincides with the plane of the upper retaining wall, which extends to the left and to the right of the façade. The portion of wall that appears to the left, and that is no longer visible today, seems to have prevented access to the western terrace. This, in fact, is not visible in

Fig. 20. Biagio d'Antonio Tucci (attributed), *Annunciazione* (late fifteenth century), detail. Rome: Accademia di San Luca. Scala/Art Resource, New York.

either of the late fifteenth-century paintings.[225] As we have seen, however, the garden mentioned by the archival sources can be identified with the upper eastern terrace, and since it is described as being "behind" the palace, it is likely that entrance to the villa was from the west side. This side, on the other hand, does not seem to have included a garden, neither at the time of Lorenzo nor earlier. If we compare the two paintings reproducing the Medici villa we notice that a change in the dimension of the terraces occurred in the time frame between the Ghirlandaio fresco and the Tucci painting. In fact, the upper terrace in the Tornabuoni lunette appears much shorter than it does in the painting by Biagio d'Antonio. The zigzag outline of the retaining wall in the first painting disappears in the second in favor of a straight line. It is likely that the terrace was extended at the time of Lorenzo, considering that the tax return from 1480 shows that a number of meadows and tilled fields with vines had been added to the property, in addition to a farmhouse and an oil mill that are absent in the previous documents.

The inventory from 1492 speaks for the first time of the building as *palagio* instead of *casamento*, thus suggesting that the building too had been extended at that time.[226] Moreover, the inventory describes a few elements that composed the garden on the upper terrace. This included a number of *orticini*, probably flowerbeds, and a bosquet of cypresses and firs. It is not possible, on the sole basis of this source, to formulate a reconstruction of the garden's layout, for the document does not describe the shape, position, and spacing of the flowerbeds, nor does it say where exactly the trees were planted. However, as in the case of the previous Medici villas, scholars have assumed that the garden at Fiesole must have been a *giardino all'italiana* and, more precisely, "the first formal garden in the Renaissance to be conceived as an extension of the house."[227] Thus, for example, the phrase "orticini murati e ricinti di mura" is often interpreted as "formal walled garden divided into beds."[228] Moreover, it has been argued that the geometric pattern organizing the *orticini* reflected the cosmological theories of someone like Nicholas of Cusa, and the artificial space of the garden, with its regular parterres and evenly spaced trees, has been interpreted as mirroring the structure of the universe.[229] In addition, because the Italian garden is usually thought of as including a leveled terrace followed by a grove of trees, the view is usually held that the firs and cypresses at Fiesole constituted a bosquet that spatially followed the flowerbeds, that is, that formed the backdrop to the secret garden.

It is not uncommon to read that the Medici villa anticipates later developments of Italian garden architecture, especially with regard to the articulation of the gardens into three terraces linked by a single path. The only element that makes the gardens at Fiesole a still somewhat timid example, according to some authors, is the fact that the steps connecting the terraces are not designed in a grandiose manner, as will be the case in later Renaissance villas. Now, if on one hand there is not enough evidence to substantiate a reconstruction of the garden layout that separates the *orticini* from the *boschetto*, on the other hand the fact that fifteenth-century sources never mention the presence of a connecting walkway is very telling, in that it may demonstrate that the terraces were likely to be independent of each other. Therefore, as we shall see, the gardens at Fiesole too fail to fit the stereotypical model of the *giardino all'italiana* characterized by a formal layout and continuous path. But this does not mean that the unconnected terraces at Fiesole, contained by massive retaining walls, were less innovative.

It is my opinion that the garden and the bosquet on the upper terrace were not distinct from each other. We do not actually know whether or not the beds were laid out according to a regular pattern and if a wall surrounded the garden. In fact, the phrase "ricinti di mura" that appears in the 1492 inventory is but a repetition of the adjective *murati* that is used to stress and emphasize that the beds were surrounded by low "walls" or curbs; and the fact that the adjective is in the plural indicates that it refers to the *orticini* and not to the *giardino*. Scholars who argue otherwise usually report Aby Warburg's transcription of the document along with his added punctuation: "et uno pezzo di terra in detto giardino con arcipressi, abeti et altro a uso di boschetto."[230] By comparing this to the most recent transcription by Marco Spallanzani, we see how the position of a comma can lead to a totally different interpretation: "e uno pezzo di terra in detto giardino con arcipressi, abeti e altro, a uso di boschetto."[231] Whereas in Warburg's transcription the word *altro* could stand for "another garden," in Spallanzani's it means "other trees," and we can interpret the whole phrase as follows: "and a piece of land within the abovementioned garden with cypress trees, firs etc., which is used as a bosquet." Now, we can't determine with absolute certainty where the comma should go, because the original document, like most fifteenth-century inventories and tax returns, does not have punctuation. However, I am more inclined to believe that the *giardino* and the *boschetto* were not yet separated from each other—as they will be in later Medici villas. We cannot, in fact, rule out the possibility that the bosquet followed the garden spatially, but if the word *giardino* referred to the whole, *boschetto* referred only to the use to which a portion of that garden was put.[232] And the use was likely hunting, as the presence of *ragne da tordi* also suggests.[233]

Another argument for the separation of the garden from the bosquet is the claim that in the fifteenth century orange trees were planted along the north wall of the upper terrace, like today. Scholars endorsing this thesis rightly affirm that orange trees, or *Citrus aurantium*, used to be cultivated—and still are—along walls with a southern exposure. Thus, they identify as orange trees the trees in Biagio d'Antonio's *Annunciazione* (see fig. 20), planted both along

Fig. 21. Telemaco Bonaiuti, *Veduta della Villa Mozzi, già de' Medici* (early nineteenth century). In Giuseppe del Rosso, *Guida di Fiesole e suoi dintorni* (Florence: Luigi Pezzati, 1846).

the upper retaining wall and the wall separating the property from the via Vecchia Fiesolana. Another source, the nineteenth-century representation of the Medici villa by Telemaco Bonaiuti (fig. 21), according to these authors, also shows orange trees along the retaining wall of the upper garden and the boundary wall of the upper terrace.[234] That these are orange trees seems to be confirmed by the fact that the painting reproduces sheds along the walls, which were used to protect the trees from the cold.[235] Therefore, if tall trees, such as conifers, had been planted in the garden, they would have cast their shadow on the orange trees, which need full sun. Hence the argument that the bosquet must have been adjacent to the garden, instead of being integrated with it.[236]

The trees represented in the *Annunciazione* along the retaining wall of the upper garden are not dissimilar from the trees beyond the Medici property, in the middle of the landscape. Moreover, these trees are almost as tall as the wall itself, and they are not protected by sheds; also, the trees present on the upper terrace could not be orange trees, for they are aligned along the wall, on the edge of the via Vecchia Fiesolana, which is far lower than the trees themselves and thus can offer neither protection from the north wind nor the possibility of installing sheds against hail. However, orange trees are indeed mentioned in the primary sources, as in a letter written by Giovanni di Luca Rossi to Giovanni di Cosimo: "Bartolommeo Serragli will be going to Naples in eight days and I made a note for him of everything that we need for Fiesole, that is, pomegranates, orange trees, lemon trees . . . and some other things."[237] In my view, it is possible that orange trees were planted along the retaining wall of the upper garden, that is, along the perimetric wall of the *ortaccio*—in which case we should consider Biagio d'Antonio not very accurate in the representation of plants—but there is no proof of their presence on the upper terrace. Therefore, there is no reason why the cypresses and firs of the bosquet could not have cast their shadows in the garden.

As we have seen, the garden also included flowerbeds that must have hosted the precious flowers of which Giovanni was fond. In fact, there is evidence that besides ordering plants from Naples, such as pomegranate, orange, and lemon trees, the young Medici was involved in the exchange of cultivars. In a letter written to him Giovan Francesco della Torre asks the young Medici to send him a variety of rose called *alba "incarnata,"* for its color resembling human flesh, and white (probably the *dianthus*) and red carnations: "Send me many rose cuttings of the white and pale pink variety and similarly if you could send me some cuttings of those white and pale pink carnations with lots of leaves and the beautiful red ones for there should be many over there, and if you don't find cuttings send me the seeds, and I will be very grateful."[238]

Apart from the knowledge of the species that were cultivated at Fiesole, the archival sources do not offer a precise description of the Medici gardens' layout, whose "design," notwithstanding the lack of information about it, is usually considered groundbreaking. The first scholars to draw attention to the innovative character of the gardens at Fiesole were John Shepherd and Geoffrey Jellicoe in 1925. In their *Italian Gardens of the Renaissance* they wrote, "As a work of garden architecture, it was a thoroughly sound conception, and one of the most important foundations of the future garden design."[239] Georgina Masson specifically addressed the gardens at Fiesole in her *Italian Gardens*, saying that the fundamental lines of the garden terraces had remained intact since the day when they were built, and that the clumsy way in which they are connected shows that the design of these gardens was still at an elementary stage, "which did not yet envisage the exploitation of a hillside site as an opportunity for the spectacular use connecting stairs and ramps that was to become a *tour de force* of later Renaissance garden architects."[240] Masson's view is generally accepted today.[241]

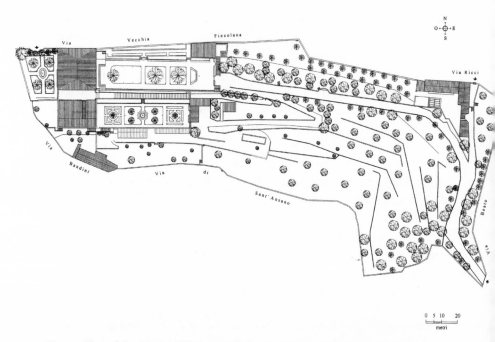

Fig. 22. Plan of the Medici Villa at Fiesole by Donata Mazzini. In Donata Mazzini, ed., *Villa Medici a Fiesole: Leon Battista Alberti e il prototipo di villa rinascimentale* (Florence: Centro Di, 2004), 20.

While these scholars suggest that little transformation, both architectural and mineral, took place at the villa during the course of several centuries, Clara Bargellini and Pierre de la Ruffinière du Prey, following in the footsteps of James Ackerman,[242] have proved that the appearance of the villa at Fiesole was greatly altered, especially in the years between 1776 and 1779, when the property belonged to Margaret Rolle, Lady Orford. She was the wife of Robert Walpole, Earl of Orford and eldest brother of Horace Walpole.[243] When she died in 1781, Lady Orford left the villa to her companion, Giulio Mozzi.[244]

As Bargellini and Ruffinière du Prey have demonstrated, one of the major transformations carried out for Lady Orford was the construction of a "new road cut through the mountain,"[245] which became the main access to the villa and thus changed the hierarchy of the façades by prioritizing the east side.[246] This road still leads to the main entrance of the villa today (fig. 22), and it is used as a driveway lined with cypress trees linking the via Beato Angelico to the eastern garden.[247] The construction of the new carriageway must have transformed what was probably the secret garden, private and intimate, into a place more outward-looking, apt to receive the countess and her occasional guests. Moreover, the addition of a *limonaia*, or orangery, to the northeast corner of the upper garden, and of a belvedere to the southeast, inevitably altered the proportions of the original terrace by stretching it nearly fifteen meters.[248] In addition, Lady Orford wished to facilitate the entrance of carriages to the stables of the villa along the road leading to Fiesole from Florence.[249] The stables corresponded to the service buildings located on the western side of the lower terrace. It is likely that more service buildings were added at this time to the east side of this garden, since these buildings are aligned both with the new portion of retaining wall and with the *limonaia* on the upper terrace. The presence of quoins, which are still visible today along the retaining wall of the upper garden, shows precisely the point at which the terrace was extended (fig. 23). The quoins, which are located at the beginning of the raised footpath on the lower level, also correspond to the threshold of a pergola (figs. 24 and 25), and they separate two sections of wall obviously constructed at different times. Considering that the length of the retaining wall from the house to the quoins matches the length of the garden's perimetric wall to the north side, that is, from the house to the orangery, we can deduce that the position of the quoins indicates the original length of the garden terrace extending eastward from the façade of the house; the portion of wall to the right of the quoins marks the eighteenth-century extension.[250]

Another transformation of the villa exterior during the eighteenth century was the addition of a footpath at the base of the higher retaining wall (fig. 26). The path, which was later covered by the pergola,[251] serves as the terraces' connective element in that it leads to the eastern garden on the upper terrace by means of a tortuous path that connects to the entrance gate of the villa (fig. 27); on the opposite side the walkway leads to the western garden— a few steps compensating for the difference in elevation (figs. 28 and 29); and finally, at approximately its midpoint, the path connects to the lower, southern garden by means of a stone staircase (fig. 30).

In an effort to prove that the gardens at Fiesole—especially the articulation of the terraces—have remained unchanged since the Quattrocento, some scholars claim that the raised walkway has always existed, and that it was built in the fifteenth century to help absorb the thrust of the mass of earth retained by the wall to which it is attached: "The upper terrace is notable in its inventive construction, in that it allows a reduction of the earth's thrust and at the same time [it creates] a gradual arrangement of terraces and also the possibility of a connection between the different levels, which resulted from the daring adaptation—breathtaking at that time—of the steep hill of Fiesole."[252] However, none of the letters sent to Giovanni de' Medici,

Fig. 23. Medici Villa at Fiesole, detail of the upper retaining wall.

Fig. 24. Medici Villa at Fiesole, detail of the pergola and the wall.

Fig. 25. Medici Villa at Fiesole, pergola.

Fig. 26. Medici Villa at Fiesole, hanging footpath.

Fig. 27. Medici Villa at Fiesole, entrance to the villa from the east.

especially those that express concern about the structural condition of the re-taining wall, mentions the construction of a raised path as a remedy. In one of the letters, Giovanni Macinghi wrote to the younger Medici that his brother Piero, who used to supervise the work at Fiesole when Giovanni was away, wanted to seek the opinion of three experts about the retaining wall. Thus, he called Antonio Manetti, Lorenzo da San Frediano, and Pagolo Calaffi.[253] Also, a letter written by Ginevra degli Alessandri reports that Piero expressed the need for caution: "Piero says that he wants to understand fully before beginning [the work] for he says that one would not want to rush im-patiently in similar things."[254] In another letter to Giovanni, Macinghi wrote that Piero had decided to accept the advice of the architect and engineer Manetti, namely, "to dig down to bedrock ("fino al sodo") to construct new foundations around the wall and a supporting arch strengthened with lime mortar."[255] The appearance of the higher retaining wall shows precisely that Manetti's advice must have been followed, for protruding rocks are visible at the base of the wall, which was the point at which digging would have stopped; moreover, the wall is stepped along its height, as if it had been en-veloped with another wall or foundation (figs. 31 and 32). A close examination of the wall reveals also the presence of arches reinforced with mortar, which

Fig. 28. Medici Villa at Fiesole, walkway under the pergola.

Fig. 29. Medici Villa at Fiesole, entrance to the western garden.

Fig. 30. Medici Villa at Fiesole, steps leading to the *ortaccio*.

Fig. 31. Medici Villa at Fiesole, protruding rocks at the base of the retaining wall.

Fig. 32. Medici Villa at Fiesole, retaining-wall foundation.

Fig. 33. Medici Villa at Fiesole, wall detail.

correspond to Manetti's advice (fig. 33). At this point, it seems that Manetti's plan was carried out, and the structural problem was solved without the need to construct a raised footpath.[256]

These considerations lead me to conclude that the walkway was constructed later than the fifteenth century, insofar as it is never mentioned as a remedy for the structural problem concerning the retaining wall; therefore, the gardens at Fiesole were probably not linked to each other by a single path, as they are today. In addition, the assumption that the pathway may be a fifteenth-century invention is contradicted by the fact that Biagio d'Antonio did not represent it in his painting of the Medici property (see fig. 20), which dates to the end of the century. However, the walkway does appear in three visual sources, namely, the engraving by Telemaco Bonaiuti from 1826 mentioned above (see fig. 21); a sketch of the villa titled *Veduta della collina di San Francesco* drawn by Emilio Burci in 1842 (fig. 34); and a nineteenth-century painting by an anonymous artist (fig. 35). It is likely that the pathway was built sometime in the eighteenth or early nineteenth century.[257] The above sources, moreover, show an uninterrupted path linking the eastern garden to

Fig. 34. Emilio Burci, *Veduta della collina di San Francesco* (1842). GDSU 1119P. By permission of Ministero per i Beni e le Attività Culturali.

Fig. 35. Anonymous, *Veduta di Villa Spence* (1860). Private collection. In Donata Mazzini, ed., *Villa Medici a Fiesole: Leon Battista Alberti e il prototipo di villa rinascimentale* (Florence: Centro Di, 2004), 57.

Fig. 36. The Medici Villa at Fiesole from the southeast (c. 1907). American Academy in Rome, Photographic Archive.

the western one, but not to the southern terrace. This means that the steps connecting the southern garden to the raised walkway were probably designed later.

A photograph of the property taken from the southeast at the beginning of the twentieth century shows the appearance of the villa before Lady Sybil Cutting commissioned from Cecil Pinsent the design of the lower garden in 1915 (fig. 36). This garden included a large greenhouse, which had been created for the growing of exotic plants toward the end of the nineteenth century, as a sketch drawn by Joseph Pennell in 1883 shows (fig. 37).[258] The greenhouse flanked the raised path throughout its entire length, thus preventing access to the lower garden.[259] A sketch of the Medici villa by Edward G. Lawson (fig. 38), the first landscape architecture fellow at the American Academy in Rome, reproduces Pinsent's design in 1915.[260] The English architect reduced the dimensions of the greenhouse, "a marble-covered garden-house,"[261] and split it into two by adding a few steps in line with the new axis of the garden. He also replaced the posts of an existing pergola, with stone pilasters.[262] This is how Norman T. Newton described the pergola a few years later: "A long

Fig. 37. Joseph Pennell, *Veduta di Fiesole* (1883) GDSU 1610P. By permission of Ministero per i Beni e le Attività Culturali.

arbor, covered with grapes and roses, nestles at the foot of the high retaining-wall of the arrival terrace. At the far end of the arbor is another small gateway, from which a sloping path runs up between vine-covered walls to regain the entrance road. A few feet below the arbor is the lower terrace, recently laid out as a garden in the old manner—a placid area of gravel, box, turf, and roses, with a stone-coped fountain splashing merrily in the center."[263] It is clear that a fundamental element of this new *old* Italian garden was the path connecting the three terraces, joined together as to form one work of garden architecture.

In sum, if the steps leading up from the southern garden were designed in 1915; if the raised walkway is a late eighteenth- or early nineteenth-century invention; and considering that there is no mention of such elements in fifteenth-century visual and written sources, we may assume that the gardens mentioned in the 1492 inventory were independent from each other, rather than "designed" according to a specific aesthetic and coordinating principle. In fact, it is likely that in the Quattrocento the contiguity of the terraces was only visual, and that the eastern garden, being the most private, was accessible

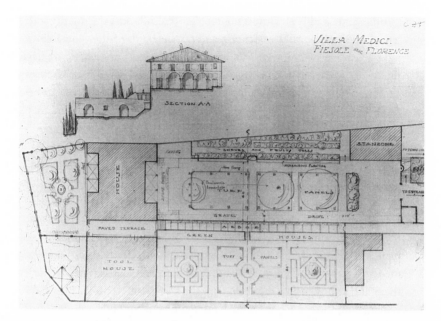

Fig. 38. Edward G. Lawson, sketch of the Medici Villa at Fiesole (c. 1915). American Academy in Rome, Photographic Archive.

only through the main room on the first floor of the villa. On the other hand, the lower garden, or *ortaccio*, was accessible from the ground floor of the service buildings located on the lower level and to the southwest of the villa, whereas the garden to the west did not yet exist. It follows that the gardens that we see today are the result of numerous transformations that took place throughout the centuries to meet the needs and changing taste of the people who owned and inhabited the Medici villa.[264]

If it is true that the construction of the gardens' retaining walls in the second half of the fifteenth century is an admirable work of structural engineering, this was not, in fact, the only enterprise of the kind being undertaken at that time. The closest example is probably the Badia Fiesolana, whose reconstruction was commissioned from Michelozzo by Cosimo de' Medici, and whose hanging gardens are described by Filarete in the twenty-fifth book of his treatise on architecture:

> Here [at Fiesole] the abovementioned Cosimo has had a noble monastery of canons regular of St. Augustine built. It is called the Badia of Fiesole. [It is called this] because there was a Badia here at one time which

through time had been almost obliterated. It also lacked the dignity it deserved. He was moved by devotion and by the words of the venerable monks, among whom was the aforementioned Don Timoteo. As we have shown above, by his good words Cosimo knew that he was a satisfactory and worthy person and gave him full permission to spend as freely as he thought best in this affair. . . . Together with Cosimo he [Don Timoteo] arranged a fish pond one hundred and twenty *braccia* on one side and sixty on the other. In the middle of it a bridge was arranged with a cataract. I mean to say a coffer. Whenever fish were needed, one had only to raise the cataract. All the water from the other side ran into the middle of this bridge. It was arranged in such a way that the fish stayed there. Thus one could take them as one pleased with ease and quickness when they were required. He told me that many kinds of fruit trees were planted round it, that is, figs, pears, apples, plums, cherries, sorb-apple, medlars, and similar fruits. When they were ripe, they fell. The fish ate them and also the roots that held firm the banks of this pond. It had a wall all around set back from the bank ten *braccia* and high enough to keep out people who did not have permission to enter. This goes from the foot of the perimeter of the garden, where it is near a little stream that runs beside it. The water from it flows into the pond. Thus the garden is surrounded by a wall so high that one cannot enter it. I do not wish to say more about the nature of this place. It is such, however, that it is worthy of being praised with all the other noble ones, for it is most beautiful.[265]

Also in Alberto Avogadro's description of the Badia we find reference to the construction of retaining walls and hanging platforms.[266] According to Franco Borsi the plan of the Badia was governed by a simple rule, which was based not on symmetry but rather on functional exigencies and visual panoramas.[267] The works for the renovation of the Badia started in 1456, as we learn from the record of payments dated from the month of September of that year.[268] These payments refer to the initial earthworks and substruction of the building, which were required by the very steep slope of the terrain on which the new convent was going to be built.[269] In fact, according to Vasari: "It is important to consider that having to create a level surface for the building on a steep slope, he [Brunelleschi, who was in charge of the project, says Vasari] made use, judiciously, of the basement by creating cellars, lavatories, bakeries, stables, kitchens, rooms for the storage of wood, and many other comforts, such that it is not possible to see better ones: therefore he put the plan of the building on a level surface and then he could build loggias, the refectory, the infirmary, the novitiate, the dormitory, the library and the most important rooms of a monastery."[270]

Apparently, the complexity of the work derived from the fact that the nature of the terrain required multiple rooms located on several floors, in a kind of giant stepped structure. The intermediate level was the entrance to the friars' convent as well as that of the church, which was located on the same level. Both above and below the intermediate level were two more levels, with specific functions.[271] On the intermediate level of the Badia were the guest quarters and the abbot's quarters, which were two cubic structures separated by a hanging garden to the south. To the north side this garden was once limited by a loggia connecting the two buildings and looking over the valley of the Mugnone. It is likely—although Borsi does not mention it—that another hanging garden existed between the two buildings of the *dormitorio dei canonici* and the building including the kitchen on the ground floor and the library and the *dormitorio dei novizi* on the upper floors. In fact, the relationship between these two elongated bodies, separated as they are by a loggia and a terrace to the east side, resembles the symmetrical relationship between the two cubical buildings to the south side of the complex.

As we learn from the primary sources, the Badia was not built out of nothing. In fact, Cosimo had decided to restore and expand an existing early Christian building, the former cathedral of Fiesole, which had been founded on the site of a *martyrium* dedicated to Saint Romolo, a martyr from the fourth century A.D. It has been ascertained that the church Cosimo expanded was already a building of considerable proportions, which occupied most of the central nave of the church that we see today. A large monastery flanked the church. The excavations carried out by a group of archaeologists in 1876 revealed that the perimetric walls of the Romanic church rested on two large walls of rusticated ashlar, connected by a similarly wide transversal stone wall. It is known that the Etruscans used this technique for the construction of the terraces on which they built their temples, and it is likely that whoever built the church in early Christian times, prior to the intervention sponsored by Cosimo, adopted precisely a building technique that was already observable in situ.[272] It is possible, in fact, that Fiesole itself evoked the structure, or morphological configuration, that was most appropriate for both the Badia and the Medici gardens. The topography of Fiesole is characterized precisely by a stepped settlement system, formed by a sequence of terraces that from the bottom of the via Vecchia Fiesolana ascend to meet the Medici villa and the hill between Saint Francis and Saint Apollinaris. And, as we learn from archaeological studies and ancient sources, this system was of Etruscan origin.[273] Fiesole, or *Fesulae*, was one of the first Etruscan settlements, founded around 474 B.C., of which we still see today the remains of the ancient city walls. It was subject to the domain of the Romans and was mentioned for the first time by Dionysius of Halicarnassus in his *Roman Antiquities* (7 B.C.); the Greek historian Polybius also mentioned Fiesole in his history of Rome, and so did Livy in his *Historia Romae* (book XXII) at the point in which he tells of the passage of Hannibal from Gaul to Tuscany across the Ligurian Apennines and the fertile Etruscan fields between Fiesole and Arezzo.[274]

Now, given the fact that, as Filarete tells us, Cosimo spent a fortune to reconstruct the Badia, which even prior to Cosimo's intervention stood on the steep slope of its site, and considering also that the new building included one or more hanging gardens, which were being built at the same time as the Medici villa's terraces, it follows that the villa's terraces cannot be regarded as a unique example. In fact, the construction of the terraces was not the first of its kind, although it was the first such construction to be undertaken for a private house, rather than a large monastery.

Bargellini and Ruffinière du Prey have also mentioned the possibility of a more illustrious precedent for the Medici villa, that is, the gardens described in classical literature, for example in the poems of Statius and in the epistolary exchanges of Pliny the Younger and Cicero. In almost all these sources we find descriptions of suburban villas from which it is possible to enjoy wonderful views of gardens and *loci amoeni*. As we deduce from the descriptions in Statius's *Silvae* and in the letters of the younger Pliny,[275] these ancient villas were characterized by a visual accord between the building and its surroundings. The interior of a villa was usually designed in such a way that each room had its own special view or optical connection with a specific place/garden outside it. Even more important, however, are the frequent references to terrace gardens in Pliny's letters, which may remind us of the terraces at Fiesole.

In sum, Pliny's correspondence contains many elements that could have offered a Florentine humanist plenty of ideas for the construction, and especially location, of his villa.[276] And it is known that Giovanni di Cosimo de' Medici had a strong inclination toward the classics.[277] For example, in 1453 Giovanni ordered a series of twelve heads for his study, which are likely to have represented the Caesars, as he possessed the major literary source accounting for the appearance of the Roman emperors, namely, Suetonius's *De vita Caesarum*.[278]

Also, it appears that Giovanni acted as a newborn Cicero, who had his friend Atticus send him works of art from Athens.[279] In fact, the young Medici put his half-brother Carlo and Giovanni Serragli in charge of sending him antique and well-preserved marbles from Rome. And the sources show that he commissioned many works of art for the decoration of his villa at Fiesole. A letter written in October 1453 by Bartolommeo Serragli suggests that Giovanni would have liked to incorporate ancient Roman marble heads into the walls at Fiesole: "Surely these old things incorporated into the walls will look very good. Think about it for Fiesole, before we are done with the works."[280]

It is reasonable to conclude that for the construction of his villa Giovanni di Cosimo put to good use his knowledge of classical literature, and his sensitivity toward the site, including his consideration of the preexistent Etruscan civilization, which had modeled the landscape with the construction of terraces long before him.[281] In addition, Giovanni was a connoisseur of the finest horticultural specimens, and, as the sources report, he possessed a copy of Theophrastus's *De plantis* and Columella's *De re rustica*.

Many critics have often placed the Medici villa at Fiesole in opposition to the older Medici properties, such as Trebbio, Cafaggiolo, and Careggi. In particular, they have argued that, unlike the older villas, Fiesole was not a farm but rather a pleasure place, surrounded by gardens. James Ackerman wrote, for example, that the villa at Fiesole "was dramatically dissimilar to its predecessors in symbolism as well as in form. This is due less to its later date and the evolution of Renaissance architecture than to its distinct role as a suburban villa without an agricultural function, the scale and form of which was accommodated to the choice of a site with a panoramic view. . . . The Fiesole villa is an abstract, purist structure designed . . . to stand off from rather than to merge into its natural environment."[282] To the contrary, Amanda Lillie opposed this nonutilitarian approach, arguing that the notion of beauty in fifteenth-century villa ideology was linked to the concept of *utilitas*, not to pleasure. In an effort to prove the possibility of rural pursuits at Fiesole, however, Lillie claimed that no intellectual urge had an impact on the design of the villa. She argued that "for those who wish to make a strict division between humanist villas and farm houses, it was the menial and agricultural functions of the household, rather than intellectual pursuits, that were incorporated into the design and specially catered for in an ingenious and modern way."[283]

Although I agree with Lillie's view that at Fiesole the Medici did not ignore the possibility of making a profit, on the other hand I think that the two pursuits, the economic and the intellectual, are not mutually exclusive, as

Lillie seems to believe, for they could very well have been pursued at the same time. If it is true that the urge to make a profit drove the Medici to invest in those arable portions of land existing at Fiesole, although detached from the villa, the sources also confirm that Giovanni di Cosimo was a man of learning, who appreciated classical literature and drew inspiration from it. Moreover, the presence of a garden with rare imported specimens shows that he also valued eye-pleasing delicacies that did not yield any profit.

Even if it is very likely that the site at Fiesole was chosen because of the spectacular view it offers, the lack of a farm is to be ascribed only to the hilly topography of the site, and not to a deliberate choice of the Medici. In fact, had Giovanni had the possibility of enjoying both a great panorama and flat, arable land, he would have not been dissatisfied. Nonetheless, it is true that he gave precedence to the panoramic view over agriculture. However, we know that the lack of extended fields around the villa was compensated for in other ways. First of all, the *orto et ortali* mentioned in the tax return from 1457 served, at least, the needs of the family,[284] and the great effort demonstrated in the search for water at Fiesole testifies to the need for water for irrigation, as there is no record of the creation of fountains.[285] Moreover, it appears that between 1457 and 1458 Giovanni di Cosimo bought a large wooded area at Fiesole, which he had cleared of trees and divided into three smaller farms that yielded wine, wheat, beans, barley, spelt, and wood.[286] After Giovanni's death, his brother Piero continued the purchase of land at Fiesole, especially vineyards and olive groves.[287] When the property passed down to Lorenzo efforts were made to increase its productivity. In the 1492 inventory, for example, we read that the ground floor of the service building on the lower terrace was "used for the grape harvest, it fits four tubs on four wooden benches with six stone pilasters; they yield about one hundred and twenty *barili* [one *barile da vino* equals 45.58 liters; twelve gallons] and six small tubs to be used for the said tubs, holding about fifty *barili*."[288] We read too that on the first floor of the same building were: "Six barrels for red wine on stone benches hold forty-one *barili*. Six *barili* and two half *barili* of red wine. In the adjacent cellar, called the summer cellar, six barrels on two rows of benches, holding almost fifty-one *barili*."[289] This means that the Fiesole property produced about 7,748 liters of wine (2,047 gallons), of which 4,400 liters (1,162 gallons) were red wine. That the wine was produced at the villa is demonstrated by the fact that the grape harvest, or *vendemia*, used to take place there, as the inventory reports. From the same document we learn that another service building was used for the storage of olive oil: "Thirty-six pots for oil and three barrels and two half barrels [one *barile da olio* equals 33.42 liters; 8.8 gallons],"[290] which was produced at the nearby oil mill: "A farm of one-hundred and sixty *staiora* [5.6 *staiora* equals 1 hectare], located in the parish of Santo Romolo at the presbytery of Fiesole with a house for the farm overseer."[291] This farm of about eighty-four thousand square meters belonged to the family and produced: "Forty eight *staia* of wheat [1,169.3 liters; 265.45 gallons; one *staio* equals 24.36 liters], six *staia* of fodder [146 liters; 33 gallons], forty five *barili* of wine [2,051 liters; 542 gallons], twenty two *barili* of oil [713.24 liters; 188.4 gallons], fruit."[292]

Other information that we can draw from the 1492 inventory is that Lorenzo de' Medici owned four quarries of *pietra serena* at Fiesole: "Several stone quarries follow and masses of stone, part of which are sold for the extraction of stone in a certain amount of time and part are rented for a certain amount per year, that is, two quarries are sold to Mattio di Manno and to Marcho di Sandro Ferrucci in order to extract stone in four years, and if they do not make any extraction in the agreed time, the stone will remain in the quarry; these are located in the parish of Sancto Romolo and presbytery of Fiesole, at a place called the palace of Fiesole."[293] It appears, then, that the Medici would sell a few of their quarries on condition that the buyer extracted the stone within four years. But as the time allowed for the extraction was evidently too limited, the Medici conveniently remained the owners of the quarries. The fact that the quarries were rented to other people shows that they yielded an income with which the Medici would make up for those profits that they could not gain from agriculture, apart, of course, from any surplus production of wine, oil, and wheat that they could sell.[294] That the property at Fiesole was productive is also proven by a letter written by Lorenzo to the *ufficiali delle imposte* in which he asked for a reduction of his taxes in consideration of the fact that some of his revenue was donated to the poor: "I can attest to this by the writing of a third person, the abovementioned alms [those of his father, Piero] have greatly increased by means of my own deeds; in addition, my mother Lucrezia, in the name of God distributes a generous amount of money, and particularly all the income from Fiesole, since my father, before he died, expressed the wish that all the revenue from Fiesole be distributed for [the sake of] God."[295] And, of course, had Fiesole constituted for Lorenzo only a negligible source of income, he would not even have mentioned it to the officials as evidence of his charity.

Finally, it appears that the villa at Fiesole was not a farm like the older Medici properties, only because the site chosen was too hilly to allow for extensive cultivation; nearby properties, as we have seen, could yield produce, such as oil, wine, and wheat. Moreover, the primary sources show that the Medici exploited all the intrinsic qualities the site had to offer, including taking full advantage of the quarries they owned. From the point of view of the "design," however, the layout of the villa did not fully exploit the challenge of a stepped terrain, insofar as there was not a single path that would connect the different levels of the terraces. The innovative character of the villa lies in the fact that for the first time the garden at a villa was spatially distinguished from the kitchen garden, and the very existence of the terraces, built "per forza,"[296] with the different views they offer, shows that the villa was carefully researched, and was probably inspired by ancient sources and testimonies, such as the Etruscan and the Roman, with which Giovanni di Cosimo was very familiar. In addition, Giovanni's appreciation of the solitude of country life could have also been instilled in him by his reading of Petrarch, as a letter written by Bartolomeo Scala shows. Here the Florentine chancellor refers to visiting Giovanni at Fiesole and talking with him about Francesco Filelfo, whom Giovanni convinced to write a commentary on Petrarch's lyric poems: "I set out in the afternoon for Fiesole where Giovanni was rusticating, absorbed in his building. . . . I eventually gave him your greetings, in your own words, and showed him your letter and your poem. He read them very carefully and then spoke most warmly in your praise, saying he had written to you that very day, and urging you, if you thought him worthy of the kindness, to undertake the work of interpreting Petrarch's poems."[297]

All this shows, ultimately, that the Medici villa as well as the way of life conducted there incorporated both intellectual pursuits, such as learned ideas and philosophical discussions, and agricultural or economic ones. Thus, at Fiesole the distinction was not so much between material interests and humanistic ones as between farming and dwelling, in that the house was no longer at the center of a large agricultural estate as it had been, for instance, at Careggi; and this was a separation (but not an opposition) that Lorenzo de' Medici would continue at Poggio a Caiano.[298]

Archival documents related to the four fifteenth-century suburban gardens of the Medici do not support the assumption that these places corresponded to the "Italian garden" type. Moreover, as we have seen, both the architecture of the villas and their outdoors underwent a number of transformations throughout the centuries; thus, they hardly can fit the stereotypical definition of a work of art that is not affected by the passing of time. It is also telling that none of the documents cited above mentions the name of a single architect, or better yet, *ingegnere*, as being put in charge of the gardens' design. On the other hand, the utilitarian function of the *orti*, which often carries with it an idea of beauty, at least in the language of early modern Italy, suggests that these places were not at all designed, let alone by the hand of a single man. And if their layout obeyed geometrical discipline, this resulted more from the advent of sharecropping than the application of some design theory for, as we shall see in the ensuing chapters, such theory was yet to be written.

CHAPTER TWO

From Work of Nature to Work of Art

THE PRACTICE OF garden making in early modern Florence was a perfunctory activity, resulting both from an oral tradition and from the application of the principles of good husbandry extracted from agricultural handbooks. These texts were manuals more than treatises in that their authors' main objective was to share their horticultural knowledge, which was the result of years of direct experience. This knowledge did not include the methodological principles related to garden design, however, for it is likely that a concept of design intended as process (the series of actions performed by the designer), rather than as end product (the object of design), did not yet exist. This means that the *scriptores* did not conceptualize, for example, about the use of drawings and models in order to define a certain spatial configuration, nor did they theorize a process of design as temporally separate from actual implementation. Therefore, it is likely that their gardens were laid out directly on the land, not first on paper. In addition to the literature on husbandry, gardens were also mentioned in relation to architecture. But if the process of designing buildings was indeed addressed by the authors, that of designing gardens, as we shall see, was not. Within architectural treatises, gardens often appear as accessories, whose implementation is described in terms of know-how.

One of the most frequently published works on agriculture is the *Liber ruralium commodorum* written by Pier de' Crescenzi between 1304 and 1306.[1] The book, originally written in Latin, was translated into Tuscan in 1350. In total there were eleven published editions in Latin, and twenty-seven editions had been published in Italian by 1852.[2] The author was a learned man who had studied logic, medicine, natural science, and law at the University of Bologna but was forced to leave his hometown in 1275, probably because of his Ghibelline leanings. For thirty years Crescenzi traveled throughout northern Italy, serving as a lawyer; all the while he read the books of the ancients and witnessed the diverse practices of cultivating the land.[3] When in 1299 he was able to return to Bologna, he settled down as a farmer on the outskirts of the city and began writing his *Liber*, which benefited from his knowledge of the ancient authorities and from his direct experience.[4] Crescenzi derived the structure and content of the book from Columella's *De re rustica*, and the section dedicated to gardens, book 8, closely replicates a similar section in Albertus Magnus's mid-thirteenth-century *De vegetabilibus et plantis*.[5] This is so in particular for the first chapter, dedicated to the small garden of herbs.

Crescenzi says that a small garden can be made of herbs only, trees only, or both. He addresses the *verziere dell'erbe* first, giving practical advice on the choice of the site and the tilling of the soil that will allow for the growing of "fine and delicate grasses that greatly please the sight."[6] Further, he describes how to sow the seeds. As for the morphology of the garden, he says: "The site of the garden should be square and of such a size as may suit those that are expected to live there."[7] Along the perimeter of the garden he recommends planting aromatic herbs, such as rue, sage, marjoram, basil, and mint, "since they not only delight by their odor, but also refresh and delight the sense of sight."[8] Further, he suggests the pruning of a bush in the shape of a seat. For the sake of providing shade, trees can be planted, and he adds that "shade more than fruit is sought from those trees."[9] Trees should not be planted too close to each other or too plentifully, in order to allow for the circulation of air. Moreover, they should not be planted in the middle of the lawn, for the formation of spider webs between their branches would be a nuisance to strollers.

In the second chapter Crescenzi makes clear that the size of the garden depends on the social status of its owner; a medium garden is fit for people of moderate means. Once the area of the site is established, trenches should be dug and thorn bushes planted along its perimeter. Trees must be planted in rows according to species, and vines of different kinds—"which will bring delight and usefulness"[10]—can be planted between the trees. The rest of the garden can be a meadow of thin grasses. He also suggests the creation of pergolas and pavilions. Both the small garden of herbs and the medium-sized bosquet for people of average means can be created as part of a larger estate, such as the garden of a king or other illustrious people, which he describes in the third chapter. High walls should surround this garden, and wild animals may inhabit it. These should be able to retreat into a *selva*, or woodland, planted on the north side of the property. The southern side is where the *palagio* of the king should be located, so that during the summer its walls will cast a "dilettevole ombra" (pleasing shade) onto the garden.[11] Crescenzi explains how to build a house made of trees and vines shaped in such a way as to form rooms and hallways. Also, there should be evergreen trees, planted in an orderly way according to their age.

The next two chapters are dedicated to the ornamenting of gardens and fields—"things to be made for the sake of pleasure."[12] Crescenzi points out, however, that the pleasure of the fields, unlike that of gardens, derives from usefulness: "Usefulness should take precedence over delight in the fields, although in gardens the opposite must be preserved."[13] Finally, the last three chapters deal with vineyards, trees, and kitchen gardens.

Because of the frequent use of the word *diletto*, or pleasure, scholars have often read Crescenzi's eighth book as an anticipation of the aesthetic sensibility that is usually associated with gardens, as if this were a necessary condition for the existence of medieval pleasances.[14] The application of modern aesthetics to Crescenzi's ideas on gardening is also encouraged by the many illustrations, especially woodcuts, in existing copies of the book.[15] According to Robert Calkins, "The emphasis that Crescenzi places upon the aesthetics of pleasurable settings in his discussion of the *vergier*"[16] in fact encouraged the production of miniatures with which artists, especially the Flemish, tried to capture the author's "sensitivity to the aesthetics of light and shade, texture of foliage, mixture of odors and colors, and the quality of gentle breezes."[17] Calkins admitted, however, that the illuminations and woodcuts illustrating the numerous copies of Crescenzi's work published over the centuries reflect more the "period and locale in which the pictures were made rather than a direct dependence upon the early fourteenth-century text."[18]

The miniatures executed during the fourteenth century are more faithful to the author's text in that they simply portray the tending of the soil and its plants. For example, the earliest copy containing illustrations, namely, the Latin manuscript from about 1330 housed in the Vatican Library, shows only historiated initials, and its single-column illuminations represent the typical iconographical motifs associated with agricultural practices to be carried out month by month: sowing the fields, harvesting produce, picking herbs, and so forth. In short, during Crescenzi's own time, labor was emphasized more than the setting itself.

The paucity of illustrations dating to the fourteenth century, and the fact that the few existing ones emphasize the making of the garden rather than the garden's layout, suggest that medieval pleasances were not yet considered to be art objects. It is more likely that they reflected the ethical values associated with agriculture rather than anticipated the aesthetic qualities of modern gardens, which would require a theorization of the beautiful as distinct from the good.[19]

In more than one instance throughout the text, the ethical meaning that Crescenzi attributes to agriculture, and to gardens in particular, acquires theological overtones. In the *proemio*, for instance, he remarks that the practice of cultivating the land is fit for good people, and it is because of this practice that they earn God's love.[20] Further on he makes clear that the practice of agriculture brings usefulness in addition to pleasure: "The exquisite discipline of agriculture, through which it is easier to receive usefulness and delight more abundantly . . . this is what good men, who wish to live justly by the revenue of their farms without harming anyone, should deservingly seek; [thus] I turned my mind and soul to the tending of the villa."[21] This concept is repeated in the section on gardens, which Crescenzi defines as those places "that give pleasure to the soul and preserve also the health of the body, since the proportion of the bodily humors is always closely related to the disposition of the soul."[22] Therefore, besides pleasing the soul of men, gardens are also beneficial to their bodily health, and in fact Crescenzi remarks that there cannot be any delight without health. Also when he speaks of the vines to be planted between the trees in the garden of medium size, he says that these "daranno diletto e utilitade" (will bring pleasure and usefulness). At last, when describing the garden fit for a king, he says: "And the king will not delight in such a garden at all times, but only when he will have performed his obligatory business glorifying God on high, who is the origin and cause of all good and legitimate delights, will he [the king] be renewed in it. For, as Cicero wrote, we were not born to delight, but rather to carry out noble tasks. Although it is true that sometimes it is legitimate, once we have attended to the necessary and more useful things, to let go."[23] Hence it is clear that even a princely garden must be deserved, meaning that the king will delight in it only after having carried out his duty. It is precisely because the enjoyment of nature cannot be detached from the moral, religious, and practical content of the book that it is inappropriate to speak of an aesthetic sensibility in the Kantian sense in relation to fourteenth-century gardens.

Crescenzi, however, does acknowledge and appreciate the sensitivity of the bodily senses to external stimuli, such as sweet scents and shiny blades of grass, and although he does not conceptualize it, he mentions beauty in a few instances throughout his text. In the eighth chapter, for example, he writes: "In the fields the beauty of the site itself delights most of all, especially when there are not several irregular small fields, but when a great number are gathered into one,"[24] and further, "It delights most of all to have beautiful vineyards . . . bearing grapes of different types."[25] In both cases the word is used in a context that does not involve gardens directly but rather addresses fields and vineyards, which are both productive.

The only time in which the word *beauty* is used in the context of the garden and is not linked to the good is when Crescenzi mentions a fountain with running waters that provides *diletto* with its beauty: "A very pure spring should be diverted into the middle of the garden, because its beauty would bring delight and gaiety."[26] But it is significant that this passage was, in fact, added to the later editions of the *Liber* (i.e., the *Trattato dell'agricoltura* printed in Naples in 1724), since it is not to be found either in the Latin *editio princeps* of 1471 (*Ruralia commoda,* Augsburg: Johann Schüssler) or in the Latin edition of 1538, in which we read: "Si aut—possibile sit fons purissimus derivetur in medio, quia ipsius puritas multam affert iocunditatem."[27]

As Kristeller has remarked, the branch of philosophy that deals with art criticism and is called aesthetics was born in the eighteenth century; it "can be applied to earlier phases of Western thought only with reservation."[28] In particular, it is problematic to apply it to a historical period in which authors, such as Crescenzi, were concerned more with technical precepts than with general ideas, and in which even the term *arts* was used to mean crafts, or technique, rather than fine arts. In fact, the making of gardens in Crescenzi's work participates in the ethical rigor that informs the practice of cultivating the land, an activity that had both moral and spiritual implications. This shows that in the fourteenth century gardens were not yet considered to be an artist's exclusive concern; rather, they were by and large a matter of praxis in which any anonymous citizen could be involved. Within the context of medieval culture, the making of gardens was learned through direct experience, and through the reading of earlier writings. Crescenzi's sources show that for the writing of his book he drew as much inspiration from Albertus Magnus's mid-thirteenth-century *De vegetabilibus et plantis* as from Avicenna's eleventh-century book on the practice of medicine, the *Liber canonis.* Thus, Crescenzi's handbook had a strictly technical character and showed no tendency to link the practice of agriculture with the liberal arts or with philosophy.[29]

We have to wait until the early Renaissance to see a change in the position that garden making held vis-à-vis the other arts, both mechanical and liberal. The fifteenth-century architect and theorist Leon Battista Alberti was the first to include a chapter on gardens in a treatise that dealt with something other than agriculture, namely, architecture.[30] This was a step backward, considering that since the Middle Ages gardens had been included in the realm of agriculture, which was one of the seven principal mechanical arts, and now they were included within the discipline of architecture, which, along with painting and sculpture, was listed as a subgroup of *armatura*, one of the mechanical arts.[31] Therefore, gardens came to occupy quite a subordinate place among the other arts. However, because Alberti's intention in writing the *De re aedificatoria* was to promote the position of architecture to the rank of a liberal art, he contributed, albeit indirectly, to modifying the consideration accorded to gardens in the previous century. In fact, by addressing not only architects and craftsmen but also princes and patrons, Alberti claimed for the architect a high position in the social fabric of the early Renaissance. This is probably why he wrote his treatise in Latin and did not provide it with images, which were considered as pleasing the eyes of the ignorant more than those of the learned.[32] Also, he probably wanted to fix attention exclusively on the nobility of his language, where there was no room for Vitruvius's technical neologisms.[33] But if on the one hand Alberti adapted to architecture the theoretical dignity of classical rhetoric, on the other hand his attitude toward the making of gardens within the *De re aedificatoria* was rather different.

Gardens are discussed in the section on the ornamentation of private houses. The *orti suburbani* are not to be located too far away from the city, so that they can be reached often by the city dweller. The main elements composing Alberti's garden are porticoes, which allow for shade, fountains, and evergreen hedges. He also advises on the kind of trees and bushes to be planted. But the most important idea, as Lise Bek has noted,[34] is that of composing the plan of the garden in the manner of the plan of the building, that is, by means of geometrical figures, such as circles and semicircles. The planting of trees too should follow geometrical arrangements, such as divisions into triads and quincunxes.

Throughout the section on gardens, Alberti never tells us how to choose between the geometrical forms that are most appropriate for a garden, that is, he does not dwell on a process of design, nor does he address the design tools by means of which an architect can make an informed decision, rather than choosing arbitrarily among templates. Thus, besides the more or less disguised

material from classical authorities, which at times Alberti reinterprets according to his personal observations, the chapter on gardens is more a list of instructions on garden making than an attempt to formulate a theory of design,
which, on the other hand, he does develop with regard to architecture.[35]

Alberti's prescriptions for the making of gardens were followed by other
architectural theorists, such as Francesco di Giorgio Martini, who wrote
about gardens in his *Trattato di architettura* of 1482. Martini's section on gardens, however, can also be viewed at the level of a reference book, offering
templates for flowerbeds or for the layout of entire gardens.[36] Like Alberti in
his *De re aedificatoria*, Martini never made reference to a design process before the construction of a garden. He explained the geometry for planning a
garden in these terms: "The deviser of it must reduce it to some sort of perfect figures such as circles, squares, or triangles; after these, pentagons, hexa-
gons, orthogonal forms, etc., can be applied."[37] It follows that both the single
divisions and the garden as a whole are regulated by a formal structure, in
particular a centralized one, but how one reaches the ultimate form, the author does not say. The most immediate model for this, as Lucia Tongiorgi
Tomasi has pointed out, is the ideal city that goes back to Vitruvius, "planned
according to a rational scheme, but also conceived as a 'symbolic form,' connected with the theories of the microcosm."[38] In his 1464 treatise on the ideal
city of Sforzinda, for example, Antonio Averlino, also known as Filarete, described his ideal garden as formed by a number of terraces, built around a
palace and enclosed by a large square labyrinth of which it forms the center.[39]
Although the gardens of Sforzinda are described minutely, Filarete was not
interested in explaining the process of their creation. A reason for this may be
that his gardens exist solely in the imagination of the author, for they often
turn into fantastic and symbolic flights of fancy, which anticipate the descriptions of imaginary gardens found in Francesco Colonna's *Hypnerotomachia
Poliphili*.

Sebastiano Serlio, who published the fourth book of his *De architectura* in
Venice in 1537, and with it provided four specific plans for beds and labyrinths,
limited himself to saying that these plans can also be used for other purposes:
"Gardens are part of a building's ornament, therefore these four figures below
[can be used] as compartments for the gardens and they can also be used for
other things, in addition to the two labyrinths illustrated above, which serve
that function [that is, they are examples of garden labyrinths]."[40] Serlio's
fourth book included a few plates illustrating templates to be used either for
ceiling decoration or for gardens. These engravings can be regarded as printed

sketches, and the book itself as a visual compendium rather than a philosophi-cal treatise.[41]

In sum, even though during the course of the fourteenth century the making of gardens was discussed within writings on agriculture, it was not until the fifteenth century, with Leon Battista Alberti, that architectural dis-course began to address the issue of manipulating vegetal materials vis-à-vis mineral ones.[42] However, the making of gardens was never singled out as an autonomous discipline, nor were gardens considered to be works of art, as we tend to view them today. On the contrary, the tendency of present-day schol-arship to describe gardens as objects of aesthetic appreciation has lead to the search for precedents of a modern aesthetic sensibility in the gardens and gar-den writings of the fourteenth and fifteenth centuries. Therefore the writings of Crescenzi, like those of Petrarch, as we shall see in the following chapter, have come to constitute for most scholars the origin of an appreciation of beauty, whether of a garden or a *locus amoenus*, for its own sake: "De' Crescenzi and with him Della Cornia [an author of a poem on agriculture] dwell on the ways to make pleasurable a courtyard, a kitchen garden, a cultivated field, a vineyard . . . revealing a certain sensitivity for man's new attitude towards na-ture which was being born at that time and was going to have a determining role in the subsequent history of the garden. [This sensitivity] anticipated one of the main principles of the landscape garden that would be developed more than four centuries later. . . . The writings of Petrarch and Boccaccio reveal the participatory attention with which a learned man conceives both the natural environment and the designed garden. With them the aesthetic feeling of the landscape is born."[43]

If on the one hand it may be legitimate to point to the origin of an ap-preciation of beauty—albeit not beauty for its own sake—in the pages of Crescenzi's text, on the other we need to recover the fact that the experience of gardens changed over many centuries.[44] In "Some Medici Gardens of the Florentine Renaissance: An Essay in Post-Aesthetic Interpretation"[45] Edward Wright expresses his dissatisfaction with the scholarship on Italian Renais-sance gardens. This scholarship, he suggests, is informed by a modernist out-look characterized by the opposition of art versus nature, and by the exclusive use of formal or visual analysis, which he finds reductive. This modernist ap-proach, he rightly claims, is incompatible with the gardens themselves, which he interprets as the product of know-how. And he adds that historians' exege-sis of gardens is "confined to issues of style and aesthetic intentionality."[46] In fact, Wright laments that with the rise of modern epistemology the simple skill of laying out gardens became a sort of conceptual abstraction that stood as the antithesis of nature.

In opposition to that kind of approach to garden studies, Wright interprets art as technique, and he claims that the gardens of the mature Renaissance, such as Castello and Boboli in Florence, were structured by a know-how (*ars* or *techné*) that "was a matter of skills accumulated, handed down, and enlarged over many generations through a continuing intimacy with natural materials. . . . Renaissance gardens were for the most part a collaborative effort among patrons and technicians . . . Niccolò Tribolo was first hired at Castello only to design and make the fountains. Besides it hardly took an artistic genius to come up with the quartered square plan of the Giardino del laberinto at Castello or the regular lawn bordered by evergreens at the Boboli."[47] Therefore, Wright concludes that sixteenth-century Florentine gardens were "works of Nature," a matter of "habits and habitats, and of human Convention, timeless or topical."[48]

Claudia Lazzaro too acknowledges the existence of a traditional garden practice in her book *The Italian Renaissance Garden.*[49] However, unlike Wright, she explicitly pushes back the simple know-how of garden making to a period that precedes the fifteenth century, and claims that from the Quattrocento onward gardens began to show a geometrical layout that resulted from a design practice: "Ordering and regularizing, imposed on traditional garden practice, is what distinguished the gardens of the fifteenth and sixteenth centuries from earlier ones."[50] She insists on this point by saying that "the consistent application to the whole [garden] of the order and measure that is epitomized by the quincunx is one of the principal features that distinguished Italian gardens of the fifteenth and sixteenth centuries from earlier ones."[51] However, not only do the sixteenth-century gardens she examines to prove her point greatly outnumber her fifteenth-century examples, the few Quattrocento pleasances she describes are not, in fact, actual gardens. They are the fictional gardens imagined by Colonna in the *Hypnerotomachia Poliphili,* which was published in Venice as late as 1499.[52] Even if Lazzaro claims that "over the two centuries of the Renaissance, there were undoubtedly clearly distinct types [of gardens]," she also admits that "little is known of fifteenth-century designs for compartments, but evidence from the sixteenth century suggests that a basic repertoire was in currency throughout much of the later period."[53] Therefore, she accepts the use of later evidence for the analysis of earlier gardens, as when she says: "The evidence does not permit an equal treatment of all topics, and again later examples must be used to illustrate earlier developments."[54]

Lazzaro maintains that during the fifteenth and sixteenth centuries gardens began to be laid out according to geometrical rules and principles of order. And this is what she calls design. However, design too, like planting, is for her a mere convention, that is, a practice that was carried out almost automatically. She explains the process of design in terms of a number of sequential operations, such as the choice of plants, the enclosing of the garden site, and the subdivision into compartments defined either by short hedges or low lattice fences with vegetation trained against them. One part of the garden that was not—she claims—determined by design was the *giardino segreto*, because this was distinguished by enclosure and privacy, instead of geometrically shaped compartments. In fact, she often uses the word *design* to mean *layout*.[55] It is obvious, then, that Lazzaro takes the issue of design in the context of Renaissance gardens as self-evident. Wright, to the contrary, denies altogether the existence of a design practice, and interprets Renaissance gardens only as the consequence of the practical knowledge of garden making handed down over many generations.

If on the one hand Wright's analysis of the influence of modern epistemology on garden studies is accurate, on the other his "either/or" bias does not do justice either to the gardens themselves or to their "designers." In fact, sixteenth-century gardens are both the product of a knowledge inherited from previous generations—as Lazzaro maintains—and the result of a design practice, which—contrary to Lazzaro's view—was foreign to the fifteenth-century tradition of garden making. This is so especially if by design we intend not only the thinking process aimed at the selection of certain geometrical forms but also the visual translation of that speculative moment by means of drawings and models. These are the tools recommended by Alberti for the design of buildings, and an architect is supposed to deploy them during a trial and error phase that eventually determines the final layout.

Moreover, Wright's view of sixteenth-century garden making as a conventional technique applies more to fifteenth-century gardens, that is, the Medici villas from Trebbio to Fiesole, than to the gardens of the mature Renaissance, such as those at Castello and Boboli. Indeed, these later gardens could not be simply the result of conventional rules handed down from the past—although the conventions of planting did exist—because the cultural value of these places had changed since the previous century. Therefore, Lazzaro's suggested fixity of the notion of the garden throughout the fifteenth and sixteenth centuries is also problematic.

The grand ducal gardens of the Cinquecento, unlike earlier ones, were meant to represent and authorize the political power of the Medici duke; they hosted performances, such as wedding ceremonies, that once used to take place publicly at urban venues in an effort to involve the lower classes and deter feelings of envy; therefore, these gardens' configuration required a project, that is, a design. Also, primary sources show that unlike earlier Medici villas, these later gardens were constructed after the execution of drawings and the construction of models. Thus, they were no longer the result of spontaneous operations carried out in situ, which is what Lazzaro calls the convention of design; rather, they were born out of a creative process that involved a time for thinking. In addition, it is precisely in the sixteenth century that the name of the individual who is responsible for the design of the garden is mentioned by the primary sources. In fact, even if Tribolo—as Wright claims—was not such a genius, there are many archival documents showing that he was indeed the first designer of the gardens at Castello; therefore, his gardens, the result of his drawings, cannot be regarded only as a work of nature or the simple application of know-how; they must also be considered a work of art.

On the other hand, in the fifteenth century the blurred distinction between gardens and kitchen gardens, and the silence about the garden maker, suggest that these pleasances were the product of habit, meaning an instinctive modus operandi that each generation inherited from the previous one in the form of tradition, that is, a human activity embedded in the practice of everyday life.[56] In fifteenth-century Florence, garden making coincided with an empirical knowledge. It was an oral tradition that would become the base, in the following century, for the writing of several handbooks on agriculture when their authors decided to put on paper the fruit of their own experiences, often combined with the precepts derived from the *scriptores rei rusticae*, as was the case with Crescenzi. In these works, however, the sections dedicated to gardens are usually fairly limited, especially if compared to the scope of the entire work, that is, the practice of agriculture.

CHAPTER THREE

Writing the Garden in the Age of Humanism

Petrarch and Boccaccio

The Medici *orti* of the fifteenth century were the product of an empirical modus operandi that was by and large indebted to an oral knowledge, handed down over many generations. Because garden making proceeded empirically, its tradition was subject to change, and its practice was probably revised and adjusted according to the outcomes of horticultural experiments. Petrarch's annotations on gardening reflect an artless kind of plant cultivation, motivated perhaps by an urge to imitate the classics and by a curiosity to verify the reliability of the *scriptores*' horticultural advice. His gardening notes as well as his poetry offer an example of a creative activity that was ceaselessly reexamined, just like the tradition of garden making. Moreover, in the same way the Medici gardens were both *orti* and *giardini*, the actual gardens of Petrarch defy the clarity of a concept or precise definition.

Unlike Petrarch, Boccaccio does not appear to have been a gardener. However, in the literary making of his pleasances he approximated an idea of design that was not going to be explored until few centuries later. The fact that the morphology of a garden can be separated from its matter is implied in the *Decameron*, but garden makers would fully explore this concept only when they started drawing layouts of gardens on paper before selecting the actual specimens to be planted, as we shall see in the next chapter. The writings of Petrarch and Boccaccio, as well as those of Ficino, as we shall see in the next section, also help to demonstrate that in the age of humanism gardens were not yet conceived as objects, in the same way the *orti dei Medici* were not an artist's creation and the *loci amoeni* were not considered "things" of nature, for they materialized the feelings and passions of the poet, in the case of Petrarch, and of the potential reader, in the case of Boccaccio, and can thus be interpreted as projections or emanations of the very subjects who created and/or experienced them. Ficino's literary pleasances are not mere objects of aesthetic appreciation because they act as signs that point to an absence, the transcendental existence of God. Thus, they offer clues to understanding the meaning that Ficino's contemporaries, the Medicis in particular, would have attributed to their gardens.

In what follows I shall be examining several manifestations of Petrarch's sensitivity to nature: the writings about the actual *horti* that Petrarch cultivated at Parma, Milan, and Arquà; his house at Vaucluse and the two gardens that he supposedly had there, although their status as gardens is unclear, as we shall see; the gardens in his moralistic work; and his letter on the ascent of Mount Ventoux. I shall then discuss Boccaccio's *loci amoeni* and gardens, and show that the way in which Boccaccio described them in his *Comedia delle ninfe fiorentine* and *Decameron* has been a source of inspiration for illuminators and painters depicting gardens across the centuries.

As Pierre de Nolhac has shown, Petrarch possessed a garden, or was allowed to cultivate one, in almost every city in which he lived. In his gardens he conducted horticultural experiments, the outcome of which he carefully annotated on the flyleaves of a manuscript, the codex Vaticano Latino 2193, containing a copy of Rutilius Palladius's *De agricultura* (circa fourth century A.D.).[1] It is precisely by transcribing Petrarch's annotations that de Nolhac was able to enumerate the poet's gardens.[2] Between 1348 and 1350 Petrarch cultivated vines, officinal hyssop, rosemary, salvia, rue, apple trees, and peach trees in his backyard at Parma, where he seems to have had two *orticelli*. His house in Milan—where the poet lived for eight years—had no yard, but he was allowed to do some planting at Sant'Ambrogio and Santa Valeria between 1353 and 1359, and there he grew spinach, beets, fennel, parsley, eleven laurels, and one olive tree. One of the last entries on the manuscript reports the planting of some laurels and fruit trees in the yard surrounding the house at Arquà, a village in the Euganean hills, where Petrarch spent the last years of his life, from about 1369 until his death in 1374.

The nature of Petrarch's experiments shows how empirically garden making proceeded at that time. He writes, for example, that at Parma he had cuttings planted which had been clipped some time earlier from certain vines. This, he remarks, is *contra consuetudinem communem* (against common habit), according to which vine cuttings should be planted immediately. However, he learned from a friend, who by chance had to delay the planting of his vine cuttings, that this procedure is actually successful. The cuttings grew and yielded new vines. "Therefore," remarks Petrarch, "the fruit of chance became rule and constant practice, and since then [it was] an ever pleasant habit. Hence, I too enjoy experimenting."[3] It seems that the pleasure of putting his horticultural knowledge, or that of Virgil, to the test urges him to transplant several trees and plants on his properties. In 1349 in his garden at Parma he transplants an apple tree, from a shadowy place far from the house to a closer and sunnier location. Unfortunately, the tree dies. A few days later he has two peach trees transplanted. An older one close to the house is substituted with a younger tree planted farther away. This experiment also fails. Later on he has sage plants moved from the center to the perimeter of his *orto* at Parma. And at Arquà he tries to transplant laurel trees. For each experiment Petrarch annotates the conditions that are considered favorable and those that are traditionally considered unfavorable. He carries out his plans even when the unfavorable conditions outnumber the favorable ones, the main reason being that he enjoys experimenting, *sed placet experiri*, and waiting to see the outcome.

In addition to showing the experiential nature of garden making, and the continuous testing of traditional horticultural knowledge, Petrarch's annotations are valuable for what they do not say. In his entries, as in the *orti* of the Medici, one looks in vain for consciousness of spatial design. It is likely that Petrarch's "gardens" were probably just orchards or kitchen gardens, whose layout was not decided at a drawing table. Moreover, all the planting the poet carried out involved officinal herbs, vegetables, and fruit trees, whose function is not ornamental, especially according to opinions that were widely diffused at that time.

Crescenzi's *Liber ruralium commodorum* was very well known in Petrarch's time and also to following generations. In the eighth book, which deals with the pleasures deriving from trees, grassy lawns, and fruits, Crescenzi distinguishes between *viridaria* and *horti*.[4] In the introduction he explains what kind of *diletto* or pleasure is to be derived from green places. It is the pleasure of the soul, which is a consequence of the pleasure of the senses.[5] For example, in the first chapter, on gardens with lawns, the sight of thin grasses gives pleasure to the eye, whereas odoriferous plants, such as the aromatic rue, sage, basil, and marjoram, give pleasure to the sense of smell. Crescenzi suggests also the use of a few trees—to be separated from the lawns—because they yield *diletto* with their shade. Trees too have to emanate sweet scents and bear flowers, so

Crescenzi recommends apple and pear trees, laurels, pomegranates, cypresses, and so on. Moreover, because the function of the *viridarium* or *verziere* is to provide *diletto* and not *frutto*,[6] the garden is to be exposed to northern winds, for these prevent trees from bearing fruit. The eighth chapter of the same book is called *De delectationibus hortorum*. Crescenzi here distinguishes a kind of pleasure that kitchen gardens—unlike gardens—yield, that is, the pleasure that comes from usefulness, for, as he says in the chapter about fields, "pleasure cannot come before usefulness, the opposite being true for gardens."[7] *Horti*, in fact, are filled with officinal and edible herbs,[8] such as rue and basil, and vegetables like pumpkin, radish, lettuce, watermelon, cucumber, and the like. Thus, *horti* probably correspond to our kitchen gardens.

Petrarch's annotations about plants are very far from Crescenzi's words. He does not say, for example, why he cultivated rue and sage: for their smell, for cooking, or for both? In the same way, we are not told whether his fruit trees bore fruit and flowers, only flowers, or neither.[9] Moreover, whereas Crescenzi's gardens are definitely square,[10] Petrarch does not make any reference to the geometry of his properties. There is one letter, however, in which the poet gives an account of the two small gardens he apparently owned at Vaucluse, and hints at their formal characteristics. This is the letter Petrarch wrote to Francesco Nelli, the prior of Santi Apostoli, in 1352, in which he mentions that one of the gardens at Vaucluse has a more cultivated aspect, and is vine-clad. Maybe he is referring to its regular layout, especially considering that he compares it to a wilder garden where—as he says—"nature conquers art."[11] The wilder garden, which he dedicates to Apollo, is shady and suitable for study. It is close to the point where the Sorgue gushes forth, and there is nothing beyond it except rocks accessible only to birds and beasts. Below the steep rock he has found a confined but very stimulating spot, "where even an inert mind may rise to lofty thoughts."[12] The other garden is sacred to Bacchus, surrounded by water and connected with the house by a bridge; here too he can easily study, for native cavelike rocks form a shelter that protects him against the summer heat. We cannot exclude the possibility that the latter pleasance may embody Crescenzi's definition of a garden. But we do not, in fact, have enough evidence to be able to identify the exact nature of the two pleasances. Incidentally, it may be useful to note that the gardens at Vaucluse do not figure among the entries on the flyleaves of Petrarch's *Palladius*, where all his other existing *hortuli* are mentioned. Therefore, it is legitimate to ask whether these gardens ever existed.[13] To complicate the matter further, there is a letter that Petrarch wrote to Luca Cristiani in

1351, in which he says that he cultivated the gardens at Vaucluse with his own hands, whereas the letter to Nelli addresses the gardens but does not make any mention of horticultural activities. Thus, the question arises not only as to the existence of the gardens at Vaucluse but also, if they did exist, as to the use to which they were put, and whether or not Petrarch was directly involved in their cultivation.

If we look at the context in which these gardens are mentioned, however, and keep in mind the fact that Petrarch's description of them in his letters is quite inconsistent, we may suggest that they were possibly as real as a literary metaphor. The use of horticultural imagery, in fact, is not uncommon in fourteenth-century Italian literature, where plants and gardens are given symbolic significance in order to compensate for something other, which is usually absent. Of course it is possible that the gardens at Vaucluse enjoyed both an actual and a metaphorical existence, but it is the latter I shall consider here, as the evidence to prove the former is too slim. Moreover, the analysis of the metaphor will help discern the message and meaning Petrarch attributed to gardens at a conceptual level. And this will ultimately allow us to draw a parallel with the way gardens were interpreted in the fifteenth century, when the Medici built the first of their villas.

One of the passages in which Petrarch writes about gardens, or *viridaria*, without referring to an actual place, is included in his *De remediis utriusque fortunae* (1354–1360). In this philosophical work, Petrarch's ideas on the remedies for adverse fortune are expressed in the form of a dialogue between the allegorical characters of Reason, on the one hand, and sentiments such as Joy, Hope, Fear, and Sorrow, on the other.

In the chapter on gardens, Reason says to its interlocutor, Joy: "Your happiness cannot be found in gardens or in other possessions of any kind, but only in your mind. . . . How many holy men have flourished in rugged caves, how many loathsome fornicators have luxuriated in lush meadows? Moreover, it is known that such verdant places have not only been hurtful to men's minds, but also to their bodies and their lives—not due to immoderate exposure to fresh air, but due to the naked sword and unexpected assault."[14] Petrarch here hints at a long tradition of so-called gardens of love that, starting with French literature of courtly love in the thirteenth century, had been the locales of many erotic literary enterprises (fig. 39). It is also possible that he had been familiar with several frescoed gardens that were being painted in some Florentine palaces and that served as a background to tales of love—such as the legend of the *Castellana di Vergi* at the Palazzo Davanzati (fig. 40).

Fig. 39. Master of the Prayerbooks, *Romance of the Rose: Lutenist and Singers in a Garden* (c. 1500). London: British Library, ms. Harley 4425, fol. 12v. By permission of the British Library.

Fig. 40. Detail of the fresco reproducing the *Castellana di Vergi* legend (c. 1348). Florence: Palazzo Davanzati. Scala/Art Resource, New York.

The reason for Petrarch's disdain of gardens is to be found in the very context in which he lived. In fact, Saint Augustine—Petrarch's most respected authority—had said, "Do not love the world nor the things that are in the world, for that which is in the world is concupiscence of the flesh, and concupiscence of the eyes, and craving of the world."[15] A similar admonition preoccupies Petrarch in the famous letter in which he describes his ascent of Mount Ventoux, in southeast France. Whether or not the letter is the diary of a day actually lived by Petrarch is unimportant,[16] because the document describes for the first time the ascent of a mountain for the sole purpose of experiencing the famous altitude of the place.[17] But the view from the top of Mount Ventoux is so surprisingly overwhelming that the poet is actually left speechless.

It is a moral meaning, according to medieval principles of rhetoric, that Petrarch portrays in this letter, when, having reached the top of the mountain, he opens at random his copy of Augustine's *Confessions*, only to read that one should not spend so much time admiring beautiful mountains and rivers, the waves of the sea, and the movements of the stars but rather should look into the depths of one's inner soul. The teaching of Saint Augustine implies a

Platonic reference, in that according to Plato the materiality of what surrounds us is but a pale reflection of an ideal reality that contains the absolute models, or ideas, that our souls contemplate before we are born. Thus, paradoxically, the fruit of Petrarch's ascent is the discovery that it is useless, and even dangerous, to observe and explore the external world at the expense of introspection and ethical reflection on one's own nature.

As Manlio Pastore Stocchi has pointed out, Petrarch's reflection on Mount Ventoux is intrinsic to the very definition of humanism;[18] however, the consequences that Petrarch and the humanists of later generations derived from the premises mentioned above were neither rigorous nor coherent enough to eliminate any interest in the external and material world. Petrarch was introduced to the bishop of Hippo's writings by Dionigi da Borgo San Sepolcro, an Augustinian friar he had met in Avignon in 1333. The lesson that Petrarch derived from the learned theologian was that the place of man is still in the world, and therefore one has to learn how to live in it according to moral principles. Thus, it is to Dionigi that Petrarch turns in order to find a remedy for his divided nature, torn between attraction to the world and withdrawal from it, and to whom he addresses his letter on the ascent of Mount Ventoux. Hence, Petrarch's rejection of the material reality around him is never definitive. In fact, not loving the world is no easy task for the poet, and for his personification of Reason in the *De remediis*. In her effort to comfort Sorrow, who complains of always being dejected "because of all the misery in this life," Reason says:

> Now, considering essentials, it is so small a joy to know that there is the likeness of God the Creator depicted within the human soul . . . that so many inventions and arts are here to serve your soul and body, whose needs are all provided for by the good Lord; that great opportunities and desirable things are supplied in His marvelous and ineffable ways, not just for survival, but for your delight? So many efficacious roots and juices of herbs, the pleasant variety of so many flowers, the harmony by contraries of scents, colors, tastes and sounds. . . . Add here the beckoning hills, the sun-drenched valleys and shady glens, the icy Alps, and the mild seashore, the wholesome bubbling waters and the springs, some sulfurous and steaming, some clear and cold. . . . Add lakes as big as oceans, swamps, the waters rushing through mountain gorges and those flowering edges, the cushioned riverbanks and meadows fresh with streams, as Virgil says. Think of the foaming cliffs, the dank caverns, and fields of

golden wheat, the budding vineyards, the ease of cities, and the quiet of the countryside, the freedom of the wilderness.[19]

Reason's point of view seems to contradict what she previously said about gardens. This may be due to the fact that her strategy is to juxtapose contraries to each proposition advanced by the four passions in the two books of the *De remediis*. Petrarch's objective is to raise doubts in the minds of his readers, to present them with all the possibilities and let them make their final, supposedly enlightened, decisions, for it is through doubt that we obtain knowledge. This is Saint Augustine's teaching.[20] In a passage from his *De civitate Dei* (IX, 2), we read:

> It is a great and unusual thing for a man, after he has contemplated all creation, corporeal and incorporeal, and found it to be subject to change, to pass beyond it by concentrated thought and so to arrive at the unchangeable substance of God, and there to learn from God himself that all nature that is not identical with himself has been made by none other than he. For so it comes that God speaks to man, not by means of some material creation, making a noise for material ears . . . nor through a spiritual agency that takes on the form and likeness of bodies, as in dreams. . . . No, he speaks with the voice of truth itself, if anyone is attuned to hear him with his mind, not using the body. He speaks to that in man which is superior to all the rest of his substance, and which has no superior save God alone.[21]

It follows that contemplating the world, or enjoying the material beauty of a garden, are not sins in themselves, but that indulging in the pleasure of the senses without searching for the truth, or attuning one's mind to the contemplation of what is neither visible nor audible through bodily means, is immoral. Therefore, after those moments of weakness when Petrarch is assailed by such a passion toward the beauty of the landscape—not to mention his love for Laura, his idealized object of affection—he abandons himself to a feeling of guilt, because the pain of guilt, that is, the painful awareness of being what he should not be, can somehow redeem him. And he shows his redemption at the end of the letter on Mount Ventoux when, at dusk, he is filled with a sudden confidence fallen upon him through grace. He begins the descent, and, penitent, gives a new meaning to his adventure: the journey of a man who reaches God through physical and mental fatigue, and worn-out pride.

If on Mount Ventoux the effect of Saint Augustine's teaching is Petrarch's silence, in the *De remediis* nothing restrains Petrarch from spelling out his contempt for gardens, however contradictory this may seem vis-à-vis Reason's admiration for the natural landscape. The explanation for this may be that gardens—as Crescenzi, Petrarch's contemporary, remarked—are purposefully created by men for the enjoyment of the eye, and so seem to represent for Petrarch a human weakness that is greater than love for untouched nature. However, the final words of Reason in the *De remediis* show that Petrarch had actually found a possible way of relating to a beautiful garden without necessarily feeling guilty. In fact, Reason suggests the possibility that even a place as invidious as a garden can be ennobled by a lofty mind: "No more happily [will you, Joy, stroll in your gardens] than wild boar and bear. It does not matter where you are, but what you do where you are. The place does not ennoble you, but you the place, [in] no other way than by striving to accomplish something admirable and noteworthy in that place."[22] Also, a few pages earlier Reason remarks that gardens, and solitary retreats in general, "are useful only when the mind is properly attuned, not otherwise . . . for, what good is it to put a stinking ointment into a fine ivory case, [or] to have a foul mind in beautiful places?"[23]

Considering the words of Reason, it is useful to note that in the letter to Francesco Nelli mentioned earlier the description of the two gardens at Vaucluse is preceded by a long narration of Petrarch's lifestyle. He lives alone and eats sparingly. He has only a dog and two servants—having sent the others to Italy. As for his clothing and footwear, he says that he no longer likes to be distinguished among his fellows, and that now he looks more like a peasant or a shepherd. This humble lifestyle, morally impeccable, is necessary in order to attune his mind and accomplish something remarkable in the solitude of the country. Finally he writes about his two gardens. But he does not say what they look like—except for the fact that one is controlled by "art" and the other by "nature"—rather, he tells Nelli what it is that he does there: he studies. Thus, Petrarch's intellectual occupation somehow justifies the presence of these gardens in his writing, because a noble mind can ennoble a place, even if it is a garden. Besides the fact that the two gardens are not morphologically described, what is missing is any reference to horticultural activity, which is another occupation that Petrarch sometimes condemns, especially if compared to the study of the *humanae litterae*. As he says in the *De remediis*: "I, most certainly, cannot disapprove of agriculture. However, neither the excellence of the writers [on agriculture] nor the fear of famine can make me consider it superior to the liberal and respected arts or, even, equal to them."[24]

Nevertheless we know, from the *Familiares* XI.12 written to Luca Cristiani in 1351, that the gardens of Vaucluse were cultivated with his own hands.[25] So why is there no mention of this activity in the letter that he later writes to Francesco Nelli? An answer may be found in the *Bucolicum Carmen*, Petrarch's bucolic song, in which his views are expressed in the form of poems "sung" by shepherds. In the tenth eclogue Petrarch opposes two allegorical images: his *aridulum rus* and the *silvae apricae*. The *aridulum rus* is a field that the poet had begun to cultivate but that gave him little harvest. According to Enrico Carrara,[26] Petrarch's arid field would stand for any activities whose only end is wealth and mundane success. And all the arid field can yield is spiritual poverty. In the eclogue Petrarch says that he has given up his *aridulum rus*, because it made him poor, and as fatigue was only followed by need, he decided to wander through the *silvae* instead. These stand for the abode of the poets, that is, for the disinterested study of the classics. It is here, Petrarch remarks, that he will find true glory, symbolized by the cultivation of a laurel. *Rusticus*, or inexpert, says Petrarch, is the love that he nurtures for the laurel at the beginning, when he has not yet subjected himself to hard discipline—the study of Roman poets as well as Homer. But once he has disciplined himself he finds that nothing but study can give him pleasure, not even the idea of those material goods, or futile activities, that he used to pursue in the past. Thus, his renouncing the cultivation of his field has yielded the peace of the soul, which, he makes clear, is true delight, richness, and possession.[27] Of course Petrarch is talking about an ideal assessment, not an economic one; as Carrara remarks, "His new richness is to be identified with his inner satisfactions brought about by literary studies."[28]

I want to suggest that the two gardens of Vaucluse also have an allegorical meaning, like the *Bucolicum Carmen*. In the letter written in 1351, Petrarch excuses himself for being at Vaucluse again, although he had promised never to return to Provence because it is too far away from Italy and too close to Avignon. The latter is the place where he spent most of his youth, and where at one time he enjoyed the worldly and refined, but not very spiritual, life of the papal court. In Avignon the elegance of his culture and his first poems were very well known and amply admired. There, Petrarch might have also been exposed to the richness of the papal palace that a few years earlier had been frescoed with naturalistic scenes. In particular it is the frescoes in Pope Clement VI's room—painted around 1343 by Giovannetti—that might have inspired the poet's naturalistic allegories. The walls of the room, called Room of the Deer, or of the Wardrobe, are covered with hunting and fishing scenes mixed with other rural amusements, where the tasteful costumes of the characters, together with their shining swords and slender greyhounds, stand out against a background of luxurious vegetation.[29] Also, Avignon was the place where Petrarch came into contact with the noble Roman family of the Colonnas, who enabled him to travel across Europe and Italy. However, later in life, probably following the example of Dante, he found that all the French city reminded him of was papal exile, and so he addressed the place with hostile words: "Sentina profundissima vitiorum . . . fetorque ultimus orbis terre," whereas Rome was considered "mundi caput . . . arx fidei catholice, fons omnium memorabilium exemplorum."[30] It follows that Avignon may be the place Petrarch has in mind when he mentions his *aridulum rus* in the tenth eclogue, or in the letter XI.12 when he asks his addressee to bear with him if he wants to revisit those "gardens"—*hortuli*—that he had planted with his own hands, and that are now more than he needs and more than really befits him.[31]

By contrast, in the letter that Petrarch writes later to Nelli he seems to have already entered the *silvae*, in that he is no longer "cultivating" or "writing" his own poetry, nor is he engaged in trivial activities, but rather he is studying the works of his Greek and Roman predecessors with great humility.[32] Material satisfaction is not pursued in the letter to Nelli. This is probably why Petrarch mentions that his eyes no longer guide him "along the road that leads to disaster," they no longer see "gold or gems or ivory or purple raiment" but "behold only the sky, mountains, and streams."[33] For the same reason he mortifies his ears: "Where is the sweetness of song, of the flute, of the lyre, whereby I was wont to be rapt out of myself? All that sweetness is gone with the wind; now I hear only the lowing of cattle or the bleating of sheep or the songs of birds, and the continual murmur of the river."[34] Moreover, his tongue has no one to talk to except himself, and he eats the food of a peasant, for "habit has become satisfaction,"[35] in the same way that the studying discipline to which he subjects himself—as he says in the eclogue—is the only occupation that he now enjoys.

The latter considerations help to explain why, in the *Familiares* XIII.8, one of the gardens is dedicated to Apollo and the other to Bacchus. In the Middle Ages and the Renaissance the allegorical figures of Apollo and Bacchus were meant to stand in opposition, with Apollo representing reason and temperance, and Bacchus license and passion.[36] However, both gods had something in common: Apollo was the god that bestowed poetic inspiration, the grantor of the poet's laurel; but Bacchus was also considered a source of inspiration because of the pun on his other name: Liber, which entailed liberation.

No wonder, then, that Petrarch dedicates his gardens—the allegories of his literary activity and life—to these two gods. However, one of the two gardens seems to need more control, and indeed it has "a more cultivated aspect." It is precisely the garden that Petrarch dedicates to Bacchus, the allegorical figure that stands for worldly desires in general. In fact, throughout the whole letter XIII.8 Petrarch shows that he has succeeded in controlling his bodily senses, and his former passions. Thus, in this letter, the restrained garden of Bacchus would correspond to the poet's abandonment of the *aridulum rus* in the tenth eclogue of the *Bucolicum Carmen*. In contrast, Petrarch's rationality, with its moral and spiritual values, that is, the garden of Apollo, does not need to be restrained, and therefore it reminds us of Petrarch's free wandering in the eclogue's *silvae*.

The possibility that the gardens at Vaucluse may be nothing more than a metaphoric invention is suggested by yet another letter in which the poet uses a horticultural image to visualize his thoughts. In the *epistola metrica* III.1 written to Cardinal Giovanni Colonna in 1346 Petrarch tells of a struggle over a stony field, again at Vaucluse, between himself, his Muses, and the Nymphs that personify the river Sorgue. Because Petrarch considers the field as an appropriate abode for his Muses, the nine ancient companions of Apollo, we can identify the *agellus* with the wilder garden that Petrarch dedicates to the god in the *Familiares* XIII.8. And, in fact, he works to transform this field into a pleasurable garden. But as soon as the grass that he has planted starts to grow, the Nymphs flood his lawn, and he is forced to withdraw. When the Nymphs' siege comes to an end, Petrarch goes back to his field and sees that no sign remains of his previous toil. Thus, he is full of anger and woe, and renews his attack, which is successful only so long as the summer lasts.[37]

Now, the question is why would Muses (poetic inspiration) and Nymphs (natural energy) be at war over the possession of a garden? My suggestion is that the abode of the Muses, who, as Fred J. Nichols has pointed out,[38] represent the rigid rules of Latin poetry, can only be the garden of Apollo, the god of Reason. On the other hand, the Nymphs, besides being the personification of the force of nature, are also the poet's vital energy, which, as we have seen, wants to live freely. It follows that the perfect place in which they can dwell is the garden of Apollo, a garden in which, as Petrarch says in his *Familiares* XIII.8, art does not control nature. Thus, the Nymphs are but another side of Petrarch's self, the side that wants to express freely its creativity, without having classical poetry channeling it with its fixed rhythms and meters. Eventually, these two sides of Petrarch's self, that is, the Muses and the Nymphs, will live together harmoniously, but it takes considerable effort to have literary art, Latin poetry in particular, coexist with natural freedom.

To conclude, throughout these letters the gardens at Vaucluse have the flavor of an allegory shaped by psychological implications; thus, they are far from the sense of actuality that the green abodes of the poet at Parma, Milan, and Arquà possess. Even if we accept the physical existence of these verdant places, their exact nature, or function, remains vague. It was Ernest Wilkins who documented the actuality of these places and called "gardens" what Petrarch had called *hortuli* in the *Familiares* XIII.8. And, in fact, in his Italian translation of the letter, Giuseppe Fracassetti translates the Latin *hortuli* as *orticelli*, or "little kitchen gardens."[39] It could also be possible that the "garden" in which "nature conquers art" was nothing but a shady *locus amoenus* that Petrarch found conducive to study, while the other *hortulus* might have been either a vegetable garden or a pleasure garden, or, more likely, both. Another possibility is that the two *orticelli* were indeed one—as Boccaccio mentions in his *Genealogie*[40]—transformed into two by Petrarch's desire to represent two different sides of the same unique self. In any case, the poet was only interested in portraying an allegorical meaning, rather than in describing verbally the actual features of the place, or any possible horticultural activity he might have carried out there.

Ultimately, the fact that there are virtually no pictorial illustrations of Petrarch's pleasances, and that none of their references alludes to any regular morphology, is perhaps more important than establishing whether his green abodes were *giardini* or *orticelli*, for the lack of detailed visual illustrations of these so-called gardens already suggests that the art of gardens could have not begun with Petrarch, and his verdant places can hardly be considered precedents for later Italian Renaissance gardens.[41] There is only one attempt in which the poet offers a visual rendering of Vaucluse. It is a pen-and-ink sketch (fig. 41) found in Petrarch's copy of Pliny the Elder's *Natural History*, precisely at the point, in book XVIII.51, at which Pliny mentions the river Sorgue.[42] However, the few strokes depicting Vaucluse—a river flowing forth from the base of a rocky height with reeds growing on its banks, a few trees and bushes on the mountain suggesting the presence of vegetation—were meant to represent the *locus amoenus* par excellence, the place that reflects, as Petrarch pus it, "transalpina solitudo mea iocundissima" (my most delightful transalpine solitude) more than a man-made garden.[43]

It is true that Petrarch's writings inspired the work of many illuminators, but it is significant that none of them chose to illustrate his gardens. At most

Fig. 41. Fontaine de Vaucluse, pen-and-ink sketch. Paris: Bibliothèque Nationale de France, ms. Lat. 6802, fol. 143v.

they represented the places that are usually associated with the poet's life.[44] The reasons for this may either be that the illuminators lacked a set of formulae for the visual representation of gardens or that they perceived Petrarch's descriptions of nature in his lyrics and narrative works precisely as descriptions of *loci amoeni* rather than gardens. The most common illustration, to be found especially in manuscripts of the *Canzoniere*, represents Petrarch himself as the personification of poetry at the moment of his coronation as a poet laureate (1341). This event often takes place in an open landscape, suggestive of Vaucluse, with the river Sorgue flowing through it, and laurel trees on the banks of the river. Other illustrations of Petrarch's work are the early illuminated *Trionfi*, in which we only find deserted landscapes that are not identifiable with any specific place. Even the most famous painting Petrarch owned, the so-called *Virgil Frontispiece* (fig. 42), does not illustrate any of his existing *orticelli*. However, this painting is important, for it offers a visual interpretation of Petrarch's

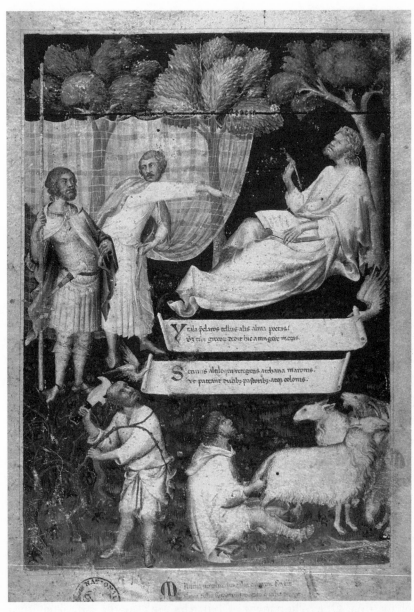

Fig. 42. Simone Martini, *Virgil Frontispiece* (1340). Milan: Ambrosiana Library, ms. Petrarcae Codex A. 79 inf., fol. 2v. Scala/Art Resource, New York.

poetic and horticultural endeavor. Petrarch commissioned the *Frontispiece* from Simone Martini in 1340 to illustrate the cover of his collection of Virgil's works: the *Eclogues*, the *Georgics* (from fol. 17v), and the *Aeneid*, commented upon by Servius, the fourth-century grammarian.[45] In the painting, Servius is shown pulling the veil away from Virgil, revealing the poet, at the moment of his inspiration, to three figures: a knight holding a lance, representing the *Aeneid*; a farmer, who stands for the *Georgics*; and a shepherd, representing the *Eclogues*. Each of the three figures looks toward Virgil, who is reclining in a grove and composing his verses under a tree.[46]

By imitating the *Aeneid* in his *Africa* and the *Eclogues* in his *Bucolicum Carmen*, Petrarch identified himself with the great Latin poet and sought to restore to his own day the glory of poetry at the time of Caesar Augustus. Although he did not set out to imitate the *Georgics*, he at least tried to live according to the principle that the book on husbandry teaches, namely, moral virtue mediates between the humility of the shepherd and the loftiness of the knight. In the *Frontispiece*, in fact, the figure of the husbandman is located at an intermediate position between the standing knight and the seated shepherd. Thus, the practice of agriculture represented for Petrarch a path to salvation through righteous living, according to the same moral principles that would urge Cosimo de' Medici to cultivate the land and provide for his family. Both for Petrarch and later for Cosimo, gardens are not solely objects of aesthetic appreciation, and their presence, either in poetry or in actuality, is somehow justified by a noble activity, such as the writing of poetry, the reading of philosophy, and the direct involvement in the cultivation of plants. We have to wait until Boccaccio before the appreciation of nature, and especially of gardens, can be expressed without conflict. In fact, it is only when it starts to show itself in poetry and painting, such as in the numerous illustrations of the *Decameron*, that the art of gardens—at least in Italian discourse—finally becomes conscious of itself.

In the *Genealogie deorum gentilium*, Boccaccio's dictionary of Greco-Roman mythology, we find a few lines on the *locus amoenus*, which was, by then, an established *topos*, especially after Petrarch, and Dante before him,[47] had so insistently connected it with poetry. Boccaccio writes: "All the works of nature are truly genuine. Here are the beech trees rising toward the sky, and the other trees that, with their opacity, provide refreshing shade; here is the soil covered with green grass and with flowers of a thousand colors; the clear springs and silver brooks flowing down from the mountains with a pleasing sound; here are the colorful singing birds and the branches moved by the breeze resonate."[48] And in the following lines the *locus amoenus* turns into a bucolic landscape: "Here are the huts of the shepherds . . . and everything is full of tranquility and silence. And by filling the eyes and the ears, these beautiful sights not only soften the soul, but also seem to let the mind concentrate upon itself and if the intellect were tired, they invigorate and inspire it with the desire of contemplating sublime things and composing; and these activities are suggested, with earnest appeal, by the company of books and the songs of the Muses."[49] Such a full description of the *locus amoenus* could apply, for instance, to Petrarch's beloved and inspiring Vaucluse, with the only difference being that any sense of guilt for the appreciation of the material world has finally gone. This suggests that Boccaccio, unlike Petrarch, does not show any uneasiness toward the beauty of nature (from landscapes to gardens). Moreover, he often uses a horticultural image to portray his moral lessons. And he is able to do so by combining and modifying different sources, both medieval and classical, that form an eclectic and original new beginning in the history of literary gardens. It is precisely by admiring the amenity of the landscape and of a garden—not to mention the bodily beauty of women—that Boccaccio's characters undergo a metamorphosis and turn from luxurious beasts into wise men. In this respect, the *Comedia delle ninfe fiorentine* is paradigmatic.[50]

The protagonist, Ameto, is a young, uncivilized man who delights in wandering and hunting with his dogs in the woods of Mount Corito, the site of present-day Fiesole. Ameto is attracted to the beauty that surrounds him and even more to the beautiful sound of a voice—*graziosa voce*[51]—that he hears singing in the woods, and that he decides to follow. Walking amid tall grasses and abundant flowers, he discovers a group of young and beautiful nymphs bathing at a creek. Boccaccio narrates how Ameto, astonished at the sudden sight of such beauty, steps back and kneels down in near adoration. As Vittore Branca has pointed out,[52] it is the beauty of the nymph Lia that transforms Ameto's love from sensual and carnal to spiritual and moral, and that makes him say at the end of the story that he has "turned from beast to man."[53] Because Lia is born from the water of a river, which symbolizes baptism, and belongs to the retinue of the celestial Venus, the goddess who mediates between the human mind and God,[54] she stands allegorically for Christian faith. Therefore, she is capable of love and guides her loved ones, such as the rude Ameto, toward eternal happiness along the road of contemplation.

However, it is not just feminine beauty that activates Ameto's moral metamorphosis; the beauty of the place in which Lia dwells also contributes to it. The adjectives with which Boccaccio describes the landscape show that it is material beauty—of nature as well as of women—that is finally accepted and no longer charged with men's deviation from moral rectitude. Boccaccio describes Etruria—a region extending over part of today's Tuscany and Umbria before the Roman conquest in the third century B.C.—as a region of "uncommon beauty . . . pleasant with its beautiful villas and full of cultivated fields,"[55] and his description of the place becomes full of adjectives and details as the narration proceeds. On the slopes of Mount Corito grow a great variety of trees, including oaks, cedars, and firs, that provide the place with beautiful shadows—*ombre graziose*[56]—which resonate with Lia's *graziosa voce*. Boccaccio's lexicon is far from the formulaic descriptions of anonymous *loci amoeni*. The pleasance where Ameto wanders has woods that host more animals, the rays of the sun are brighter than in any other place, and the air is so fresh that it relieves one from tiredness. Grass and flowers grow here more than is usual everywhere else and testify to the coming of divine presences. But more important, the beauty of the landscape and that of the female body are united by the same language. In fact, when Boccaccio says *piacevoli seni* to describe the pleasing topography of the region,[57] he is using figuratively a word that usually refers to a woman's bosom.[58] Moreover, Lia herself makes clear that she belongs to a certain environment, a specific context outside which the transformation of Ameto could never take place: "And this place, which more than any other is worthy of my pleasure, I command."[59] Thus, the place where Lia lives is the only one that is worth her beauty and, if she did not dwell in her exclusive *locus amoenus*, Ameto's sudden encounter would lose its magic: he would never turn into a virtuous man. It is significant that the presence of the nymph is linked also to a specific season, that is, springtime, which is an essential attribute of every *locus amoenus*. Ameto is, in fact, denied the sight of his beloved nymph during the winter, when the place where she used to appear to him is stripped bare and covered with snow. Yet when the spring returns, Ameto goes to those places that are "di quella fedelissimi renditori," that is, that always bring her back to him.[60] "In this place"— says Ameto—he will await his beautiful nymph, and there he will give her the gifts he has collected.[61]

Another example of the positive effect of the landscape can be appreciated in the *Decameron* (1349–1351). Critical commentaries have often focused on the structure of the collection of stories, and have made a clear distinction between frame and tales (i.e., between the storytellers and the characters they invent). Such a distinction, as Marshall Brown has aptly observed,[62] is suggested by the dichotomy between actions and words that Boccaccio subtly modulates throughout the work, creating a precarious balance. In what follows I shall show that the "art of composing an organic book"[63]—as Brown calls Boccaccio's writing—is also reflected by the *Decameron* gardens and *loci amoeni*. In fact, as Brown has implied, the subtle equilibrium that Boccaccio establishes between the orderliness of the *brigata*, expressed by their actions, and the license of the stories, spelled out by their language, is reflected as well by the coexistence of different, but balanced, settings: the gardens of the tales' *cornice*, or frame, that host the storytellers, and the gardens of the *novelle*, which are created and described by the vivid imagination of Boccaccio's own characters, and which provide settings for their tales. In fact, the doubly fictional pleasances of the tales can be considered gardens of love in the courtly sense, meaning that they materialize the wrongdoings of both men and women, protagonists of the *novelle*. On the other hand, the gardens in which the stories are told convey a moral message that Boccaccio ultimately seems to deliver.

The first novel of book V tells the story of Cimone, a rude man without manners, who lives in the woods almost as a beast but is turned into a gentle man after his encounter with Efigenia, a beautiful woman with whom he falls in love. In this tale, the method of presenting the affinity between the beauty of the female body and that of the *locus amoenus*, which Boccaccio renders in the *Comedia* by using human attributes to describe the topography— *piacevoli seni*—is reversed. Here Boccaccio describes the nudity of Efigenia as if she were one with the landscape, and he uses such terms as *vestimento*—"a very beautiful young woman wearing such a thin vesture"—and *coperta*— "covered by a very white blanket from the waist down"[64]—which could apply, respectively, to a canopy of trees or to a plain covered with snow. The fact that at the moment of the encounter with Cimone she is almost naked and is sleeping "on the green lawn,"[65] as if the green grass were her natural element, allows the reader to include her among the other creatures of nature. Moreover, the attribute *bellissimo* that is repeated three times within one short paragraph to describe the little grove that Cimone enters, the fountain that he sees, and the sleeping lady on the grass cannot but emphasize the kinship between the *locus amoenus* and the human body. Thus, here too, as in the *Comedia delle ninfe fiorentine*, the landscape participates in the redeeming process of the protagonist, for, were those beautiful women not encountered in a *locus amoenus*, the protagonists' catharsis would never occur.

Another token of Boccaccio's unconditional appreciation of the beauty of nature derives from the fact that a *locus amoenus* is never thought of as an enticing place or as embodying negative values. In fact, when Boccaccio wants to portray the wrongdoings of men, the landscape, far from being *amoenus*, becomes frightening, and suggests only terror and discomfort. For example, in the *novella* V.8 from the *Decameron* Boccaccio transforms nature from beautiful to horrifying in order to accommodate the most tragic episode of the tale. Upon entering a pine grove in Chiassi, a small town on the Adriatic coast, the young protagonist Nastagio degli Onesti witnesses a horrendous scene. He sees a knight on horseback galloping after a naked young woman, who is trying to escape two mastiff dogs running after her. The knight discourages Nastagio from trying to defend the woman, because—as he tells him—he and the woman are just carrying out a divine command. Being guilty of having taken his own life in order to put his love sufferings to an end, the knight is condemned to kill the woman that was once his beloved, and the woman, guilty of taking pleasure in the death of her suitor, is condemned to be bitten by two dogs that satisfy their hunger with her organs, which the knight pulls out of the victim after stabbing her in the back.

It is as if Nastagio were witnessing a scene that would ordinarily take place in the *Inferno Dantesco*, where suicides are located. Boccaccio describes the innermost part of the grove as inhospitable, full of thick bushes and prickly shrubs that wound the bare flesh of the fugitive woman. Also, the woman's screams fill the place as the lamentations and groans of the damned fill the thick atmosphere of hell. However, the horrid place exists only for the brief time span of the vision in which the two ghostly characters appear, and it then vanishes together with the vision as in a dream, taking the beholder back to his actual reality, the *locus amoenus*. Although Boccaccio does not describe Chiassi, the very name of this place must have reminded his readers of the famous description of its beautiful shore and pine grove that Dante gave in his *Divine Comedy* in order to convey his mental image of a pleasant earthly Paradise: "The divine forest green and dense . . . / as gathers from branch to branch / through the pine forest on Chiassi's shore."[66]

If any discomfort related to the appreciation of *loci amoeni* is gone from Boccaccio's works, gone also is any uneasiness toward artificial beauty, such as that of gardens created by people. The rich and appealing vocabulary with which Boccaccio depicts his literary gardens in the *Decameron* bears this out. In the collection of stories the three suburban gardens included in the narrative context of the plot offer a refuge from plague-stricken Florence to a group of young people—three men and seven women—who recount a hundred tales to each other in the time span of ten days. First the company retreats to a villa in the country, where a building is surrounded by several gardens. On the first Sunday—the third day of storytelling—they move to a second place, where they enter a walled garden with freshly cut lawns and a marble fountain carved with bas-reliefs. Lastly, on the ninth day of the *brigata's* gathering, they visit the so-called Valle delle Donne, or valley of the ladies, a remote and secluded place approachable only along a narrow path. After a day's sojourn in the valley, the group moves back to the second garden and, finally, to the city.

Like the *locus amoenus* in the *novella* of Nastagio degli Onesti, the gardens of the *cornice* embody an ethical meaning, which is reflected by Boccaccio's final words in the *Decameron*. The concluding chapter, in fact, gives a reason for the dichotomy between the *cornice* gardens and the *novella* gardens. Here the author reveals the double nature of his work, which can be read both as a fourteenth-century ideology of natural love and as a manifesto of medieval ethics extolling the institution of marriage. The interpretation depends on whether the reader weighs the words of the characters more than their actions, or vice versa. Boccaccio admits that the *novelle* told by his characters may sound too licentious to those readers who "give more weight to words than facts,"[67] and he pleads that freedom of writing be conceded to him as freedom of painting is granted to the painter. However, if readers consider that the *novelle* are but uttered inventions, and that the behavior of the *novellatori* within the three garden settings of the *cornice* could not be more chaste and appropriate to the medieval moral code, then they will be able to grasp the ethical message of the *Decameron*. Readers are ultimately free to choose their own sinful or virtuous path either by surrendering to the charm of overtly fictional gardens or by deciding to behave like the ten young storytellers, who are "non pieghevoli per novelle,"[68] that is, not corrupted by their own fables. Also, it is precisely by directing the reader's attention toward the dichotomy between fictional gardens and actual gardens that Boccaccio makes his own advice on how to lead a virtuous life available to his readers.

Let us consider first the gardens of the *cornice*. Although the three gardens are typologically different from each other, they can be read as part of a homogeneous ensemble: one, for instance, in which the settings are all linked by a progressive conformity to the principles of rational order and human culture.[69] The first setting embodies, in its gardens and villa architecture—and even in the words being spoken there—those qualities of order and measure that will be exploited, and made progressively more explicit, in the second and third settings, when the allegorical apparel will start to fade away. In order to perceive these qualities, it is important not to separate the gardens of the first setting from the architecture of its villa.[70] First, in this setting the *allegra brigata* spends as much time in the indoor space of the villa as it does in the numerous gardens surrounding the building. Also, *giardini* and *palagio* are not given different paragraphs in the text; rather, their descriptions tend to blend with each other: "The abovementioned place was on a little hill . . . with various trees and plants full of green branches and pleasant to see; on top of the hill was a building with a large and beautiful courtyard at its center, and with loggias, living-rooms, and bedrooms . . . surrounded by little lawns and marvelous gardens, and wells with fresh waters and cellars of precious wine."[71]

Few words in the text allow us to identify the typology of the villa: on the top of a hill covered with plants stands a building that unfolds around a courtyard at its center, with loggias connecting to beautiful rooms; the villa is surrounded by lawns and beautiful gardens. Then Boccaccio mentions the wells of fresh water and the vaulted wine cellars, as if water and wine, wells and cellars, stand in a sort of reciprocal equilibrium. He also remarks that the rooms inside the building are clean and in perfect order: "The place had been swept, the beds made, and there was plenty of flowers blooming in that season and reeds."[72] Boccaccio makes clear that everything is perfectly organized, including the gardens that seem to enter the rooms of the building with their spring flowers.

As soon as the young storytellers arrive at this place, two of them, Dioneo and Pampinea, give voice to the rational order of the architectural setting: the man, in fact, remarks that it was the *senno* of the women, that is, their intellect, that lead them out of the city so that they could flee from Florence and from death.[73] Pampinea's words are even more telling. She suggests that even their leisure time, spent in telling stories to each other, needs order and structure, for anything that lacks these qualities is bound by fate to a short life span.[74]

In the second setting, garden and building are clearly detached, although adjacent to each other. The storytellers do not enter the building but only go into the walled garden, of which Boccaccio gives a detailed description, with greater emphasis on the geometry imposed on it: "It was surrounded and crossed at its center by large paths, all straight and covered with vine arbors,"[75] and the distribution of plants in this garden shows so much order that "it would take too long to describe it."[76] At the center is a grassy lawn whose colors are almost—we would say—impressionistic, with the infinite hues of the flowers amid the grass, and the deep green of the grass that appears, at times, as dark as black. As Millicent Marcus has pointed out,[77] Boccaccio increasingly stresses human artifice: from the layout of the garden, to the marble fountain at the center, carved with bas-reliefs, to the water channeled "artificially"[78] outside the garden in order to serve two mills, and finally, to the "almost petlike"[79] animals that dwell in it. Man's art thus results from a rationally controlled and ordered setting, which very much contrasts with the libertine stories that are told within it.

The Valle delle Donne, or last frame setting of the *Decameron*, is the apotheosis of rational order and geometry. However, the valley is also the utmost celebration of the perfection of nature that, in this third setting, is far from any sign of human intervention, that is, far both from the architecture of a villa—although six *palagi* are visible in the distance on the top of six little hills—and from the city itself. The valley is in the shape of a circle, so exactly round that it looks as if it has been drawn by means of a compass, "although it looked like an artifice made by Nature rather than man."[80] Also, the hills surrounding the valley slope down gradually in the form of tiers of steps, "ordered progressively,"[81] that look like the seats of an amphitheater. The top half of these tiers, starting from the middle step to the top one, and facing south, is filled with plants, such as vineyards, olive trees, fig trees, almond trees, and cherry trees, in such a way that not even the smallest piece of soil is left uncultivated. The remaining part of the tiers, from the bottommost step to the middle one, contains firs, cypresses, laurels, and pines, "arranged and ordered so well that they looked as if the best artificer had planted them."[82] It is clear from these last words that nature is seen as the artificer of itself, or as a secular divinity, for, as Boccaccio repeatedly stresses, the order governing the valley is not imposed by man.

As Marcus suggests, Boccaccio simply applies to the valley of the ladies the artistic principle used by Giotto in his painting: mimesis in the Aristotelian sense, that is, not so much the imitation of the "things of the natural world" as the replication of "nature's own mode of creation."[83] Because nature is considered "the divine source of all cosmic order,"[84] and the natural world receives the imprint of its art, it follows that one way of imitating nature's poietic process is to make its intrinsic order visible. This is why Boccaccio stresses the geometric perfection of the valley of the ladies: the perfectly circular circumference and the rows of trees planted in a grid, which, in addition, is visible all year long, as the trees are evergreens.[85] Now, if we read the frame-story settings backward, that is, starting from the valley to the first villa, we can see that Boccaccio applied Giotto's mimesis not only to the last setting but also to the first two,[86] with the only difference being that in the second garden a human artificer imposes a geometrically ordered layout over nature, and the first setting too has a human protagonist. In the first setting, however, the order imposed by man is less geometrical, for it stems from balance and measure, like that of the built and the open areas within the villa, and of the water fountains and wine cellars that Boccaccio mentions in the same sentence; but order is also hierarchy, like that which structures the enjoyable occupation of the *brigata* during the time they spend together.

These considerations suggest that the order governing the three settings makes the *cornice* of the *Decameron* one whole homogeneous ensemble with which Boccaccio presented his moral lesson. As Edith Kern has pointed out, unlike the gardens of the *novelle*, the frame gardens are "stripped . . . of all supernatural elements,"[87] for no allegorical character, including the god of love, inhabits them. Only the ten young Florentines give life to these pleasances. Thus, the contrast between *cornice* and *novelle* is one between actual reality and creative imagination, or restraining order and licentious freedom. Recalling what Boccaccio says in his concluding chapter about paying more attention to the facts, that is, to the righteous behavior of the storytellers, instead of following the example of their novels, the reader can understand that to "imitate" the *allegra brigata*, whose behavior reflects the ordered garden settings in which they dwell, means to restrain one's instincts in order to live according to the common moral principles of the medieval world.

This becomes all the more clear if we consider that the *novelle* gardens, whose inhabitants often do not have any regard for moral standards, do not present an ordered and geometrical layout. Paradigmatic is the tale of Madonna Dianora (*Decameron* X.5). She is a married woman who, in order to put an end to the solicitations of her suitor, Ansaldo, tells him that she will give herself to him only when he is able to show her a garden that blooms during the winter months as if it were spring. Not understanding that the request of the woman, being impossible to fulfill, is yet another denial, Ansaldo hires a magician who is actually able to produce the illusion. Drawing from more than a century of courtly love literature, Boccaccio could have described this garden in every detail. But all he says about the enchanted place is that it has flowers, trees, and fruit, and that it is one of the most beautiful gardens ever seen.[88] The same happens in all the other tales, where garden settings are simply named. Thus, the morphological freedom of the tale gardens cannot but reflect the self-indulgence with which the protagonists lead their lives.

In the conclusion to the *Decameron*, Boccaccio remarks that the tales have been told not in the church of Santa Maria Novella, where the members of the *brigata* originally meet, and not in the schools of the philosophers, but rather in gardens—"ne' giardini, in luogo di sollazzo, tra persone giovani"— that is, in pleasurable places, among young people. Besides associating these words with the tradition of courtly love—as many commentators have done—I think it is important to highlight a fact that, although self-evident, has often been overlooked: namely, that gardens are acknowledged as distinct places. They are, for example, clearly distinguished from orchards or kitchen gardens, for, as Boccaccio's characters explain, all that these pleasances allow is idleness—no toil is contemplated in these fictional gardens. Thus, the existence of the latter is finally legitimated. Also, in his description of the second garden setting Boccaccio says what the distinguishing characteristic of gardens is vis-à-vis *loci amoeni*: "When they saw this garden, with its beautiful order, its plants and fountain with the little brooks coming out of it, all the women and men of the group loved it so much that they said if they were to create Paradise on earth, they would not know what other shape to give it besides the one they had admired in that garden."[89] These lines contain in embryo a distinction between matter and form and thus establish the parameters that will lead to a concept of the art of gardens as that which bestows order, in the form of human control, over nature. And it is this concept that anticipates the later developments of the Renaissance.

The way in which Boccaccio employed gardens in his writings shows us that gardens can be regarded as narrative elements that materialize the actions and passions of multiple selves, such as the fictitious characters of the *Decameron*. Thus, Boccaccio's gardens, like those of Petrarch, cannot be read solely as objects of aesthetic appreciation. Petrarch's gardens, however, are often accorded value only in relation to the poet's self—probably due to his writing in a different genre. In addition, most illustrations of Petrarch's *loci amoeni* show the poet within them, for all the pleasances named in his literature are places where he, in fact, lived (fig. 43).[90] In contrast, the visual representations related to Boccaccio's writings, besides being more numerous, do not show the *Certaldese* in any one of his fictional pleasances.

Boccaccio's works do not include illustrations of fourteenth-century Florentine gardens. The *Decameron*, which was well known and read by the Florentine bourgeoisie, found a limited visual translation in the Trecento.[91] The earliest manuscript presenting the illustration of a garden is the codex that Giovanni d'Agnolo Capponi, a member of a mercantile family, transcribed

Fig. 43. Petrarch in the landscape of Vaucluse (late fifteenth century). Florence: BML, ms. Strozzi 172, fol. 1r. By permission of Ministero per i Beni e le Attività Culturali.

sometime before the year 1365, that is, ten years before Boccaccio's death.[92] The sixteen miniatures of the codex, drawn in pen and brown watercolor, illustrate forty-two scenes and are situated in the upper margin of the leaves, following one another without interruption. As Ciardi Dupré has demonstrated, it is possible that Boccaccio knew Capponi and also took part in the illustrative project—as in the choice of the passages to be illustrated. It would not be surprising if Boccaccio drew the vignettes himself.[93] After all, unlike Petrarch, he had a tendency toward figurative visualization, and he practiced drawing throughout his life. Moreover, in the *Decameron* It. 482 manuscript the illustrations precede the first story of each day—with the exception of the introduction to the second day and the conclusion to the work—as if they were meant visually to introduce the reader to the atmosphere of each of the ten *novelle*. Such a careful project might indicate the presence of the author himself as the illustrator. However, Boccaccio must not have been interested in the literal representation of the contents and settings of his *novelle*, for the miniatures tend rather to illustrate the moral meaning the stories embodied. Thus the early illustrations served the function of glosses. For example, the frontispiece of the manuscript (fig. 44) depicts the charming place where the storytellers tell their tales. The illustration shows a building surrounded by a grassy lawn and a hexagonal fountain embellished with a tiny nude Venus on a slender column. However, in the text this fountain appears not in the first garden—whose illustration we would expect to find in the frontispiece—but in the second, which Boccaccio describes at the outset of the third day. Furthermore, of this second garden, the illustration depicts only the fountain, not the geometrical layout of the setting. The geometric order characterizing the second garden is nonetheless present in the illustration, embodied by the square shape of the *palagio*, the geometry of the fountain, and the perfect circle around which the *brigata* sits. The illustration is thus a conflation of the first two gardens of the *cornice*. Now, whereas the presence of Venus anticipates the reading of tales about love, the pine trees behind the storytellers and beside the fountain remind the reader of Venus's servants, whose labors are often more bitter than pleasing. The conflation of the two garden settings has the power of portraying the double possibility that Boccaccio offers his readers: follow the example of the chaste members of the group and live happily ever after or follow that of the characters they invent and risk experiencing the pain of love.

The lack of a literal visual illustration of Boccaccio's surely unintentional definition of gardens in the *Decameron* shows that they were not yet regarded

Fig. 44. Capponi *Decameron*, drawing of the *brigata* in a garden (c. 1365). Paris: Bibliothèque Nationale de France, ms. It. 482, fol. 4v.

as art objects. The formal order and symmetry of his gardens was, as we have seen, only a representation of the power that people have to dominate nature, and especially their own sinful nature, symbolized by both the chaos brought about by the plague and the lack of order typical of the fictional garden settings. On the other hand, if Capponi was the illustrator of the manuscript instead of Boccaccio, it is possible that he lacked the pictorial model of a garden, that is, a representative tradition from which to draw inspiration. As Millard Meiss writes—especially in cases where the illustrators and the authors were different persons—the less specific the instructions given to the illuminators the more they tended to draw from their repertoire those figures that seemed better to suit the requested subject.[94] This could explain why the visual illustration of the gardens does not correspond to the way they are described in the text. Nevertheless, unlike other illustrations of profane literature, the miniatures of the Capponi manuscript seem to be enriched by realistic elements, such as those provided by the description of Florence given by Filippo Balducci in the prologue to the fourth day of storytelling, where trees, rocks, and caves are no longer just symbols but rather fresh and shady environments that belong to the reality of men and women.

In 1427 a new manuscript of the *Decameron* was transcribed by Lodovico Ceffini, and it included an illustration for each *novella*, as well as fifteen for each part of the *cornice*.[95] Located in the upper and lower margins of the leaves, the illustrations were executed by multiple, probably five, illuminators. It is very likely that Ceffini knew the Capponi manuscript, as the illustration of the introduction, representing the seven women and three men gathering together in a garden, is identical to that of the earlier manuscript—namely, a miniature that does not closely follow the sequence of events as they unfold in the text. Only one of the original illustrations showing a *novella* garden gives a faithful visual translation of Boccaccio's words. It is the miniature, in pen, ink, and watercolor, representing the garden in which the young Gabriotto dies on the lap of his lover Andreuola.[96] The figures of the two characters are plastically rendered and immersed in a homogeneous space, which is hinted at with only a few strokes. In the text the garden is described as an enclosed space, which in the illustration is rendered by means of a crenelated wall.

Later in the century, Florence lived an atmosphere of austere morality deeply influenced by the reforms of Savonarola (1452–1498). Thus, it would have never been possible to publish in Florence an edition of the *Decameron* with all the visual appeal the book suggested to people's imagination. In a time that was restrained by the laws of morality, centered on the civic rigor propelled by Leonardo Bruni, the *Decameron* was considered light reading for leisure. Florentine readers had to wait until July 29, 1516, to see a new illustrated copy of the *Decameron*, printed by Filippo Giunti. However, the woodcuts published along with the text did not have any Florentine features, as they derived from the Venetian edition printed by Giovanni and Gregorio De' Gregori in 1492.[97]

The illustrations of the De' Gregori *Decameron* adopted the tradition of illuminated manuscripts, where the illustrations followed each other as a commentary on the narration. They were realistic vignettes: realism, in fact, mirrored the attitudes and behavior of the rich mercantile bourgeoisie who had started to appreciate the luxury of beautifully illustrated books with costly bindings. Unlike the foreign editions of the book, in which landscape

Fig. 45. De' Gregori, *Decameron*, frontispiece with xylography reproducing the *brigata* in a garden setting (1492). BNCF, ms. Banco Rari 365, fol. 1r. By permission of Ministero per i Beni e le Attività Culturali.

had hardly been represented, reduced as it was to few schematic trees and blades of grass, the Venetian illustrations, and in particular their gardens, had already inspired some of the minor arts. The De' Gregori edition includes a sequence of sumptuous arbors, gardens, rose trellises, and fountains in multiple shapes. It opens with a frontispiece representing the merry *brigata* seated under a pergola of latticework (fig. 45). The woodcut is possibly a representation of the second garden setting of the *cornice*. Thus, bearing in mind the rigidly geometrical and symmetrical features of the garden described by Boccaccio in the text, we can say that illuminators of the late fifteenth century tended to illustrate the *Decameron* more literally than earlier illustrators did. Therefore, it is to these late illustrations that we have to look for examples of a figurative translation of the early definition that Boccaccio gave of gardens. In the sixteenth century, as Branca has remarked, the late medieval message that formed the ideological key of the *Decameron*, which centered on the dialectic relationship between the force of Providence and human willpower,

Fig. 46. Antonio Vivarini (b. c. 1415, d. c. 1476–1484), Italian. The *Garden of Love*,
c. 1465–1470, oil, tempera, and gold on wood. 152.5 x 239.0 cm. Felton Bequest,
1947. National Gallery of Victoria, Melbourne.

was irremediably misunderstood; in the late Renaissance, artists tended to
blend the dichotomy of *cornice* and *novella* by merging the moralistic outcome of the story collection with an Apollonian atmosphere.[98]

A great change in the illustrated gardens of the *Decameron* took place
with the publication in 1542 of the edition by Gabriele Giolito. The vignettes
are influenced by the typical Venetian taste for narration. With an attention
to details characteristic of Flemish painters, the illustrator represents the ten
storytellers as all wearing oak leaves, their hands full of odoriferous herbs and
flowers. These late illustrations, although richer than the literary gardens that
we find described in the *Decameron*, for the first time represent that order and
rigid geometry that Boccaccio put forth as an allegory of medieval moral
standards. In fact, unlike in the earlier illustrations, in these prints gardens
show more explicitly the work of human artifice, and even the amorphous
nature of plants disappears to leave room for rose-clad trellises, arbors, and
other signs showing that the garden is a human product. Gardens are thus
filled with classical constructions, such as lawns surrounding fountains of
love, that had already entered the engraving and painting traditions of the fifteenth century thanks to the workshop of Antonio Vivarini (fig. 46).

However, toward the end of the sixteenth century, illustrated editions of the *Decameron* were no longer appreciated in Venice as elsewhere. Boccaccio's work in itself began to be considered unworthy of expensive paper and elegant illustrations, especially because of the perceived triviality of its content. Those who expressed such concerns were, of course, being influenced by the new regimen imposed by the Inquisition. Thus, the only floral and vegetal motifs present in the editions of the *Decameron* printed in Venice in 1582, "Per li Giunti di Firenze," are those decorating the initials. The illustration of entire gardens could have been too compromising.[99]

In conclusion, Petrarch's writings revealed the poet's fondness for nature and uneasiness with material beauty, especially beauty molded by human artifice. Moreover, Boccaccio's individuation of gardens as distinct places in which form shapes matter shows that the *Certaldese* was well aware of the distinction between nature and artifice, which he spelled out in the *Decameron*. Thus, Boccaccio's unintentional definition of gardens has offered artists of later centuries a great source of inspiration for the visual rendering of these pleasances. This conclusion has been corroborated by the paucity of visual illustrations of gardens included in Petrarch's works, and by the numerous illustrations of the *Decameron*. However, the fact that the most imaginative, but also the most literal, illustrations of the *Decameron* occurred at a later date shows that it is the reception of Boccaccio's work through the miniatures of later illustrators, rather than—as some garden historians maintain—Boccaccio himself, that has a greater claim to be considered a precedent for the art of gardens.

Marsilio Ficino and the Neoplatonic Pleasance

The writings of Petrarch, and alternatively those of Boccaccio, are often singled out as the source of inspiration for the "design" of early Renaissance gardens in general, and Medici gardens in particular.[100] In addition to Petrarch's influence, Neoplatonic philosophy is often said to have contributed to the layout of a garden like Careggi: "The influence of Petrarch as well as the progressive affirmation in Florence of the theories linked to the ideology of the Neoplatonic Academy had an impact on the configuration of the garden."[101] But even in this recurrent theme in the historiography of the early Medici villas the relationship between the Florentine Neoplatonic Academy and the gardens of Careggi is often simply mentioned rather than fully explored. Moreover, if Petrarch's conception of actual gardens, or *horti*, as we have seen, is difficult to pin down, Ficino does not write about existing gardens at all, not even about Careggi, where he composed, in 1489, the most important of his original works, the *De vita libri tres*, or three books on life.

However, Ficino's train of thought, and especially his considerations about the ontology of the natural world and man's ability to take part in its formation and manipulation, make us long for an elaboration on the word *garden* in his writings. And it is understandable that many scholars should have convinced themselves and their readership that they have come across an account of Neoplatonic gardens in Ficino's philosophical writings; for all the so-called elements of a garden, among which plants and flowers, sunlight and shade, are indeed mentioned by the philosopher, together with his praise of human creativity and ability to manipulate such elements, as a close reading of Ficino's *De vita* and *Platonic Theology* bears out. Such a reading highlights how different the role the so-called *locus amoenus* played in philosophical writings was from the role it played in works of literature, such as those of Petrarch and Boccaccio. If the pleasances of the poets, as we have seen, can be interpreted as other subjects, that is, as projections of the poets' own selves and characters, the pleasances of Ficino lack the objectlike quality of the work of art because they are intended as intelligible signs that point to the existence of God. In the *De Sole*, or book on the sun, Ficino maintains that light, colors, and scents, all arguably elements of a garden that are perceptible through the senses, allow us to grasp a superior meaning that goes beyond the limits of sense perception.

While Ficino, like Boccaccio, distinguishes form from matter, he does so in accordance with Neoplatonic philosophy, and therefore he believes that form is not altogether separate from matter but actually abides in it. Every material or substance that exists on this earth already possesses in itself its most appropriate form, and our task seems to be simply that of revealing it, rather than imposing it on matter.[102] This perhaps explains why Ficino is not interested in discussing what form to give a garden but dwells instead on the function of garden elements (i.e., plants and flowers), which is to soothe both the human body and the human spirit. Thus, if on one hand it is unlikely that Ficino's writings inspired the layout of a garden at Careggi, on the other his philosophy must have offered his fellow humanists a key to understanding the meaning and purpose of their green abodes in relation to, for instance, the hierarchical framework of the world. Moreover, the relevance of Ficino's thought for our understanding of Medici gardens lies in the philosopher's theorization of human making as an instinctive activity that does not require discursive reasoning. Thus, Cosimo de' Medici pruning his vines could serve as an example of that artificer who according to Ficino lives in every person, and the *orto* at Careggi can be thought of as the most immediate product of an individual's toil.

In the second book of the *De vita*, Ficino has Venus suggest that "the nature of green things . . . is not only [that they are] alive but even youthful and abounding with very salubrious humor and a lively spirit; and because of this a certain youthful spirit flows to us through the odor, sight, use, and frequent habitation of and in them."[103] If everything that is green is alive and all the elements of the world "live not so much by their own life as by the common life of the universal whole itself,"[104] it follows that a *locus amoenus* too participates in the unity and lively harmony of the cosmos. In the *Theologia Platonica*, Ficino makes this concept clear: "Think of plants and animals: their separate parts are so designed that the position of one is to the advantage of another; they serve each other. Certainly, when one is removed, the whole structure is virtually destroyed. Next, all their parts are arranged for the sake of the composite whole, and the composite itself, that is, the plant or animal, is equipped with the instruments it needs to do the works of its own nature."[105]

It follows that, in the same way as for plants and animals, all the different parts of the world contribute to the harmony of the entire universe. The analogy with a bodily structure, whether vegetal or animal, allows Ficino to say that the world is also a replica—on a different scale—of the human body, and thus it constitutes a living ensemble in which each element has its own function and is indispensable to the structure of the whole, "from which nothing can be subtracted and to which nothing can be added."[106] Therefore, Ficino compares plants and trees to the hair of the body and metals and stones to its bones and teeth, whereas the celestial bodies are like the head, heart, or eyes of the world.[107] A consequence of this way of thinking would be that a garden, like anything that exists, has its own peculiar role within the organism of the world, but Ficino does not say this explicitly.

The philosopher's medical recommendations, based on the same analogical method with which he illustrates the cosmos, lighten the prose of *De vita*, dense and rich in allegorical symbols. His recipes are based on sympathetic associations or *congruitates*, whose efficacy derives from the fact that, as he says in the third book, they exert on each other a sort of reciprocal influence, which may work on us to the highest benefit.[108] By means of the analogical method Ficino explains to his readers the importance of plants and flowers.

Their bright colors and hues of green help a person avoid melancholy, which is a feeling that is brought about by anything that is dark and by whatever offends sight, smell, and hearing. It follows that the sight of the color green and the pleasant smells of fruits, such as lemons and oranges, flowers, such as roses and violets, and trees, such as myrtle, camphor, and sandalwood, are very useful.[109]

The panegyric on the color green that Venus utters to old people in the fourteenth chapter lauds the beneficial power that a *locus amoenus* bestows on the sense of sight. The goddess says:

> While we are walking among the green things, let us figure out why the color green more than others foments the sight and healthfully delights it. We will discover at last that the nature of sight is bright and friendly to light but volatile and easily dissipated. . . . The sight wants to use light in such a way that through its friend it may be amplified, indeed, but not at the same time dissipated. Now in whatever sort of color there is more of darkness or blackness than of light, the visual ray is not dilated, and therefore not delighted, as it would like. Conversely, where there is more of a shining color than a black, it is scattered more widely, distracted by a harmful pleasure. On which account the color green, tempering most of all black with white, furnishes the one effect and the other, equally delighting and conserving the sight.[110]

But verdant places are beneficial not only to people's eyes. Because plants are living things—especially plants that are still clinging to mother earth with their roots[111]—it follows that, according to Ficino's principle of likeness, they are essential for people who wish to live a long life. Ficino advises his fellows to take long walks through groves and meadows and to breathe the "lives" of these pleasances, in order to enhance their own. Because, to be more precise, what is inhaled during a walk through an open and green place is the scents of plants, the next question to be answered is how those odors can enhance human life.

Ficino identifies one's life with one's spirit.[112] The reference to the idea that life equals spirit is probably to be found in the second chapter of the book of Genesis, which accounts for the importance of the act of breathing. Here it is told that man was created from the earth,[113] and that he only became a living creature when God breathed into his nostrils.[114] Therefore life, for Ficino, is something to be inhaled, a sort of immaterial vapor not dissimilar to spirit. In order to lend his point authority, Ficino reports a passage from the *Historia naturalis* in which Pliny the Elder tells of a people at the extreme boundary of India, who live only on the air they breathe and the scents they inhale through their nostrils. They need neither food nor drink, only the different odors of roots, flowers, and such fruits as wild apples. Hence, life is enhanced by odors, and, according to Ficino, the reason for this is that odors share the incorporeal nature of life and, because like is nourished by like,[115] the scents of plants constitute the basic nourishment of man's existence. Because of their ethereal nature, one's spirit and life are also nourished by anything that is as insubstantial as odors, such as air. The quality of the spirit is the quality of air, for air, eternally moved by the sublunar and celestial powers, penetrates us on all sides, affecting both our vital and our animal spirit.

If we consider what Ficino says about inhaling only odors and air with certain characteristics, we can probably list the qualities of the perfect pleasance from which a fifteenth-century stroller would have derived the greatest benefit. First of all, odors and air need to be suitably mixed. Variety prevents boredom, which is evil for the spirit, and brings pleasure, "through which, so to say, Venus herself the friend of pleasure, comes into the spirit, and as soon as she has entered it she propagates it as is her function."[116] Moreover, a quality that odors should have is temperateness, which accounts for the importance of selecting only certain species of plants. Excessive odors could in fact have a destructive effect: the people of India of which Pliny writes, for example, are so sensitive to scents that too strong an odor could be fatal. In the first book, Ficino explains that the most pleasant smells are "those verging toward warmth if coldness prevails and those tending toward cold, if warmth dominates. Therefore smells must be tempered from roses, violets, myrtle, sandal . . . which are cold; and again from cinnamon, citron, orange, cloves, mint, melissa, saffron . . . which are warm. Spring flowers are especially useful and the leaves of the citron or of the orange, and fragrant fruits."[117] Hence, temperateness results from various scents of vegetal species, which must be chosen carefully in order to grant the human spirit the most "fruitful" nutriment. Also, among the trees, the best ones are the evergreens, planted in groves: pines, olives, and laurels, for "if they stay green even in winter, [they] will help you live long by their shade, their vapor, their fruit when new, their wood, and any timely use."[118]

For the sake of always breathing fresh air, the ideal pleasance ought to be exposed to the wind, yet moderately: there should be no "winds that come from a swamp," and no drafts; "likewise [to be avoided are those] places where the air moves violently or does not move at all."[119] Also, Ficino says to "avoid" the clouds and to prepare yourself daily to receive the light of the sun, so that "you live in the light as continually possible without sweating and dehydration, or at least in sight of the light, both at a distance and near, both covered and open to the sky . . . always breathe living air, air living with light."[120] Thus, both sunny and shady areas are useful, but it seems that they should be separated from each other, for, as Ficino writes to Giovanni Cavalcanti, God "has shed into physical matter light unmixed with darkness."[121] Ficino also recommends certain plants that are more solar than others, in that they better retain the sun's beneficial power. The most Phoebean of all is the laurel, then the palm, but also the lotus, because of the roundness of its leaves that unfold during the day and fold back up at night. Similarly, to the sun belong all those flowers and herbs that close up when the sun is absent, unfold as soon as it returns, and continuously turn toward it. The light and heat of the sun are nourishments as precious as odors and air, for they too feed the human spirit, thanks to their incorporeal nature.

It appears that the primary function of Ficino's *locus amoenus* is a medicinal one, in that it contributes to prolong a person's earthly life. However, this ideal philosophical pleasance is also endowed with a deep symbolic meaning that makes it a point of contact between the Christian religion and Platonic philosophy. Ficino says that the scents of plants are not only salubrious for the spirit but also nourish the soul, in that the spirit is in fact a mediator between the body and the soul.[122] As Plato admonishes in the *Timaeus*,[123] the soul should not be promoted at the expense of the body, or vice versa; each should receive its proper nourishment, otherwise, says Ficino, if a man feeds and trains just one of the two, ignoring the other, he will do considerable damage to his life. Therefore, a way to simply take care of both of them at the same time is through the cure of the spirit, which is nourished by the sight of green things, temperate scents, and moderate winds.

Further, Ficino advocates the consideration of two examples: that of Paradise, and that of the mode of life posited by Plato in the *Phaedo*.[124] In Genesis 2:15 we read that God created the Garden of Eden, where man could live and be nurtured by the fruits of its trees. The fact that Ficino uses the word *Paradisus* instead of Eden accounts for his knowledge of the myths regarding this place: at the center of Paradise stands the tree of life, whose fruit, if eaten continuously, grants immortality. In the biblical account, the paradisal place bestows spiritual pleasure, harmony, and freedom from suffering on those who dwell in it. Interestingly enough, Ficino mentions the tree of life and the abundance of its fruit but not the only tree that in the book of Genesis is singled out from the many: the tree of knowledge of good and evil, whose fruit is forbidden. Therefore, instead of pointing out the obedience to the command of God that the tree of knowledge would represent, Ficino stresses God's Providence: God forbids Adam to eat that fruit only because it is harmful, whereas all the other fruits are good. Thus the description of life in Paradise, which Ficino urges his readers to reflect upon, mirrors a conception of the *locus amoenus* as an indefinitely pleasant place that is not overshadowed by the bitter sense that its inhabitants are going to "fall" from it.

In his *Phaedo*, Plato has Socrates explain the importance of conducting a fair life and taking care of one's own soul. Because the soul is in fact immortal, and there is no escape from evil or salvation, it follows that men ought to take care of their souls not just for a beneficial earthly life but for the sake of eternity. Those who live a pious life will then be rewarded with freedom: they will be released from the hollows of the earth in which they live and will be allowed to live on the surface. This is described as a sort of earthly paradise, with a hilly topography, where trees, flowers, and fruits are not spoiled by decay. People who dwell in this place know that theirs "is the true heaven, the true light and the true earth . . . they see the sun, the moon and the stars as they are,"[125] while we, who live in the hollows, can only see them dimly, as if sitting at the bottom of the sea and looking at them through the water. As these two examples show, for Ficino the relationship between a *locus amoenus* and the human soul is reciprocal. The former soothes the human body and spirit (Genesis); those who take good care of their souls are rewarded with a pleasance, where their souls will rejoice eternally (as Plato argues). In both cases the *locus amoenus* is synonymous with well-being and pleasure. More evidence for this assumption is given by the speech of Venus that Ficino introduces in the fourteenth chapter of book 2. Here the goddess says: "Liber[126] himself always hates slaves, and that life which he promises by wine, he gives . . . only to the free . . . select from my garden [*hortis*] rice [*risum*], but let the fig alone."[127] The fig tree is a scriptural emblem, behind which stands a whole series of anterior images, which point back to Genesis, where the tree suggests the estrangement from God: in the Old Testament, Adam uses fig leaves to cover his nakedness before God. The fig tree thus represents the primordial shame, the feeling of guilt that Adam experienced when he longed for what was forbidden, and that caused him that innermost disturbance that tears apart the unity of body and spirit. If the fig tree is the bitter memory of the Fall,[128] and Venus's plea in her green abode is that of preferring *risus* to the fig, it follows that the *locus amoenus* is for Ficino an image of gaiety and lightness, which reflects more the harmony of body and soul than a feeling of shame and burdensome fear.

The question now is what the nature is of the pleasure that green places bestow upon their strollers, and what significance an avid reader of Ficino, such as his patron Cosimo de' Medici, may have attributed to his most important pleasance, the *orto* at Careggi. As we have seen, the presence of Venus calls forth an allegorical dimension of meaning, with which Ficino endows his imaginary pleasances. In her speech the goddess, called "almam Venerem" (nursing mother), addresses the elderly as well as Ficino, who remarks that he is already old. Venus's *locus* is not clearly defined. There are flowers that were planted as lilies but instead grow as crocuses (saffron), and those that originally were lilies but are plucked as violets. At last, Venus pronounces: "Let the rose be your morning star, the myrtle your evening star,"[129] and with these words she concludes her oracle.

In the goddess's speech, the *locus amoenus* seems to be a place where men could spend their entire existence on earth, from the dawn of their youth to their vespertine senility, but its virtual gates are open also to the simultaneous presence of youth and old age.[130] To pluck violets (*Viola odorata*), which, blooming in the winter month of February, may represent old age, as if they were lilies (*Lilium candidum*), which blossom in the spring and usually symbolize virginity, might allude to the importance of conducting a chaste life even in old age. Also, to pluck the lilies of the place in springtime (youth) at the same time as the crocus (*Crocus sativus*), which is an autumn flower, probably signifies that youth and old age can benefit from their reciprocal companionship. Ficino already mentions young and old people keeping company with each other a few chapters earlier, when he suggests consulting Socrates in order to know "how the frequent companionship of youths avails for a while to hold back old age."[131] But the pleasure that green places provide is not of a promiscuous kind. In fact, the adjective *chaste* with which Ficino describes Socrates is used to assure the reader that the relationship between the old philosopher and his young companions was entirely Platonic, in that it transcended both physical promiscuity and licentiousness.[132]

In the context of early Renaissance culture, Ficino suggests that, far from escaping, with the restless wonder that someone like Petrarch betrays, the uncomfortable and tense state provoked by the desires of the senses, people should learn how to cope with them and to discover, in the agitation stirred by sensual beauty, the very reward of their existence: people must remain open to the power that sensual beauty has on the soul, because the virtue of sensual beauty is precisely that of helping people transcend the very materiality of the world. In his commentary on Plato's *Symposium*, Ficino says more precisely that one must transcend visible and tangible matter, for beauty cannot reside in physical bodies, and that which cannot endure eternally in matter—the beauty of the human body itself decreases with time—cannot depend on it either. It follows that beauty depends only on the superior Artificer, who employs his angels and souls in order to beautify the matter of the world. Thus the *locus amoenus*, and especially the rose that Venus mentions at the end of her speech—the flower that in literary tradition connotes the most erotic allusions—can well stand for the sensual pleasure of the youth (who tends to perceive a lesser degree of beauty, however) but not for lechery or for feminine beauty. In the macrocosmic-microcosmic sphere of Platonic correspondences, the rose turns into the living symbol of an ideal beauty, which is grasped with the myrtle (*Myrtus communis*)—flowering in winter—representing the wisdom that comes with old age. Hence, if the relationship between old age and youth is not promiscuous, and if, as Venus suggests, her abode is a place open to both, and far from hosting the human vicissitudes of *amour courtois*,[133] the pleasure that her pleasance represents is a purified enjoyment of the senses, which leads to the joy of the intellect that comes from the superior understanding of the infinite beauty of God.

The very essence of God, that is, luminosity, is in fact another quality that pleasances should have, one that further stresses the metaphysical implications of the *locus amoenus*. It is extremely important that people take long walks in these lofty, clear and open places, when the rays of the sun and the stars can reach them on all sides, and their spirits can thus be filled by the spirit of the world shining from their rays, which will nourish them with the motion and power of the world.[134]

Ficino explains in his *De Sole* that light is a sign of love and goodness.[135] However, he argues that men must venerate not the sun per se but the principle that moves it, that is, God. Ficino's light, like the sun, is a sign that, though existing in the real world, points to an absence, the idea of God. In fact, the sun that we see moves, whereas God is immobile, for stillness—intended as beginning, rule, and end of motion—is the most perfect of any movements. Now, because human intelligence can only grasp whatever is corporeal, or at least perceptible through the senses,[136] God lets us sense his existence through something that is intelligible, like the visible sun, or the colors and scents of flowers, and visible light. Hence, the affinity between God and the sun that Ficino spells out in the *De Sole* is to be regarded not as the result of an equation but rather as a chain of correspondences in the hierarchical network of the cosmos, in which the elements of a garden too may have their own place and function. Ficino's *topos* of light serves to justify the presence of green places in this world, a justification that transcends the mere fact that it is the sun that activates the efficacy of the pleasance on the human being, in that the heat of the sun enhances the smell of plants.

The panegyric on light explains the descent of the *locus amoenus* from the light of the sun, and further endows the former with metaphysical signif-icance: anything that Ficino says in the *De vita* about green places, the life of men, and the cure of their spirit is confirmed, though on another, higher level of meaning, in his *De Sole*. Here vegetal species belong to the triplet of lives born from the heat of the sun, which is equated to the *Spiritus Sanctus*, whereas the sense of olfaction derives from the light of the sun,[137] which stands for the Son. The very nature of the ideal *locus amoenus*, which is made of mixed species and scents, depends on the fecundity of the sun, which is as-sociated with the Father. It follows that every pleasance partakes of the three-fold pattern of the sun, which so closely resembles the holy Christian Trinity.

Both in the *De vita* and in the *De Sole* Ficino speaks of vegetal species but does not make explicit reference to any man-made gardens. In the ninth chapter of the book on the sun Ficino says that when God pervades anything by means of natural light, all that is ineffable becomes partially intelligible to the human intellect, which feels stirrings of the urge to make use of what it sees: "God continuously surrounds them with light through which the virtues of that which is intelligible and those of the intellects are urged to act[138] and come together by their action."[139] Light, then, is what makes people active. David, says Ficino in the *De Sole*, started to play his lyre at dawn and said that it is not useful to wake up before the morning dawn, for the sun has the power of compelling the human spirit to produce sublime things (or perform sublimely). Also, human operations taking place in sunlight serve to reveal and exploit those magical sympathies that inform the fabric of the cosmos.

In the *De vita coelitus comparanda*, or third book of the *De vita*, Ficino says that the spirit of the man who is intent on creating an image of the uni-verse, and who has been concentrating upon his work and the stars through his imagination and emotion, is joined to the very spirit of the world and to the rays of the stars with which the world spirit acts.[140] Further, he adds that odors, especially if the rays of the stars enhance them, strongly influence the air and the spirit toward capturing the gifts of the sun, when the work is done opportunely under its rays.[141] The harder the material with which the maker—*operans*—works, the less possibility there is that it catches the mini-mum from scents and that it reflects the imprint of the maker's imagination.

Finally, in the thirteenth chapter, he says: "If a hundred gifts of the Sun or Jupiter were scattered throughout a hundred plants . . . and you discovered them and were able to compound them and work them up into *one form*, in this you would actually seem already to possess completely the Sun or Jupiter"[142] (emphasis added). If we pushed this argument further, we could say that a garden, following Ficino's logic, would represent for the philosopher the most powerful of the works of art, for its essential components are naturally odoriferous and their textures are so rough and airy as to both seize and retain the gifts of the sun, and reflect the imagination of its creator. But nowhere in his treatise on life does Ficino speak explicitly about man-made gardens. As we have seen, he advises people to take long walks in verdant places because these can greatly improve their health, but he never tells us whether these places are *loci amoeni* or gardens. Judging from the few details we are given, they could be both.

In his *Platonic Theology* Ficino places greater emphasis on men as active creatures, that is, as makers, more than as passive strollers whose experience among green places is merely sensory. In fact, it is men's making that brings them closer to God. As Michael Allen has pointed out, man imitates God "when he too makes things from the sensible objects of the sublunar realm that God made in imitation of the Ideas of such objects in His own Mind."[143] In the third chapter of the *Theology*'s thirteenth book Ficino says that man "uses all the world's materials and uses them everywhere as though they were all subject to him: he uses the elements, stones, metals, plants, and animals, fashioning them into many forms and figures, which the beasts never do. . . . He [man] tramples on the earth, furrows the water, ascends into the air in the tallest towers. . . . Man not only uses the elements, he adorns them."[144] Ficino seems particularly enthusiastic about the idea that man not only uses but also adorns the elements of the world: "Throughout the whole globe how marvelous is [man's] culture of the earth! How stupendous is the construction of his buildings and his cities! How skillful is his use of water in irrigation! In inhabiting all the elements and cultivating them all, he performs the office of God."[145] Ficino's objective is to prove that because man "handles, changes, and forms" all the materials, he rules over them, and if he can do so he is a kind of god, and therefore, like God himself, he is immortal.[146] As we have seen, Ficino mentions plants among the natural materials that are available to man. Therefore, it would be legitimate to argue, following his logic, that the making of a garden, which consists of the manipulation of natural elements, is also a form of art that would prove man's similarity to God. And this is even more so if we consider that a garden is not only made of natural materials but also constitutes a perfect example of men's adornment of them.

Ficino began this chapter of the *Platonic Theology* by saying that while animals are "drawn by the law of fate" to deploy a single art or skill and "they never improve over time in doing what they do, men, by contrast, are the inventors of numberless arts that they pursue at their own choosing. This is evidenced by the fact that individual men practice many of the arts and they develop and become more skilled as a result of daily practice; and what is marvelous is that human arts make on their own whatever nature itself makes: it is as if we were not her slaves but her rivals."[147] At this point he could have mentioned such an exemplary garden as that of the famous villa Lo Specchio at Quaracchi, which belonged to his contemporary Giovanni Rucellai, where the works of *ars topiaria* had been described by the owner with a profusion of details.[148] Instead, Ficino mentions painters and sculptors whose works looked so realistic as to provoke the most astonishing reactions from their observers: "Zeuxis so painted grapes that the birds flew up to them. . . . Praxiteles sculpted a marble statue of Venus in a temple of the Indians that was so alluring that it could scarcely be kept safe and unspotted from the lustful gazes of passersby."[149] He goes on to praise the pyramids of the Egyptians and the edifices of the Romans and the Greeks, whose perfect geometry and mathematical proportions are examples of man's attempt to imitate "all the works of divine nature" and to perfect "all the works of lower nature [i.e., matter], correcting and emending them."[150]

In an earlier book of the *Platonic Theology* Ficino explains that "all art, since it organizes its work with a definite reason towards a definite end, is a rational faculty."[151] Moreover, this rational faculty is innate not only in humans as a species but also in nature: "How artfully do the elements make for their proper location. . . . With what architectural diligence does the rain contract itself into spherical drops!"[152] Further on Ficino speaks of two kinds of arts:

> Some are concerned with a material that does not have the work's effective principle within itself. Clay or stone, for instance, are subject to the potter or sculptor in such a way that they have to await the artist's hand. . . . But there are other arts whose matter, with the help of some form, is actually moved to effect the work, which in this case should be called a natural rather than an artificial work. Thus earth submits to the farmer, the human body to the doctor. The fertility of the soil for

producing crops and the role of the body's complexion or temperament in recovering health are what most help the farmer and the doctor, and so much so that often a field produces crops without cultivation and our body's complexion fights off diseases without a doctor's attention. . . . In the first kind of art, therefore, the artist is called the lord and master of the matter, but in the second, he is just the stimulator and minister of nature.[153]

The art of making gardens, as we understand it today, would probably lie between the two categories described by Ficino, in that plants are living things and as such have the capacity to grow even without the help of the gardener; however, the arrangement of them in space, like the design of a building, would pertain to the first category, in that the arrangement is dependent on "the artist's hand." However, it is more likely that fifteenth-century garden making belonged to the second category, given the often blurred distinction between gardens and kitchen gardens. Moreover, as Ficino never speaks about the appearance of a garden, it is possible that the layout was not an artist's concern, and also not the object of a separate study meant to anticipate the actual implementation of the garden on site.

Finally, as we have seen, Petrarch rejected material beauty for fear of its sensual allurements. Therefore, he spoke of gardens (*horti*) only in terms of the toil involved in the cultivation of them, and used them as elements of a figurative speech meant to visualize his literary endeavor. Boccaccio, on the other hand, used his fictional gardens consistently as narrative elements, whose morphological structure obeys the logic of a secular ethic veiled by allegory.[154] Ficino's prose, like Boccaccio's, is dense with allegorical correspondences that point to something other than that to which they apparently refer. However, in the case of Ficino's pleasances, these correspondences act as signs, or symbols, pointing to something invisible, that is, the transcendental idea of God and divine beauty. Therefore, with Ficino allegory becomes Christianized—although sometimes this was a necessity due more to the difficult religious atmosphere of the time than to severe Christian orthodoxy.

Unlike Boccaccio, Ficino did not speak of the morphology of any earthly pleasances. In tune with his philosophical theory of magic expressed in the third book of the *De vita*, he believed that the power forms have of attracting celestial influence depends more on the material to be manipulated than on some intrinsic quality these forms may possess. Moreover, because stellar rays can penetrate matter while this is being "shaped" or given form, we could say that the act of making a garden, and the creative imagination involved in the process, is more important than the actual morphology of the final product.[155]

There is one instance in which Ficino refers to an actual place, namely, when he discusses with Pico della Mirandola the qualities of the ideal site for a villa—of which he writes in a letter to Filippo Valori (November 1488).[156] In this letter, Ficino recounts a walk he and Pico took on the hills of Fiesole, when they identified as the most salubrious of the sites around Florence the place where Boccaccio lived. During the stroll they discussed the characteristics of the ideal site: first of all, it should be as far away as possible from the mists of the Arno and also be protected from the cold Boreas. Moreover, the villa should have a southern exposure and abundant springs. Suddenly, while Ficino and Pico are talking about the salubriousness of the site, the villa of Pier Filippo Pandolfini, which had been built for Leonardo Bruni precisely on the site where Boccaccio used to live, materializes before their eyes. Surprised, Pico points out that the forms they were just so earnestly imagining and hoping for have appeared as if in a dream, and he asks whether the villa they have before their eyes has always existed or if it has been created by the power of their imagination.[157] Unlike Boccaccio in his *Decameron*, Ficino does not, in fact, describe the ideal "forms" of the villa and its setting; however, he has Pico say that they conformed to the right and natural rule of building: "recta et physica aedificandi ratio."[158] Thus, the philosophers conclude that only a wise man could have built the villa in such a manner. A few lines later, it appears that the power of imagination takes over once again, for the villa is now called a sacred shrine—*aedem sacram*—in the same way that the groves surrounding it are sacred. The attribute of sacredness is therefore justified by the perfection of the architecture and of its site, which cannot but reflect a higher concept of perfection. For this reason the artificer who created the villa and chose its site must have been a sage. The ambiguity between actuality and illusion, or dream, to which Pico's words refer, suggests that Neoplatonic philosophers, even more than humanist poets, clothed the world with the veils of allegory, for anything that exists on this earth—writes Ficino in his translation of Synesius's *De somniis*—points to something other: "per omnia significantur omnia."[159] Therefore, in order to understand what the meaning of the *locus amoenus* in Neoplatonic writings is, one has to look beyond appearances, as Boccaccio had suggested his readers do.

Ultimately, in his works Ficino addresses both the experience of being in a green place, which, for all we know, could either be untouched nature or a man-made garden, and the experience of making use of garden elements, such as plants and odoriferous flowers. Every man is for the philosopher a potential artificer who is naturally prone to make use of the natural elements of the world. However, Ficino places a greater emphasis on the performance of an action than on the material product that results from it. In the context of fifteenth-century Florence, therefore, we could interpret garden making as one of the skills that people naturally possess and improve as a result of daily practice. By cultivating and manipulating the elements of nature men become nature's rivals, and act in imitation of God the Creator.

CHAPTER FOUR

Practice and Theory

The Design of the Garden

The tradition of garden making that produced the Medici *orti* of the early Renaissance did not operate by means of drawings and models. It appears that a concept of design vis-à-vis the "art" of gardens did not yet exist, and that the layout of Quattrocento pleasances resulted from an empirical modus operandi. This may have taken into account such elements as sense perception, that is, the sense of olfaction, which would dictate the choice and grouping of odoriferous plants—as Ficino's recommendations suggest—or the sense of sight, which would call for the choice of sites totally open to the landscape—as is the case with Fiesole. Moreover, utilitarian reasons would often dictate the proximity to the house of kitchen gardens and fruit gardens, or *pomarii*, whose layout, as many scholars have already pointed out, was inherited from the agricultural tradition. At any rate, the appearance of the garden would be decided in situ, that is, on site, and not at a drawing table or in some *bottega*, where models of buildings were produced.

Grazia Gobbi Sica has called attention to the fact that the making of gardens in fifteenth-century Florence, just as in the Middle Ages, is not linked to a design practice, and such examples as the villa Lo Specchio at Quaracchi, whose garden has been described in plenty of detail by its owner Giovanni Rucellai—and is usually interpreted as the result of an overall and elaborate design scheme—are but exceptions.[1] On the other hand, according to Gobbi Sica, toward the middle of the sixteenth century gardens reflect literally the design principles, based on geometry, put forth in the treatises written toward the end of the Quattrocento, such as Francesco di Giorgio Martini's *Trattati di architettura, ingegneria e arte militare,* or by sixteenth-century works on architecture, such as Sebastiano Serlio's *De architectura.*[2] However, whether the application of geometric principles extracted from theoretical works by itself originated a design practice is questionable, as we shall see. Gobbi Sica also seems to imply that these gardens are designed, insofar as they are no longer composed of an "episodic succession of parts" but are rather "the object of a coherent composition . . . space of pure volumes, linked by precise relationships, better still, by numeric ratios in addition to symbolic meanings and *topoi.*"[3] Yet, a few lines later she claims that these gardens from the first half of the Cinquecento are not particularly innovative, especially when compared with their Roman counterparts. She writes that sixteenth-century gardens still bear an old-fashioned appearance "in the layout of the garden interpreted as parterre, as outdoor extension, more or less enlarged, of the house, basically developed in two dimensions."[4]

By focusing exclusively on the "guida totalizzante del disegno da parte della geometria" (the absolute control of the layout by means of geometry), Gobbi Sica overemphasizes the role of geometry and overlooks the role of *disegno* vis-à-vis the design of the garden. I would argue that sixteenth-century gardens differ from their predecessors in that for the first time they are drawn before being made. In fact, the application of geometry to garden making took place long before these gardens started to be designed (see, for example, the ordered layout of medieval cloister gardens); therefore the innovative aspect of Florentine gardens in the Cinquecento is not so much geometry as it is their being designed by means of tools (i.e., drawings and models) previously used in other disciplines, such as the making of buildings.

One of the earliest garden drawings, although very schematic, is included in a plan of the villa at Poggio a Caiano that dates to the years 1513–1534 (fig. 47). The drawing includes a handwritten note saying that the proportions of the gardens will be increased according to the wishes of the pope, who was probably Leo X.[5] Drawings of other Medici gardens were also produced later on. For example, in his account of the life of Niccolò Pericoli—called Il Tribolo—Vasari tells how in 1538 the Duke of Florence, Cosimo I, "wanted Tribolo to begin working at the ornamentation of that place [Castello] according to the drawings and models he had previously shown him."[6] According to Vasari's testimony, the trees and boxwood hedges of these gardens were so precisely aligned and pruned that they appeared as if they had been painted by an artist: "And in the middle of this garden [was] a bosquet of very tall and

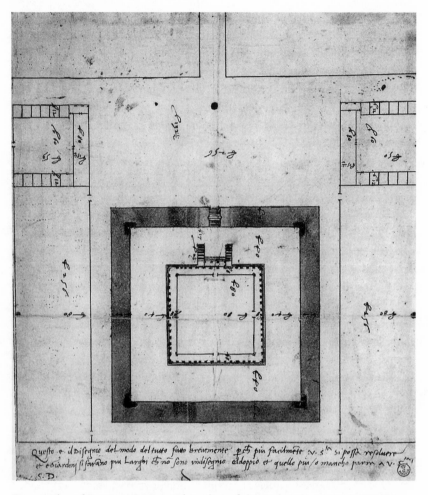

Fig. 47. Plan of Poggio a Caiano with outline of the gardens (1513–1534). GDSU, 4016r A. By permission of Ministero per i Beni e le Attività Culturali.

thick cypresses, laurels, and marjoram, which planted in a circle give shape to a labyrinth surrounded by boxwood, two and a half *braccia* high [4.8 feet; 1 *braccio* equals 58.3 cm], and with their surfaces so even and beautifully clipped that they seem to be the work of a painter."[7] As we shall see, this remark is important, in that gardens are compared for the first time to a product of artistic craftsmanship—painting in this case—which results from a number of sequential operations, such as drawing and the application of pigments.[8] Moreover,

Vasari's statement suggests that the garden is no longer considered a microcosm reflecting the beauty of the entire universe created by God; rather, the perfection of the labyrinth reveals the presence of man as the artificer, whose skills allow him to manipulate nature according to his own wishes. Therefore, drawing becomes as necessary for the making of a garden as it is for the making of a painting, or of a building, because drawing allows the artificer to exercise a greater control over his work and thus better reveal his virtuosity for the appreciation of the beholder.

The design of the garden also coincides with the formation of the garden designer. This does not mean that a new professional figure is created out of nothing, as the artists from whom the duke commissioned his gardens were not only able to design gardens but could also master the disciplines of architecture, military art, and hydraulic engineering. And all these fields required an expertise in the *arte del disegno*, and in the making of models.[9] We know, for instance, that Tribolo constructed a wood model representing the city of Florence, which Clement VII commissioned from him in 1529, so that he could follow from Rome the unfolding of the siege of Florence by Charles V's troops. Also, it seems that Benedetto Varchi's accurate description of Florence in his *Storie fiorentine* is indebted to a very peculiar topographical survey of the city (now lost) that Tribolo conducted together with Benvenuto della Volpaia; according to Vasari, "It was Tribolo who suggested that a plan be drawn, [because he thought that with a plan] it would have been easier to record the height of the mountains, the level of the plains, and other important details."[10]

It is likely that among the drawings of Tribolo mentioned by Vasari there was a topographical survey of the land for the construction of the gardens at Castello. Drawings were a necessary tool to study the positioning of underground water channels, which would connect the various fountains and ponds of the villas.[11] Tribolo laid out the gardens along the slope of the hill, so that "all the longitudinal alleys have a slight and comfortable slope, the transversal ones are straight and level," as we learn from the description given by Michel de Montaigne in his *Journal de voyage en Italie par la Suisse et l'Allemagne en 1580 et 1581*.[12] Incidentally, the design scheme adopted by Tribolo obviously prioritized the visual effect versus the practical, insofar as the laying out of the gardens along the longitudinal slope of the hill on the one hand favored the movement of the water through the channels toward the fountains, but on the other hand contributed to the phenomenon of soil erosion by speeding up the ground waters.[13] At any rate, the calculation of the different levels, and the unusually large scale of the villa, which needed a comprehensive design scheme, were enough to justify the production of drawings and models not only for the study of the final layout of the gardens but also, as we have seen, for the purpose of showing the overall plan to the duke. Moreover, drawings were needed for the study of those sculptures that would ornament the garden. Unfortunately, little has been done to trace and record the location of Tribolo's drawings dedicated to gardens, and only the drawings dedicated to garden sculptures and fountains have so far attracted the attention of scholars.

To my knowledge, Philip Foster was the first to point out the existence of a drawing in which a portion of the gardens at Castello is outlined (fig. 48).[14] The drawing, which represents a detail of the *orticini*, was later published by Giorgio Galletti, who pointed as well to the similarity between the hedges flanking the fountain of Hercules and Antaeus, the plan of which is represented on the Uffizi drawing, and the hedges that were represented by Giusto Utens in 1599.[15] Now, since we know that the Hercules and Antaeus group was sculpted by Ammannati between 1558 and 1559, it is likely that he followed Tribolo's drawings and models not only for the execution of the fountain but also for the design of the garden. In any case, the measurements recorded on the folio show that the outline of the hedges was carefully thought through, that is, it was designed instead of simply "made," as was the case in earlier gardens.

Even if the attribution of the Uffizi drawing to Tribolo is uncertain, and Vasari's testimony is not to be taken for granted, there are other primary sources suggesting that the layout of the gardens in the sixteenth century was being addressed by means of drawings, during a speculative phase of design that preceded the gardens' implementation on their villa site. This is what Tribolo says, for instance, about the garden at Poggio a Caiano in a letter written to Pier Francesco Riccio in 1549: "This morning His Excellence commanded that I see to it that that grove and the garden toward the road are planted. And [he told me] that I must draw it so that work can begin. And I started immediately . . . and considering how much he wants what he asked for, today I made a drawing on paper, and this evening at our convenience I will show it to you"[16] (fig. 49). Later in the letter Tribolo explains that the works involved the planting of sixty orange trees and four hundred other trees that had been ordered for the garden and the grove. In another letter, written a few years earlier, the word *disegno* is used both to indicate an actual drawing and to mean the mental elaboration—*disegniato e liberato*—of the villa's outdoors. In this letter, Cosimo I himself appears to have drawn, perhaps mentally,

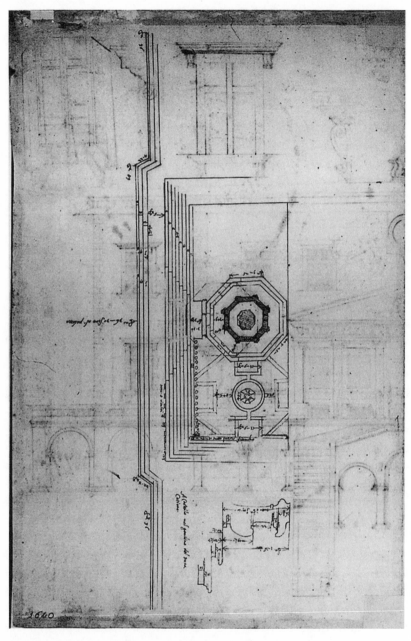

Fig. 48. Tribolo (attributed), drawing of a garden detail at Castello (1520–1536).
GDSU, 1640v A. By permission of Ministero per i Beni e le Attività Culturali.

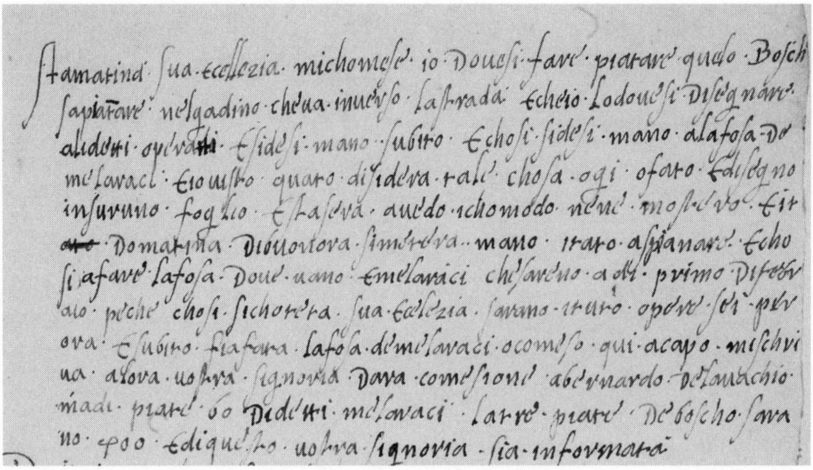

Fig. 49. Letter of Tribolo to Pier Francesco Riccio (1548). ASF, *Mediceo del Principato* 1171, ins. 6, fol. 292r. By permission of Ministero per i Beni e le Attività Culturali.

a sketch of the garden at Poggio a Caiano—*gli è parso disegniare uno giardino*—even before entrusting Tribolo with its design.[17] The duke's direct interest in the design of Poggio a Caiano is attested by the fact that a series of drawings were made of the villa during his rule. One of them is a measured sketch that includes in a corner a rough detail of what the center of the garden may have looked like, a detail that seems to have resulted from an extemporaneous gesture (fig. 50).[18] The difference between this rough sketch and the plan mentioned above (see fig. 47), in which the perimeter of the gardens at Poggio a Caiano is outlined (though not on the right scale), is that the sketch shows a design idea that was not meant to be shown, unlike in the earlier plan with its handwritten note for the pope. This sketch of a garden detail was probably put on paper as an aid to the mind, suddenly thinking about the design of the garden, while also carrying out the plan of the building.

The design of the Boboli gardens, which Cosimo I also commissioned from Tribolo, provides more evidence in support of the production of garden drawings. On September 27, 1550, three weeks after Tribolo's death, Cosimo requested a retainer to make sure that Francesco di Ser Jacopo, the Provveditore of the Fortezza da Basso, and Davide di Raffaello Fortini, who was supervising the works at Castello, provided him with "all the garden drawings and all the instructions left by poor Tribolo so that we may give the order that the planting be completed."[19]

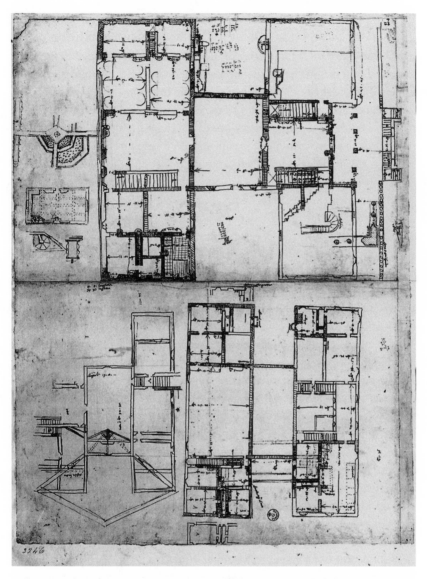

Fig. 50. Sketch of Poggio a Caiano with detail of the garden (c. 1550). GDSU 3246r A. By permission of Ministero per i Beni e le Attività Culturali.

The duke's wish to bring his gardens to completion according to Tribolo's design shows not only that the early project for the Boboli gardens was put on paper but also that that particular design was accorded special value by Cosimo I. On the one hand, this would oppose the belief of some garden historians that it was not customary at that time to retain a design project once the designer had passed away.[20] On the other hand, the preference accorded to a specific design concept bears witness to a change in the way gardens were thought of in the sixteenth century, that is, they were now regarded as objects of design. And this change is precisely what distinguishes these "designed" gardens from those "made" gardens of the Quattrocento.

A document in the State Archives in Florence refers to garden drawings produced at the time when Vasari was involved with the construction of the so-called *vivaio* at Boboli between 1557 and 1564: "Construction works must be carried out in the garden of the Pitti, both outside and inside where the two niches are located, according to the drawing by Giorgio Vasari and also the stone slabs should be cut for the plane where the niche of the fish-pond is located, on the outward side, five *braccia* [9.5 feet; nearly three meters] wide and ten and a quarter *braccia* [19.6 feet; nearly six meters] high."[21] Besides the use of drawings as design tools, it appears that Vasari also commissioned a basswood model—now lost—of his *vivaio* from the carpenter Luigi di Matteo.[22]

In addition to the production of both technical and illustrative drawings, or models, and to the formation of what we might call the garden designer, the design of sixteenth-century Medici gardens is dependent on another factor, that is, a new urge expressed by the Medici to authorize their own power and make a public display of their wealth for the benefit of their continued political rule. For example, unlike earlier Medici gardens, those at Castello embody a narrative that illustrates the vicissitudes of its owner, and are designed for propagandistic purposes. In particular, these gardens represent the fortunate series of events that, from January to August 1537, led the young Cosimo di Giovanni de' Medici, a descendant of the cadet branch of the family, to be elected first duke of Florence. Therefore, the design of the gardens at Castello also involved the study of a coherent allegorical program.[23] One of the themes the gardens were to represent was the city of Florence itself, because, according to a prophecy formulated when Cosimo was still very young, he would become the ruler of the city. Moreover, his election coincided with a rare meteorological event, namely, an early but short spring that brought relief from the chills of the winter. Therefore, the vernal season was the second motif that the garden embodied, standing for the eternal political and artistic spring brought

to Florence by the duke. Also, the allegorical program for the garden was corroborated by the use of the aforementioned sculptures and the construction of
grottoes.[24] For instance, the personification of Florence was identified with a
statue of Venus; the association of Florence with both Venus and spring was
meant to suggest a parallel between Cosimo's renovation of Florence and the
Roman emperor Augustus's *renovatio imperii*. This is probably the reason why
the two famous Botticelli paintings representing Spring and the birth of Venus
were also brought to the villa.[25]

Another recurring theme in the garden was the call for order, which we
find especially clear in the grotto of the animals, where the two statues of Nep-
tune and Pan from Tribolo's project represent order after chaos, in particular
the restoration of civil and political order in Florence after a period of political
anarchy. The same can be said for the group of Hercules and Anteus, where
the former represents Cosimo defeating his enemy Antaeus, who stands for the
anti-Medicean party. According to Vasari, who was among those best ac-
quainted with Castello and with Tribolo's plan, the artist, following the advice
of Benedetto Varchi, designed sculptures representing the cosmic theme of the
four seasons. Spring, Summer, Fall, and Winter were to be personified by statues placed in the four corners of the garden. Varchi also devised six other allegories, whose sole purpose was to glorify the Medici. According to Vasari these
six figures represented "the greatness and magnanimity of the Medici family,
and all the virtues of the duke Cosimo, and these are Justice, Piety, Courage,
Nobility, Wisdom, and Liberality."[26] These statues were to be located in
gabled niches in the labyrinth garden. They symbolized the greatness and
goodness of the Medici house, and, at the same time, indicated that these
virtues were all combined in the person of Cosimo.[27] Moreover, Tribolo proposed that in front of the opposite garden wall there be represented those elements of civilization that had come to thrive in Florence under the wise rule of
the Medici: *leggi, pace, armi, scienze, sapienza, lingue,* and *arti.*

In sum, from a political point of view, the garden became a propaganda
vehicle for sovereignty, as city palaces had been in the past. And the fact that
at Castello such a role is attributed solely to the gardens is proven by Tribolo's
choice of a more sober language for the architecture of the villa.[28] (But this
may also be explained by the fact that the architect had to deal with a preexisting *palagio merlato,* as the building is described in the notarial deed of
1477.)[29] At any rate, Tribolo's design for the gardens at Castello was not
brought to completion, first because he was distracted by other commissions,
and ultimately because of his death.

The need for a designer and a design for the Medici gardens, from the sixteenth century onward, was also dictated by a change in the sort of activities that used to take place in those pleasances,[30] and these activities in their turn reflect a shift in the cultural and political life of Florence. In the fifteenth century making sure that the lower classes were called to participate in public banquets and other festivities organized by the wealthy was a means for the latter to earn public consensus.[31] Giovanni Rucellai, a learned member of the elite, thought that wealth concentrated in the hands of a few people was an injustice vis-à-vis the common good. According to Rucellai, the rich were aware of the reasons behind the hatred and envy of the poor, and they also knew that wealth was a cause of violence and injustice. Therefore he advised his peers to earn the respect and gratitude of the lower classes by adopting behavior comparable to that of the administrator of common wealth, rather than acting as the sole proprietor of it. Therefore, an important task (especially as it was a moral one) of the rich man was to donate in abundance to people in need.[32] Showing an interest in the well-being of the lower classes was also a way to shun any accusation of antirepublican behavior at a time in which the Florentines were weary of people who acted as tyrants, whether they be foreigners, such as the Milanese Visconti, or citizens of the republic. Thus, in his *Ricordi* Giovanni di Pagolo Morelli advised: "Be with your fellow citizens as a parent, love them all, and bring love to them; and, if you can, be kind toward them. Attend their company often; at times feed them and satisfy their thirst, and not the least be caring of the people, the good ones more often than the wicked ones."[33] For these reasons, in the Quattrocento such events as the weddings celebrated by the members of aristocratic families were thought of less as private celebrations than as occasions to display and contribute to the civic décor of Florence. It is useful, in this regard, to read about the marriage of Nannina de' Medici and Bernardo Rucellai in 1466, which was celebrated for three days on the small triangular plaza facing the Rucellai palace on the via della Vigna, and which was described by Bernardo's father, Giovanni, as follows:

> On June 8, 1466, we celebrated the wedding of my son Bernardo with Nannina, Cosimo de' Medici's daughter, who was accompanied by four escorts . . . the celebrations took place on a wooden platform which was one and a half *braccia* high from the ground and about sixteen hundred square *braccia*, which occupied the whole square in front of our house [palazzo Rucellai] which is in the shape of a triangle, [we ornamented it] with a beautiful display of fabrics, tapestries, benches and espaliers and with a sky made of turquoise fabrics to protect us from the sun,

Fig. 51. Cassone Adimari, Florence: Galleria dell'Accademia. Alinari/Art Resource, New York.

decorated with garlands, and roses and shields, half of which with the Medici coat of arms and the other half with the Rucellai coat of arms. . . . And there, on that platform, the guests danced, ate, drank, while young knights made any kind of *armeggeria* on the via della Vigna, and music sent its notes to the sky, so that not only the guests enjoyed it, but also the whole people of Florence did.[34]

Obviously the prodigality of celebrations, and their taking place in a more or less large section of the city, depended on the economic and social status of the wedding couple's families.[35] An exemplary wedding is represented on the *cassone* painted on occasion of the wedding of Lisa Ricasoli and Boccaccio Adimari in the first half of the century: from the portico of the Bigallo, a number of people are shown walking toward the Piazza di San Giovanni, underneath a long red and white canopy, while the trumpeters of the Signoria sit on the steps of the Loggia del Bigallo (fig. 51).[36]

At the turn of the century collective festivities slowly turned into private events. This was due in part to the influence of the Dominican friar Girolamo Savonarola, who disapproved of all profane festivities and bacchanalia, which regularly used to take place in Florence, and who also limited the traditional *feste di San Giovanni*, which were celebrated in spring and were dedicated to love.[37] Later on, when Tuscany became a ducal state, members of the elite, and the Medici probably more than any other family, no longer needed to worry about the happiness of the less fortunate. Nor was self-promotion condemned; rather, as in the case of Cosimo I, it was a necessary tool used to lend authority to the duke's political hegemony. The first complete celebration of the Medici was carried out precisely between 1556 and 1558 in the Salone dei Cinquecento at the Palazzo Vecchio, where Vasari painted a cycle of frescos intended to extol the figure of Cosimo I. It is at this time that the Medici gardens became the venue for celebrating events that formerly took place in the streets of the republican city, and were now a luxury shared only among the acknowledged members of the aristocracy.

Already on June 27, 1539, the wedding of Cosimo de' Medici to Eleonora of Toledo was celebrated in the garden of the Medici Palace. Tribolo designed the scenery for the comedy called *Il Commodo* in collaboration with Aristotle da Sangallo, which was performed, reports Vasari, "in the large courtyard of the Medici palace, where the fountain is located."[38] However, on that specific occasion the scenery, described by Vasari, consisted of temporary structures meant to represent the city of Pisa, and Vasari does not mention any details suggesting that the garden itself was part of the scenery or contributed to the setting of that ephemeral theater, as would be the case, some time later, with the amphitheater at the Boboli gardens.[39] Another example of the privatization of an event that a century earlier could have been public is the wedding of Maria de' Medici and Henry IV, king of France, in 1600. On that occasion the Florentine Riccardo Riccardi offered his palace and garden—called the *giardino di Valfonda*—for the celebrations. Besides a ball that took place in the courtyard of the palace, the guests witnessed a dance and a parade of triumphal chariots in the garden, and finally took part in a hunt that occurred in the park surrounding the garden.[40]

In the same period, that is, during the reign of Grand Duke Ferdinand I (1587–1609), a shift at the center of Medici governance occurred. As Malcolm Campbell has pointed out, this shift was witnessed by the fact that the Pitti Palace and the Boboli gardens became the primary venue for the "representation of the grand duke as the divinely authorized dispenser of justice and mercy," and as guarantor of the prosperity and peace of the Tuscan state and its people.[41] When the grand duke married Cristina of Lorraine, Bernardo Buontalenti, who at the time was in charge of the Pitti's extension—organized a naval battle in the form of a theatrical mise-en-scène staged in the courtyard of the palace. This courtyard was visually and physically linked to the amphitheater, which was meant to host such events as tournaments and horsemanship.

The *teatro di verzura* was, in fact, a rectangular grass meadow originally laid out by Tribolo in the form of a horseshoe, ringed by rows of evergreens planted on the slopes of the rounded valley, and with canals bringing water onto the meadow. Aligned on the central axis of the palace, this rustic amphitheater culminated in a wide alley ascending through the trees to a marble fountain and fishpond, called *peschiera di Nettuno*. All around it was a cluster of orchards, muscatel vineyards, and vegetable plots interspersed with groves

Fig. 52. Stefano Buonsignori, detail of a plan of Florence (1584). Uffizi 21918 st.sc.
By permission of Ministero per i Beni e le Attività Culturali.

for bird hunting. As I mentioned earlier, however, Tribolo did not live long
enough to see the amphitheater completed, and his project was carried out by
Bartolomeo Ammannati, whose contribution is still visible in the plan of Florence drawn by Buonsignori in 1584, and in the lunette painted by Utens in
1599 (figs. 52 and 53). An earlier drawing of the "giardino e del palazzo . . . reale
e imperiale" seems to have been produced in 1563, but unfortunately it is no
longer extant.[42] That the amphitheater was part of a specific design project is

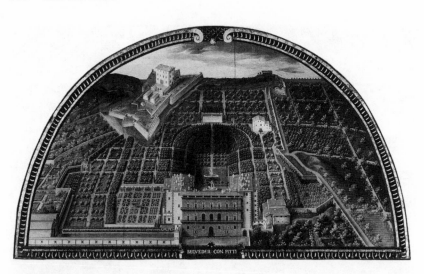

Fig. 53. Giusto Utens, *Belveder con Pitti* (1599). Florence: Museo di Firenze Com'era. By permission of Ministero per i Beni e le Attività Culturali.

demonstrated by the fact that it was "structured along sight-lines leading inward to a central point" from the perimeter, in the interest of maximum visibility.[43] In the seventeenth century Giulio Parigi transformed the *teatro di verzura* into an amphitheater made of stone. In addition to this, he emphasized another aspect of the amphitheater as seen from outside, that is, he put it in direct visual relation with the *piano nobile* of the palace in such a way that the spectators sitting around the amphitheater became part of the scene for the grand duke and his guests watching the performance from their apartments on the first floor. The amphitheater was finally inaugurated only in 1637, with a *festa a cavallo*—apparently designed by Giulio Parigi himself—on the occasion of the wedding of Ferdinand II and Vittoria della Rovere.[44]

Finally, the importance of the Boboli amphitheater lies in the fact that its construction further encouraged the production of models and drawings of gardens—especially scale drawings—which were also exchanged between those Italian courts in which jousts were popular entertainment. For instance, in a letter written in 1608, Giovan Battista Aleotti asked Cesare d'Este of Ferrara to send him the drawing of his garden, because he wished to build a garden amphitheater for the wedding celebrations of the duke's son:

> I wish that Your Illustrious Excellency would allow me to serve Your Highness and that whenever you decided to organize some cavalry

entertainment for the wedding of the Serene Prince, Your Highness be pleased to send me the drawing of your garden recording the fishpond, and those hills toward the city walls, with the scale in order to be able to measure it, so that I can try to find some striking invention for a *Barriera* or a joust . . . in fact, I would like to know whether the said fishpond can be dried out entirely or in part, and how much water it holds, since I am thinking of organizing a great *Barriera* with plenty of marvelous things, and a magnificent amphitheater.[45]

Ultimately, it appears that the Medici gardens of the Cinquecento performed a representative function that was foreign to previous gardens. Moreover, their function as venues for private and costly entertainment indicates that the garden maker was now given a greater responsibility, which involved the study of the garden layout by means of tools previously used in other disciplines, such as the *arti del disegno*. This means that sixteenth-century gardens were no longer, or at best not only, the result of a tradition of garden making, which had informed the gardens of the Quattrocento, for their construction also required time for intellectual speculation, or design.

The Writing of Tradition

When the gardens of the Medici began to be designed, as we have seen with Castello and Boboli, the tradition of garden making was also recorded in written form.[46] During the course of the sixteenth century, and throughout the seventeenth, appear several texts on agriculture, and on gardens in particular, in which it is possible to perceive an evolution in the writing of this tradition: from a recording of modes and practical rules, relating to the "agricoltura dei giardini,"[47] to the birth of a body of theoretical literature oriented toward the design of gardens.[48]

Among the sixteenth-century manuals on garden making written in Tuscany are the works of Luigi Alamanni, Giacomo Firenzuola, Agostino del Riccio, and Giovanvettorio Soderini. In the same category of reference books we can include two texts written in Lombardy by Agostino Gallo and Bartolomeo Taegio. It is in Rome, however, that the first treatise on gardens is published in the seventeenth century. This is entitled *De florum cultura* and was written by the Sienese Jesuit Giovan Battista Ferrari. Unlike his predecessors, Ferrari addresses for the first time what he calls the "architettura del giardino,"[49] which he considers a new discipline, and for which he provides the principles of design.

Luigi Alamanni, a Florentine man of letters, published his *Coltivazione* in Paris in 1546.[50] The fifth book, which deals with the cultivation of gardens, opens as in Virgil's *Georgics* by citing Priapus, according to Greek mythology the god of fertility who was thought to protect the crops. Alamanni's verses describe the development of a contemporary fashion concerning gardens—a fashion, however, that dates to the botanical garden at Pisa[51]—which involves importing exotic plants from foreign countries. The reason why these plants, originally accustomed to living in different climates and soil conditions, are able to adapt to their new environment is that "nature / surrenders to skill and for a long time / continuously transforms itself every hour and invigorates."[52] Therefore, Alamanni emphasizes the ability of humans, particularly their skill and technical knowledge, which allows them to control nature: "But the wise gardener, who understands / the wish of each [plant], can with beautiful art / operate in such a way that, little by little / he will make [the plants] forget their old habits / and renew for him their uses and wishes."[53] People exert the same sort of control over nature when planting a garden, as when sowing seeds attached to a rope so that they will grow as trees that will be perfectly aligned—as Columella also suggested—"such that by looking at it the eye would not be offended."[54] Alamanni, however, does not dwell on the creative process of designing a garden, and his poem is more an attempt to imitate Virgil, Columella, and Palladius than a real innovation.[55]

An exemplary text on agriculture and gardens that also dates to the first half of the sixteenth century was written by Giacomo Gatteschi da Firenzuola.[56] The "Trattato di agricoltura" is divided into seven books and opens with a letter written by the author to the Florentine captain Gianbattista Martelli on September 16, 1552. It was Martelli, as Firenzuola writes in the *proemio*, who asked him to put on paper the conversations they used to have on agriculture: "Therefore I put into writing those experiences, which I enjoyed having and that concern the grafting and planting of diverse fruits, vines, and other things, all belonging to . . . the great art of Agriculture, [experiences] that I had at the villa, occasionally, in order to pass time . . . as you asked me to do when in those days we discussed such things, and while we talked we decided to write down the experiences I had, although I don't judge them worthy of being published."[57]

Although Firenzuola's work was not published until the nineteenth century,[58] it probably circulated in manuscript form during his lifetime. Bernardo

Davanzati implicitly referred to it in the preface to his *Toscana coltivazione delle viti e delli arbori*, where he wrote that his treatise was going to teach readers how to cultivate "according to the modern fashion and with our own terms, which is more useful to us than are the [texts] of ancient or foreign authors, and [this book] is also good and trustworthy as the work written by someone who was knowledgeable in it"[59] Although Davanzati does not mention Firenzuola directly, it is likely that he relied precisely on the latter's text, which he judged too prolix, not well written, and not well ordered. Thus, he set out to summarize the content of his predecessor's book on agriculture—"ne ho spremuto questo sugo"—and to improve its language. In fact, the structure and content of the *Toscana coltivazione* are very similar to the work of Firenzuola, and Davanzati at least appreciated the fact that it had been written by an expert.[60]

The importance of Firenzuola's text was that he put into writing—"in nota"—his own experience, formerly a subject matter that he only addressed orally—"discorrendo"—and in order to do so he used the modern language, instead of simply translating the work of the ancients, which was no longer considered very useful. Moreover, as Davanzati's remarks imply, and as Firenzuola himself writes in the *proemio*, his "Trattato di agricoltura" was the result of knowledge accumulated through direct experience.

The sixteenth chapter of the fifth book of Firenzuola's treatise is dedicated to gardens. These, the author recommends, should be subdivided into smaller but regular compartments. He advises the reader to "have different kinds of beautiful vines planted, starting from the entrance of the garden, and subdivide the vines' beds in this way . . . and also control the vines [growing along] the paths . . . with order and method, in the same way as for all the other paths . . . and then in the square compartments of the said garden, divided by a cross, create certain paths for the growing of grass, and subdivide these again by a cross."[61] In addition, Firenzuola mentions a "meadow proportionately oval"[62] that is also subdivided by two straight paths intersecting at a right angle. He recommends terminating these paths with walls that are covered with ivy and are painted or sculpted in a way that the figures could be discerned through the climbers' foliage. A path separates the meadow from "a grove and bosquet, planted with measure,"[63] beyond which is a *verziere* with evergreen plants. And on the other side of the meadow are two green chambers, one of them used as a kitchen, the other as a storage room, "well made, well kept, and pruned, in which one would enter through only one door, which would be located on the path toward the ivy espalier . . . with some holes in the espalier toward the garden, carefully positioned in order to bring the dishes to the table during a meal."[64] Among the elements of Firenzuola's garden are the so-called *spalliere*, or latticework, of which he mentions a great variety that testifies to direct experience. These elements are often referred to as *componimento*. In the same way the author speaks of the paths through the garden: "Once the grove is made, the paths must be composed in order to subdivide the garden with a cross."[65] Moreover, when speaking of the flowerbeds to be laid out all around the garden, and of the kind of flowers and medicinal herbs to be cultivated there, Firenzuola concludes that all this needs to be done in order to make a "varied composition, pleasing and distinct."[66]

Other elements that contribute to the *piacevolezza* of the garden are scent and color. Firenzuola stresses how important it is to choose plants that will improve these two qualities. He disapproves of the use of boxwood for hedges, because this evergreen is not fragrant enough and is melancholic— probably because of its grayish hue of green; he suggests the use of marjoram, because "it has a very good scent and a beautiful hue of green."[67] Moreover, orange, lemon, and cedar trees are recommended for hedges, because "they are much more beautiful and pleasing to the eye."[68]

The recurrent use of the words *componimento* and *comporre*, as well as *studio*, suggests that the making of a garden also requires a time for reflection, although the two stages of design and implementation are not yet clearly distinguished from each other, at least verbally, as the use of the verb *creare* in conjunction with *fare* seems to show: "Moreover, it is necessary to *make and create* a convenient distance between the curbed flowerbeds in the garden"[69] (emphasis added). In fact, whereas the verb *fare* simply means making, *creare*, besides making, also implies thinking. However, the design principles of Firenzuola's modus operandi are not explicitly spelled out in his writings; therefore his book can be regarded more as a manual than a treatise. On the other hand, from his attention to the composition of a garden in terms of form, proportions, and color we can infer that in his manual the garden starts to be considered a work of art, such as a painting, as Alessandro Tagliolini suggested.[70]

Although Bernardo Davanzati was familiar with Firenzuola's text, it was not known outside a small circle of Tuscan connoisseurs. In fact, in the second half of the century a new comprehensive work on agriculture was still in demand, especially in the north of Italy, as we see in a letter written by the Paduan Giovan Battista da Romano to Agostino Gallo from Brescia. In this letter, Giovan Battista tells Agostino about the need for a treatise on agriculture in which the author would not limit himself to the translation of the classical

works, such as Cato's or Varro's, with the consequent transliteration of their critical technical terms, which none of the moderns—complains Giovan Battista—
is able to fully understand. The ideal treatise would include, according to Giovan
Battista, a commentary on the classical texts, with an explanation of their ter-
minology and systems of measurement, comparing them with modern vocabulary and measuring systems. In addition to this, he says that the author of the
treatise should make his own experience available to readers and compare it
to that of the classical writers: "And first of all, I think that one of the most
important things that we might ask of our author is that he write clearly and
explicitly that he is going to recount his own experience, which is more trustworthy and does not generate dissent. The witness of experience has not been
treated by any of the moderns, nor has it been revealed to the world."[71] Therefore, in this letter Giovan Battista urges Agostino Gallo to write about his experience in order to make it available to numerous others. Perhaps the most
important aspect of the letter is the claim that writing on agriculture can also be
beneficial to the vulgar tongue, insofar as the subject matter of the treatise will
contribute to the enrichment of the spoken language, in this case the Lombard
vernacular. And, according to Giovan Battista, the "modern author" who em-
barks on this enterprise will be praised for his beautiful rhetoric as well: "Now
I believe that if a book on Agriculture that takes into account all these suggestions is published, our language will be enriched by a beautiful and very useful
text and the publisher Arrivabene will be proud of it as Giolito is of the always
praised Retorica [written by] the very famous and highly celebrated Caval-
vanti.[72] . . . And if you, Agostino . . . will be able to write such a rare, and perfect work, you will gain the equal benefit of immortal glory."[73] In sum, the art
of agriculture is now compared to that of rhetoric, and this by itself demonstrates that the making of gardens, which was once only a matter of agricultural
knowledge acquired through experience and passed down orally from one generation to the next, is now regarded as not only simply a mechanical discipline
but also as a liberal art. Nonetheless, the glory promised by Giovan Battista
does not persuade Gallo to write the ideal treatise. He believed, in fact, that
most of the classics' precepts were out of date, and therefore not useful to agriculture, even if translated and commented upon:

> But do not expect from me that I explain the names, numbers, meas-
> ures, Calends, Ninths, Ides, Solstices, Equinoxes, Stars, and winds,
> about which the very famous authors have written satisfactorily, and
> knowledgeably. For not only was I never very knowledgeable in these

matters, which pertain only to the scientists, but also I would not waste time to write them down in my work even if I knew them, for I think that such subtle things are not necessary to farmers. . . . In the same way do not expect from me that I set out to comment upon the many works that have been written and translated, because I think that most of them would not be of any use for the modern cultivation of our land, since it is too remote from the famous authors of those times.[74]

As Gallo mentions in his reply to Giovan Battista, he had started collecting his thoughts on agriculture eight years earlier. He is, in fact, the author of *Le dieci giornate della vera Agricoltura*, a work written *in lingua Lombarda* that circulated in manuscript form for many years before being published by Bozzola at Brescia in 1564.[75] Although one of the treatise's *giornate*—day five—is dedicated to gardens there is little in it that compares to the way gardens are treated in Firenzuola's text. In fact, for Gallo a garden is "cosa utile,"[76] and as such it is more a *pomarium* filled with fruit trees, such as pear and apple trees, than a flower garden that only contributes to the recreation of the eye. On the other hand, like Firenzuola's text, Gallo's reads like a reference book rather than a treatise. In fact, his intention in writing is made clear in his reply to Giovan Battista, where he says: "My thoughts (which I have collected for eight years) are very far from the things you look for, since I always concerned myself with the pure practice of useful agricultural activities, leaving the theory to others, whose intellects are more sublime, and excellent than my own."[77] Only in the sixth *giornata*, part of which is dedicated to the beautiful "gardens . . . made for recreation,"[78] does Agostino speak briefly of what we may call "gardens": "Gardens should be made, if at all possible, on the northern side of the owner's house in order to comfortably enjoy seeing [them] through the windows, and especially when [the garden] is made more for pleasure than for usefulness."[79] He also recommends that the *horti* be surrounded by a wall or tall hedge, and that they be square and subdivided into four smaller areas by two paths intersecting at right angles. However, a few lines later he adds that he also appreciates other forms, such as the circular, the triangular, and so on, and further describes a few examples that he has seen with his own eyes.[80] At any rate, the section dedicated to gardens, or *horti belli*, within the whole treatise is not very significant.

Agostino's lack of interest in this subject may be due to the fact that a dialogue on gardens, entitled *La villa*, had already been written by the Milanese lawyer Bartolomeo Taegio and been published in 1559.[81] Among the existing gardens that Taegio describes in his text is that of Cesare Simonetta at his villa of Castellazzo:

> Around its sides, and through the middle in many parts it has been well-ordered with right proportions and drawn with a sure eye; so that corners being the same, and sides equal, the eye by looking cannot see anything wrong,[82] nor are the alleys too wide, nor very narrow; but such that they agree nicely with the delicate garden. The other parts then of this pleasant place, where the flowers and the herbs are obliged to dwell, give rise to squares of beautiful appearance, both distinct one from another, and equal. . . . Moreover, the plants are placed with marvelous order, and of those that are praised so much and that don't thrive in our land, here they grow in the greatest abundance; here the ingenious grafts are without end that show with great wonder to the world the industry of a wise gardener, who by incorporating art with nature brings forth from both a third nature, which causes the fruits to be more flavorful here than elsewhere.[83]

In this passage Taegio describes a square and well-proportioned garden, whose paths are neither too wide nor too narrow but such that they agree well with the delicate garden. The agreement of all the garden parts seems to be achieved by the use of geometry and proportion, but most of all by means of the skill—*industria*—of the gardener, who molds nature with expertise and therefore "makes"—*fà*—a third nature. However, this third nature does not seem to imply a purely "aesthetic" connotation, especially if we consider that its main responsibility is to make the fruits of this garden taste better.[84] Therefore, it appears that the word *arte* is used to mean technique, more than art; thus, in Lombardy too as in Tuscany the making of gardens seems to be indebted to reference books, which provide readers with the instructions for planting a garden rather than with the principles for its design. Moreover, Taegio's vocabulary is not dissimilar to Firenzuola's and Alamanni's. In fact, in *La villa* we also read about compartments, to be traced with order and measure. In addition, the fact that both Gallo's and Taegio's horticultural experiences are written down in dialogue form is a reminder that these texts too aim to record a georgic tradition that was previously passed down orally.[85] However, a novelty in both texts is that they describe existing places, unlike their Tuscan predecessors. This may appear to be a contradiction, given that in

Tuscany the Medici villas offered paradigmatic examples of garden elements that could be reproduced in other villas for the enjoyment of their owners and their guests.

We have to wait until the second half of the sixteenth century to see the influence of the Medici gardens emerge through the pages of a text on agriculture. The text in question consists of the "Agricultura sperimentale" and "Agricultura teorica" by Agostino del Riccio, a Dominican Florentine friar.[86] The first part, which includes a list of activities to be done month by month, is dedicated to those readers who lack specific horticultural knowledge, whereas the second part is for the experts, or those who are well versed in the practice of agriculture. The second part includes a detailed description of the plants and flowers that were cultivated in Florence at the time.

In the chapter called "Del giardino di un re" Agostino describes an ideal garden, which includes a flower garden, a dwarf fruit garden, and a bosquet. The *giardino dei fiori* is a square walled garden subdivided into eight smaller squares; at its center is a small octagonal island reachable by a drawbridge. And at the center of the island is a sculpted fountain. The *giardino dei frutti nani* is also a walled garden, and it is subdivided into four squares by two intersecting paths. At its center is a fountain surrounded by a *vivaio*, or fishpond. Agostino points out that the trees of this garden should not be taller than a man's shoulders, so that the whole garden can be perceived at a glance. The *bosco regio* too is square and walled, but kneeling windows—so-called because of the form of their supporting brackets—open its walls at regular intervals. The bosquet is divided into four squares, each of which has a labyrinth with eight grottoes and fountains. At the intersection of the two main paths of the bosquet is a large plaza, which "should be square as we said above, two times larger than the one at Santa Croce in Florence where, in order to please everybody, almost all the festivities and public shows are organized as our fathers the Romans used to do."[87] The remark about the size of the central square of the bosquet confirms the fact that gardens, as we saw in the previous section, became the new venues for celebrating formerly public events. In fact, Agostino says that the function of the *piazza* is that of hosting jousts and games, such as the popular *gioco del calcio* (soccer), while a century earlier both these activities used to take place mainly on the Piazza di Santa Croce in Florence.[88]

The description of the ideal garden has numerous affinities with the Medici properties of Castello, Boboli, and Pratolino. For instance, the fact that the ideal garden belongs to a fortified palace, which is located close to the city walls, seems to have been inspired by the location of the Pitti residence and the Boboli gardens, with the fortress of the Belvedere looking over them. Moreover, the numerous grottoes described in the treatise are indebted to the grottoes of Castello and Pratolino, the only difference being that in Agostino's ideal bosquet they are placed at regular intervals. Finally, the flower garden seems to have been inspired by the Giardino dei Semplici, the botanical garden of Florence.[89] When describing the ideal garden, Agostino makes clear that its beauty depends not only on its layout but also on its plants, the choice of which must be dictated by the time of the year in which they flower, in such a way as always to have plants in full bloom that can better define the outline of the compartments, or *quadri*, subdividing the garden. This is not what happens, however, at the Giardino dei Semplici during the time of Grand Duke Ferdinando:

> But I, who was many times in the said garden both for my pleasure and refuge, considered . . . that having planted all the Greek mosses in one compartment, the tulips or anemones in another, once they have bloomed we do not see any beauty in such compartments; in fact, it would be better if in each compartment in the shape of a heart or a star and other shapes you planted other plants that would always be in bloom, and this task must be assigned to an expert gardener . . . in this way, the garden of the king would always be beautiful throughout all the months of the year.[90]

Hence, it appears that Agostino's primary concern is not praising the Medici; rather, it is teaching; and the reason why he offers the Giardino dei Semplici as a negative model is that the flowers planted there all bloom at the same time. Moreover, even if he draws inspiration from existing examples, such as the Medici properties, he combines what he believes are the best features of their gardens, and through a process of abstraction that allows him to eliminate flaws—such as the unequal layout of Castello, which is not perfectly square—he defines the appearance of the ideal garden. This, in turn, will serve as a model, not of a garden but rather of design. As the author himself points out, he was not an architect, nor was he an artist: "Although I do not really know how to draw, however, I know a few principles, and I feel that I am a painter, a sculptor and an architect because I often attend the company of such virtuous men."[91] Here Agostino makes clear that even if he does not know how to draw, he knows the principles of design, among which is that a garden should be "subdivided in an orderly way"[92] by means of a rigorous symmetry that shapes the place by means of axial paths. Moreover, a garden should be square, "otherwise, if the site of the garden is not square, but has another shape, it would not be possible to see the fruit trees and plants from every angle . . . and everything is done so that the whole garden can be appreciated at a glance."[93]

Another principle that Agostino puts forth is that a garden should aim at the embodiment of beauty in the same way beauty is the foremost quality that a building is supposed to have; therefore, the parts of which a garden is composed should be as well proportioned as the parts of a building: "A body is called beautiful when all of its parts are proportional to each other, and those who can draw know this general rule, as also do the followers of painters, sculptors, and architects."[94] It is evident from this statement that Agostino draws his principles of garden design from the canonical *arti del disegno*. Moreover, as Detlef Heikamp has indicated,[95] there is a striking similarity between some garden plans drawn by Giorgio Vasari the Younger in his *Città ideale* and some descriptions of Agostino's ideal garden.[96] Therefore, it appears that this treatise constitutes a first example of how the art of gardens in the late sixteenth century evolves from being a mere practical discipline to a more theoretical concern.[97] Moreover, in his treatise Agostino explicitly refers to drawings, as, for example, when he describes the first labyrinth included in the bosquet: "Now I insert the drawing, so that you can use the drawing of the labyrinth that is painted at the garden at Bagnaia, or [at] that garden at Tivoli, which is beautiful and well studied, if I will be able to bring this work to completion, but at the end there will be drawings of numerous kinds of labyrinths."[98] It seems that the author would have liked to add an iconographic section to his text but, as he himself explains in the introduction to the second volume of the "Agricultura sperimentale," this was too expensive an enterprise. He also adds that his work would have needed some eighty drawings.[99] Later on, thanks to the economic support of the Sommaia family, Agostino could commission from the painter Vincenzo Dori the illustration of some of his works, among which a "Libro dei fiori" (now lost) to be added to the "Agricultura sperimentale." Unfortunately, Dori's drawings are missing, so it is not possible to assess whether or not, besides the reproduction of flowers, they also illustrated the ideal garden, or some of its parts.

Another Tuscan writer on agriculture and gardens is Giovanvettorio Soderini. Toward the last decade of the sixteenth century he wrote a treatise in four volumes in folio subdivided into the following sections: "Di agricoltura"; "Della coltivazione delle viti"; "Della coltura degli orti e dei giardini"; "Degli alberi"; and "Degli animali domestici."[100] Besides addressing such issues as the nature of the soil, the winds, the choice of the site, and the making of cisterns, the author includes a section dedicated to the architecture of the villa: "First of all, each part of the site on which the building is going to be constructed must be examined and squared: and in order to have a successful building worthy of praise, it must be comfortable, useful, beautiful and durable."[101] The author explains further that by *perpetuo* he means solidly built. It is likely that Soderini drew inspiration from both Vitruvius's three principles of *firmitas, utilitas,* and *venustas* articulated in his *De architectura,* and Alberti's definitions of *pulchritudo* and *concinnitas* in his *De re aedificatoria.* When he explains his principles of design, Soderini says: "Beauty derives from a graceful shape and from the correspondence of the whole to the parts and these to the whole and [the correspondence of] the parts within themselves, since buildings must be and appear as a whole and predetermined body, each member of which must correspond to the other, and each member must carry out a function for which it is necessary. These things must be accounted for in a drawing on paper or in a wood model that should be constructed on site, with proportional measurements."[102] The use of drawings and models, however, is not limited to the study of the building, for "not only the model of buildings, but also of anything else that relates to invention and cleverness needs to be large, so that such a reasonable and moderate size would allow one to judge the entire work."[103] In fact, the author explains that the importance of the model, "be it a model or a drawing,"[104] is that of studying how the human being relates to the newly created place, "so that I can relate myself to those parts."[105] Moreover, it is important that all the parts of the building be located in their appropriate places, "according to their function and the worth of the place and the character of the client, always keeping in mind that the villa's exterior should not surpass the building, nor should the building [surpass] the outside; in other words, the house should not seem to need more outdoor space than the one it has, and in the same way the outside [should not seem to deserve] a larger building, but the one should correspond to the other."[106] It follows that the house and the fields surrounding it should be in proportion to each other.

After a long section dedicated to the materials for construction, and the choice of the site, which should be dictated mainly by the presence of water, Soderini explains how to position the house vis-à-vis the whole property. He says, "The house of the villa and the whole building of the property should be always placed in a way that allows it to see and be seen, [located] far away from any deep valleys enclosed by mountains . . . the house of the villa, however, should be comfortable within the property and it should be placed in the middle of it, thoroughly visible, in such a way that the owner can easily discover and appreciate the surrounding places."[107] He explains that one reason for allowing a view of the whole property from the house is: "It will be easier to enjoy the subdivision and layout of the alleys and paths, which need to be located with due reason so that they correspond both to the fields and the house."[108] Therefore, it seems that both the cultivated fields and the house should obey the same proportions, materialized and made visible by the paths and alleys that run through the property. This point is taken up again in the discussion about gardens:

> Have the delicate gardens, kitchen gardens and fruitful fields located
> close at hand and visible; they should be subdivided into equal compart-
> ments by wide and spacious paths, and the square compartments should
> be visible, and should be traced according to the position of the windows
> and the loggias; also the trees, both those planted by men and the wild
> ones, must be aligned all around; and while they are growing, they must
> be pruned with scissors, scythe . . . , in such a way that one does not
> grow taller than the other; and a meadow of green grasses should be seen,
> and the square compartments should correspond in size to the corners
> and façades of the house.[109]

Further on, Soderini says that the house should be surrounded by evergreen trees, in order to protect it from the winds, and other trees should be planted in circles, or other geometrical figures, in accordance with the plan of the house:

> Circles of laurels, cedars, and juniper, interwoven, wrapped up, and
> mixed with each other can also be made, according to those layouts
> that are used for the plants of buildings. Moreover, vases are a great
> ornament and tasteful delight along the alleys, with plenty of dwarf
> fruits of every kind . . . today we see in the main gardens alleys covered
> with barrel vault pergolas of ivy, open in the center to the air, sustained
> by columns on both sides. . . . Trees, or better fruit trees, must be
> planted in a quincunx, in the same way as the number five is marked
> on dice.[110]

Although Soderini suggests the quincunx for the planting of trees, he generally considers the square as old-fashioned and suggests instead another form, the oval, both for the architecture of the villa and for the garden:

> But in order to avoid this triviality and often-used habit of building in angles and squares, it is perfectly possible and with equal benefit of the sight, beauty and comfort, usefulness and easiness . . . to change shape . . . and build in an oval shape . . . court and courtyard, squares, meadows and garden . . . nonetheless everything should be controlled by the rules of good architecture in relation to heights, lengths, and widths and graceful proportion and dimension of the rooms, in such a way that the whole composition corresponds to the parts and the parts to the whole, no more no less well and aptly than to resemble the structure of the human body.[111]

It appears from these words that the author considers the villa a homogeneous composition, in which both house and gardens follow the rules of the "buona architettura": all the parts correspond to the whole, and the whole to the parts, as in the human body. Last, he mentions the possibility of creating a hanging garden on the roof of a house.[112]

Although Soderini does not explicitly recommend the preparation of drawings in order to study the layout of the garden, a series of documents housed at the Uffizi shows that he used drawing as a design tool.[113] In one mid-sixteenth-century example, which was published for the first time by Gabriele Morolli (fig. 54),[114] we see how Soderini proceeded in the design of a casino and garden. These are contained within two adjacent squares of equal size: in the casino he prioritizes the diagonal direction, along which he places an octagonal *sala* and an oval *cortile*, whereas the garden has a centralized plan, with a circle inscribed within a square and the two diagonals given equal importance by the placing of semicircular elements along the vertices of the square; moreover, although the garden is not subdivided into four squares, the middle point of each side of the square is marked either by a door, a fountain, or a niche, as if to mark a cross supposedly inscribed in the square. For the center of the garden Soderini provides several options, which he annotates on the drawing: a pond, a square, a *praticello*, a mount with rock formations crowded with flowers and water flowing underneath it. He also specifies by means of notes written in the margins, and arrows connecting them to the flowerbeds, each vegetal specimen to be planted in the garden.

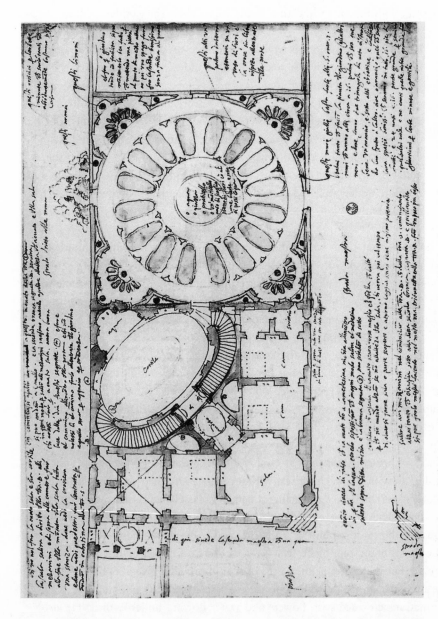

Fig. 54. Giovanvittorio Soderini (attributed), plan of casino and garden (mid-sixteenth century). GDSU 3888r A. By permission of Ministero per i Beni e le Attività Culturali.

The fact that Soderini includes a garden, with plenty of details of both its outline and its plants, in his drawing of the casino shows that he considered the garden as *cosa d'invenzione e d'ingegno*,[115] worthy of being studied on paper. Moreover, his reference to the villa as a homogeneous ensemble, in which house and garden are linked by geometrical correspondences, and his continuous application of the principles of architectural design to the whole composition show his eagerness to include gardens within a theoretical more than a practical discourse. However, his attempt is never fully carried out, and that gardens should be designed is an implicit statement that is never spelled out in his treatise.

We have to wait until the following century to see a first attempt to go beyond the writing of manuals about the modes and practical rules regulating the tradition of garden making. This is when the Jesuit Giovan Battista Ferrari from Siena wrote a treatise in four books called *De florum cultura*, published in Rome in 1633.[116] Unlike sixteenth-century treatises, Ferrari's was written in Latin and also included a number of woodcuts engraved after drawings by Pietro da Cortona, Guido Reni, Andrea Sacchi, and Giovanni Lanfranco, illustrating allegorical and mythological tales dedicated to Flora. Six drawings illustrated flowerbeds and were inspired by cosmic imagery; a labyrinth was also represented, as were agricultural tools and flowers. The expensive edition and the use of the Latin indicate that the treatise was meant to address an aristocratic audience.[117]

Unlike any one of his predecessors Ferrari dedicates his treatise solely to the art of gardens, and he points out that he is the first to address such a task: "I am the one, who, before anything else, is going to teach the sweet toil of tending the flowering gardens, which was born in the past, and by many people has already been performed, but by no one has it yet been written in detail."[118] This is the first time that an author of *res rusticae* spells out that he is going to put into writing, and therefore teach, an art that hitherto had only been the result of habit. He does not say, though, that he is actually going to provide this practice with a sound theory that previously had been applied only to the art of building. But this is, in fact, what he finally does. That Ferrari's text is not just a manual is made clear by the author's own words:

> Two things I neglect and naively say cannot be obtained from me. One is to cover all the precepts of this art: who, in fact, being the first to engage in such an enterprise, can claim to have seen everything and who will not want to leave behind something to those who will be willing to continue [the work] after him? I think it will be sufficient for me to

show the most important things. The second thing is that I will not please everybody: in fact, who is that man, not foolish, who will hope to please the great number of men of all different kinds, mostly in opposition with each other and in discord, with just one work? I will make myself happy if I can please but a few men, provided they are wise ones.[119]

Therefore, by deciding to be selective and leave out, for example, those precepts related to the cultivation of simples, or other practices that have already been discussed by his predecessors, Ferrari acknowledges the fact that his is not a manual on the cultivation of the land: "If I did not know that this has already been done, I would write a catalogue of the writers who have addressed this discipline, and I would add the topics they have addressed in their substantial treatises in order to prove what I say."[120]

Perhaps the most interesting chapter is the one called "Architettura del Giardino." First of all, it appears that a garden results from the collaboration of an "avveduto coltivatore" (wise gardener), who is responsible for the choice of the site, and "uno che buono sia in disegnare" (one who can draw), who is also called a "wise architect of this [apparently] simple beauty."[121] But the separate tasks of the *coltivatore* and the *architetto* are not so clear-cut. In fact, the *coltivatore* is also responsible for deciding the overall layout of the garden: "In addition to this, the outline of the garden must be chosen in such a way as not to lose anything or to lose little of the quality of the site."[122] And this can be considered a first principle of design, in that Ferrari does not recommend a specific geometrical figure—"Anyone can choose any outline, which can be square, or oblong, or circular, or with many angles"[123]—instead, he says that one should choose a figure that is in accord with the site itself, that is, that brings out the intrinsic qualities of the place, rather than being simply imposed on it. Once the general layout is established, the *coltivatore* should proceed to the subdivision of the garden: "Hence the garden should be surrounded by a wall or hedge, as if it were the seat of flowered ranks, so that it will be safe and impenetrable . . . the Garden, of which, as if it were a City of flowers, you will protect the borders, according to the old way of erecting cities."[124]

We notice here the association of gardens with military art, which suggests that for Ferrari the making of gardens is drifting away from the practice of agriculture with its image of regularly subdivided fields and plots of land, and is appropriating the image of the Roman *castrum*, that is, the regular layout used by the Romans for the planning of their cities.[125] All this means that the subdivision of the garden into compartments must acknowledge such factors as the movement of the sun and the orientation of the main axis of the garden and the city in relation to it. Therefore, a garden is not a matter of habit, or at least it is no longer just that, but is the result of a design process that involves a separate time for thinking and planning. This stage is emphasized by Ferrari's recommendation of making several sketches on paper. And this seems to be the architect's task: "Subdivide and diligently take measures by first drawing a sketch on paper, according to which the garden will be outlined";[126] or, even better, the architect will make "many drawings of these compartments and he will choose the most beautiful."[127] It is important that the architect have before his eyes "various garden layouts, so that his drawing, more than his words, will describe the architecture of the gardens."[128] Hence, drawings are better than words for the making of gardens.

The drawing of garden compartments is important not only as a way to study the geometry of the garden but also as a tool to test the colors of different flowers and to choose the ones that can be planted side by side. This is, according to Ferrari, the procedure adopted by Francesco Caetani, the Duke of Sermoneta, at his Horti Cisterniani (at Cisterna, Rome): "Each flowerbed is filled with one or two species of flowers, so that if the flowers are different in nature, and color, they are planted in separate places, whereas the flowers of the same species and those of similar ones are placed in front of each other or in such a way as to correspond to each other diagonally."[129] Moreover, Caetani "records the very colors of two or three kinds of flowers on a sketch, or drawing on paper, and paints and highlights each flowerbed with the same colors of the flowers that are going to be planted there."[130] The necessity for such a design tool as the drawing is also dictated by the fact that when the flowerbed surrounded by hedges is without flowers, that is, for example, when flower buds have not yet bloomed within the *aiuola*, this needs to maintain a beautiful appearance, if not by means of its color then at least with its outline, "so that we will be able to say that [when] these Elysian fields of ours [are] without flowers [they] will still bloom with their stars, which the very beautiful blooming of the flowers highlights even more than the remote influence of the stars is able to do."[131] Therefore, the use of geometry in the shaping of clipped hedges will guarantee the appropriate degree of beauty when the colorful flowers are missing. In some cases bricks instead of hedges are used to surround the flowerbeds and form a curb around them. This is what Marc'Antonio Specchi, for instance, did at his Roman garden: "Make a drawing on paper of a square site, or oblong, or with right angles, and draw the lines in every direction as if [you were forming] a grid, measuring each distance in such a way as to make it correspond proportionately to whole bricks."[132] From this statement we can infer another interesting principle of design that gardens derive from architecture, that is, the use of a modular measure—in this case, the size of a brick— to determine the size and shape of flowerbeds.

Ultimately, in *De florum coltura* Ferrari does more than simply record a series of procedures for the making of gardens. He theorizes the principles according to which gardens should be designed, and describes the tools that architects should use in order to test their choices. Unlike earlier works on agriculture and gardens, therefore, Ferrari's treatise is not just about the writing down of a tradition that used to be passed down orally, from one generation to the other. His text acknowledges the creative process that informs the design of gardens. Hence, with Ferrari the art of gardens evolves from the level of know-how to that of a liberal art.

Conclusion

IN THE SIXTEENTH century, by the time the technique used to lay out a garden had been assimilated into garden practice as thoroughly as grammatical rules had been into rhetorical performance, the *scriptores rei rusticae* started to codify in writing the relationship between the elements of the garden. That is, they started to put into writing a tradition of garden making, which had resulted from the modus operandi of their predecessors. The result of this process was the production of manuals, or reference books, that would facilitate the implementation and maintenance of a garden. The purpose of these texts was to commit to memory, through writing, the writers' own horticultural experience and expertise. Their aim, however, was not to produce a garden theory, that is, the definition of a series of concepts, or principles, that would address the design of a garden. And the reason for this is perhaps that a concept of design had not yet been articulated either orally or in written form.

Existing gardens of the sixteenth century, such as those at the Medici villas of Castello and Boboli, show that the process of making a garden evolved from pure habit, or repetition, to what we might call "design." Artists like Tribolo and Buontalenti adapted to the configuration of their gardens the methods they used in the design of buildings or in the sculpting of statues. And they made use of design tools, such as drawings and models. Hence, with these artists actual gardens became objects of art, endowed with representative power, and meaning. However, whereas these artists were already designing gardens, contemporary writers were still producing manuals on agriculture; and we have to wait until the following century to read that the making of gardens is part of a creative process, which involves knowledge of design principles. This means that, in the same way the writing of manuals occurs after garden praxis has already been established, a theory of gardens is written down only after the most important gardens—such as those of the Medici grand dukes—have been designed. The reason for this may be that the new generation of *scriptores* is no longer directly involved with the practice of garden making, as were, for instance, Agostino del Riccio, Agostino Gallo, and Giovanvettorio Soderini. Agostino del Riccio, for instance, was in charge of the cultivated fields at the convent of Santa Maria Novella, where he lived. Soderini's texts were born of his experience at his villa called "Il Giardino" at San Salvi, on the outskirts on Florence.[1] Agostino Gallo's *giornate* were also the product of the author's experience, accumulated through the cultivation of his own property at Poncarale in the province of Brescia. When he addressed his readers in *Dieci giornate* Gallo admitted to employing a "basso stile" and the "lingua lombarda," which he used to address "those who love the villa and agriculture so that they can more easily understand the things that are appropriate to such a pleasing discipline."[2] Moreover, as his biographer wrote, "Our Gallo was not versed in the study of languages and sciences and he never engaged himself either in poetry, or in philosophical discussions."[3]

Giovan Battista Ferrari, on the contrary, was a humanist, a man of learning who wrote in Latin, and it is significant that he addressed his *De florum cultura* to another learned man, Cardinal Francesco Barberini. Moreover, his treatise is indebted not so much to direct experience as it is to the experience of others, such as two garden owners in Rome: Tranquillo Romauli and Giovan Battista Martelletti, who possessed a garden on the Gianicolo. It is true that Ferrari defined himself as a "rozzo giardiniere," but he also called himself "agricoltore di città," thus emphasizing his being a city dweller more than a countryman.[4] Therefore, the garden upon which Ferrari commented was not something he had created with his own hands. Rather, the garden with its palette of colors and fixed geometry was an object of knowledge, which no longer had anything to do with skill but instead entailed seeing.

Skill, and by and large an oral tradition, on the other hand, produced the gardens and/or kitchen gardens of the fifteenth century. As we have seen, at that time gardens were not yet conceived as works of art, and interpretation of them as objects of aesthetic appreciation is mostly due to some historians' method of back formation. In the writings of Petrarch and Boccaccio, fictional gardens are not mere objects used as backdrops for the writers' stories and poems; rather, they express the passions and actions of the human being and thus perform as eloquently as other literary characters. In addition, Petrarch's engagement with horticulture, as it emerges from the extemporary annotations on his *Palladius*, have a better claim to be regarded as a precedent for fifteenth-century gardens, not in terms of the origin of an aesthetic feeling but rather as an example of that empirical practice of garden making that will characterize the implementation of the Medicis' *orti suburbani* in the Quattrocento. What is remarkable in Petrarch's notes is precisely the poet's writing about the outcome of his horticultural experiments after they have taken place, his record of whether or not they were successful. Moreover, practice does not seem to follow theory for Petrarch, who remarks: "All of this goes against Virgil's teaching. But I like to experiment."[5] The fact that Petrarch does not write these notes in the vernacular, however, invites us to consider that even while gardening the poet was concerned with literary significance,[6] and the laurels that he tried with so much effort to grow, and whose planting Boccaccio, "a great friend of theirs,"[7] witnessed on a Saturday afternoon in 1359, turn into an allegory of his great desire for poetic recognition. Like his literary gardens at Vaucluse, Petrarch's laurels warn us against too literal a reading of his work, for it is a *fabula*, as the poet often called it, that he consciously molded in order to bequeath to posterity an image of himself that coincided with his poetic persona.[8]

There is no doubt that Boccaccio's gardens, on the other hand, are fictitious. In the *Decameron* the author uses gardens and *loci amoeni* as narrative elements, whose morphology and position within the text convey different messages to the readers. Moreover, with Boccaccio gardens are singled out as distinct places, but whether the author was conscious of this is open to question. The storytellers gather in not just any garden but in gardens outside the city walls, and the apparent motivation for this is that the city is being struck by the plague. However, the contrast between the devastation brought by the disease and the lightheartedness of the storytellers, who completely forget about the horror that is taking place in Florence, suggests another level of interpretation that involves an allegorical, and not only literal, dimension of meaning. By locating his characters outside the city walls, Boccaccio wants the reader to notice that the countryside is the appropriate venue for the *novellatori* to tell their stories because they are, in fact, poets. Moreover, by regarding them as poets, whom he defines as "story-tellers, that is, they invent fables,"[9] Boccaccio forces the reader of the *Decameron* to look for an allegorical level of meaning, always disclosing a moral lesson behind the apparent licentiousness of the *novelle*. Therefore, the singling out of gardens does not imply that Boccaccio had started to see them as the pleasurable places modern commentators want them to be, or that through his writing the art of gardens finally becomes conscious of itself. One may argue that if Boccaccio, like Plato, placed the poets outside the city walls, he was not hinting at the need for allegorical interpretation but rather was parting company with those jurists, theologians, and philosophers who had joined Jerome and Boethius in condemning the poets as despicable liars, who deserved to be exiled from the city. But this does not seem to be the case.

First of all, Boccaccio's characters in the *Decameron* are not exiled; they leave the city voluntarily. Moreover, Boccaccio himself felt compelled to defend his fellow poets from their detractors in the fourteenth chapter of his *Genealogie*,[10] in which he defines poetry as a divine gift that stirs the imagination and urges the intellect of a chosen few to a longing for the expression of its visions, by means of words and thoughts orderly woven in such a way as to form fables concealing the truth. In the case of the *Decameron* the "truth" is precisely the moral message Boccaccio hints at in the conclusion to the work: "Any thing is in itself good to any other thing, but if it is evilly employed it can harm many things, and I can say the same of my stories. Whoever will want to derive an evil message and action from them, they will offer no opposition, if they by chance have it, and they can be turned and twisted till they get it; but whoever wants to make good use of them, they will not deny it."[11]

Therefore, it seems that in addition to the impeccable conduct of Boccaccio's *novellatori* mirrored by the orderly gardens of the *cornice*, a righteous reader can also learn a moral lesson from their *novelle*, and from their amorphous settings, the only difference being that the good behavior of the storytellers is explicit in the prose, whereas the ethical meaning of the tales is disguised under the poetic veil of allegory. Hence, Boccaccio's pointing out in the conclusion to the *Decameron* that the tales have been told neither in the church of Santa Maria Novella nor in the schools of the philosophers, but rather in the gardens, is another indication that the author was consciously and purposely pointing to the fact that his storytellers were outside the city walls, rather than in the gardens themselves; with this he was implicitly warning his readers that the tales should not be taken literally. Moreover, that Boccaccio was more interested in illustrating the moral meaning embodied by his tales rather than the garden settings themselves is demonstrated by the miniatures of the *Decameron* It. 482, which he probably executed himself. The conflation of the first two gardens of the *cornice* in the frontispiece miniature, and the fact that the resulting setting lacks the geometric layout described in the text, ultimately shows that gardens are not yet conceived as objects of art. They are different from sculptures, such as the hexagonal fountain and the statue of Venus, and they do not have the objectlike quality of buildings, such as the cubic palace represented in the miniature. For this reason, the reception of the *Decameron* through the illuminated codices executed in Venice one hundred years after the writing of the text, may perhaps represent the origin of the *giardino all'italiana*. But to read Boccaccio's fictional gardens as prototypes is equivalent to using later evidence to prove that the fifteenth-century Medici gardens were the earliest examples of the national garden style.

Ficino's philosophical pleasances, in addition to being endowed with allegorical significance, like Boccaccio's, can be interpreted as an emanation from God, or else as signs that allow us to perceive a lesser degree of beauty than that of the divine light, which is by itself unapproachable through bodily senses. Therefore, like the pleasances of the poets and the early *orti* of the Medicis, Ficino's *loci amoeni* are no mere objects of aesthetic appreciation. In fact, if we consider that the garden maker is a craftsman, and the craftsman, according to Ficino, creates as a direct consequence of his spiritual structure, then the product of his toil, the garden, rather than being just an object, is the materialization of cosmic influences.

Although Ficino's account of verdant places and his apology for the color green do not by themselves add to our understanding of the man-made gardens of his day, such as those of the Medicis, his theorization of human creativity, or *consilium*, as immediate and intuitive rather than discursive parallels what I have described as the extemporary implementation of fifteenth-century gardens, in the same way his definition of man as artificer more than artist recalls the possibility that Quattrocento gardens may have been produced by one or more anonymous makers, rather than by a single garden designer.

Ficino's knowledge of magic brings him to emphasize the creative process involved in the manipulation of matter, such as plants and trees. In fact, being green and permeable to the light of the sun, plants are capable of attracting the influence of the most powerful star, and this influence is bestowed also upon whoever works with or manipulates them. Whoever is involved in a creative process acts not by his own discursive reason, says Ficino, but rather by intuition for, as he remarks in his *Platonic Theology*, "People who are unskilled usually seek counsel about making something. But a consummately skilled craftsman no longer deliberates: he works from habit just as nature does with its forms."[12] Moreover, as a species humans possess all the arts, in addition to the rules relating to them, which are implanted in their minds together with the species of things,[13] and each individual has the potential—*habitus*—to practice any of the arts, although in actuality he exercises—*actus*—only one or a few.[14] This line of thinking leads us to conclude that Ficino did not grant the artist any privileged position among other men, considering the fact that according to him all men are artists by their very nature and are also images of God the artist.[15]

The Medici gardens of the early Renaissance, as at Careggi and Fiesole, can be interpreted as an example of that work of art that, according to Ficino, should be created intuitively. And, in fact, the lack of primary sources concerning the exact layout of these gardens confirms that the making of the garden in the Quattrocento was not as willed and as logically elaborated (i.e., by means of drawings) as the meaning the interpreters of the garden—literary scholars and philosophers in particular—have bestowed upon it; rather, garden making resulted from a peculiar habit of repetition. However, if the tradition involved in the making of gardens can be compared to Ficino's notion of *consilium*, this does not mean that garden makers were necessarily Neoplatonists or actually believed that by making their gardens they were creating an image of God. There seems to be a tension associated with early Renaissance gardens, which involves on one hand the tacit modus operandi concerning the actual gardens and, on the other, the explicit interpretation and communication related to fictional gardens, such as the pleasances of poetry and philosophy.

Finally, it is fairly common among garden historians to try to reconstruct the appearance of the early Medici gardens, for which we lack visual evidence and only have scanty written sources. The objective is usually to prove that these early gardens can be considered the prototypes of the *giardino all'italiana*, whose definition was spelled out by the first exhibition of the Italian garden held in Florence in 1931. However, the sources used by historians offer little or no help for the reconstruction of this typology. For example, Braccesi's description of the garden at Careggi, as well as the verses written by Alberto Avogadro and the letter by Galeazzo Maria Sforza, yield little information about the morphology of the gardens. Moreover, it is problematic to read these sources literally, for their authors made use of a rhetoric that had more to do with praising the Medici—and encomia often required mythological references—than with an accurate description of place.

The notion of style applied to the Medici gardens has also led to anachronistic associations, like those between the 1599 Utens lunettes and the fifteenth-century properties at Trebbio and Cafaggiolo. As the archival sources show, the *horti*, which were declared for tax purposes, were so called insofar as they yielded produce both for the needs of the Medici family and for sale; however, they were occasionally referred to as gardens, and the reason for this may be that they were at times venues of pleasurable activities or were in themselves considered as pleasurable as a French *jardin*. At any rate, even if the *horti* were sometimes called gardens, this by itself does not prove that they were early examples of the Italian garden style. And if they did have a regular layout, this was probably to facilitate their maintenance and cultivation, as their being surrounded by hedges was a means to protect them against both wild animals and cattle.

Compared to the earlier Medici properties in the Mugello, or to Careggi, Fiesole has often been considered an anticipation of later Renaissance villas. The reason for this is the absence of extensive portions of cultivated land, and also the fact that the gardens here are arranged in terraces connected by a single path. The only difference between the Fiesole gardens and later Renaissance gardens, some scholars have argued, would be that at Fiesole the connecting path is still somewhat timid, in that it is not axial and does not make use of monumental staircases. This view results from the belief that the late fifteenth-century appearance of the gardens at Fiesole has been preserved until today. But this, as I hope I have demonstrated, is not so, for the path linking the terraces was a later addition; originally the terraces were accessible only through the villa's interior. Moreover, even if cultivated land was not immediately adjacent to the site of the villa, the Medici owned several *poderi* at Fiesole, and they also exploited the existing nearby quarries. Hence, Fiesole was not exclusively a *luogo di villeggiatura*, as it has been described, although it is true that it was different from the other Medici properties. But this has more to do with the fact that the house was not at the center of a large agricultural estate than with the layout of the gardens and the structure of the terraces.

Ultimately, the use of eighteenth-century aesthetic theory for the interpretation of early Renaissance gardens has encouraged the reading of these gardens as art objects, such as paintings, fixed and immutable. In this book I have tried to avoid forcing the Medici gardens into predetermined patterns, or types. That is, rather than comparing them to the fixed idea of the *giardino all'italiana*, I have used archival and primary sources to analyze them as a flexible concept shaped by the passing of time and the evolution of culture.

Letter by Galeazzo Maria Sforza

Letter of Galeazzo Maria Sforza in Florence to his father
Francesco in Milan; April 23, 1459 (Paris, Bibliothèque Nationale,
Fonds italien 1588)

Anday a Caregio pallatio bellissimo di esso Cosmo quale visto da ogni canto
et delectatomene grandemente non mancho per la polidezza di giardini, che
invero sono pur tropo legiadra cosa, quanto per il degno edificio dela casa, ala
quale et per camere et per cusine et per sale et per ogni fornimento non mancha piu che si facia ad una dele belle case di questa cita, disnay [desinai] insieme con tuti li sudetti salvo Giohanne di Cosmo, che non volesse sedere ala
tavola mia ne anche mangiare, quando laltri per fare servire ognuno. Dopo el
disnare essendo immediate partito el S.re M. Sigismundo reductome in una
camera con tuta la compagnia oldite cantare con la citara uno Maestro Antonio, che credo che V.Exc.ia debba se non cognoscere, al mancho havere oldito
nominare, quale principiato da le prime cose, che V.Exc.ia fece et venuto non
solo al fine di quelli nele quale interpuose de grandissime laude di M. Tiberto,
ma poy disceso anche in commendatione mia narro ogni cosa con tanta
Dignita et modo, chel magiore poeta ne oratore che sia al mundo sel havesse
havuto a fare tale acto, forse nonne saria usito con tanta commendatione
da ogni canto del dire suo, che in vero fu tale, che ognuno fece signare che
maraviglia et maxime quilli che piu docti sono, vedendo loro ultra arte com-
paratione chel fece, del quale non so se Lucano, ne Dante ne facessero may alcuna di piu bella, miscolare tante hystorie antiche, nome de romani vechi

innumerabili, fabule, poeti et il nome de tute quante le muse, or a dire di co-
stuy saria grandissima impressa. Ma questa sia la conclusione, ad ognuno e
parso che lhabia dicto tanto bene che meglio non si possa dire. Oldito questo
trovay apparechiata una festagliola di done per certo bella, dove erano la
moglie di Piero, quella di Giohanne, una fiogliolla grande di Piero di Cosmo,
la moglie di Piero-francesco, una giovane di Strozi, quale se non e la piu bella
di questa cita, almancho e avanzata da puoche et cosi alcune villane et quivi si
ballo per tute queste ala fiorentina con salti e scambieti a la polita.

I went to Cosimo's beautiful house at Careggi and saw every corner of it, and I
very much enjoyed it not only for its beautiful gardens, which are indeed an ex-
ceedingly graceful thing, but also for the honorable building, which has as
many bedrooms, kitchens, rooms, and comforts as the beautiful houses of the
city; I ate together with everyone except for Giovanni di Cosimo, who did not
want to sit at my table even for eating because he took care that everyone
would be served. After eating, right after M. Sigismondo had left, I retired to a
room with the whole company in order to listen to a certain Maestro Antonio
play the guitar, and I think that your Excellency either knows him or has heard
of him. He started singing of those deeds that your Excellency has done and he
mixed it with very great praise of M. Tiberto, then at my request he narrated
every thing with such Dignity and skill that if the greatest poet or orator in the
world were asked to do the same thing maybe he would not be able to achieve
the same mastering of each detail of his speech; indeed he made the most
learned men marvel at his analogies, in relation to which I do not know if
Lucan or Dante ever made anything more beautiful, mixing so many old tales,
with numerous names of Roman men, fables, poets and the names of all the
muses, which according to him is a great undertaking. But finally, everyone
thought that he spoke so well that it is not possible to speak better. After listening to him I found that the women had organized a beautiful party, [here] were
Piero's wife, Giovanni's wife, an older daughter of Piero di Cosimo, the wife of
Pier Francesco, a young woman of the Strozzi family, who, if [she is] not the
most beautiful woman of this town, only a few [other women] can surpass her
[for her beauty] and also some countrywomen, and here we all danced together
in the Florentine manner, with leaps and beautiful turns.

The text of the letter is from Benjamin von Buser, *Die Beziehungen der
Mediceer zu Frankreich während der Jahre 1434–1494 in ihrem Zusammenhang
mit den allgemeinen Verhältnissen Italiens* (Leipzig: Verlag von Duncker &
Humblot, 1879), 347–348. My translation.

Metric Letter by Alessandro Braccesi

Ad eundem [Bernardum Bembum] descriptio
horti Laurentii Medicis

Alexander Braccius

Ne me forte putes oblitum, Bembe, laboris
Propositi nuper cum Meliore mihi,
Decrevi Medicum quaecunque legantur in horto
Scribere, quod Melior non queat ille tuus.
Prodeat in campum nunc et se carmine iactet:
Nanque mihi validas sentiet esse manus,
Cumque viro forti, cum bellatore tremendo,
Milite cum strenuo proelia saeva geret,
Victorique dabit victus vel terga potenti,
Me vocitans clarum magnanimumque ducem,
Vel captiva meos augebit praeda triumphos,
Afferet et titulos Crescia palma novos.
Nunc hortus qui sit Medicum placido accipe vultu—
Perlege nunc iussu carmina facta tuo!—
Villa suburbanis foelix quem continet arvis,
Caregio notum cui bene nomen inest.
Non fuit hortorum celebris tam gloria quondam
Hesperidum, iactet fabula plura licet,
Regis et Alcinoi fortisque Semiramis horti

Pensilis, aut Cyrum quem coluisse ferunt,
  Quam nunc est horti Laurentis gloria nostri,
  Inclyta fama, decus, nomina, cultus, honor.
Hic olea est pallens Bellonae sacra Minervae,
  Et Veneri myrtus, aesculus atque Iovi;
  Hic tua frons est, qua sese Tirynthius heros
  Cinxit honoratum, popule celsa, caput.
Est etiam platanus vastis ita consita ramis,
  Illius ut late protegat umbra solum.
Hic viridis semper laurus, gratissima Phoebo,
  Qua meriti vates tempora docta tegunt.
Ante Mithridatis quam non dum Roma triumphum
  Viderat, hoc surgit hebanus ampla loco;
  Hic piper et machir, gariophilon, assaron, ochi,
  Mellifluens nardum, balsama, myrrha, loton;
  Intubus est etiam therebintus, casia, caedron,
  Hic et odoratus nobilis est calamus.
Thus quoque fert sacrum superis hic terra Sabaeum,
  Fert cithisum, clarum laudibus Antiochi.
Est abies, pinus, buxus, viridisque cupressus,
  Nascitur hic quercus, robora, taeda, larix;
  Est suber, est cerrus, fagus, quin carpinus, ilex,
  Fraxinus, et quicquid silva nemusque ferunt.
Sunt ulmi, salices, dumi, fragilesque genistae,
  Sambucusque levis, sanguineusque frutex,
  Cornus, lentiscus, terrae quoque proxima fraga,
  Praedulces siliquae, castaneaeque nuces.
Sunt et quae Romae dederat tua poma Lucullus,
  Cerase, mora rubens, acida sorba iuglans.
Hic et Avellanae sunt, Appia mala, pirumque
  Omnigenum, ficus, persica, chrysomila,
  Punica mala et cotona, cidoneumque volemum;
  Turbaque prunorum vix numeranda subit.
Vicia, panicumque, fabae, farrago, lupinum,
  Pisa, cicer, milium, far, triticumque bonum,
  Ervum, fasellus, lens, sisima, oriza, siligo,
  Thiphe, similago sunt aliae segetes.
Quin cucumis, melopepo, cucurbita longa, papaver,

Allea, caepa rubens, porraque cum raphanis,
  Angurium, coriander, eruca, nepeta, et anesum,
    Marubium triste est, asparagusque simul,
    Serpillum, petroselinum, amaratus, onyx,
      Beta, cicoreum, brassica, menta, ruta.
    Quid dicam varias uvas dulcesque liquores,
    Qui mage sunt suaves nectare, melle, sapa?
    Quid violas referam, celseminos bene olentes,
    Quid niveas memorem purpureasque rhosas?
  Cur te, Bembe, moror? Sunt hoc plantata sub horto
  Quicquid habent Veneti, Tuscia quicquid habet.
    Pomorum speties hoc omnis frondet in horto,
    Hortus et hic olerum fert genus omne virens;
    Hic florum poteris cunctorum sumere odores,
      Hic, si tu quaeras, omne legumen erit.
  Haec nos pauca tibi de multis scripsimus: at, cum
    Plura voles, melius lumine cuncta leges,
    Lustrabisque oculis excelsa palatia regum
    Instar et egregia quaeque notanda tuis;
  Nam, si cuncta velim perstringere versibus, o quam
    Difficile atque audax aggrederemur opus!

To the Same [Bernardo Bembo]. Description of Lorenzo de' Medici's Garden

Alessandro Braccesi

So that you don't think that I forgot, Bembo, about the work with [the one who is] Migliore suggested to me recently, I decided to write about whatever things are gathered in the garden of the Medici, because that Migliore of yours is not able [to do so].

Let him go out into the field and boast of his poem: since he will feel that my hands are powerful and he will fight ferocious battles with a vigorous soldier, with a robust man, with a dreadful warrior, and he will either turn the tail to the powerful winner or surrender, calling me famous and magnanimous leader, or the captured prey will make my victories greater, and the defeat of [Migliore] Cresci will bring new honors.

Now hear with a pleasant face what the garden of the Medici is, now read the poems written by your command. The garden which the productive villa contains in the suburban fields, to which belongs the famous name of Careggi. There was no glory of the gardens of the Hesperides of long ago, although the myth boasts many things, or of the hanging garden of Semiramis and of the strong king Alcinoos, or of the one they say Cyrus cultivated—none with glory as celebrated as that of the garden of our Lorenzo, highest fame, splendor, name, cult, and honor.

Here is the bright olive tree sacred to Minerva the goddess of war, and here is the myrtle sacred to Venus, and the oak to Zeus; here is your leafy bough, with which the hero of Tirynthius garlanded his honored head. Also [here] the plane tree is planted with its large branches whose shade broadly protects the ground. Here is the evergreen laurel, dearest to Apollo, with which the deserving poets cover their learned temples. The magnificent ebony has been growing in this place since before Rome saw the triumph of Mithridates; there the pepper and carnation, the basil and wild spikenard, the honey-dropping nard, balsam trees, the myrrh tree, the lotus tree [or water lily; Italian persimmon]; also [there] is the endive, the terebinth, the wild cinnamon, the cedar; here is the famous sweet flag [calamus]. Here the soil bears also the Sabaean incense sacred to the gods, it bears the clover famous because of Antiochus's praises.

There is the fir, the pine, the boxwood tree, the green cypress, here the oaks spring forth [*quercus* and *robora*], the pitch pine, the larch; there is the cork oak, there is the turkey oak, the beech, why not mention the hornbeam, the holm oak, the ash, and whatever the wood and the grove bear.

There are the elms, the willows, the brambles, and the fragile broom plants, and the light elder, the mastic, also the strawberries nearest to the ground, the sweetest carob, nuts, and chestnuts. There are your fruits, and cherry tree, which Lucullus gave to Rome; making the cherries red, the tart service-cherries. There also are the Avellan nuts, and the Appian apples, and pears of all kinds, peach trees, quinces, pomegranate trees, black briony, and the Cydonian wonder pear and the almost innumerable variety of the plum tree follows.

There is the vetch, and panic grass, horse beans, fodder, lupine peas, chickpea, millet, spelt [barley], and the good wheat, the bitter vetch, the phasel [kidney beans], the lentil, sesame rice, winter wheat, one-grained wheat, *thiphe*, the finest wheat flour and other fields.

Why not mention the cucumber, the cucumber melon, a long gourd, the poppy, the red onion, and the scallions with radishes, watermelon, coriander, colewort, catnip and anise; there is the bitter hore-hound, and at the same time the asparagus, thyme, rock parsley, beet, endive, cabbage, mint, rue.

What more can I say of the various grapes, and sweet wines, which are sweeter than nectar, honey and must? What more can I tell about the violets, the good-smelling jasmines, what can I mention about the white or red roses?

Why am I detaining you, Bembo? Everything the Venetians have, everything that Tuscany has is planted in this garden. The whole assortment of fruit trees puts forth leaves in this garden, and this garden bears every verdant species of it; here you will be able to enjoy the scents of all the flowers, here should you seek there will be every kind of leguminous plant.

We wrote to you these few things about many things: but, you will survey the lofty palaces after the fashion of kings, and all of the magnificent things you should note with your eyes. For if I wanted to go over all the things briefly in verses, oh what a difficult and bold work it would be to undertake.

The Latin text is from *Alexandri Braccii Carmina*, ed. Alessandro Perosa (Florence: Libreria Editrice Bibliopolis, 1943), 75–77. My translation.

NOTES

The following abbreviations appear in the notes.

ACF   Archivio Storico Comunale di Fiesole
ASCF   Archivio Storico Comunale di Firenze
ASF   Archivio di Stato di Firenze
BML   Biblioteca Medicea Laurenziana
BNCF Biblioteca Nazionale Centrale di Firenze
GDSU Gabinetto Disegni e Stampe degli Uffizi
MAP   Mediceo Avanti il Principato

INTRODUCTION

1. Margherita Ciacci, "Non tutti i giardini di delizie sono uguali," in *I giardini delle regine: Il mito di Firenze nell'ambiente preraffaellita e nella cultura americana fra Ottocento e Novecento,* ed. Margherita Ciacci and Grazia Gobbi Sica (Florence: Sillabe, 2004), 12–28.

2. The quotation from Harold Acton is in Ciacci, "Non tutti i giardini di delizie sono uguali," 18.

3. It is telling that in an effort to preserve the medieval appearance of Florence, most foreigners opposed the destruction of the city walls on the right bank of the Arno. The urban intervention, which was proposed in 1864, was carried out from 1865—when Florence became the new capital of Italy after Turin—to 1869.

4. On Stanhope's villa at Bellosguardo see A. M. Wilhelmina Stirling, *Life's Little Day: Some Tales and Other Reminiscences* (New York: Dodd, Mead, 1924), 145ff.

5. In the book she focuses mainly on the architecture of the villas, and the vicissitudes of their owners, rather than on their gardens.

6. Vernon Lee, "Old Italian Gardens," in *In Praise of Old Gardens* (Portland, Me.: Thomas B. Mosher, 1912), 44. Lee's essay was also published in an early history of Italian gardens included in her *Limbo and Other Essays* (1897). Vernon Lee—pseudonym of the English novelist Violet Paget—lived on the outskirts of Florence at the Villa del Palmerino (Maiano, San Gervasio).

7. Edith Wharton, *Italian Villas and Their Gardens* (1904; reprint with introductory notes by Arthur Ross, Henry Hope Reed, and Thomas S. Hayes, New York: Da Capo Press, 1988), 11. In the United States, these scholars' ideas found fertile ground, especially because the Columbian Exposition of 1893, which took place in Chicago to commemorate the four-hundredth anniversary of Columbus's landing in America, had already contributed to raising interest in the classical tradition of Western art in general, and in the art of the Italian Renaissance in particular.

8. Exemplary are the residences commissioned by John Pierpont Morgan, Andrew Carnegie, and Egisto Fabbri in the United States. See Ciacci, "Non tutti i giardini di delizie sono uguali," 23. Edith Wharton's own house, called The Mount, in Lenox, Massachusetts, was designed by her niece Beatrix Jones (later Farrand) according to the principles Wharton had described in her influential book.

9. Wharton, *Italian Villas and Their Gardens*, 12.

10. Sir George Sitwell, *On the Making of Gardens* (1909; reprint, with a foreword by John Dixon Hunt, Boston: David R. Godine, 2003), 8, 7. Sitwell was a member of the Florentine Anglo-American colony whose members had purchased land and villas in Florence and its surroundings at the turn of the century. In particular, at his castle of Montefugoni, near Montagnana on the Tuscan hills, he created a small garden according to the principles of the Italian tradition.

11. Ibid., 14.

12. Pinsent's interpretation of the Italian Renaissance garden was partly influenced by the formal garden revival that had begun in Great Britain in the 1880s. Discussion of the architectural garden of the late Victorian and Edwardian eras used in part the same vocabulary as discussion of the historic Italian gardens, with a few differences described by David Ottewill in "Outdoor Rooms: Houses into Gardens in Britain at the Turn of the Century," in *Cecil Pinsent and His Gardens in Tuscany*, ed. Marcello Fantoni, Heidi Flores, and John Pfordresher (Florence: Edifir, 1996), 1–13.

13. According to the Berensons, Italian architects were to be considered untrustworthy until proven otherwise. The Berensons had initially hired an Italian architect for the renovation of I Tatti, but they soon dismissed him for "every conceivable reason: shoddy work, cost overruns, cheating workmen." See Richard M. Dunn, "An Architectural Partnership: C. Pinsent and G. Scott," in *Cecil Pinsent and His Gardens in Tuscany*, 39. It is true, however, that the Berensons were often frustrated with Pinsent's work, too. However, their professional relationship managed to continue over more than twenty years. Moreover, it was the Berensons who introduced Pinsent and Scott to Charles Strong when the American philosopher was looking for an architect to build his villa at Fiesole. Pinsent himself listed his works for an article by John Fleming that was never published. Pinsent's list was partly published by Erika Neubauer, "The Garden Architecture of Cecil Pinsent, 1884–1864," in *Journal of Garden History* 3, no. 1 (1983), 35–48.

14. Archival documents related to the organization of the exhibition are at the Archivio Storico Comunale di Firenze (hereafter ASCF), "Mostra del giardino italiano, 1931," buste 5087–93, and C.F. 9260. See also Biblioteca della Facoltà di Architettura di

Firenze, Fondo Roberto Papini, filza 117, Mostra del giardino italiano. I analyze these archival sources in my essay for the 2008 Dumbarton Oaks Symposium on Italian gardens, *Recent Issues in Italian Garden Studies: Sources, Methods, and Theoretical Perspectives.*

15. Among the exceptions see Georges Gromort, *L'Art des jardins* (Paris, 1934). He was the author of a three-volume work entitled *Jardins d'Italie* (Paris, 1922–1931). Also Mario Recchi, "La villa e il giardino nel concetto della Rinascenza italiana," in *Critica d'arte* 2 (1937), 131–137.

16. Arturo Jahn-Rusconi, *Le ville medicee: Boboli, Castello, Petraia e Poggio a Caiano* (Rome: Istituto Poligrafico dello Stato, 1938), 12.

17. In an article written earlier, called "Il giardino inglese," in *La vita britannica* (September–October 1919), 372–375, Dami explains that one of the reasons why the English garden was so successful was the fact that it offered an alternative to the dull and prosaic designs of the French, who had theorized the principles of the Italian garden and turned them into sterile and repetitive academic exercises.

18. The book by Dami (Milan: Bestetti & Tumminelli, 1924), as well as the earlier one by Maria Pasolini Ponti, *Il giardino italiano* (Rome: Ermanno Loescher, 1915), relied on Edith Wharton's study. By Dami see also *Il nostro giardino* (Florence: Felice Le Monnier, 1923).

19. At the beginning of the century, when most British and Americans were buying properties in Florence, the greatest number of working-class Italians was emigrating to the United States as a consequence of the economic crisis the country underwent at the turn of the century. Between 1900 and 1914 nine million Italians immigrated to the major cities of the East Coast, such as New York, Philadelphia, Boston, and Providence. In 1910 New York became the city with the fourth-largest Italian-speaking population, after Rome, Milan, and Naples. See Giovanna Ginex, ed., *L'Italia liberale (1870–1900)* (Rome: Editori Riuniti, 1998), 6.

20. D. Medina Lasansky, *The Renaissance Perfected: Architecture, Spectacle, and Tourism in Fascist Italy* (University Park: Pennsylvania State University Press, 2004), 57. Considering that the idea of a Tuscan identity was centered around the notion that Florence had been an intellectual capital during the Middle Ages and the Renaissance, the regime sought to promote the study of the Renaissance among Italian scholars in order to reclaim Florence's old primacy. Thus, in 1937 the Centro di Studi Rinascimentali was created in Florence with the purpose of encouraging research and coordinating publications on the Italian Renaissance. The Centro's "seemingly transparent agenda of cultural propaganda hid a more subtle purpose allied to the government's growing xenophobia. 'It is time,' as an editorial noted in 1937, 'to liberate the study of the Renaissance from foreign control.' . . . A particular motivation for these developments was the continued success of foreign institutes such as the German Kunsthistorisches Institut [founded in 1897]," 80.

21. Comune di Firenze, *Mostra del giardino italiano: Catalogo*, 2nd ed. (Florence: Comune di Firenze, 1931), 23.

22. Ibid., 45.

23. Ibid., 71.

24. The others were dedicated to the gardens of ancient Rome, Venice, the Piemonte region, and Lombardy, and to the Romantic garden, shown solely to provide an example of what was considered the antagonist style.

25. A "Mostra augustea della romanità" was organized in Rome in 1937 in order to celebrate the two-thousandth anniversary of Augustus's birth.

26. This may explain why the celebration of the Italian garden tradition, which was traced back to the Renaissance, took place in Florence, whereas Rome was not considered an appropriate venue for the first exhibition of late Renaissance and Baroque Roman gardens, which was curiously organized in Turin in 1928. This exhibition included the recreation of gardens that once existed as part of the most important Roman villas of the seventeenth and eighteenth centuries, such as the Villa Borghese. The patriotic spirit pervading the exposition, and the influence of this on the reception of the garden, becomes apparent in the catalogue *Mostra del giardino romano al Valentino nella esposizione di Torino MCMXXVIII*, published soon after the exhibition by the City of Rome.

27. It is useful to remember that the political and geographical unity of the country had been achieved only recently, in 1861, after Giuseppe Garibaldi had seized the Kingdom of the Two Sicilies and turned it over to Vittorio Emanuele, who then proclaimed the Kingdom of Italy and established Florence as its capital. Rome became part of the unified state only in 1870.

28. Giulio Cesare Lensi Orlandi Cardini, *Le ville di Firenze* (Florence: Vallecchi, 1954), 1:xx.

29. This is not to say that guidebooks were no longer written and published at the same time. See, for example, Frances Margaret McGuire, *Gardens of Italy* (London: Heinemann, 1965). This book is mostly an account of the gardens the author visited in Italy while her husband was the Australian ambassador in Rome. The Pitti Palace is the only Florentine villa she describes, and of the Boboli gardens she writes: "They have remained virtually unchanged since their founding. They were the model and inspiration for those Renaissance gardens which made the sixteenth century so notable a period in the evolution of garden architecture," 70.

30. Camillo Fiorani, *Giardini d'Italia: Arte, carattere e storia del giardino italiano* (Rome: Edizioni Mediterranee, 1960), 202.

31. Georgina Masson [Barbara Johnson], *Italian Gardens* (New York: Harry N. Abrams, 1961), 71.

CHAPTER ONE. MEDICI GARDENS

1. Domenico Moreni, *Notizie istoriche dei contorni di Firenze dalla Porta al Prato fino alla Real villa di Castello*, 6 vols. (Florence: Cambiagi, 1791–1795). Guido Carocci, *La villa Medicea di Careggi: Memorie e ricordi* (Florence, 1888). Guido Carocci, *I dintorni di Firenze*, 2 vols. (1906–1907; reprint, Rome: Multigrafica, 1968). Giuseppe Baccini, *Le ville medicee di Cafaggiolo e Trebbio in Mugello oggi proprietà Borghese di Roma* (Florence: Baroni e Lastrucci,

1897). The scholarly tradition established by Moreni, Carocci, and Baccini was continued by Lensi Orlandi Cardini, *Le ville di Firenze*, 2 vols. (Florence: Vallecchi, 1954) and more recently by Luigi Zangheri, *Ville della provincia di Firenze* (Milan: Rusconi, 1989).

2. Luigi Dami, *Il giardino italiano* (Milan: Bestetti and Tumminelli, 1924), 31 n. 4. Earlier books on Italian gardens rely solely on Vasari's testimony. See for example, Julia Cartwright, *Italian Gardens of the Renaissance* (London: Smith, Elder, 1914): "Cafaggiolo was another villa which Michelozzo built for Cosimo. Vasari describes this as a castle with moat and drawbridge, built for defense, but surrounded with ilex-woods, gardens, fountains, aviaries, and all that makes a villa fair and pleasant," 13.

3. Rose Standish Nichols, *Italian Pleasure Gardens* (New York: Dodd, Mead, 1931), 100–101.

4. See, for example, Alessandro Tagliolini, *Storia del giardino italiano: Gli artisti, l'invenzione, le forme dall'antichità al XIX secolo* (1988; reprint, Florence: La Casa Usher, 1994), 65–66; Mariachiara Pozzana, "Il giardino del Trebbio," in *Giardini medicei: Giardini di palazzo e di villa nella Firenze del Quattrocento*, ed. Cristina Acidini Luchinat (Florence: Federico Motta Editore, 1996), 148, 150–151, 155.

5. Although the descent of the family from the Mugello is widely accepted, it has also been opposed by a few scholars. In "Il committente: La famiglia Medici dalle origini al Quattrocento," in Giovanni Cherubini and Giovanni Fanelli, eds., *Il Palazzo Medici Riccardi di Firenze* (Florence: Giunti, 1990), 2–7, Massimo Tarassi says that the Medici were originally from Florence, and that only at a later stage did they choose the Mugello as the base for their expansion toward the countryside. In a contrary view, Gaetano Pieraccini, *La stirpe dei Medici di Cafaggiolo*, 3 vols., 2nd ed. (Florence: Vallecchi, 1947), claims that the early Medici belonged to that lower social class that moved to the city from the countryside, attracted by the lure of urban activities. However, as Johan F. Plesner maintains in *L'emigrazione dalle campagne alla città libera di Firenze nel XIII secolo* (Florence: Papafava, 1979), these new citizens were not at all poor and uncivilized; rather, they were rich land owners who saw the city as a new opportunity for their economic and political activities.

6. Emanuele Repetti, *Dizionario geografico, fisico, storico della Toscana* (Florence: Repetti, 1833–1845; anastatic reprint, Rome: Multigrafica, 1972), 5:584–585.

7. Father Lino Chini, *La storia antica e moderna del Mugello* (Florence, 1875; anastatic reprint, Rome: Multigrafica Editrice, 1969), 2:39.

8. Repetti, *Dizionario geografico*, 1:379: "Cafaggio, Cafaggiolo, (Cafagium): Nome generico restato a varie contrade sino dai tempi dei Longobardi, i quali appellavano Cafaggio e Cafaggiolo una più o meno estesa possessione territoriale vestita di alberi, e recinta da siepi, o da fossi, o da altri ripari."

9. With this document, endorsed by the notary Lotheringo Pucci, Averardo de' Medici's properties were subdivided among his six sons: Jacopo, Giovenco, Salvestro—also called Chiarissimo—Francesco, Talento, and Conte. The document contained in the *fondo* is not an original but a copy made in the sixteenth century. ASF, MAP, 151, n. 7, fol. 53r: "Frates et filii Averardi de Medicis . . . volentes pervenire ad divisionem plurium bonorum casolarium, domorum, terrarum, vinearum . . . fecerunt comuni concordia . . . sex

partes et ad sortes cum sex cedulis de istis sex partibus pervenerunt." (The brothers and sons of Averardo de' Medici ... being willing to divide the multiple goods, buildings [sheds], houses, fields, vineyards ... agreed to [divide the property into] six parts and to assign them by drawing lots consisting of six pieces.) From the deed it seems that Francesco was the only inheritor of Trebbio: "In secunda vero parte posuerunt et designaverunt partem de Trebio cum omnibus bonis et terris et rebus, scriptis et confinatis positis et designatis in ea et post eam. Que secunda pars de Trebio venit in partem Francisco predicto, datis, receptis et apertis sortibus predictis." (Ibid.) (Moreover, the second part was established and designated as that of Trebbio with all its annexed goods and fields and things, recorded and confined and designated within it and beyond it. This second part of Trebbio was assigned in part to the said Francesco, the aforementioned lots having been given, received and opened.) Cafaggiolo was probably the place where the brothers lived with their father Averardo, and so they must have decided to share the building and its annexes: "Item a Chafagioulo palatium in quo morabatur Franciscus . . . [et] Chiarissimus . . . [et] Jacobus. Et unum ortum cui a primo quod via per quam iter sit Campolitardi, a ij° via, a iij° Averardus, a iiij° via per quam iter venit de super ad cappannas sit largum iuxta aias brachiis decem et iuxta viam de cappanis brachiis decem et via que est in medio infra eam et foveam sit larga brachiis quattuor vel plus." (Ibid., fol. 54v.) (Also at Cafaggiolo a building in which Francesco lived . . . [and] Chiarissimo . . . [and] Jacopo. And one kitchen garden which [should be bordered by] the road leading to Campolitardi to the first side, [by] the road to the second side, [by] Averardo to the third side, to the fourth side by the road running beyond the sheds, which should be ten *braccia* [5.83 meters] near the threshing floor, by ten *braccia* near the road away from the sheds, and the road which is between it and the moat should be four *braccia* wide [2.33 meters] or more.)

10. ASF, *Signori, Missive, I Cancelleria*, 12, fol. 84v: "I Comuni di Villanuova e di Campiano deputammo a la guardia e fortificatione di Cafaggiuolo, e a quello vogliamo stieno fermi. . . . Et però non gli gravare per guardia o fortificazione di altro luogo." The letter is also mentioned by Baccini, *Le ville medicee di Cafaggiolo e Trebbio*, 9. Whenever there was fortification or restoration of the castles of the *contado fiorentino*, the Signoria used to nominate a few officials to be put in charge of inspecting and supervising the works, the structural condition of the buildings, and their supplies and ammunitions, and also to supervise the military and civil personnel whose task it was to monitor specific areas of the countryside.

11. ASF, *Signori, Responsive*, 5, doc. n. 58: "E' già più dì che fumo a Chafagiuolo de' Medici e troviamo che v'à entro intorno di dugiento moggia tra grano e biada. Anolo chominciato ad achonciarlo no[n] ci pare che sieno isstudiosi ad achonciarlo chome e' doverebono e però mandate se vi pare per messer Giovanni e per i suoi egevano a fare e solecitategli che l'achoncino od eglino lo sghonbrino."

12. Although Conte is not mentioned among the sons of Averardo who shared Cafaggiolo, it is possible that he acquired the property, or part of it, from one of his brothers, who all died before him. In this way Conte's son Giovanni could have inherited Cafaggiolo after his father's death in 1349.

13. In a letter written on March 5, 1359, two officials write to the Signoria that another Medici property, namely, Schifanoia, needed to be fortified, since "parci che aforzandola

sarebbe grande sicurtà del paese." Cited by Baccini, *Le ville medicee di Cafaggiolo e Trebbio*, 9. These documents therefore testify to the degree of control the city of Florence exercised over private properties in the countryside, especially if their geographic position was deemed strategic for the defense of the city.

14. ASF, MAP, 152, fols. 1r–95v. Filigno was Averardo's grandson and brother of Giovanni. His memoirs were edited in part by a Medici descendant, Giovanni Biondi de' Medici Tornaquinci, *Libro di memorie di Filigno de' Medici* (Florence: Spes, 1981). The editor, however, skips the whole section dedicated to the Mugello. On Filigno's book see Gene A. Brucker, "The Medici in the Fourteenth Century," *Speculum* 32, no. 1 (January 1957), 1–26. The importance of this book of memoirs derives from the fact that, as a nonofficial document written only for family members, it records facts, purchases, matrimonial contracts, and the true value of the possessions, a level of detail not easily found in other documents, such as those contained in the *Catasto*, whose compilers are often people whose interest was in declaring less than they possessed, in order to gain fiscal benefits. See Elio Conti, *I catasti agrari della Repubblica fiorentina e il catasto particellare toscano* (Rome: Istituto Storico Italiano per il Medio Evo, 1966), 59.

15. As it appears from this document, Averardo, whose possessions were divided among his sons in 1319, had bought at least nine fields at Cafaggiolo between the years 1270 and 1303, but there is no mention of a fortified building built there, or purchased, during those years (ASF, MAP, 152; esp. fols. 23r, 24r, 25r, 26r). However, we know from the previous deed that a *palagio* existed there as early as 1319. Thus, it could have been built or purchased either before the year 1270 or between 1303 and 1319. From this document we understand that the property was shared by Averardo's grandsons, as it had been shared by his sons: "La metà d'un palagio chon chase intorno, chon corte e loggia e mura e foso, con un peço d'orto di fuori, posto in Chafagiuolo, nel popolo San Giovanni in Petroio cholla sesta parte della chorte di drento ale mura vecchie e chon ogni altra apartenença che nelle dovise si chontiene e de' esser la via larga quatro braccia intorno al cerchiuito vecchio di Chafagiuolo siché i figliuoli di messer Giovencho non ci posono vietare la via lungo il palagio e lungo il muro loro infino al ponte. E' nostro tutto il foso d'intorno a Chafagiuolo chome tragono le nostre mura." (Ibid., fol. 88r). (Half of a palace with surrounding houses, with courtyard, loggia, walls and moat, with a kitchen garden outside the walls, located in Cafaggiolo, in the parish of San Giovanni in Petroio, with the sixth part of the courtyard within the old walls, and with everything that belongs to it. And the path within the circuit of walls at Cafaggiolo must be four *braccia* wide [2.33 meters] so that the sons of Giovenco cannot deny us passage along the building and along their wall up to the bridge. The moat around Cafaggiolo is ours.) In the fourteenth century the *contado* around the city of Florence was divided into *popoli*, or parishes, each of which had its own church, depending on the major *pieve* of the *contado*. Thus, for instance, Cafaggiolo and its surroundings belonged to the church of Santa Maria a Campiano, which, in its turn, belonged to the *piviere* of San Giovanni in Petroio. See Luigi Santoni, *Raccolta di notizie storiche riguardanti le chiese dell'arci-diocesi di Firenze* (Florence: Mazzoni, 1847; anastatic reprint, Bologna: Forni, 1974), 242. Also, Silvio Pieri, *Toponomastica della valle dell'Arno* (Rome, 1919; anastatic reprint, Bologna: Forni, 1985), 354.

16. ASF, MAP, 152, fol. 88v: "Anche uno peço di terra chon chapana e aia e cho' molti frutti e viti poste nel detto popolo fuor della piaça di Chafagiuolo, il qual si dice giardino, a j°, a ij°, a iij° via, a iiij° de' figliuoli di Biccio che fu di Malatesta de' Medici è 'ntorno a cinque staiora." One *staioro* corresponds to 525 square meters, so five would be 2,625 square meters.

17. See note 9.

18. The presence of *orti* is recorded for most rural properties; among the vegetables grown there were pumpkins, cabbage, onions, garlic, lettuce, radicchio, spinach, carrots, beans, peas, chickpeas, saffron, and the like. Among the fruit trees were fig, citrus, almond, walnut, pomegranate, apple, pear, and cherry trees. On manor farms and agricultural techniques in use during the late Middle Ages and early Renaissance see Centro Italiano di Studi di Storia e d'Arte, Convegno internazionale, *Civiltà ed economia agricola in Toscana nei secc. XIII–XV: Problemi della vita delle campagne nel tardo medioevo* (Pistoia: Centro Italiano di Studi di Storia e d'Arte, 1981).

19. See note 16.

20. Giovanna Casali, "Le proprietà medicee nel Mugello," in *Il Mugello, un territorio, una presenza culturale* (Florence: Edizioni all'Insegna del Giglio, 1983), 159–168. In 1386 Giovanni and his brother Francesco legally divided the estate they inherited from their father Averardo (called Bicci) di Chiarissimo, one of the six sons of Averardo de' Medici. It is likely that Giovanni di Bicci inherited Trebbio from his mother. In fact, when Bicci died in 1363 his wife Jacopa was one of the executors of his will (a copy of Bicci's will is in the ASF, *Atti Notarili* L. 290, III, fols. 20r–22v). With this document Bicci restored his wife's dowry and allowed her to enjoy the usufruct of his property. On August 13, 1384, Jacopa made her own will (Biblioteca Nazionale Centrale of Florence, henceforth BNCF, *Capponi*, 262, fol. 53r), dividing all of her property equally among her five sons: Matteo, Francesco, Michele, Giovanni, and Paolo.

21. In her book (written in collaboration with Vittorio Franchetti Pardo) *I Medici nel contado fiorentino: Ville e possedimenti agricoli tra quattrocento e cinquecento,* (Florence: CLUSF, 1978), 49, Casali mentions that in the year 1386 Giovanni de' Medici acquired the property of Trebbio, but she does not say where this information can be found. When I contacted Casali in reference to the *lodo divisorio*, I learned that the document is included in the *Possessioni Medicee* 4112. However, the collection in the ASF contains only forty numbered folios (of which fols. 23–40 are blank), which include solely the 1456 *lodo divisorio* between Cosimo and Pierfrancesco.

22. ASF, MAP, 81 doc. 8, fols. 20–24. The document is a petition that was presented to the Sei di Mercanzia from a notary on behalf of Lisa de' Pulci, daughter of Filigno de' Medici. With this document she claimed her rights over some of the properties of her brother Michele. The dispute involved Lisa and Francesca, the wife of Francesco di Bicci, Giovanni's brother, on account of her two sons Malatesta and Averardo.

At folio 2r of Filigno's memoirs we learn that he inherited his possessions, including Cafaggiolo, from his brother Giovanni di Conte, who died in 1372. In particular, Filigno possessed half of the *palagio*. When he died the property passed down to Filigno's only son, Michele, and when the latter died, to his grandson Giovanni, whom Michele had nominated as his universal heir. But Giovanni died in 1400 and left no male descendants. When the branch descending from Conte de' Medici—one of the six sons of Averardo de' Medici—died out after Giovanni's death, his portion of Cafaggiolo was put on sale by the *sindachi et uficiali* of Florence. Although Lisa won the dispute and her brother's properties were not put up for sale, we know that almost two decades later Cafaggiolo came to be recorded as a property belonging to Averardo di Francesco, that is, to the Medici branch descending from Chiarissimo. It is thus possible that Averardo acquired, or was assigned at some point, the property of Cafaggiolo inherited by Giovanni di Michele, on account of which property the dispute between Averardo's mother, Francesca, and Michele's sister Lisa had begun.

23. "Uno palagio overo fortezza con corte, logge, volta, piazza et colombaia et altre cose . . . luogo detto in Cafagiuolo." Ibid., fol. 20r.

24. "Anchora uno giardino di staiora cinque o circha a seme posto nel detto popolo, al quale d'atri parti la via, a iiij° del detto Francesco di Bicci. Anchora un pezzo di terra ortiva posto nel detto popolo, luogo detto in su' fossi del detto castello, al quale da j° e ij° e a iiij° Francescho di Bicci, a iiij° il detto fosso." Ibid.

25. Averardo was also the legal tutor or foster parent of Papi, the son of Niccolò di Francesco di Giovenco de' Medici. This position allowed him to administer the portion of land at Cafaggiolo that belonged to Papi, who had inherited it from his father Niccolò. ASF, *Catasto*, 142.

26. ASF, MAP 149, doc. 3, fol. 5r: "Uno abituro acto a forteza con certe case di fuori acte a stalle e habituro da famiglia, posto in Mugello, luogho decto Cafaggiuolo nel popolo della pieve di San Giovanni in Petroio con certi ortali a uso della casa e per mio habetare e però non tragho fuori stima."

27. ASF, *Catasto,* 60, fols. 81r–94r: "Uno abituro acto a forteza posto in Mugello luogo decto Chafaggiuolo . . . e d'atorno e' fossi di decto luogho chon più masserizie per mio uso e più una chasetta di fuori di decto luogho chon abituro da famiglia e stalle che da j° la piaza, a ij° Antonio e Albizo de' Medici, iij° fossato e più ortali per uso della chasa che da j° foddi del luogho, ij° e iij° via, a iiij° fossato, posto nel popolo di San Giovanni in Petroio, cioè della pieve di lungi di qui miglia XIII." (Fol. 82r.) (A fortified building located in Mugello, at a place called Cafaggiolo . . . and around the moats of the said place are many farms for my own use and a small house outside this place with a family house and stables, which is limited by the square on the first side, by Antonio and Albizo de' Medici on the second side, by the moat on the fourth side, and kitchen gardens for the use of the household that are limited by [?] on the first side, by the road on the second and third sides, by the moat on the fourth side, located in the parish of San Giovanni in Petroio, which is thirteen miles away from the parish church.)

28. "Una chasa posta in Chafaggiuolo, popolo decto, da cittadino con staiora quindici di terra incirca tra ortali, vigne e terre lavorative . . . choll'uso della chasa, dell'orto e delle vigne, cioè la reddita di quella . . . sono a vita di Monna Filippa. . . . Una chasa ad uso di lavoratore chon chapanna murata e con aia, posta in sulla piaza di Chafaggiuolo in decto popolo che da j° e ij° piaza, iij° rede di Niccholò di Francesco de' Medici

con j° chasolare, a iiij° fossato con più pezi di terre lavorative chon ortali, vigne, pasture, boschi, querce, sodi che da j° piaza, ij° via, iij° Sieve." (Ibid., fol. 83r.) (A house located at Cafaggiolo, in the said parish, with about fifteen *staiora* [almost two acres] of land, including market gardens, vineyards, and cultivated fields. The use of the house, market garden and vineyards, that is, the usufruct of the property belongs to Monna Filippa . . . a farmhouse with a stone shed and threshing floor, which is limited by the square to the first and second sides, by Niccholò di Francesco de' Medici to the third side with one small outbuilding, by the moat to the fourth side, with many cultivated fields, with market gardens, vineyards, pastures, woods, oaks . . . which are limited by the square to the first side, by the road to the second side, by the Sieve to the third side.)

29. ASF, *Catasto*, 49, fol. 1140. See Casali, "Le proprietà medicee nel Mugello," 159–160. Also Cornelius von Fabriczy, "Michelozzo di Bartolomeo," in *Jahrbuch der Königlich Preuszischen Kunst Sammlungen* 25 (1904), 54. A copy of this document can be found at ASF, *Monte Comune o delle graticole* (the funded debt of the commune that was established in 1345), serie: Copie del Catasto; pezzo: 83. This document was compiled by Lorenzo and Giovanni di Pierfrancesco de' Medici, who listed the properties that Giovanni di Bicci possessed in 1427, and that were later given to their father Pierfrancesco, Giovanni's grandson, by Cosimo de' Medici in 1456. See fol. 515v. A copy of the will formulated by Pierfrancesco di Lorenzo di Giovanni de' Medici can be found in the *Scrittoio delle Regie Possessioni*, 821, fols. 13v–14r. The document was endorsed by Ser Antonio di Ser Battista Bartolomei on July 18, 1476. In it, Pierfrancesco names his two sons, Lorenzo and Giovanni, and their male descendants, as his heirs. But if his sons found themselves *sine filiis et descendentibus masculis*, Pierfrancesco's legal heirs would be Piero di Cosimo il Vecchio's sons, namely, Lorenzo and Giuliano de' Medici.

30. The *popolo,* or parish, of Santa Maria a Spugnole was included in the *piviere* of S. Giovanni a Petroio, which was in its turn included in the *giurisdizione* of Scarperia, belonging to the *diocesi* and *compartimento* of Florence.

31. ASF, *Monte Comune o delle Graticole*, serie: Copie del Catasto; pezzo: 83, fol. 512v: "Un luogo ridotto in fortezza per nostro habitare con più masserizie a nostro uso con orto corti pratello e cisterna e altri hedificii posto nel popolo di Santa Maria a Spugnole luogo detto a Trebbio che da j° da ij° ¹/₃ via a ¹/₄ noi medesimi colla vigna del chancello e quella del posticcio, rende nulla perchè saranno cho poderi scritti di sotto." A *posticcio* is a piece of land where young trees, including vines, are grown before being transplanted somewhere else. See Niccolò Tommaseo, *Dizionario della lingua italiana* (Turin: Unione Tipografico-Editrice Torinese, 1865–1879), s.v. *posticcio. Cancello,* on the other hand, may refer to a piece of land surrounded by a fence, and gated.

32. ASF, *Monte Comune o delle Graticole*, serie: Copie del Catasto; pezzo: 83, fol. 513r.

33. See for example the cadastral documents from 1433 (MAP 88, n. 382, fols. 477–488).

34. ASF, MAP 83, doc. 89, fols. 504r–505v. "In Mugello a Trebbio et suoi dintorni. Uno luogho adatto a fortezza per nostra abitatione posto in Mugiello luogho detto Trebbio con più masserizie a uso della casa posto nel popolo di Santa Maria a Spugnole chon orti

prati e chorte con tre pezzi di vignia che faciamo a nostre mani." (Fol. 504r.) (At Mugello, Trebbio and its surroundings. A fortified place used as our residence, located in Mugello, at a place called Trebbio, with many farms for the use of the household, located in the parish of Santa Maria a Spugnole, with kitchen gardens, meadows, and courtyard, with three vineyards which we cultivate with our own hands.)

35. The document also lists the number of cows that were bred at Trebbio.

36. The enclosure of fields, the so-called *campi chiusi*, is a fifteenth-century practice that arises precisely from the need to protect the fields from cattle, especially from sheep, oxen, and pigs. Thus, hedges and ditches would surround vineyards and cultivated fields; vineyards alone could also be surrounded by thorn bushes.

37. "Con assai acqua v'abondi di prata, / Che me' si possin mantener gli armenti." Michelangelo Tanaglia, "De agricultura," in *Scritti teorici e tecnici di agricoltura,* ed. Sergio Zaninelli (Milan: Il Polifilo, 1995), 1:10. The meadows were usually mowed in June and July. Once dried by the sun, and after having been exposed to the air, the grass was carried to the *casa del lavoratore* for storage. For the definition of meadow see Tommaseo, *Dizionario della lingua italiana,* s.v. *prato*: "Propriamente quel campo, il quale non lavorato, serve per produrre erba da pascolare bestiami e da far fieno. 'Prato' propriamente, se il foraggio si falcia; 'Pascolo' se quello lasciasi pascere dal bestiame sul luogo. La 'Prateria' è d'ordin. più ampia e più coltivata. 'Prato naturale,' se formato e conservato dallo svolgimento di semi che trovansi naturalmente nel terreno. 'Prato artificiale,' se seminato periodicamente dall'arte." (Meadow: it is a field that, if not tended, is used to grow grass for the cattle and hay. It is called precisely "meadow" if the fodder is mowed; "pasture" if it is left for the cattle to graze on. A "prairie" is a larger extension of grassland. A meadow is called "natural" if it is formed and preserved by the seeds that are naturally found in it, and "artificial" [lawn] if it is periodically sown by [man's] art.)

38. ASF, *Catasto,* 410 (microfilm 1045), fol. 4v: "Con più ortali per uso della chasa." Since the *ortali* are for the use of the household, I translate the term as "kitchen gardens," instead of "market gardens." Another document from the *Catasto* dates to 1433, and is again written by Averardo di Francesco (ASF, *Catasto,* 500 [microfilm 1240], fol. 58r). The description of the property is here even stingier with details than is the previous description; the author is probably so concise because nothing has changed in his possessions from the last declaration. In the same year, another document was written that is very similar to the cadastral description (ASF, MAP, 88 doc. 382, fols. 477–488). However, we learn from this document that the fields of the property were seeded and yielded mainly wheat, whereas the vineyards produced both red and white wines.

39. Cosimo and Pierfrancesco probably acquired Cafaggiolo from Averardo's grandson Francesco de' Medici. Averardo's son, Giuliano, in fact, died only a year after his father, and Francesco di Giuliano was probably too young to administer the property. This hypothesis is proven by the tax return filed by Piero di Cosimo de' Medici in 1469, ASF, *Catasto,* 924, fol. 299v: "Apresso scriverremo e' beni posti in Mugiello pervenuti dall'eredità di Francesco di Giuliano di Averardo de' Medici." For the patrimonial situation of Pierfrancesco after his father's death see ASF, MAP, 161, fols. 1–7v. When Cosimo's brother,

Lorenzo, died in 1440, his wife yielded the custody of her son to Cosimo, who became the tutor of Pierfrancesco, and because of this he was allowed to administer his nephew's properties until he turned twenty. When Pierfrancesco became old enough, disputes between him and Cosimo began regarding the administration of the land owned. There are four documents, dating from December 13, 1440, to February 20, 1442/3, in which Cosimo listed the possessions belonging to the patrimony that Lorenzo had left to his son. See ASF, MAP, *Inventario*, ed. Francesca Morandini and Arnaldo D'Addario (Florence: 1951–1963), 4:431–432.

40. ASF, *Catasto*, 622 (microfilm 1520), fol. 618v: "Uno abituro adatto a forteza con orti per nostro uso, posto in Mugiello, luogho detto in Chafaggiuolo." A very similar version of this document is in MAP, 82, 182.

41. ASF, *Catasto*, 76: "Quartiere di San Giovanni, Gonfalone del Leon d'Oro, Portata di Cosimo e Pierfrancesco de' Medici," fol. 4v: "Chosimo di Giovanni de' Medici et Pierfrancesco di Lorenzo mio nipote aprestanziate in detto gonfalone. . . . Uno luogho adatto di fortezza per nostra habitazione posto in Mugiello luogho detto Trebbio con più masserizie ad uso della chasa poste nel popolo di Santa Maria a Spugnole con orto, prato e chorte con due pezzi di vigna fanosi a nostre mani chen chostano l'anno di chotanti che quelle sene chava." (Chosimo di Giovanni de' Medici and my nephew Pierfrancesco di Lorenzo . . . a fortified place used as our residence, located in Mugello, a place called Trebbio, with many farms for the use of the household located in the parish of Santa Maria a Spugnole with a kitchen garden, meadow, and courtyard, with two vineyards that we tend with our own hands, and we invest in it as much as we earn from it.)

42. In the declaration from August 1451 by Cosimo and Pierfrancesco the description of Trebbio is repeated almost invariably. ASF, *Catasto*, 712: "Quartiere di San Giovanni, Gonfalone del Leon d'Oro, Portata di Cosimo e Pierfrancesco de' Medici," fol. 640r.

43. By the end of 1451 the disputes between Cosimo and Pierfrancesco made it necessary to have recourse to a notary. On November 17 a *lodo divisorio* was formulated by Carlo di Gregorio Marsuppini and Bernardo di Antonio Medici—elected arbiters of the controversy—and it was made effective on July 9, 1456. Probably the original version of the *lodo* is the document contained in the *Scrittoio delle Regie Possessioni,* 4112; there is also a Latin copy, with no date, in MAP, 150, doc. 41; an excerpt of it is in the *Scrittoio delle Regie Possessioni*, 821; and other copies are in MAP 159; MAP 81, doc. 59, cc. 562r–564v (this one, written in Latin, also contains a brief description of Careggi, fol. 562r) and MAP 161, doc. 16, fols. 24r–27r). The following excerpt is from ASF, *Scrittoio delle Regie Possessioni* 4112, "Campione dei beni patrimoniali della famiglia Medici, 1456," fol. 6r: "A Pierfrancesco. . . . Uno chasamento a Trebbio per nostra abitatione ridotto in forteza chon chorte, loggia interna, volte, sale et altri [e]difici, chon una torre in becchatelli sopra la porta, chon ponte levatoio et po . . . to attorno merlato, et altri [e]difici tutti ridotti in forteza, et chon due pratelli, l'uno dinanzi murato intorno, l'altro di verso la Scarperia, chon istalle et uno orto allato a detto chasamento di verso Spugnole murato intorno chon pergole et alberi fruttiferi di staiora 3[?] incircha, chon una chiesa et una fonte et una chasa in volta[?] chon granai et stalla et cella da tina per la vendemia, muratavi di j° appiè della

detta abitatione di verso Schantalone, posta nel Popolo di Santa Maria overo di Santo Niccholo a Spugnole, luogho detto A Trebbio, chon da j° via, da ji° jii° jiii° noi medesimi.
Con più boschi di querciuolo et chon . . . et chastagneti et altri legnami appartenenti alla
detta habitatione et chon una vigna che si dice a posticci la quale si fa a nostre mani che ci
rende l'ano in parte bo[tti] 60 di vino sterzato la rendita da. . . . Et chol detto chasamento
e apicchato di verso Chafaggiuolo uno parcho overo chiuso da fiere selvatiche fatto di legname il quale gira intorno uno miglio incircha. Il quale chasamento overo sito tocchò a
Giovanni di Bicci de' Medici in parte insino l'anno . . . quanto si divise da Francesco suo
fratello et ragionossi che valesse f . . . et dipoi visè murato per insino a questo dì sopradetto
di modo che Chosimo lo chonsegnò a Pierfrancesco suo nipote per rhagione della sua
parte per f . . . et chosì trago fuori, et la vigna si fa che renda f. 18. . . . Appare . . . delle
possessioni di Giovanni di Bicci." (To Pierfrancesco. . . . A fortified building at Trebbio
used for our residence with courtyard, inner loggia, cellars, rooms and other buildings,
with a tower above the entrance, with a drawbridge . . . and other fortified buildings, and
with two small meadows, one of which is in front [of the building] and it is walled, the
other is oriented toward Scarperia, with stables and a kitchen garden to the side of the said
building oriented toward Spugnole. It is walled and has pergolas and fruit trees; it is about
three *staiora* in size [1,575 square meters; 0.39 acres], with a church and a wellspring and a
house with granaries and stable and storage room for the tubs used during the grape harvest built at the foot of the said building toward Schantalone, located in the parish of
Santa Maria, that is, Santo Niccholo a Spugnole, at a place called Trebbio, which is bordered by the road to the first side, and by ourselves to the second, third, and fourth sides.
With many oak woods and chestnuts and other trees belonging to the same property, and
with a vineyard that is called *a posticci*, which we tend with our own hands and yields sixty
tubs of wine per year. Adjacent to the said building at Cafaggiolo is a park, which runs
for at least one mile and houses untamed animals. Giovanni di Bicci gained possession of
this property . . . when his brother Francesco subdivided it and its value was estimated . . .
and then construction works took place until today so that Cosimo gave to his nephew
Pierfrancesco the part that was due to him . . . and the vineyard yields eighteen florins . . .
it seems . . . from Giovanni di Bicci's possessions.)

44. As reported by Casali, with the *lodo divisorio* Cosimo obtained all the estates of
Careggi, where he had already made some investments, and where, in 1457, he had put
Michelozzo in charge of the restoration project (Franchetti Pardo and Casali, *I Medici nel
contado fiorentino*, 52–54). Cosimo also obtained Cafaggiolo with the surrounding *poderi*
and the neighboring properties of Campiano, Comugnole, Lucigliano, San Piero a Sieve,
and Fagna, which together formed a large and probably uninterrupted estate. He was also
assigned a number of *poderi* that were located along a road that links Cafaggiolo with Gal-
liano, Rezzano, and Montecarelli; in this way Cosimo could easily control the whole property. Moreover, as these lands were located along the major communication roads, they
offered easy access to the farming markets and the city.

45. ASF, *Scrittoio delle Regie Possessioni* 4112, fol. 1r: "A Choximo. . . . Uno luogho in
Chafaggiuolo da habitare ridotto in forteza con due torri et ponte levatoio et fossi intorno

et una piazza dinanzi et orto dirietro con cinque chasette in sulla detta piaza et una chiesa titolata Santo Jachopo assieve, posta nel popolo di Santa Maria a Champiano di stima di f. 2000, stimata secondo lo 'nventario fatto fino l'anno 1440, et più vi se speso per muramento fattovi di poi f. 1000 sicchè in tutto si stima detto luogho f. 3000." (To Cosimo: A fortified place used as a residence with two towers, drawbridge and moats, and a square in front of it and kitchen garden behind it, with five small houses bordering the said square and a church dedicated to Saint Jacob at Sieve, located in the parish of Santa Maria a Campiano, it is worth two thousand florins according to the inventory compiled in the year 1440. Later on we spent one thousand florins in some construction works, therefore the whole place is worth three thousand florins.)

46. ASF, MAP 161, doc. 16, fols. 24–27 and 28–31. "Unum palatium positum in forteça positum in popolo Sancte Marie a Campiano de Mugello comi[ta]tu florentino, loco decto Cafaggiuolo cum habitatione pro domino cum duabus turribus et ponte levatoio et fossis circa et cum orto ex parte posteriori et cum pratello sive piaça ex parte anteriori et cum quinque domunculis super dicta platea. Et cum una ecclesia iuxta Sevem que dicitur Sancto Jacopo et cum pluribus boschis, castagnetis et torrentatis et sodis et pastures pertinentibus et consegnatis dicti habitatione." (Fol. 24r.)

47. "Pars adiudicata per dictum laudum dicto Pierfrancischo proprio. . . . Unum palatium in forteça positum in comitatum florentino et in popolo Sancte Marie sive Sancti Nicholai a Spugnole de Mugello comitatum florentino loco detto a trebbio cum habitatione pro domino, cum turri et pratello et orto et stalla et alii[s] hedifitiis, cum una clausura sive clauso pro animalibus silvestribus, cum una domo ibi ppe [?] apta per retinemdo granum, et talia, et stalla, et cum pluribus nemoribus, et cum vinea que vocatur a posticci, cum castanetis, cum vect[or]ia [?] iuxta dictu palatium et cum fonte." (Ibid., fol. 28r.) A Latin description of Trebbio is found in *Carte Strozziane*, series I, pezzo 10, fols. 59v–61r.

48. See note 45.

49. ASF, MAP, 87, doc. 61, fols. 406r–430r. "Uno abituro grande hedifichato a ghuisa di fortezza chon fussi murati intorno et chon antimuri et chon due torri et chon altri edifici dentro ad esso sichondo s'aspetta a ttale abitazione possto nel pivieri e popolo di San Giovanni in Petroio vocato Chafagiuolo, chon piaza grande dinanzi murata intorno da due lati et dall'altro lato più abitazioni murate a una dirictura e lunghezza per bisongni e chomodità di detto abituro overo fortezza, cioè chapanna et stalle et vendemmie et granai et quatro chase de' abitazione, che detta piazza murata chon detti abituri fassciano detta forteza, overo abituro da tre lati et drieto ad esso v'è horto di circha istaiora quattro a seme murato da tre lati et dall'altro v'è istechato. La quale tengiamo per nostro abitare cholle masserizie che s'aspetta ad esso per nostri bisongni et per la chomodità et bisongnio delle nostre possessioni di Mugiello." (Fol. 406v.) (A large fortified building with walls and moats and with two towers and other houses within it as it is appropriate for such a residence, located in the *piviere* and parish of San Giovanni in Petroio, called Cafaggiolo, with a large square in front of it walled on two sides, and to the other side is a row of many houses to satisfy the needs and for the comfort of the said fortified building. These are: a shed with stables and places

for the grape harvest and granaries and four houses for dwelling. The said walled square and the said houses surround the fortified building on three sides, and behind it is a kitchen garden of about four *staiora* [2,100 square meters; half an acre], seeded and walled on three sides; the fourth side is bordered by a fence. We use this property as our residence with the farms that belong to it for our needs and comforts and for those of the other properties in the Mugello.) In the *Catasto* 924 of 1469 the property of Cafaggiolo is still declared by Piero de' Medici, who gives a brief description of it at fol. 299v: "Abituro e ch'un orto dirieto et pratello overo piazza dinanzi." Piero mentions also that they inherited Cafaggiolo from Francesco di Giuliano di Averardo de' Medici.

50. ASF, *Catasto*, 1016 (microfilm 2462): "Uno abituro adatto a ffortezza posto nel popolo di Santa Maria a Chanpiano di Mugiello, luogho detto Chafaggio[lo] cholle masserizie apartenente a detto abituro et chon orto dallato he pratello hovero piazza dinanzi il quale tongiamo per nostra abitazione hovero popolo di Santo Johanni in Pretorio." (Fol. 455r.) (A fortified building located in the parish of Santa Maria a Chanpiano in Mugello, a place called Cafaggiolo, with the farms belonging to the said building, and with a kitchen garden to the side of it, and a meadow or else square in front of it. We use it as our residence in the parish of San Giovanni in Petroio.) A copy of this document reports a different version of Lorenzo's property, in which the *orto* appears again at the back. It is found at ASF, *Monte Comune o delle Graticole*, 83: "Uno abituro adatto affortezza posto nel popolo di Santa Maria a Champiano di Mugiello luogho detto Chafaggiolo cholle masserizie apartenenti a detto abituro et chon horto di drieto et pratello hovero piazza dinanzi il quale tenghiamo per nostra abitazione hovero popolo di San Giovanni in Petroio." (Fol. 536v.) (A fortified building located in the parish of Santa Maria a Chanpiano in Mugello, a place called Cafaggiolo, with the farms belonging to the said building, and with a kitchen garden behind [the building], and a meadow or else square in front of it. We use it as our residence or parish of San Giovanni in Petroio.)

51. ASF, MAP, 104, doc. 8, fols. 84–88: "Uno palagio in fortezza chon fossi intorno, antimuri, ponte levatoio, chon due torri, ballatoi, chorti, sale terrene, loggie, chamere, antichamere, chapella, chucina, forno, pozzi, volte da vino, ortho murato da due lati e dall'altro stechato chon piazza dinanzi murata intorno et chon un filo di case in su detta piazza fuori di detto palagio, dove sono granai, cielle da tina per la vendemia chon tina e strettoio, stalle, chapanna, forno et tre chase che s'apigionano et uno ve n'è per uso del factore, possto nel popolo di San Giovanni in Petroio hovero di Santa Maria a Chanpiano, luogho detto Chafagiuolo cho' poderi che apresso si dirà, in prima chonfinato, da primo via, secondo, $^1/_3$ venditori, $^1/_4$ fossato di Chaf°." (Fol. 86r.) (A fortified building surrounded by moats, with walls, drawbridge, two towers, hanging walkways, courtyards, ground floor rooms, loggias, rooms, anterooms, chapel, kitchen, bakery, wells, wine cellars, kitchen garden walled on two sides with a fence on the other side, with a walled square in front of it, and with a row of houses overlooking the square in front of the building, which include granaries, storage rooms for the tubs to be used during the grape harvest, stables, shed, bakery; three houses are rented and one is the house of the farm overseer. It is located in the parish of San Giovanni in Petroio or Santa Maria a Campiano, a place called Cafaggiolo

with the farms listed below, bordered by the road on the first side, by the shopkeepers on the second and third sides, by the moat of Cafaggiolo on the fourth side.) Less accurate versions of the arbitration award are in: MAP, 150, doc. 39, fol. 65r; MAP, 159, fols. 55r–62r (this copy was made in the sixteenth century).

52. ASF, MAP, 129, fols. 480–528: "Una casa su la piazza di Trebbio a uso di granaio con una stalla di sotto e una ciella dove stanno le tine per le vendemie. Una capanna grande . . . nella quale capanna se tiene lo stramo. Una fonte murata su la piazza . . . una casa hovero fortezza castello in forteza con ballatoi atorno, corte, logia, cisterna, volte, stalle, chamera, con una torre grande, . . . colombaia, cucina, forno, stalla, pollaio, orto murato et altri soi edifici luogo detto Trebbio. Valli. Un palazzo in fortezza post[o] nel popolo di Santa Maria a Spugnole luogo detto Cafagnolo co' balatoi intorno, corthe, logie con dua torre grande, fossi intorno, sale, camare, volte, cucina, pollaio, forno, colonbaie e altri soi edifitii, oratraio dove se dice messa, orto murato et una piazza murata intorno. Fuori de detto castello, valle. Uno filare di case post[e] sula piazza di Chafagiuollo, che in una parte di dette case stanno per nostro uso, dove se tien le tine per le vendeme et per le stalle, per cavalli, e per mulli di orxa et dov è un forno per uso di la vicinanza, con un pozo di fuori o una capanna per lo stramo in detto fillaro." (Fol. 542v.) (A house on the square of Trebbio used as a granary with a stable on the ground floor and a storage room for the tubs used during the grape harvest. A large shed . . . in which we keep the hay. A walled wellspring on the square . . . a house or else fortified castle surrounded by hanging walkways, with courtyard, loggia, cistern, and cellars, stables, rooms, and a large tower, dovecote, kitchen, bakery, stable, henhouse, walled kitchen garden and other houses belonging to it, place called Trebbio. Valleys. A fortified palace located in the parish of Santa Maria a Spugnole, place called Cafaggiolo surrounded by hanging walkways, courtyard, loggias, with two large towers, surrounded by moats, rooms, cellars, kitchen, henhouse, bakery, dovecotes and other houses belonging to it, oratory for the celebration of Mass, walled kitchen garden and walled square. The place is in a valley. A row of houses located on the square of Cafaggiolo; some of them are for our own use; we use them as storage rooms for the tubs, as stables for horses and mules, and as a bakery for the neighborhood, with a well and a shed for the hay.) A similar document is included in the *Decima Repubblicana*, 27, fols. 573r–589v.

53. ASF, MAP, 146, fols. 13–34v: "Uno casamento a uso di palagio in fortezza con fossi intorno et una piazza grande dinanzi con uno filare di case in su decta piazza a uso di granai et vendemmia et stalla et altre sue apartenentie poste nel populo di Sancta Maria a Spugnole o vero della pieve di San Giovanni in Petroio luogho detto Cafaggiuolo di stima di . . . non mettendo tre case che s'appigionano in decto filare tuct'a tre. Uno podere posto nel popolo di sopra, luogo decto in Cafaggiuolo da l'orto con suoi vocaboli et confini. Lavora Giovanni di Pollonio Cierrota." (Fol. 14v.) (A fortified palace surrounded by moats and a large square in front of it with a row of houses overlooking the said square used as granaries, and used for the grape harvest and as a stable, with everything else that belongs to it; located in the parish of Santa Maria a Spugnole or parish church of San Giovanni in Petroio, place called Cafaggiolo, which is worth . . . excluding three houses in the said row that we rent. A farm

located in the abovementioned parish, place called Cafaggiolo with a kitchen garden and everything that belongs to it. The farm overseer is Giovanni di Pollonio Cerrota.)

54. "Uno palazzo con una torre auso di fortezza merlato et con procinto intorno con granai et stalle et tinaie et capanna intorno fuor di detto procinto et una cappella in sulla piazza posta nel popolo di Santa Maria a Spugnole di Mugello luogo detto a Trebbio. Un podere posto nel popolo di Santa Maria a Spugnole vicino al detto palazzo con suoi vocaboli et confini lavoralo Matteo di Jacopo. Un podere posto nel sopradetto popolo luogo detto alla fonte di trebbio con suoi vocaboli et confini lavoralo Matteo di Francesco Francini." (Ibid., fol. 23v.) (A fortified crenellated building with tower, surrounding walls, granaries and stables, cellars for the tubs and shed outside of the walls and a chapel on the square located in the parish of Santa Maria a Spugnole in Mugello, place called Trebbio. A farm located in the parish of Santa Maria a Spugnole close to the said building with everything that belongs to it within its boundaries. The farm overseer is Matteo di Jacopo. A farm located in the abovementioned parish, called Trebbio's wellspring, with everything that belongs to it; the overseer is Matteo di Francesco Francini.)

55. "Casa con una bottegha sotto con uno pezzo d'orto posta sotto l'orto di Trebbio luogo detto a Malborghetto tienla in . . . [?] le [e]rede di Pergiovanni." (Ibid. fol. 26r.)

56. "Una casa con uno pezzo d'orto et capanna posta nel sopradetto luogo di Malborghetto sotto l'orto di Trebbio apigionasi a Giovanni et Agnolo di Niccholò fornaciari insieme cholla infrascripta fornace." (Ibid. fol. 26v.)

57. ASF, *Scrittoio delle Regie Possessioni*, 4113: "Uno palazo da signore con sua abiture et appartenenze posto nel populo di San Giovanni in Petroio, luogho detto Cafaggiuolo con sua fossi et antimuri con horto dentro [?] a detto palazo di staiora otto. Una macchia da uccellare di staiora dieci posta in detto populo con el fossato di Rotona che passa per esso. Un prato atorno a detto palazo di staiora sei con muriccioli intorno a detto pratello, confina a primo via che va a Barberino, a secondo via che va al Trebbio, a terzo fossato. Una casa con bottegha posta in detto populo con cantina et horto detta la casa de' vasellari, a primo piaza di Cafaggiuolo, a secondo fossato. Tienla Jacopo di Stefano vasellaio. Una casa et bottegha a uso di fabro con cantina et horto, posto nel populo di San Giovanni a Petroio, confinata come la detta di sopra. Una casa con bottegha posta in detto populo, confina a primo piaza di Cafaggiuolo, a secondo fossato, a terzo granaio di Cafaggiuolo." (Fol. 34r.) (A landowner's palace with its houses and annexes located in the parish of San Giovanni in Petroio, at a place called Cafaggiolo, with moats and walls, with a kitchen garden within the building of eight *staiora* [4,200 square meters; one acre]. A wood of ten *staiora* [5,250 square meters; 1.3 acres] for bird hunting located in the said parish with the moat of Rotona passing through it. A meadow of six *staiora* [3,150 square meters; 0.77 acres] around the said building with curbs around the said meadow, it is bordered by the road to Barberino on the first side, by the road to Trebbio on the second side, and by the moat on the third side. A house and shop located in the said parish, with cellar and kitchen garden, called house of the potters, is bordered by the square at Cafaggiolo on the first side, and by the moat on the second side. Jacopa of Stefano the potter is in charge of it. A house and shop used by a blacksmith, with cellar and kitchen garden, located at San

Giovanni a Petroio and bordered as the above one. A house and shop located in the said parish, bordered by the square at Cafaggiolo on the first side, by the moat on the second side and by the granary at Cafaggiolo on the third side.)

58. "Una vendemmia posta in sulla piaza di Cafaggiuolo con un granaio . . . una stalla posta in su detta piaza." (Ibid., fol. 34v.)

59. ASF, *Scrittoio delle regie possessioni*, 4115: "Un palazzo da signore con sue habiture et apartenentie posto nel popolo di San Giovanni in Petroio, luogo detto Cafaggiuolo con sua fossi et anitmuri con horto drieto al palazzo di staiora otto di terra." (Fol. 38r.) (A landowner's palace with its houses and pertinences located in the parish of San Giovanni in Petroio, at a place called Cafaggiolo with moats and walls, with a kitchen garden of one acre [4,200 square meters] behind the building.)

60. On the terminological distinction between *casa da signore* and *casa da lavoratore* see Amanda Rhoda Lillie, *Florentine Villas in the Fifteenth Century: An Architectureal and Social History* (Cambridge: Cambridge University Press, 2005) 58-59.

61. It is known, for instance, that Leon Battista Alberti's Latin was largely influenced by Isidore's *Etymologiae*, which was printed for the first time in 1472.

62. "Hortus nominatus quod semper ibi aliquid oriatur. Nam cum alia terra semel in anno aliquid creet, hortus numquam sine fructu est." *Etymologiae*, XVII.10.1. I use the Latin-Spanish edition *Etimologías*, ed. José Oroz Reta and Manuel A. Marcos Casquero (Madrid: Biblioteca de Autores Cristianos, 1994), 2:376.

63. "Orto. Nel plurale orti e al femminile ortora. Aff. al latino hortus. Campo chiuso da muro o siepe nel quale si coltivano erbaggi, e piante da frutto." Tommaseo, *Dizionario della lingua italiana*. s.v. *orto*.

64. "Graziosi e abbondevoli orti, i quali sovverrebbono al bisogno del nostro vivere con poca fatica di corpo." Ibid.

65. The Academy, whose aim was to purify the Italian language, was founded in Florence in 1582.

66. "Mes li François font maisons grant et plenieres et peinte, et chanbre lees por avoir joie et delit sans guerre et sans noise, et por ce sevent il miels fere praiel et vergiers et pomiers entour leur abitacle que autre jent, car ce est une chose qui mult vaut a delit d'ome." Brunetto Latini, *Li livres dou Tresor*, ed. Spurgeon Baldwin and Paul Barrette (Tempe: Arizona Center for Medieval and Renaissance Studies, Arizona State University, 2003), 107.

67. The word *verziere*, from the Latin *viridarium*, was rarely used after the 1320s, and it was not even listed in Isidore's *Etymologiae*.

68. Vittore Branca, ed., *Mercanti scrittori: Ricordi nella Firenze tra Medioevo e Rinascimento* (Milan: Rusconi, 1986), 106–115.

69. "Appresso, vedrai il paese . . . situato nel mezzo d'un bellissimo piano dimestico e adorno di frutti belli e dilettevoli, tutto lavorato e adornato di tutti i beni come un giardino . . . I terreni presso all'abitazioni vedi dimestichi, ben lavorati, adorni di frutti e di bellissime vigne, e molto copioso di pozzi o fonti d'acqua viva . . . abituri di cittadini posti in vaghi e dilettevoli siti, bene risedenti, con vaga veduta, sopra istanti a' vaghi colti, adorni di giardini e pratelli." Ibid., 108–110.

70. "Vedi nel piano del Mugello e migliori e più fruttiferi terreni che sieno nel nostro contado, dove vedrai fare due o tre ricolte per anno e ciascuna abbundante di roba: e di tutte le cose che sai addomandare, ivi si fanno perfette. E appresso, ne' poggi hai perfetti terreni, e favvisi su grande abbondanza di grano e biada e di frutti e d'olio, e simile vi si ricoglie essai vino, gran quantità di legname e di castagne, e tanto bestiame che si crede che fornisca Firenze pella terza parte." Ibid., 112.

71. "Nella terza parte ti resta solo a vedere la bontà e utilità degli edifici: e questa si vede prima in cinque castella, com'è detto, che sono nel piano. . . . Tutto l'altro paese, cioè ne' poggi e per tutto, ha, com'è detto, molti abituri, che oltre alla bellezza sono buoni e di abituro e di buono sito e di buona aria, con molte colombaie e pozzi e tutte cose utili e buone; e simile, assai fortezze sofficienti a tenersi da tutto il mondo e in tanta quantità che a' bisogni sono, e sufficiente a raccettare [accogliere] tutto il paese con tutto loro avere: e quest'è somma grazia a tutti i cittadini di e quai esse sono." Ibid., 112–113.

72. The fresco representing the procession of the Magi was painted between 1459 and 1463 for the chapel of the Palazzo Medici (now Medici-Riccardi). The Medici residence was commissioned from Michelozzo Michelozzi by Cosimo il Vecchio in the mid-fifteenth century.

73. Franconian was a language belonging to the West Germanic group, one of the Indo-European languages.

74. "Luogo cinto di muro o di siepe, dove si coltivano fiori, alberi, ecc., per delizia e non per guadagno." Tommaseo, *Dizionario della lingua italiana*, s.v. *giardino*.

75. It is not likely that the *orti* of the Medici start to be called *giardini* because they are surrounded by walls. In fact, the word *garden* appears in the archival sources much earlier (in 1373 and 1402) than the adjective *walled*, which is used to describe the kitchen gardens at Trebbio and Cafaggiolo around the 1450s.

76. ASF, MAP 17, fol. 29r: "Charisimo fratello credo abi ricevuta la mia lettera priegoti ti ricordi di mandarmi quella cornamusa in ongni modo . . . perchè ci verrà domenica di molte don[n]e e non se ne truova una in questo paese."

77. Comune di Firenze, *Mostra del Giardino Italiano*, 28, 29, 73, 74.

78. Ibid., 28–29.

79. Ibid., 45.

80. According to recent studies, Fiesole was commissioned by Cosimo's son Giovanni. In his life of Michelozzo di Bartolomeo Michelozzi, Vasari states that Fiesole was commissioned for Giovanni by Cosimo. See Giorgio Vasari, *Le vite de' più eccellenti pittori, scultori e architettori*, ed. Gaetano Milanesi (Florence: G. C. Sansoni, 1878–1885), 2:442.

81. Adriano Gradi, "Il paesaggio agrario-forestale toscano nel XV secolo e sue trasformazioni," in *L'arte al potere: Universi simbolici e reali nelle terre di Firenze al tempo di Lorenzo il Magnifico*, ed. Domenico Conci, Vittorio Dini, and Francesco Magnelli (Bologna: Editrice Compositori, 1992), 51.

82. Georgina Masson [Barbara Johnson], *Italian Gardens* (New York: Harry N. Abrams, 1961), 63.

83. Ibid., 72.

84. André Durand, *La Toscane: Album Monumental et Pittoresque exécuté sous la direction de M. le Prince Anatole Démidoff, dessiné d'apres nature par André Durand* (Paris: Lemercier, 1863). Commentary on the plate representing Cafaggiolo is at p. 15. A copy of the *Album* is located at the Gabinetto Disegni e Stampe degli Uffizi (henceforth GDSU), 109070 NA.

85. "Qui è un giardino lungo braccia 200, largo braccia 30 [about 117 meters by 17.5; 0.5 acres]." GDSU, 4920 A.

86. Giorgio Vasari il Giovane, *La città ideale: Piante di chiese [palazzi e ville] di Toscana e d'Italia*, ed. Virginia Stefanelli (Rome: Officina Edizioni, 1970).

87. The proportions of one to six between width and length of the garden described by Vasari, however, do not seem to correspond to those of its painted version. But Vasari was not very accurate in his representations. He ignored, for example, the fact that the four perimetric walls of the house, as well as those of the internal courtyard, are not parallel to each other.

88. In addition to this, we also need to consider that Utens's representation of the villas is not exactly faithful to their late sixteenth-century appearance. The lunette representing Castello, for instance, shows a garden whose central axis corresponds to that of the building, whereas this has never been the case (it was probably Tribolo's intention to expand the building in such a way as to have the two axes coincide, but the project was never carried out). Utens also regularized the perimeter of the upper terrace at Castello in its painted representation.

89. Tanaglia, "De agricultura," 1:25.

90. This technique was especially common on the hills around Florence, where vine-clad trees would not be planted along the contour lines of the hill, but rather would be planted perpendicularly to them, with rows parallel to one another and almost concentric. See Alessandro Guidotti, "Agricoltura e vita agricola nell'arte Toscana del Tre e Quattrocento (di alcune miniature fiorentine e senesi del XV secolo)," in Centro Italiano di Studi di Storia e d'Arte, *Civiltà ed economia agricola in Toscana nei secc. XIII–XV: Problemi della vita delle campagne nel tardo medioevo*, 53–101.

91. "Agli orti come a' prati squadra e lista / . . . / Se per tramite retto e pari sesti / fien compartiti, più grati saranno, / e par che me' la terra omor vi presti." Tanaglia, "De agricultura," 1:13, 15.

92. Cosimo, the first grand duke of Tuscany, belonging to the cadet branch of the Medici family descending from Lorenzo (brother of Cosimo il Vecchio), already favored Trebbio, where he had spent most of his childhood. In 1569 he left Careggi to his son Don Pietro, who died in 1604. It is only then that Careggi was added to the properties of Ferdinand I, but by then the Utens lunettes had already been painted.

93. "Il più bello paese di villate e il meglio accasato e ingiardinato e più nobilmente, per diletto de' cittadini, che altrettanta terra che fosse al mondo." Giovanni Villani, *Cronica fiorentina*, bk. IX, chap. CCCXVI (Florence, 1537).

94. "Campus Regis . . . gareggia con quella di Fiesole per dolcezza di clima, per delizie campestri, per amenità di situazione, e per essere la più copiosa di ville signorili di quante altre fanno corona ai popolatissimi e ridenti contorni della regina dell'Arno." Repetti, *Dizionario geografico*, 1:474.

95. Ficino mentions Careggi sporadically in few letters addressed to Cosimo and Lorenzo de' Medici. See, for example, Paul Oskar Kristeller, *Supplementum Ficinianum* (Florence: Olschki, 1937), 2:87–88. In these letters, however, he does not describe the villa.

96. In "I giardini della villa medicea di Careggi," in *Giardini medicei: Giardini di palazzo e di villa nella Firenze del Quattrocento*, 157–172, Daniela Mignani claims that such primary sources as the panegyric of Alberto Avogadro, the verses of Alessandro Braccesi, and a letter by Galeazzo Maria Sforza would afford the reconstruction of Careggi's fifteenth-century garden (157). However, as information on the actual layout of Careggi included in her sources is slim, she turns to the generic description of gardens found in contemporary architectural treatises and applies it to Careggi: "On the basis of Leon Battista Alberti's theory, 'an even area for the garden, a bosquet in the background and a stepped terrain is enough' to frame a fifteenth-century villa" (159). In *Le mutazioni di Proteo: I giardini medicei del Cinquecento* (Florence: Sansoni, 1981), Mila Mastrorocco speaks of Careggi's garden as if its Quattrocento layout were well known; she says, for example, that the analysis of the garden's morphological structure (which she does not carry out) allows us to see that the structure descends from philosophical principles. Unlike Mignani, who aims at an actual reconstruction of the garden, Mastrorocco relies on a notional image of Careggi, which she interprets on the basis of Neoplatonic philosophy.

97. The phrase "second nature" was used by Cicero in his *De natura deorum* (2.152), in which he refers to agriculture—and to the infrastructures created by people—as *alteram naturam*, that is, the second of two. See John Dixon Hunt, "The Idea of a Garden and the Three Natures," in *Greater Perfections: The Practice of Garden Theory* (Philadelphia: University of Pennsylvania Press, 2000), 32–75, and Thomas E. Beck, "Gardens as a 'Third Nature': The Ancient Roots of a Renaissance Idea," *Studies in the History of Gardens and Designed Landscapes* 22, no. 4 (Winter 2002), 327–334.

98. "Cosmo predetto soleva dire, che la casa loro di Cafaggiolo in Mugello vedeva meglio che quella di Fiesole, perchè ciò che quella vedeva era loro, il che di quella di Fiesole non avvenia." Angelo Poliziano, *I detti piacevoli*, ed. Mariano Fresta (Montepulciano, Siena: Editori del Grifo, 1985), 25.

99. "La villa fa buone bestie e cattivi uomini, e però usala poco: sta a la città e favvi o arte o mercatantia e capiterai bene." Brucker, "The Medici in the Fourteenth Century," 7 n. 36.

100. Piero di Cosimo sent his sons Lorenzo and Giuliano to Cafaggiolo during the days in which Cosimo was dying at Careggi. Once Piero de' Medici had died and Lorenzo started to take an active role in the political life of the city, he sent his wife Clarice and his children to the Mugello. See the letter that Clarice sends to Lorenzo from Cafaggiolo (MAP 37, fol. 379r, transcribed by Angelo Fabroni, *Laurentii Medicis Magnifici vita*, Pisa: J. Gratiolius, 1784, 2:288), and the brief letter that Lorenzo writes to her at Cafaggiolo on July 1479 (MAP 80, fol. 132r). Poliziano too lived at Cafaggiolo for a time as tutor and educator of the children, until his relationship with Clarice Orsini became unbearable and Lorenzo sent him to Fiesole. Maria Ginevra degli Alessandri lived at Trebbio after the death of her husband Giovanni di Cosimo in 1463. See Maurizio Martinelli, *Al tempo di*

Lorenzo: Viaggio nella Firenze dei Medici dal Palazzo di Via Larga al Contado e nella Toscana del '400 (Florence: FMG, 1992), 124, 127.

101. However, as Cosimo records in his *Ricordi* written in 1433, at a time of political difficulties when he feared for his own life he retired for several months to Trebbio, which was farther away from Florence than Careggi. See "Copia di Parlamento dell'anno 1433 e 34 levato da un libro di propria mano di Cosimo de' Medici, dove scriveva i suoi ricordi d'importanza; e fu levata detta copia da Luigi Guicciardini," in Giovanni Lami, *Deliciae eruditorum* (Florence: Petr. Caiet. Viviani, 1736–1769), 13:169–183.

102. See below Cosimo's biography by Vespasiano da Bisticci.

103. About the death of Cosimo and Piero di Cosimo at Careggi see Repetti, *Dizionario geografico,* 1:474. Contessina, Cosimo's wife, also died at Careggi. Martinelli, *Al tempo di Lorenzo,* 119.

104. It is known that in the last years of his life Piero di Cosimo, unable to walk, used to be carried about in a sedan chair.

105. "Contuli heri me in agrum Charegium, non agri, sed animi colendi gratia; veni ad nos, Marsili, quam primum. Fer tecum Platonis nostri librum de summo bono quem te isthic arbitror iam e graeca lingua in latinam, ut promiseras, transtulisse. Nihil enim ardentius cupio, quam quae via commodius ad felicitatem ducat cognoscere. Vale et veni non absque Orphica Lyra." Translation is from Marsilio Ficino, *The Letters of Marsilio Ficino,* with a preface by Paul Oskar Kristeller, 2nd ed. (New York: Gingko Press, 1985), 1:4.

106. "Referas . . . latine, Marsili, quae graece Xenocrates disputat." In *Marsilii Ficini in traductionem libri Xenocratis Platonici de morte praefatio;* cited by Curt Gutkind, *Cosimo de' Medici il Vecchio* (Florence: Marzocco, 1940), 326.

107. "D'agricoltura [Cosimo] era intendentissimo, et ragionavane come s'egli non avessi mai fatto altro. Et in Sancto Marco l'orto che v'è si fece con suo ordine, che fu degnissima cosa. Quando l'ordinò quello era un campo dove non era nulla, ch'era stato di certi frati v'erano stati inanzi lo riformassi Papa Eugenio. Il simile a tutte le sua posessioni, vi sono poche cose circa all'agricoltura che non fussino ordinate dallui, infiniti frutti et nesti." Vespasiano da Bisticci, *Le vite,* ed. Aulo Greco (Florence: Istituto Nazionale di Studi sul Rinascimento, 1976), 2:194–195.

108. The *vernaccia* is a variety of grape that was used to make white wine. See Laura de Angelis, "Tecniche di coltura agraria e attrezzi agricoli alla fine del Medioevo," in Centro Italiano di Studi di Storia e d'Arte, *Civiltà ed economia agricola in Toscana nei secc. XIII–XV: Problemi della vita delle campagne nel tardo medioevo,* 216.

109. ASF, *Scrittoio delle Regie Possessioni,* 4112, "Campione dei beni patrimoniali della famiglia Medici": "Una habitatione da signori chon orto murato chon chorte, prategli loggia et una chappella posta in Chareggi chon una vigna detta la vernaccia la quale se fa a nostre mani et chon uno podere chon detta abitatione che chostò fior. 1200, et di poi vi s'è murato per insino all'anno 1440 per fior. 1300 incircha, sicché si ragiona la detta habitatione chol detto podere fior. 2500. Lavoralo Domenicho Baroni et figliuoli." (Fol. 3v.) A copy of this document is included in an anonymous description of Careggi found at the BNCF, MSS. II, I, 469. A Latin version of the *lodo* is found in MAP 161, where Careggi is described in these terms: "Unam domum pro domino cum curia et lodia [?] et cum cappella et orto

murato et pratellis et cum duodecim poderibus et una vinea que vocatur la vigna della ver-naccia que bona posita sunt partem in populo Sancti Stefani in pane et partem in populo Sancti Peeri a Careggi que duodecim poderia sunt staiora." (Fol. 26r.) A Latin description of Careggi is also found in *Carte Strozziane*, series I, pezzo 10, fols. 62r–63v.

110. "Compera la villa per pascere la famiglia tua, non per darne diletto ad altri . . . fornisci la casa di quello bisogna e di quello può forse bisognare. Compera niuna di quelle cose, quali puoi prendere da e' tuoi terreni." Leon Battista Alberti, "Villa," in *Opere vol-gari*, ed. Cecil Grayson (Bari: Laterza, 1960), 1:359–363. This vernacular text, which was probably written in 1438, is a short treatise addressing the management of country estates. The word *villa* in the title refers to both the land and the house, although the latter is not the focus of the book and in general plays a minor role within the estate. The codex in which the text is included is the *Palatino* 267 of the Biblioteca Nazionale di Parma, which was found by Grayson in 1953.

111. Albinia De la Mare, "Cosimo and His Books," in *Cosimo 'il Vecchio' de' Medici, 1389–1464*, ed. Francis Ames-Lewis (Oxford: Clarendon Press, 1992), 115–156. The earliest inventory of Cosimo's books dates to 1417/18 and is a section, titled *Nello scriptoio di Cosimo*, of a larger inventory of his father's house called *Inventario di tutte le cose trovate in casa di Giovanni de' Medici* (ASF, MAP 129, fols. 11–12). The list was published for the first time by Fortunato Pintor, *La libreria di Cosimo de' Medici nel 1418* (Florence, 1902). Reprint, "Per la storia della libreria medicea nel Rinascimento. Appunti d'archivio. I: La libreria di Cosimo de' Medici nel 1418," *Italia medioevale e umanistica*, 3 (1960), 190–199. More books on agriculture are mentioned in a later inventory of the private library of the Medici com-piled in the year 1495 and published for the first time by Enea Piccolomini in 1875. There are three copies of this inventory in ASF, MAP 84, 104, 87. The document published by Piccolomini, MAP 87, is the most complete version. The inventory contained what re-mained of the private library after the Medici palace had been sacked in 1495.

112. De la Mare, "Cosimo and His Books," 127.

113. Marcus Tullius Cicero, *De senectute, de amicitia, de divinatione*, Loeb Classical Li-brary (1923), 68. Cosimo's copy is at the Biblioteca Medicea Laurenziana (henceforth BML), Laur. Plut. 76, I.

114. Ibid., 68. For the meaning of "second flitch" see M. E. Hirst, "Two Notes on Ci-cero," *Classical Review* 24, no. 2 (March 1910), 50–51.

115. Cicero, *De senectute,* 66. It unlikely that Cato himself would have agreed with the words that Cicero makes him pronounce in his dialogue, in that Cato's writings, which date back to the republican era, are more moralistic and his philosophy is more opposed to luxury. Cicero, on the other hand, lived in the age of the empire, during which there were fewer restraints, except that sin was expected to be shunned.

116. Ibid., 62.

117. Ibid., 64.

118. Ibid., 66.

119. It is useful to read the deathbed speech of Giovanni di Bicci de' Medici to his two sons Cosimo and Lorenzo reported by Silvano Razzi, in *Vite di cinque uomini illustri* (Florence: Giusti, 1602), 115. For Cosimo's way of life ibid., 175.

120. Berlin, Staatsbibliothek der Stiftung Preussischer Kulturbesitz, Hamilton 166.

121. George McCracken, "Cicero's Tusculan Villa," *Classical Journal* 30, no. 5 (February 1935), 261–277. See Marcus Tullius Cicero, *Letters to Atticus*, Loeb Classical Library (1912–1918), letters 1, 4–6, 8–11. On the influence of Cicero in the early Renaissance see Hans Baron, "Cicero and the Roman Civic Spirit in the Middle Ages and Early Renaissance," *Bulletin of the John Rylands Library* 22 (Manchester, 1938), 72–97.

122. *Maphei Vegii Laudensis de educatione liberorum et eorum claris moribus libri sex: A Critical Text of Books IV–VI*, ed. Sister Anne Stanislaus Sullivan (Washington, D.C.: Catholic University of America, 1936), xv.

123. Ibid., 215–220. The compendium is mentioned by Philip Ellis Foster, "A Study of Lorenzo de' Medici's Villa at Poggio a Caiano" (Ph.D. diss., Yale University, 1974), 1:318 n. 38.

124. Foster, "A Study of Lorenzo de' Medici's Villa at Poggio a Caiano," 1:17.

125. The text is housed in the Biblioteca Malatestiana at Cesena (S. VI 4 CS2).

126. Florence, Biblioteca Riccardiana 639; CS 65.

127. "Mi trovai un dì a ragionare collui, che sendo in Firenze il morbo, sendo lui non di molta età, si partirono di Firenze, et andarono a Careggi, et essendo di febraio, che è nel tempo si potano le viti, faceva duo degni exercitii, l'uno, com'egli si levava andava a potare delle vite, et per dua ore non faceva altro. In questo imitò Papa Bonifacio IX, che le vigne sotto al palagio del papa, a Roma, le fece porre lui, et ogni mattina . . . andava . . . a potare di sua mano parechie vite. . . . Ritornato Cosimo la matina da potare, aveva cominciato a legere i Morali di sancto Gregorio, opera degna, che sono libri trentasette, et dissi avergli letti tutti in mesi sei." Vespasiano, *Vite*, 2:195.

128. Dale Kent, *Cosimo de' Medici and the Florentine Renaissance: The Patron's Oeuvre* (New Haven: Yale University Press, 2000), 34.

129. "[È] cosa mirabile che, con queste tutte sua occupationi, non v'era nè nesto nelle posessioni ch'egli non avessi a memoria; et quando venivano a Firenze i contadini ne gli domandava et del frutto et del luogo dov'egli era, et di sua mano si dilettò di nestare et di potare." Vespasiano, *Vite*, 2:194.

130. ASF, MAP 11, fol. 628r: "Le fosse che voi avevate ordenate che ne facesseno, non si è fornita si no' una, cioè quella che giongue fino ad Terzolla. Dell'altre due che fanno pure quegli dell'Assagiolo, che sono ancho fornite: e queste sono ambedu[e] quelle che se muorono dala strada che viene ad Chareggie e vanno enverso casa dell'Assagiolo; altre fosse non c'è comenciate. Dele melarancie n'è seccho quello picchino ch'era scontra al canto de sotto dela colombaia, el quale non aveva si no' parecchie rampolii e non faceva ancora dele mele; gli altri stanno assai bene, ver'è che manchano loro adsai fogli[e], non so si fosse perchè ebbero tre di quegli gran venti e freddo, che Biascio gli tenne ad choprire fino al primo di' de gennaio, e si non fosse io, ancho non se coprivano. . . . A esvelto quello be' mela-grano ch'era ad man mancha al secondo viottolo, che fe' ogn'anno si belle mele. Le cham-bere furono fornite circha i diece di' di febbraio." Also transcribed by Foster, "A Study of Lorenzo de' Medici's Villa at Poggio a Caiano," 1:323 n. 51.

131. ASF, *Notarile Antecosimiano, Piero Calcagni*, fols. 80v–81r: "Un podere, anzi un palazzo con sua corte, loggia, pozzo, volta, cappella, stalle, colombaia, torre, orto murato,

con due case per i lavoratori, con terre lavorative vignate, ulivate e alberate, luogo detto Careggi, posto nel popolo di Santo Stefano in Pane." See Miranda Ferrara and Francesco Quinterio, *Michelozzo di Bartolomeo* (Florence: Salimbeni, 1984), 251–252. The text that I report is a copy of the original document extracted from Giuseppe Palagi, *Della Prioria di San Pietro a Careggi e del sigillo del suo primo rettore: Notizie storiche* (Florence: Tipi dei Successori di Le Monnier, 1871). BNCF, Passerini Miscellanee 129, 5–20. Another copy that I consulted is included in an anonymous manuscript at the BNCF, MSS. II.I.469. A description of Careggi at the time of Giovanni is also found in the *Catasto* 49 (1427), fols. 1140r–1171v; 1187r–1202v. A similar description is included in the *Piante dello Scrittoio delle Regie Possessioni*, serie tomi (8-1-7ff.; 8-4/5-9ff.; 43/44-24ff., microfilm 2). These last documents report that Cosimo il Vecchio, rather than his father Giovanni, bought Careggi from Tommaso Lippi on June 17, 1417.

132. ASF, MAP 83, doc. 89, fols. 499v–501r: "Uno luogho posto a Sampiero a Chareggi overo nel popolo della Pieve di Santo Stefano in pane, il quale abitiamo con chorte et orto et masseritie per nostro uso che dal primo et ij° via, a iij° Francescho di Ugholino Rucellai a iiij° il fiume di Terzolle, con più terreni lavorati e vignati et con frutti appartenenti a detto podere il quale lavora Domenicho di Sandro vochato . . . ad prestanza fiorini 20 buoi tiene da sse / rendeci l'anno in nostra parte . . . grano, orzo, fave [?], vino, olio." Fol. 499v. (A place located at San Piero at Careggi, that is, in the parish of the parish church of Santo Stefano in Pane, in which we live, with courtyard and kitchen garden, and farms for our own use, which is bordered by the road to the first and second sides, by Francesco di Ugolino Rucellai to the third side, and by the stream Terzolle to the fourth side, with many tilled fields and vineyards and fruit trees belonging to the said farm, which is tilled by Domenico di Sandro . . . yields every year wheat, barley, fava beans, wine and oil.)

133. Amanda Lillie, "Lorenzo's Rural Investments and Territorial Expansion," *Rinascimento: Rivista dell'Istituto Nazionale di Studi sul Rinascimento* 33, 2nd series (1993): 55.

134. About the relationship of Cosimo's son Piero to Careggi, little is known. In a letter written by Contessina de' Bardi, Cosimo's wife, to her other son, Giovanni, we read that Piero and his family used to go to Careggi to cure their health problems. The letter is from *VII Lettere di Contessina Bardi nei Medici, per nozze Zanichelli–Mariotti*, 1886. Cited by Foster, "A Study of Lorenzo de' Medici's Villa at Poggio a Caiano," 1:324 n. 52.

135. On the activities of the young Medicis at Cafaggiolo see the letters written by Francesco Fracassino to Piero di Cosimo in Florence in 1468: ASF, MAP 17, fol. 642. Partly transcribed by Foster, "A Study of Lorenzo de' Medici's Villa at Poggio a Caiano," 1:325 n. 59. See also MAP 16, fol. 273, in which Fracassino tells Lorenzo's father about his son's wish "spianare la piazza qui dinanzi a Chafaggiuolo." The letter is entirely transcribed by Foster, ibid., 326 n. 60.

136. See the letter written by Lorenzo in 1488 (ASF, MAP 59, fol. 185) in which he tells his addressee about hosting a friend and dining with him at Careggi, and then being in Florence the day after.

137. See the letters (ASF, MAP 33, fols. 337, 1026) published by Foster, "A Study of Lorenzo de' Medici's Villa at Poggio a Caiano," 1:328–329.

138. "Lorenzo è a Chareggi et per fuggire la noia et il disagio che harebbe su questa venuta del Duca di Ferara se n'andrà forse insino al Poggio, non però per più che per dua dì perchè l'aria di Chareggi è migl[i]ore." BNCF, Fondo Ginori Conti, 29, fol. 35, n. 4320513. See Foster, "A Study of Lorenzo de' Medici's Villa at Poggio a Caiano," 1:331 n. 80.

139. ASF, *Monte Comune o delle Graticole*, serie: Copie del Catasto; pezzo: 83: "Uno podere chon chasa da signore et da lavoratore posto a Chareggi nel popolo di Santo Stefano in pane. Il quale tengiamo per nostro abitare, con terre lavorative, vignate, ulivate, chon orto et pratelli et chon suoi vochabuli et chonfini, lavoralo Marcho di Jachopo . . . et fratelli di detto Marcho . . . rende in parte grano . . . vino . . . olio . . . biada." (Fol. 542r.) A copy of this description is found in *Catasto* 1016, II, microfilm 2462, fols. 460r–462v. Also *Decima repubblicana*, 28, fols. 450v–453r.

140. ASF, MAP 165, fol. 64: "Palagio di Chareggi sua masseritie et possessioni et altro. Uno palagio posto nel popolo di Sancto P[iero] et luogho detto Chareggi chon pratelli et orto et più sua abituri con sua vocabuli et confini di stima." This document, which reproduces the inventory compiled at the time of Lorenzo's death, is actually a copy drawn up by Simone di Stagio dalle Pozze for Lorenzo di Piero de' Medici in 1512, when the family was allowed to return to Florence. The copy was first transcribed by Aby Warburg (the typescript, in two vols., is at the Kunsthistorisches Institut in Florenz) and published for the first time by Marco Spallanzani and Giovanni Gaeta Bertelai, *Libro d'inventario dei beni di Lorenzo il Magnifico* (Florence: Studio per Edizioni Scelte, 1992). I use Spallanzani's transcription. An earlier inventory, called "Inventario delle chose di Chareggi questo di 12 di maggio 1482," is found in MAP 104, fols. 61–72v. The inventory mentions a storage room for the tubs; a few rooms for the farmer; a chapel; a loggia overlooking the kitchen garden; and a hencoop.

141. Among Lorenzo's books were a copy of Rutilius Palladius's *Opus agricolturae*, Ficino's *De religione christiana,* and Boccaccio's *Cento novelle* (ASF, MAP 165, fol. 73).

142. ASF, MAP 165, fol. 78: "Un palagio con torre, corti e orto, loggie."

143. Ibid., fol. 80: "Uno palagio posto nel popolo di Sancto Stefano in Pane, luogho detto il Palagio di Chareggi, con orto, corte, loggie e stalle e stanze da famiglia separata, granai e forni, chucine e più altri abituri e sale e camere al primo piano e nel detto palagio habituri a secondo, o/3 piano e volte, uno pratello grande innanzi e uno dirieto con fonte e acqua viva e più luoghi che venghono per chondotto, una loggia e vendemmia in sul pratello, cioè in testa una casetta che soleva essere a uso di lavoratore e oggi è al servigio di detto palagio."

144. A record of Lorenzo's planting of mulberry trees at Poggio a Caiano is to be found in ASF, MAP 43, fol. 66: "Et ho posto tanti mori al Poggio, che ho imparato quando sono giovani et teneri non si possano difendere dal vento senza un palo più grosso et più duro" (April 1489). The document is cited by Francis W. Kent, *Lorenzo de' Medici and the Art of Magnificence* (Baltimore: Johns Hopkins University Press, 2004), 207 n. 27. Kent explains that Lorenzo's interest in agriculture was commercial, as his planting of olive groves and thousands of mulberry trees seems to demonstrate. Ibid., 120–121.

145. Lillie, "Lorenzo's Rural Investments and Terrirorial Expansion," 60.

146. Ibid., 61.

147. Raymond Adrien De Roover, *The Rise and Decline of the Medici Bank, 1937–1494* (Cambridge: Harvard University Press, 1963), 366–367. Also Alison Brown, "Pierfrancesco de' Medici, 1430–1476: A Radical Alternative to Elder Medicean Supremacy?" in *The Medici in Florence: The Exercise of Language and Power* (Florence: L. S. Olschki; Perth: University of Western Australia Press, 1992), 93–94, 96–99, and esp. nn. 91 and 94. And Lillie, "Lorenzo's Rural Investments and Territorial Expansion," 62.

148. Lorenzo was not the first to be interested in the production of silk. Before him Giovanni Rucellai had started growing mulberry trees at Poggio a Caiano. See, for example, ASF, *Notarile Antecosimiano* 1749, fols. 63r–69: "Oltre alle rendite ordinarie di dette possessioni chome di sopra detto sa a chonsiderare che nel podere grande lungho il fiume vè alberi 500 in 600 di anni 8 ovvero 7 e alberi 40 grossi da tagliare ora e *mori 3 in 4 migliaia*, di anni 3 e di anni 2. Nei prati e boschi di ontani alberi 400 in 500 di anni 5 in 6" (emphasis added; the quotation is from the "Possessioni di Giovanni Rucellai," unfoliated between fols. 67–68); see also ASF, *Ospedale di San Matteo* 30, fol. 299r: "In sul detto podere lungho il fiume ve alberi 500 in 600 d'anni 8 overo 7 d'alberi grossi da tagliare et così 3 o 4 miglaia di mori d'anni 2 o d'anni 3."

149. Alessandro Braccesi dedicated his poem to Bernardo Bembo, the Venetian ambassador to Florence in the years 1475–1476 and 1478–1480.

150. The poem was published for the first time by Angelo Maria Bandini, *Catalogus codicum latinorum bibliothecae Mediceae Laurentianae* (Florence, 1776), 3:545. Here Bandini describes the *codice laurenziano* Plut. LXXXX Sup. Cod. XXXVII. It was attributed to Camerlini by William Roscoe, who published it in his first American edition of *The Life of Lorenzo de' Medici Called the Magnificent* (Philadelphia: Bronson and Chauncey, 1803), 2:188.

151. "Felici ville, campi, e voi, silvestri / boschi e fruttiferi arbori e gl'incolti / erbette, arbusti, e voi, dumi aspri e folti, / e voi, ridenti prati al mio amor destri; / piagge, colli, alti monti ombrosi, alpestri, / e fiumi ove i bè fonti son raccolti, / voi, animali domestici, e voi, sciolti, / ninfe, satiri, fauni e dii terrestri." Lorenzo's poem is the fourth sonnet of his *Canzoniere*. See *Lorenzo de' Medici: Tutte le opere*, ed. Paolo Orvieto (Rome: Salerno Editrice, 1992), 1:33–34. Also Gabriella Contorni, "'Felice ville, campi, e voi, silvestri boschi . . .': La villa di Careggi da Cosimo il Vecchio a Lorenzo il Magnifico," in *L'Arte al potere: Universi simbolici e reali nelle terre di Firenze al tempo di Lorenzo il Magnifico*, ed. Domenico Conci, Vittorio Dini, and Francesco Magnelli (Bologna: Editrice Compositori, 1992), 136.

152. Daniela Mignani, "I giardini di Careggi," in *L'architettura di Lorenzo il Magnifico*, ed. Gabriele Morolli et al. (Cinisello Balsamo: Silvana, 1992), 74–78. See esp. 74.

153. Braccesi's poem, however, must not have left his addressee disappointed, considering the fact that his list of plants was a conventional fifteenth-century *descriptio*. Also, as the poet refers to the garden of Careggi hyperbolically, that is, he compares it to well-known mythical gardens, his contemporary readers would have also been able to understand the degree of its distinction among other pleasances. See Appendix B.

154. Bice Agnoletti, *Alessandro Braccesi: Contributo alla Storia dell'Umanesimo e della Poesia Volgare* (Florence: Seeber, 1901), 104–105.

155. Braccesi hints at Bembo's suggestion of writing a poem on the *hortus* in the very first lines of the poem: "Ne me, forte, putes oblitum, Bembe, laboris / Propositi nuper cum meliore mihi." Ibid., 105.

156. Alison Brown promised a full account of the *Collectiones*, which is located at the BML in Florence (MS. Plut. LIV, 10), but she does not seem to have published it. At any rate, upon a recent examination of the manuscript collection I was able to determine that the second poem on Careggi, supposedly written by Migliore Cresci, is not included in the *Collectiones Cosmianae*. It is possible that Bice Agnoletti made a mistake and that the poem is to be found somewhere else—after all, as Alessandro Perosa has demonstrated, Agnoletti's biography has many flaws: e.g., it does not recognize the name of Migliore Cresci within Braccesi's verses and takes the word *Melior* to mean someone who is for Braccesi a *better* poet than himself. On the contrary, Braccesi does not seem to doubt his superiority with respect to Migliore.

157. Apparently, the erudite Braccesi, who called himself Alexander Braccius, made use of the same references in his epistolary exchanges, as Paul Oskar Kristeller has pointed out in "An Unknown Correspondence of Alessandro Braccesi with Niccolò Michelozzi, Naldo Naldi, Bartolomeo Scala, and Other Humanists (1470–1472) in Ms. Bodl. Auct. F. 2. 17," in *Classical, Mediaeval and Renaissance Studies in Honor of Berthold Louis Ullman,* ed. Charles Henderson, Jr. (Rome: Edizioni di Storia e Letteratura, 1964), 2:311–342. Kristeller writes, "Aside from few references to classical mythology, there are occasional mentions of Latin prose writers such as Cicero . . . and in one instance Braccesi makes extensive use of Pliny's *Natural History* (29.I, cf. f. 139–140v). Still greater familiarity Braccesi had with the classical Latin poets, for he cites lines from Virgil (f. 120v, probably after *Aen.* 10.283), and especially from Ovid (f. 133 after *Fasti* I. 487–496) without mentioning the quotation," 329.

158. This method of composition was not uncommon in the fifteenth century. It also characterized, for instance, the lyric writings of Leon Battista Alberti (see Anthony Grafton, *Leon Battista Alberti: Master Builder of the Italian Renaissance* [New York: Hill and Wang, 2000]), and will later find its apotheosis with Angelo Poliziano. The similarity between Alberti's compositions and Braccesi's has been pointed out by Alessandro Perosa, "Note e discussioni: Miscellanea di filologia umanistica," *Rinascita: Rivista del Centro Nazionale di Studi sul Rinascimento* 5 (1942), 323–331.

159. The poem was published for the first time by Lami, *Deliciae eruditorum,* 12:117–149. However, as Ernst H. Gombrich has pointed out, the text published by Lami is corrupted by the many "transpositions and omissions" of the original, which is found in Bartolomeo Scala's *Collectiones Cosmianae* (BML, Plut. 54, cod. 10, n. LIV). Gombrich has therefore collated and edited the correct text of Avogadro's poem, which he found included in another collection of the BML (Laur. 34, 46, fol. 28r). See Gombrich, "Alberto Avogadro's Descriptions of the Badia of Fiesole and of the Villa of Careggi," *Italia medioevale e umanistica* 5 (1962), 217–229. It is surprising to note that most garden historians refer to the corrupted text published by Lami. This text, however, at the point in which the description of the villa is supposed to begin (book 2), omits twenty-three lines that are

found in the correct codex, and erroneously includes a section that relates to the church interior at the Badia Fiesolana (book 1).

160. Gombrich, "Alberto Avogadro's Descriptions of the Badia of Fiesole and of the Villa of Careggi," 229: "O speculam insignem! Resides si forte fenestrae, / Spectabis villam, ruris et omne decus. / Atque videbis uti claro de fonte fluentum / Spargitur, et parvo flumine prata rigat. / Prata, inquam, variis distincta coloribus, atque / Distincto redolet flamine [ut] missus [est] odor" (fol. 44v). My translation.

161. Ibid.: "In foribus tua signa vigent, / caelataque in auro / Stat pila, quae ardenti rubra colore micat" (fol. 43v). My translation.

162. See, for example, James Ackerman, *The Villa: Form and Ideology of Country Houses* (Princeton: Princeton University Press, 1990), 72; Mignani, "I giardini della villa medicea di Careggi," 159; idem, "I giardini di Careggi," 74.

163. "Polideza di giardini, che invero sono pur tropo ligiadra cosa." The letter was published by Benjamin von Buser, *Die Beziehungen der Mediceer zu Frankreich während der Jahre 1434–1494 in ihrem Zusammenhang mit den allgemeinen Verhältnissen Italiens* (Leipzig: Verlag von Duncker & Humblot, 1879), 347–348. See Appendix A.

164. On the celebrations that took place in Florence for the visit of both Pope Pius II and Galeazzo Maria Sforza, who was then only fifteen years old, see Guglielmo Volpi, *Le feste di Firenze: Notizia di un poemetto del secolo XV* (Pistoia: Libreria Pagnini, 1902). An anonymous description of the celebrations is also found in *Rerum italicarum scriptores: Raccolta degli storici italiani dal cinquecento al millecinquecento*, comp. L. A. Muratori, ed. Giosuè Carducci and Vittorio Fiorini, vol. 17, pt. 1 (Città di Castello: S. Lapi, 1907).

165. Gabriella Contorni, *La villa medicea di Careggi* (Florence: Lo Studiolo, 1992), 18–19. Idem, "'Felici ville, campi, e voi, silvestri boschi . . . ': La villa di Careggi da Cosimo il Vecchio a Lorenzo il Magnifico," 133–136. Despite the title, from which the reader would expect a treatment of the garden/landscape at Careggi, the article is about the correspondence between Alberti's precepts in his *De re aedificatoria* and the internal distribution of rooms at the villa.

166. See note 96.

167. On the drawing we read a handwritten note: "Pianta di Careggi, innanzi è un grand.mo prato, in testa del quale, e una loggia ed una fonte dove è il segno A." (Plan of Careggi, in front of which is a very large meadow, and at its head is a loggia and wellspring indicated by the letter A.) The plan is located at the GDSU, n. 4907A. Vasari's drawing is not very accurate, as he regularized the perimeter of the building, which he represented as perpendicular to the main road.

168. Cosimo was forced to leave Florence in October 1433. Michelozzo's works at Careggi are usually dated sometime after the return of Cosimo from his exile in 1434 and up to 1440. The *lodo divisorio* between Cosimo and his nephew Pierfrancesco (see note 109), in fact, reports that substantial funds were invested for the expansion of the property up to the year 1440.

169. The plan belongs to a volume entitled *Descrizione geografica di tutti i beni che nel presente stato gode e possiede il Sere.mo Gran Duca nostro signore nella sua fattoria di Careggi*

fatta nel anno MDCLXXXXVI da Giovannozzo Giovannozzi Ingegnere e agrimensore fiorentino.
ASF, *Piante dello Scrittoio delle Regie Possessioni,* serie tomi (8-47/48-26, microfilm 2).

170. Giuseppe Ruggieri is the author of the plan from 1742. This is part of a collection of drawings entitled *Piante de' palazzi, giardini, ville et altre fabbriche dell'Altezza Reale del Serenis. Gran Duca di Toscana,* found at the BNCF, Pal. 3.B.I.5. The 1769 plan (ASF, *Scrittoio delle Regie Possessioni,* piante topografiche, fol. 68, microfilm 1) shows a large *orto* and *prato* within the walls of the villa and two smaller *orti* to the south (left-hand side of the drawing). For the date of the drawing see ASF, *Scrittoio delle Regie Possessioni,* piante topografiche, fol. 56, microfilm 1. James Ackerman says that the drawing was the pendant to a plan, called Careggi Nuovo, representing Michelozzo's expansion of Careggi for Cosimo il Vecchio, located at the ASF, Mannelli-Galilei-Riccardi n. 315 (see Ackerman, *The Villa,* 289 n. 14). The drawing shows Careggi's southern garden subdivided into nine regular compartments called *giardino.* If the intention of the author was that of representing Careggi at the time of Michelozzo's intervention, as Ackerman suggests, then we can say that Michelozzo was also responsible for the first layout of the garden. However, I think that the drawing represents the villa as it appeared in the eighteenth century, that is, at the time it was drawn. After all, the restoration of the villa sponsored by Duke Alessandro de' Medici in the sixteenth century did not modify substantially Michelozzo's architecture, whose Quattrocento appearance remained unaltered until the 1700s. This is also confirmed by the fact that comparison with other plans of Careggi Nuovo (see for example ASF, *Piante dello Scrittoio delle Regie Possessioni,* serie tomi, 8-3-4, microfilm 2) shows that part of the gardens were used for the growing of dwarf fruit trees, whose cultivation was introduced by Cosimo I. Therefore, it is unlikely that the layout of the garden as it is shown on the plan of Careggi Nuovo can be attributed to Michelozzo. The two drawings of the old and new Careggi were published together, without commentary, by Mignani in "I giardini della villa medicea di Careggi," 161.

171. It is surprising that of the three plans only the latest one, which contains the least information about the outdoors of the villa, has been published. A reason for this may be that the two earlier drawings do not represent the "typical" Italian garden, whose design is usually attributed to Michelozzo.

172. See note 109.

173. "Mira qui di Careggi all'aure amene / Marsilio e 'l Pico, e cento egregi spirti; / E dì, se all'ombra degli Elisi mirti, / tanti n'ebber giammai Tebe et Atene."

174. Giuseppe Zocchi, *Vedute delle ville, e d'altri luoghi della Toscana* (Florence: G. Bouchard, 1744). Zocchi portrayed all of the Medici villas in a portfolio. The preparatory drawings for the engravings are housed in the Pierpont Morgan Library (New York).

175. Mignani, "I giardini della villa medicea di Careggi," 157.

176. Mastrorocco, *Le mutazioni di Proteo,* 15.

177. Ibid., 17. Here Mastrorocco says that the presence of the "bosquet (contraposition of garden and forest) and the fountain in the grotto (*ninfeo*), shows the close relationship between the design of the garden and a precise ideological program, which established literary forms nourished with a fabric of allusions and associations perfectly known to the elite

of the clients and makers." Indeed, the grotto, which according to Mastrorocco derives from a specific ideological program the client shared with the architect, was built much later, that is, around 1617, when Cardinal Carlo de' Medici commissioned the restoration of the villa from the architect Giulio Parigi. The grotto was built in place of a storage room once located under the main room on the ground floor of the villa, used to store both oil and wine. ASF, *Scrittoio delle Regie Possessioni*, 4307, fol. 6; ASF, MAP 165, fols. 64–77.

178. James Hankins, *Plato in the Italian Renaissance* (Leiden: E. J. Brill, 1990), 1:296.

179. Ibid., 296–297. From Diogenes Laertius's *Lives of the Philosophers* (III, 7) we learn that in the fourth century B.C. Plato used to teach at a place called the Academy, which was "a suburban place of exercise planted like a grove, so named from an ancient hero named Hecademus, as Eupolis tells us in his *Discharged Soldiers*." According to Dicaearchus, as quoted by Plutarch in his mythical account of *Theseus*, Academus, or Echedemus, was an Arcadian hero who revealed Helen's hiding place. He "had come to Attica on Theseus's invitation. The Spartans certainly treated him with great honor while he was alive and, in their later invasions, spared his small estate on the river Cephissus, six stadia distant from Athens. This is now called the Academia: a beautiful, well-watered garden, where philosophers meet and express their irreligious views on the nature of the gods." See Robert Graves, *The Greek Myths* (Harmondsworth: Penguin Books, 1960), 1:366–369. It may be worthwhile to point out that Plutarch, the historian, speaks of a grove, whereas in the mythical account by Diogenes, the *locus* of the Academy is a beautiful garden. Robin Osborne has pointed out that "no Platonic dialogue is set in a garden, although more than one is set out of doors as Socrates and his interlocutor or interlocutors take a promenade outside the city walls." See Osborne, "Classical Greek Gardens: Between Farm and Paradise," in *Garden History: Issues, Approaches, Methods*, ed. John Dixon Hunt (Washington, D.C.: Dumbarton Oaks Research Library and Collection, 1992), 373–391. Ficino's fullest account of Plato's Academy is given in his *Life of Plato*, composed in 1477 as a letter to Francesco Bandini and later reprinted in his *Platonis opera omnia* of 1484. See *Marsilii Ficini Opera*, with an introduction by Stéphane Toussaint (Paris: Phénix Éditions, 2000), 1: fols. 763–770. Also Ficino, *The Letters*, 3:32–48.

180. Hankins, *Plato in the Italian Renaissance*, 1:297.

181. Ficino, *Opera*, 1: fol. 769. The property that Cosimo gave Ficino was described as a *praedium*, the Latin equivalent of *podere*. Reference to a *podere* called *Le Fontanelle* donated to Ficino is found in ASF, *Piante dello Scrittoio delle Regie Possessioni*, serie tomi (8-10/11-12, microfilm 2). The document reports, however, that the property was donated by Lorenzo de' Medici.

182. Hankins, *Plato in the Italian Renaissance*, 1:298.

183. James Hankins, "The Myth of the Platonic Academy of Florence," *Renaissance Quarterly* 44, no. 3 (Autumn 1991), 429–475; 436.

184. Benedetto Colucci, *Scritti inediti di Benedetto Colucci da Pistoia*, ed. Arsenio Frugoni (Florence: Olschki, 1939).

185. Hankins, "The Myth of the Platonic Academy of Florence," 445. It is useful to point out that it was only in 1638 that the Florentine Academy was called "Platonic," that is,

when the cardinal Leopoldo de' Medici tried to bring the old *gymnasium* back to life and give it a more defined structure. See Arnaldo della Torre, *Storia dell'Accademia Platonica di Firenze* (Florence: Tipografia G. Carnesecchi, 1902), 20. The title, in fact, appeared in an oration delivered by Gaudenzio Paganini at the University of Pisa: *De Platonica Academia Serenissimi Principis Leopoldi ab Etruria: Nuncius allatus Calendis Novembris in Magna Aula celeberrimi Gymnasii Pisani.* This document is also mentioned by Hankins ("The Myth of the Platonic Academy of Florence," 430), who, however, must not find it very relevant, given the fact that he looks for traces of a "Platonic Academy" in the fifteenth century. On the other hand, the so-called Florentine Academy was formally established by Cosimo I in the first half of the sixteenth century. A document written on February 23, 1541, reports that the duke "Considerando . . . e desiderando che i fedelissimi suoi popoli ancor si facciano più ricchi e si onorino di quel buono e bello che Iddio ottimo massimo ha dato loro, cioè l'eccellenza della propria lingua . . . acciochè i virtuosi . . . nella sua felicissima accademia fiorentina . . . possano più ardentemente seguitare i dotti loro esercizi . . . delibera che l'autorità onore e privilegi, gradi salario ed emolumenti ed ogni e tutto che ha conseguito e si appartiene al Rettore dello Studio di Firenze, da ora innanzi appartenga e sia pienamente del magnifico consolo della già detta Accademia Fiorentina." The document is included in the *Notizie letterarie ed istoriche intorno agli uomini illustri dell'Accademia Fiorentina* (Florence, 1700). This work, written by Iacopo Rilli, is in two parts, only the first of which was published. The second part is a manuscript at the BNCF (Magl., classe IX, 42). Cited by Enrico Bindi, "Della vita e delle opere di Bernardo Davanzati," in *Le opere di Bernardo Davanzati*, ed. Enrico Bindi (Florence: Le Monnier, 1852–1853), 1:xviii n. 2.

186. Hankins, "The Myth of the Platonic Academy of Florence," 449.

187. Ibid., 455–456.

188. Kristeller, *Supplementum Ficinianum*, 2:87. The letter is included in the *Collectiones Cosmianae* (Laur. Ms. Plut. LIV, 10), fols. 81r–81v. See James Hankins, "Cosimo de' Medici and the 'Platonic Academy,'" *Journal of the Warburg and Courtauld Institutes* 53 (1990), 144–162.

189. Hankins, "The Myth of the Platonic Academy of Florence," 455.

190. Gentile is cited by Hankins, ibid.

191. For example, Aristotle and scholastic philosophy formed part of the curriculum at the university; moreover, Cosimo and his son Piero showed their interest in the Peripatetic school when they favored the invitation of the Aristotelian philosopher and Byzantine scholar John Argyropoulos to lecture at the *Studio fiorentino*. Hankins, "Cosimo de' Medici and the Platonic Academy," 148. As for Lorenzo, it is unlikely that he thought of applying the principles of Neoplatonic philosophy to garden design. We know that he showed an interest in Platonism only late in life (1473–1476), see *Lorenzo de' Medici: Tutte le opere*, 1:14; moreover, had he wanted to "design" a garden, he would have commissioned it from his architect Giuliano da Sangallo. And there is no record of Sangallo ever working on a garden at Careggi (we only know that he built the *loggetta ionica* on the first floor and to the west side of the villa shortly before the death of Il Magnifico. See Giuseppe Marchini, *Giuliano da Sangallo* (Florence: Sansoni, 1942), 91.

192. According to Cesare Vasoli, "Michelozzo—che scomparve nel '72—non potè neppure vedere la stampa del volgarizzamento della prima opera pubblicata dal Ficino, il *De christiana religione*, edito, prima del testo latino, forse verso la fine del '74. . . . Sicchè egli restò estraneo alla profonda incidenza delle dottrine ficiniane dell'eros e della bellezza sulla cultura artistica e sulle tradizioni iconologiche della civiltà figurativa fiorentina." Vasoli, "Michelozzo e la cultura fiorentina del suo tempo," in *Michelozzo: Scultore e architetto (1396–1472)*, ed. Gabriele Morolli (Florence: Centro Di, 1998), 15.

193. See note 165.

194. Amanda Lillie, "The Humanist Villa Revisited," in *Language and Images of Renaissance Italy*, ed. Alison Brown (Oxford: Clarendon Press, 1995), 200.

195. Hankins says that also at Lorenzo's time "Ficino was no doubt a frequent visitor at his neighbor's villa, and we know of several occasions when he 'disputed' with Lorenzo at Careggi." Hankins, "The Myth of the Platonic Academy of Florence," 455.

196. Moreni, *Notizie istoriche*, 1:52; 2:114.

197. "Servì poi sotto il Magnifico Lorenzo di asilo ai sublimi ingegni di quella fioritissima età. Ce lo fa sapere il Poliziano . . . in una lettera tra le altre del medesimo scritta al predetto Lorenzo de' Medici . . . : Sed ego quoque tuum imitatus exemplum, per istos extremae quadragesimae dies, ceu fugitivus urbis, assiduus in Faesulano fui cum Pico Mirandula, meo, Coenobiumque illud ambo Regularium Canonicorum frequentavimus, avi tui sumptibus exstructum. Quia Abbas in eo Matthaeus Bossus Veronensis, homo sanctis moribus, integerrimaque vita, sed et litteris politioribus mire cultus; ita nos humanitate sua quadam tenuit, et suavitate sermonis, ut ab eo digressi; mox ego, et Picus soli propemodum relicti (quod antea fere non accidebat) nec esse alter alteri iam satis videremur etc." Angelo Maria Bandini, *Lettere XII nelle quali si ricerca, e s'illustra l'antica e moderna situazione della città di Fiesole e suoi contorni* (Siena: Bindi, 1800), 117–118. Poliziano's letter, says Bandini, was published for the first time as a preface to the work by Matteo Bosso entitled *De veris ac salutaribus animi gaudiis*, published in 1491. Giuseppe del Rosso, in his *Guida di Fiesole e suoi dintorni* (Florence: Luigi Pezzati, 1846) uses almost the same words Bandini uses.

198. "Tu velim, quando Caregianum tuum sextili mense nimis destuat adis, rusculum hoc nostrum Faesulanum ne fastidias. Multum enim heic aquarum habemus; ut in convalle minimum solis, vento certe numquam destituimur. Tum villula ipsa devia, quum paene media silva delitescat, totam tamen aestimare Florentiam potest. Et quum sit in proximo celebritas maxima semper apud nos tamen solitudo est mera, qualem profecto secessus amat: uti poteris autem duplici spe. Nam saepius e Querceto suo me Picus invisit, improvisus obrepens, extractumque de latebra secum ducit ad coenulam, qualem nosti, frugi quidem, sed et scitam, plenamque semper iucundi sermonis, et loci. Tu tamen ad me potius: non enim peius hic coenabis, bibes fortasse vel melius: nam de vini quidem palma cum Pico quoque ipso valde contenderim." The excerpt is from *Angeli Politiani et aliorum virorum illustrium epistolarum libri duodecim* (Basel, 1522), bk. 10, letter 14. Moreni quotes only part of the letter in *Notizie istoriche*, 2:122. The Latin text of the letter is fully cited by Bandini, *Lettere XII,* 119. The translation is from Ackerman, *The Villa,* 76–77, 289 n. 22.

199. "Talia Faesuleo lentus meditabar in antro / rure suburbano Medicum, qua mons sacer urbem / Maeoniam longique volumina despicit Arni, / qua bonus hospitium felix placidamque quietem / indulget Laurens, Laurens haut ultima Phoebi / gloria, iactatis Laurens fida ancora Musis." Cited by Moreni, *Notizie istoriche*, 2:145. See also Bandini, *Lettere XII*, 118. The Latin text is from Angelo Poliziano, *Silvae*, ed. Francesco Bausi, (Florence: Olschki, 1996), 98–99.

200. "Sotto questo beato cielo, e tra gli ameni passeggi delle circonvicine colline, quasi che risorta fosse la celebre Accademia di Platone, si meditavano le più profonde scienze, e l'opere di Platone medesimo, come pure di Plotino, Iamblico, Proclo e d'altri; e se noi osserveremo il cap. I del Comento sopra il Convivio di Platone, fu rinnovellata, come in antico, la memoria di lui nella villa di Careggi da Lorenzo dei Medici . . . lo che si fece per sollevar l'animo dalle profonde applicazioni che in questa villa di Fiesole s'intraprendevano." Bandini, *Lettere XII*, 121–122. My translation.

201. Besides Poliziano, also Benedetto Varchi was often a guest at the Medici villa of Fiesole, as some of his sonnets show: "In te gradito avventuroso monte [Fiesole], / Ove del volgo ognor tanto si perde, / Adoro io di fornir tutti i miei giorni." Bandini, *Lettere XII*, 123.

202. Andrea Razzi wrote a poem, entitled "Verna profectio," in which he praises the landscape at Fiesole: "Ardua Fesulae menso fastigie molis [nolis?] / Ad Boream modico se vertice Regius affert / Mons scatebris praedives aquae, vernaque perenni, / Tergemino quae fonte cadit, strepituque canoro / Grata viatorem liquidas invitat ad umbras." See Moreni, *Notizie istoriche*, 2:122–123. Cristoforo Landino and Ugolino Verino too wrote elegies in which Fiesole is praised, and they are all dedicated to Piero di Cosimo de' Medici, as Bandini reports. Verino's poem, entitled "De liberalitate Petri Medices in omnes doctos," is at BML, Cod. 42 Plut. 39 (see Bandini, *Lettere XII*, 120, 123, 145). For Pier Crinito's poem see Bandini, *Lettere XII*, 120.

203. See note 200.

204. Repetti, *Dizionario geografico, fisico, storico della Toscana*, 2:117.

205. "E per Giovanni figliuolo di Cosimo de' Medici fece a Fiesole, il medesimo [Michelozzo], un altro magnifico e onorato palazzo, fondato dalla parte di sotto nella scoscesa del poggio con grandissima spesa, ma non senza grande utile, avendo in quella parte da basso fatto volte, cantine, stalle, tinaie, ed altre belle e commode abitazioni. Di sopra poi, oltre le camere, sale e altre stanze ordinarie, ve ne fece alcune per libri, e alcune altre per la musica." Bandini, *Lettere XII*, 116.

206. "Nel monte di Fiesole, dove che è uno luogo di romiti di santo Gironimo, lui fece fabricare una chiesa molto divota e degna secondo la qualita d'essa, e ancora uno degno luogo propinquo, refriggerio quando laire campestre pigliare voleva. E così ancora lui si dilettava in varie gentilezze, e di libri e d'intagli antichi, e ancora di strumenti e d'altre cose varie, e gentilezze, e massime in questo edificare." Filarete, *Trattato di Architettura*, ed. Anna Maria Finoli and Liliana Grassi (Milan: Il Polifilo, 1972), 2:692. Also Philip Ellis Foster, "Donatello Notices in Medici Letters," *Art Bulletin* 62, no. 1 (March 1980), 148–149. See in particular 149 n. 9.

207. "Furono si la Chiesa, come il Convento, che gl'è unito restaurati, augumentati, e quasi da fondamenti interam[ent]e rifatti insieme con il bellissimo Palazzo che gl'è sotto da Giovanni." Quoted by Ferrara and Quinterio, *Michelozzo di Bartolomeo*, 253.

208. The first biography of Giovanni appeared at the end of the nineteenth century, and was written by Vittorio Rossi, *L'indole e gli studi di Giovanni di Cosimo de' Medici: Notizie e documenti*, Rendiconti dell'Accademia dei Lincei, Classe di scienze morali, storiche e filologiche, no. 5, vol. 2 (Rome: L'Accademia, 1893), 38–60; 129–150.

209. Carocci, *I dintorni di Firenze*, 1:119. Idem, *Fiesole: Breve illustrazione dei suoi monumenti pubblicata nella circostanza dell'inaugurazione del museo e degli scavi fiesolani* (Florence, 1874), 10. Ackerman too accepts Cosimo's role. See *The Villa*, 73.

210. Foster, "Donatello Notices in Medici Letters," 148–150.

211. Amanda Rhoda Lillie, "Giovanni di Cosimo and the Medici Villa at Fiesole," in *Piero de' Medici, "il Gottoso" (1416–1469): Kunst im Dienste der Medicer*, ed. Andreas Beyer and Bruce Boucher (Berlin: Akademie Verlag, 1993), 189–206. See, for example, ASF, MAP 82, doc. 182, fol. 591r.

212. ASF, MAP 9, fol. 175, fol. 185, fol. 307; MAP 138, fol. 46; MAP 6, fol. 756; MAP 7, fol. 343; MAP 9, fol. 178; MAP 16, fol. 56. See Foster, "Donatello Notices in Medici Letters," 148–150; Howard Saalman, *Filippo Brunelleschi: The Cupola of Santa Maria del Fiore* (London: A. Zwemmer, 1980), 221 n. 9; Lillie, "Giovanni di Cosimo and the Medici Villa at Fiesole," 202–203 n. 48. Two of the overseers who used to write to the young Medici were Giovanni Macinghi and Giovanni di Luca Rossi, in the mid-1450s. Also, from 1457 onward, a canon at Fiesole, Antonio, reported on the construction of both the monastery and the villa. In addition, records show that Piero de' Medici, Cosimo's elder son, also informed his brother about the works at the villa when the latter was away (ASF, MAP 138, fol. 50; MAP 9, fols. 175, 178; MAP 7, fols. 301, 298), as did his wife Ginevra degli Alessandri.

213. Lillie, "Giovanni di Cosimo and the Medici Villa at Fiesole," 196.

214. The relationship between interior and exterior space at Fiesole has been addressed by Christoph Luitpold Frommel, *Die Farnesina und Peruzzis Architektonisches Frühwerk* (Berlin: De Gruyter, 1961), 86–89.

215. ASF, MAP 5, fol. 722v: "Bartolommeo Serragli va in fra 8 dì a Napoli; 'o gli ho fatto uno richordo di più chosse vogliamo per a Fiesole, cioè melaghrani, melaranci, limonciegli, faetri [*sic*] e alchuna altra chosa." (Bartolommeo Serragli will be going to Naples in eight days and I made a note for him of everything that we need for Fiesole, that is, pomegranates, orange trees, lemon trees . . . and some other things.) The quotation is from Lillie, "Giovanni di Cosimo and the Medici Villa at Fiesole," 205 n. 68.

216. ASF, MAP 9, fol. 307r. This is a letter from Antonio, the canon at Fiesole, to Giovanni de' Medici: "Non si fà nulla ne dà frutti e anchora de melaranci stanno molto male. Anno dato ordine di choprilli inanzi che fredo venga. Sarebbe buono facessi uno verso a'llui dicessi quello sa a fare al fatto delle siepe e dei cipressi si fare quanto ci avisasti. . . . E per 2 toppe, una per la cholonbaia e per l'uscio del lavoratore lire 1 soldi 15. [Right margin:] Tutte le sopradette opre sono misse a fare una fongna a murelle nella chorte de chavagli che riceve tutta l'aqua viene dall'orto di sopra, faccia gran danno di sotto e bisongna la facciamo fare tanto chella escha di fuori. Se voi volete e altra chosa fatta insino a questo dì" (October 13, 1457). Reference to the digging of ditches for the planting of vines is found in MAP 6, fol. 756r: "Io vi scrissi de fatti de maglioli non sono venuti se voi volessi chio mandassi per essi in nessuno luogo avisatemene per lo aportatore. Inperò, non si può fornire la fossa se

non ci sono perché'llavorino, chominceranno oggi, lasceranno voto tra la grotta el muro. Sarebbe di bisogno che Ormanno ci venisse per più chagione, prima che'lla fossa non si può fornire per amore dell'uscita sua. Vorrei la vedessi innazi che'lla fornisseno per pigliare migliore partito e anche per amore di quell'altre faciano e paesani."

217. ASF, MAP 82, doc. 182, fol. 591r: "Una chasa overo chasamento chon risedo orto et ortali tutti ridotti a uno tenere posto nel popolo della chalonicha di Fiesole luogo detto affiesole che da tutto confina a primo $^1/_2$, $^1/_3$, via, a $^1/_4$ beni della chalonicha di Fiesole, conprati i terreni da più persone." The word *risedio, resedio*, or *resede*, may indicate a grassy area located in front of the building corresponding to the main entrance. However, the term may also indicate a small service building located near the landowner's house, in which case it probably refers to the building on the lower terrace.

218. ASF, MAP, 149, doc. 21, fol. 40v: "camera sopra allorto." The inventory has been published by Donata Mazzini, ed., *Villa Medici a Fiesole: Leon Battista Alberti e il prototipo di villa rinascimentale* (Florence: Centro Di, 2004), 205–206.

219. "1 roncone da tagliare siepi." ASF, MAP, 149, doc. 21, fol. 40r. Hedges were necessary around kitchen gardens and cultivated fields because they served the function of protecting them from wild and/or domestic animals.

220. ASF, *Catasto* 1016, II, microfilm 2462, fols. 465r–466v: "Una casa, hovero chasamento chon risedio, orto e ortale ridotti a uno tenere, nel popolo della Chalonicha di Fiesole in luogho detto a Fiesole."

221. ASF, MAP 164, fols. 2r and 9r: "Una chasa overo chasamento co re[se]di orto ortoli pratelli tutti ridotti aun tenere posti nel popolo della chalonicha di Fiesole luogo detto affiesole e una chasa da lavoratore fratoio da olio e con più pezzi di terre lavorate e vitate e terre sode e luoghi da cave di sassi con tutte sue appartenenze." (A house or rather a dwelling with *risedio*, kitchen garden, market gardens, and meadows, all belong to the same property, located in the parish of the presbytery of Fiesole, a place called at Fiesole and a farmhouse with oil mill and with a number of tilled fields, vineyards, unfarmed land, and quarries with all its belongings.)

222. ASF, MAP 165, fols. 81v–86v, in Spallanzani and Bertelai, *Libro d'inventario dei beni di Lorenzo il Magnifico* (see note 140). Another inventory dated December 25, 1482, in ASF, MAP 104, doc. 4, fols. 57r–60v, does not mention the garden.

223. ASF, MAP 165, fol. 86v: "Uno giardino drieto al detto palagio con più orticini murati e ricinti di mura e uno pezzo di terra in detto giardino con arcipressi, abeti e altro, a uso di boschetto et uno pezzo d'ortaccio a piè del detto palagio, chiuso atorno chon uno stechato, tutte le sopradette chose a uno tenere di staiora 6 incircha."

224. On Biagio d'Antonio Tucci (Florence, 1446–1516) and the influence of Ghirlandaio on his paintings see Jane Turner, ed., *Encyclopedia of Italian Renaissance and Mannerist Art* (London: Macmillan Reference, 2000), 1:202–203. See also Roberta Bartoli, *Biagio d'Antonio* (Milan: Federico Motta Editore, 1999).

225. Donata Mazzini identifies the portion of wall extending to the left of the southern façade with a one-story mass completed by a terrace, whose balustrade, she claims, is visible in Ghirlandaio's painting. She also argues that this mass was added by Lorenzo de'

Medici at the same time he commissioned the extension of the house to the north of the property. It is not clear, however, why both Ghirlandaio and Tucci would omit the representation of the northern extension of the house, and limit themselves to painting the western addition. I am more inclined to believe that the two artists based their representations on earlier drawings that showed the original body of the villa as it appeared probably at the time of Giovanni, prior to Lorenzo's intervention, or else at the time of Lorenzo, but before construction work started. See Mazzini, *Villa Medici a Fiesole*, 87 ff.

226. Although it is true that the use of vocabulary in the early Renaissance is not always consistent, there is more evidence proving that Lorenzo commissioned the extension of the house. In fact, by comparing the inventory drawn up by Giovanni with that of Lorenzo, Donata Mazzini has pointed to an increase in the number of rooms, which presumes that the perimeter of the building had changed. In her reconstruction of the plans layout and elevations, however, there are some inconsistencies. For instance, the author claims that the western loggia is not mentioned in the archival sources: "La loggia e tutta l'ala ovest non è direttamente menzionata nel documento del 1482, e neppure nel secondo Inventario del 1492." Mazzini, *Villa Medici a Fiesole*, 87. However, another loggia, in addition to the eastern one, is indeed mentioned in the 1492 document: "Una loggia a uso di ringhiera con muricciuoli atorno di pietra e spalliera di mattone e dallato alla casa overo da piè et suvvi uno pozzo con chonci di pietra e dua sechie con chatene e chanapo e charruchole apresso in su detta" (fol. 81v). See Spallanzani and Bertelai, *Libro d'inventario dei beni di Lorenzo il Magnifico*, 168. Mazzini interprets this as a loggia located on the southern side of the house, but she does not represent it in her reconstruction of the southern elevation (Mazzini, ibid., 94). Moreover, it is possible that the phrase *dallato alla casa overo da piè* may actually refer to the well, rather than to the loggia. Therefore, I believe that the loggia with stone balustrade was located to the west of the building, on the ground floor, and the fact that it is said to be used as a *ringhiera* probably means that its surface was extended upward to form the balustrade of the terrace on the upper floor. Moreover, the use of a loggia on the ground floor is compatible with the function of the rooms located at ground level: a room for *vendemmia* (the term often referred to outbuildings open on their sides and used for the grape harvest) and another room called *della citerna* for the storage of water. None of these rooms required permanent enclosure on four sides. If the hypothesis of a loggia with terrace on the upper floor is plausible, then the western façade of the Medici Villa at Fiesole, added at Lorenzo's time, constitutes a precedent for the architecture of Poggio a Caiano.

227. James Ackerman, "The Medici Villa in Fiesole," in *"Il se rendit en Italie": Études offertes à André Chastel* (Rome: Edizioni dell'Elefante; Paris: Flammarion, 1987), 49–56. Ackerman's view, however, is only an assumption, since he writes that "we [do not] know anything about the garden" (ibid., 51).

228. Lillie, "Giovanni di Cosimo and the Villa Medici at Fiesole," 198.

229. Mastrorocco, *Le mutazioni di Proteo*, 13–15.

230. Lillie, "Giovanni di Cosimo and the Villa Medici at Fiesole," 198.

231. Spallanzani and Bertelai, *Libro d'inventario dei beni di Lorenzo il Magnifico*, fol. 86r.

232. D. R. Edward Wright, "Some Medici Gardens of the Florentine Renaissance: An Essay in Post-aesthetic Interpretation," in *The Italian Garden: Art, Design and Culture*, ed. John Dixon Hunt (Cambridge: Cambridge University Press, 1996), 34–59.

233. Spallanzani and Bertelai, *Libro d'inventario dei beni di Lorenzo il Magnifico*, fol. 85v.

234. The engraving by Telemaco Bonaiuti is based on one of two drawings located at the Museo di Firenze Com'era (Florence), and it was published by Del Rosso, *Guida di Fiesole e suoi dintorni*, fig. 5: "Veduta della Villa Mozzi, già de' Medici."

235. I have already argued against the misguided procedure of using later sources, in this case a nineteenth-century painting, to reconstruct a Quattrocento garden. See the first section of this chapter on Trebbio and Cafaggiolo.

236. Giorgio Galletti, "Una committenza medicea poco nota: Giovanni di Cosimo e il giardino di villa Medici at Fiesole," in *Giardini Medicei: Giardini di palazzo e di villa nella Firenze del Quattrocento*, 80–81.

237. MAP 5, fol. 722v. This is the letter cited above (note 215) from Giovanni di Luca Rossi in Florence to Giovanni de' Medici at the Baths of Petriuolo, dated April 11, 1455, in which "meleghrani, melaranci, limonciegli" are mentioned. See Lillie, "Giovanni di Cosimo and the Medici Villa at Fiesole," 197–198, 205 n. 68.

238. ASF, MAP 9, fol. 196r: "Mandami parecchi pedi de rose de quelle bianche incarnate et simelmente se havesti qualche pianton de quelli garofalli bianchi incarnati da tante foglie e deli rossi belli che ne siti molto ben forniti et se non havesti deli piantoni mandateme dele semente chel haverò ultra modo gratissimo." Cited by Galletti, "Una committenza medicea poco nota: Giovanni di Cosimo e il giardino di villa Medici at Fiesole," 75. See also Marilena Mosco, "Flora medicea in Florentia," in *Floralia: Florilegio dalle collezioni fiorentine del 600–700*, ed. Marilena Mosco e Milena Rizzotto (Florence: Centro Di, 1988), 10–18.

239. John Shepherd and Geoffrey Jellicoe, *Italian Gardens of the Renaissance*, 5th ed. (New York: Princeton Architectural Press, 1993), 4–6, pl. 5–6.

240. Masson, *Italian Gardens*, 75.

241. See, for example, Galletti, "Una committenza medicea poco nota: Giovanni di Cosimo e il giardino di villa Medici at Fiesole," 70.

242. James Ackerman, "Sources of the Renaissance Villa," in *Distance Points: Essays in Theory and Renaissance Art and Architecture* (Cambridge, Mass.: MIT Press, 1991), 303–324.

243. Horace Walpole is the author of a famous essay on English landscape gardening called "History of the Modern Taste in Gardening," published in 1780.

244. Lady Orford moved to Italy after the death of Lord Orford and of her second husband. Bargellini and Ruffinière du Prey have pointed to an important correspondence between Horace Mann, who was the British consul in Florence at the time of Lady Orford's sojourn in the city, and Horace Walpole. Some of these letters are a useful report of the transformations the villa at Fiesole was undergoing during those years, owing to the fact that the English countess considered the house too small for her needs. Clara Bargellini and Ruffinière du Prey, "Sources for a Reconstruction of the Villa Medici, Fiesole," *Burlington Magazine* III (1969), 598 n. 14; 601 n. 16. The authors report a note by Lensi Orlandi Cardini, according to whom the villa had been originally sold by the Medici

family in 1671 for the same reason, namely, that it was too small. The villa was bought by Vincenzio di Cosimo del Sera, and in 1711 passed down by inheritance to the Durazzini family. In 1722 the Borgherini bought the property and owned it until 1768. The villa was later purchased by a Colonel Albergotti, who sold it to Lady Orford in 1772. See Lensi Orlandi Cardini, *Le ville di Firenze*, 1:166. Also Mazzini, *Villa Medici a Fiesole*, 48–100.

245. This quotation is from a letter that Horace Mann sent to Walpole on November 6, 1776. Cited by Bargellini and Ruffinière du Prey, "Sources for a Reconstruction of the Villa Medici, Fiesole," 601. The 'new' road commissioned by Lady Orford was, in fact, the widening of one of two preexisting alleys that used to link the upper garden to the farmhouse at the time the villa belonged to Vincenzio Gaspare Borgherini in 1771. See ASF, *Notarile Moderno*, Atti Originali n. 13874: "Notaio Cosimo Braccini, Nota di spese generali e per muramenti e rifacimenti della Villa, giardini e poderi di Fiesole, 1772. A Spese Generali della Villa di Fiesole. . . . *Detto ß 22.6*. Portò contanti il Tosi lastricatore per saldo di un suo conto di avere incanalato l'acqua, *slargato e spianato il lastrico che ivi in questo all'ingresso della villa*" (emphasis added). The entire document has been published in Mazzini, *Villa Medici a Fiesole*, 185–186. The existence of two alleys leading to the eastern gardens of the villa before the intervention carried out for Lady Orford is attested by a document from August 20, 1771, which describes the property inherited by Vincenzio Gaspare Borgherini (ASF, *Magistrato Supremo* n. 3249, Decreto di Pubblico Incanto dei Beni dell'Eredità di Giovanni Vincenzio Borgherini): "Che da piano terreno si passa in altro giardino detto giardino di mezzo murato a torno avente a sinistra un ampia conserva, quale riceve per doccia l'acqua piovana. A destra una scalaccia scoperta di pietra che scende, et in faccia una porta per dove si passa in una ragnaia posta fra *due viali cipressati e diritti*, che conducono alla casa del lavoratore del podere, vedendosi a sinistra di detta ragnaia di bel principio una scala di pietra scoperta che sale al viale superiore di dove per altra porta si entra nel giardino di sopra, li come per la citata scala, che scende, si va nel terzo giardino detto giardino di sotto murato anche esso" (emphasis added). Published in Mazzini, *Villa Medici a Fiesole*, 187–188.

246. Many scholars have debated the original access to the villa. The most widely accepted hypothesis is that it was to the west side of the building, either through a door in the north wall of the west terrace (Frommel) or through the lower wing described by Vasari, from which an internal stairway would have led to the west terrace (Geymuller). See Bargellini and Ruffinière du Prey, "Sources for a Reconstruction of the Villa Medici, Fiesole," 601 n. 22. In either case, that the access to the villa was from the west is confirmed by the inventory drawn up in 1492 (discussed earlier).

247. According to del Rosso the architect who supervised the works was Niccolò Paoletti, who not only added a long alley to the back of the villa, but also designed the gardens. See del Rosso, *Guida di Fiesole e suoi dintorni*, 50. However, Paoletti's exact contribution to the restoration of the villa has never been ascertained.

248. James Ackerman was the first to suggest that the eastern terrace was originally shorter than it is today, although he did not explain why. Ackerman, *The Villa*, 73.

249. Archivio Storico Comunale di Fiesole (ACF), n. 108, filza 2 di lavori di strade, notificazioni 1774–1781, 35: "Rendere più facile l'ingresso con la carrozza nella scuderia

della villa proprio sulla strada maestra che da Firenze va a Fiesole." Cited by Mazzini, *Villa Medici a Fiesole*, 63.

250. The length of the upper terrace prior to its extension is said to measure six times the height of the façade overlooking the eastern garden. A study of the geometric proportions of the villa was conducted by Clemens Steenbergen and Wouter Reh, *Architecture and Landscape: The Design Experiment of the Great European Gardens and Landscapes*, 2nd ed. (Bussum, Netherlands: Thoth, 2003), 33–43.

251. That the pergola was added later is demonstrated by the fact that it covers the stone lintel of the gateway located at the east end, whose decorative carving is not visible to someone walking under it. The carving must have been visible before the addition of the pergola.

252. Galletti, "Una committenza medicea poco nota: Giovanni di Cosimo e il giardino di villa Medici at Fiesole," 79.

253. ASF, MAP 9, fol. 175: "Piero says that he wants to have a clear understanding before making any decisions because it is not wise to deal with such issues in a hurry." See transcription by Lillie, "Giovanni di Cosimo and the Medici Villa at Fiesole," 203 n. 51.

254. ASF, MAP 7, fol. 298: "Piero dicie vuole intendere molto bene inanzi vi metta mano che dicie non si vuole corre affuria in simili chose." See Lillie, "Giovanni di Cosimo and the Medici Villa at Fiesole," 195, and transcription, 203 n. 52.

255. Lillie, "Giovanni di Cosimo and the Medici Villa at Fiesole," 195, 204 n. 53. In the letter, which was written on August 19, Macinghi suggests the construction of a new foundation that would be ten *braccia* long (nearly six meters) and six *braccia* wide (about three and a half meters) and reinforced by a four-*braccia* transversal wall (two and one-third meters). He also adds that he will send drawings illustrating the proposal. ASF, MAP 9, fol. 178.

256. Galletti identifies the retaining wall mentioned in the primary sources with the one on the lower level, which used to retain the *ortaccio*. However, this wall was reinforced with buttresses and thus did not need any additional structural device. Moreover, there is no mention of buttresses in the numerous letters that were sent to Giovanni on this subject. Therefore, the problematic wall was surely the one on the upper level.

257. For the engraving by Telemaco Bonaiuti, see note 234; the drawing by Burci is at the GDSU 1119 P; the anonymous painting belongs to a private collection, and was first published in Galletti, "Una committenza medicea poco nota: Giovanni di Cosimo e il giardino di villa Medici at Fiesole," 84.

258. The greenhouse is absent in the early nineteenth-century visual sources mentioned above, thus it must have been designed after 1842 and before 1883. The *Veduta di Fiesole* by Joseph Pennell is located at GDSU 1610 P. I am grateful to Lucia Monaci Moran for showing me this drawing, which was published in the catalogue of the exhibition *La Toscana di Joseph Pennel tra Otto e Novecento*, ed. Lucia Monaci Moran (Florence: Olschki, 2004), 30.

259. The photograph (c. 1907) is from the Brogi Archives, and it was published by Norman T. Newton in his article "Villa Medici at Fiesole," *Landscape Architecture* 17, no. 3 (April 1927): 185–198.

260. On Edward G. Lawson see Vincenzo Cazzato, *Ville e Giardini Italiani: I disegni di architetti e paesaggisti dell'American Academy in Rome* (Rome: Istituto Poligrafico e Zecca dello Stato, 2004), 289–290, 376–384. The sketch belongs to the Photographic Archive of the American Academy in Rome.

261. The description of the garden is by another fellow at the American Academy, namely, Norman T. Newton. See his "Villa Medici at Fiesole," 192.

262. That the pergola was constructed before 1915, contrary to what most authors believe, is demonstrated by the fact that it appears in a drawing published in 1901 by Janet Ross in her *Florentine Villas* (London: J. M. Dent, 1901), 85, and it is also visible in the 1907 photograph from the Brogi Archives mentioned above.

263. Newton, "Villa Medici at Fiesole," 194.

264. However, the gardens at Fiesole, especially as regards their spatial organization on hanging terraces, are usually celebrated as a unique model of fifteenth-century design, as beautiful as it is rare: "The series of the terraces' large retaining walls create a unique path, both for its architectonic beauty and for its uncommon occurrence, for we find ourselves in a garden that is complete in its structure, created out of nothing in the middle of the fifteenth century by a less known member of the Medici family, Giovanni, the second son of Cosimo il Vecchio." Galletti, "Una committenza medicea poco nota: Giovanni di Cosimo e il giardino di villa Medici at Fiesole," 61.

265. "Oltr'a questo dignissimi ornamenti disse ancora avere ordinato Cosimo insieme con lui [don Timoteo]: una peschiera di cento venti braccia per uno verso e sessanta per l'altro, nel mezzo della quale uno ponte in modo ordinato con una cateratta, o vuoi dire incastro che, quando bisogno di pesce averanno, solo alzare la detta cateratta, tutta l'acqua da l'altro canto si riducerà nel mezzo di detto ponte; e sta ordinato in modo che 'l pesce in quello luogo resta, e così con abilità a prestezza avere lo possono quando a loro piace. E dicemi che intorno sono piantati moltissimi frutti di varie ragioni, cioè fichi, peri, meli, susini, giriegi, sorbe, nespole, e simili frutti: quando maturi fussino, cascando, i pesci d'essi si ciberanno, e ancora le radici de' quali terranno forte le rive d'essa peschiera. La quale ha uno muro ancora, discosto dalla riva braccia dieci, intorno, alto per lo modo che sanza licenza andare non si può. E questo è da piè dello circuito del giardino, dove che viene propinquo a uno fiumicello che appresso gli corre; del quale l'acqua d'esso in essa riflue. E così el giardino è circundato d'uno muro tanto alto che entrare non si può in esso. Dell'essere di questo luogo altro non ne voglio dire, ma tanto è, che è degno d'essere lodato intra tutti gli altri che degni sieno, perchè è bellissimo." (Fols. 189r–v.) Filarete, *Trattato di Architettura*, 695. Cosimo de' Medici financed the reconstruction of the Badia at Fiesole in 1456.

266. "Eliceres verbis—ait hic—se saxa movere / Sponte sua, et duros scindere se silices. Hinc primum in faciles fessos convertere montes / Cogit; et hinc scissus mons ruit ima petens. / Hinc mandat fieri fossas, fondareque muros, / Fondamenta quibus alta fuisse iubet, / Ne pereant: nam vult ingentia pondera gestent; Et iubet ut dentur tempora longa seni." See Gombrich, "Alberto Avogadro's Descriptions of the Badia of Fiesole and of the Villa of Careggi," 217–229. Another important source is the *Cronaca* written by Isaia da

Este, a monk who described the reconstruction of the Badia as the foreword to an inventory compiled in 1493. According to the monk, Cosimo "veniva una volta il giorno a vedere quanto si fosse fatto"; also, it appears that Cosimo had reserved a room for himself "con l'anticamera, studio, letto et altri luoghi bisognosi, ove alle volte per suo diporto si riducea, familiarmente con i concanonici nostri mangniando et bevendo et conversando, non altrimenti che egli con i proprij figlioli et famiglia mangnare, bere et conversare solea, dicendo non parergli che il monistero da lui fatto fosse terreno albergo ma celeste, et non da spirti humani ma angelici habitato." See Franco Borsi, "La Badia Fiesolana: Cultura e architettura," in Franco Borsi et al., *La Badia Fiesolana* (Florence: Le Monnier, 1976), 24–25.

267. Borsi says that the construction of a library at the Badia demonstrates Cosimo's desire to attract intellectuals and men of letters to Fiesole. We know, in fact, that Cosimo put Vespasiano da Bisticci in charge of collecting the manuscripts that a good library would have needed. And it may not be a coincidence that the first painting of the Badia by Botticini was commissioned by Matteo Palmieri, whom Alamanno Rinucini described as the "tipico e mirabile esempio di perfetto equilibrio tra virtù attiva e contemplativa." (Ibid., 31.) Thus, the Badia during Cosimo's time seems to have embodied the ideal balance between *masserizia* and *luogo di contemplazione* "in un riscatto dalla lotta politica ed economica nel dialogo con il Maffei, nell'amore della natura." (Ibid., 32.) On the other hand, the following generation, that of Lorenzo, brought Pico della Mirandola and Poliziano to the Badia, but with a different dimension of interests: without the moral tension, the subtle anxiety, and the desire to master all ambiguities, typical of Cosimo il Vecchio. (Ibid., 33.)

268. Vincenzo Viti, *La Badia Fiesolana: Pagine di storia e d'arte* (Florence: Giuntina, 1926), 31.

269. Works on the Badia were only completed after eleven years, in 1467, with the construction of the church's roof. See Borsi, *La Badia Fiesolana*, 70.

270. "E quello che importa è da considerare che dovendo egli nella scesa di quel monte mettere quello edifizio in piano si servì con molto giudicio del basso facendovi cantine, lavatoi, forni stalle, cucine, stanze per legne e altre tante commodità che non è possibile veder meglio: così mise in piano la pianta dell'edifizio; onde potette a un pari fare poi le logge, il refettorio, l'infermeria, il noviziato, il dormentorio, la libreria e l'altre stanze principali d'un monasterio." Vasari, *Le Vite*, 2:367.

271. Borsi, *La Badia Fiesolana*, 71.

272. This is precisely the same technique suggested by Macinghi for the construction of new foundations for the upper retaining wall at the Medici villa. See note 255.

273. Andrea Aleardi et. al., *Fiesole: Alle origini della città. La costruzione della carta archeologica* (Comune di Fiesole, Museo Civico, 1990).

274. Repetti, *Dizionario geografico*, 2:107–108.

275. See, for example, the two descriptions of the villas of Statius's patrons in *Silvae* I.3 and II.2; see also Pliny's letter to Gallus: Epist. II, XVII; and letter to Apollinaris: Epist. V, VI. Unlike Pliny's detailed descriptions, though, Statius's "famous poem on the villa of Volantilla gives us atmosphere rather than description." Helen H. Tanzer, *The Villas of Pliny the Younger* (New York: Columbia University Press, 1924), 4.

276. Cicero too writes of the view of green places from the windows of his villa, although he does not give as many details as the younger Pliny gives. See Cicero, *Letters to Atticus*, Loeb Classical Library (Cambridge, Mass.: Harvard University Press, 1999), 1:138–141. That a villa should be located on a hilltop site was one of the recommendations of Leon Battista Alberti in his *De re aedificatoria*, whose sources are steeped in classical literature. On Alberti's architectural theories and the Medici villa at Fiesole see Ackerman, "The Medici Villa in Fiesole," 51; idem, *The Villa*, 76. On Giovanni de' Medici's acquaintance with Alberti see Mazzini, *Villa Medici a Fiesole*, 125. Here Mazzini advances the hypothesis, quite improbable, that Giovanni commissioned from Alberti the construction of the villa.

277. Lillie, "Giovanni di Cosimo and the Medici Villa at Fiesole," 190–191.

278. Ibid., 191.

279. We learn from Cicero's correspondence that Atticus used to send him works of art that he purchased for him in Athens. For example: "I have paid L. Cincius the HS 20,400 for the Megarian statues in accordance with your earlier letter. I am already quite enchanted with your Pentelic herms with the bronze heads, about which you write to me, so please send them and the statues and any other things you think would do credit to the place in question." Cicero, *Letters to Atticus*, 1:37.

280. MAP 8, fol. 366: "E per cierto queste chose antiche a murale i' muro giètano molto bene. Fateci un pocho di pensiero a Fiesole, avanti si tiri a fine." The letter was partly transcribed and published by Gino Corti and Frederick Hartt, "New Documents concerning Donatello, Luca and Andrea della Robbia, Desiderio, Mino, Uccello, Pollaiuolo, Filippo Lippi, Baldovinetti and Others," in *Art Bulletin* 44, no. 1 (1962), 157 n. 12. The quotation is from Foster, "Donatello Notices in Medici Letters," 149 n. 9. Also quoted by Lillie, "Giovanni di Cosimo and the Medici Villa at Fiesole," 204 n. 57.

281. On the fifteenth-century knowledge of the Etruscans in Italy see Gabriele Morolli, *"Vetus Etruria": Il mito degli Etruschi nella letteratura architettonica nell'arte e nella cultura da Vitruvio a Winckelmann* (Florence: Alinea Editrice, 1985).

282. Ackerman, *The Villa*, 74.

283. Lillie, "The Humanist Villa Revisited," 205, 207.

284. ASF, MAP 82, doc. 182, fol. 591r.

285. We only know of the presence of a cistern and of two wells (ASF, MAP 165, fols. 81v, 86). On the search for water at the time of Giovanni see ASF, MAP 9, fol. 146r; MAP 10, fol. 141r; MAP 138, fol. 50r.

286. Lillie, "The Humanist Villa Revisited." The document is partly transcribed at 202–203 n. 27. ASF, *Catasto* 924 (1469), fol. 308v.

287. Lillie, "The Humanist Villa Revisited," 203. ASF, *Catasto* 924 (1469), fol. 308v.

288. ASF, MAP 165, fols. 81v–86v: "A uso di vendemia, entrovi 4 tina in su 4 sedili d'albero con 6 pilastri di pietra, rendono barili 120 incircha e 6 tinelle per uso di dette tina, di tenuta di barili 50 incircha." See Spallanzani and Bertelai, *Libro d'inventario dei beni di Lorenzo il Magnifico*, 168.

289. ASF, MAP 165: "Sei botti da vermiglio in su sedili di pietra, di tenuta di barili 41. Sei barili e 2 mezzi barili da vermiglio. Nell'altra volta allato a questa, detta quella della state sei botti in su sedili in dua filari, di tenuta di barili 51 incircha." (Fol. 82r.)

290. Ibid.: "Trentasei orcia da olio e 3 barili e 2 mezzi barili."

291. Ibid.: "Podere di staiora 160, posto nel popolo di Santo Romolo a Chanonica di Fiesole chon chasa da lavoratore."

292. Ibid.: "Grano staia 48, biade staia 6, vino barili 45, olio barili 22, frutte" (fol. 86r).

293. Ibid.: "Appresso note di più chave e massi di pietra, che parte se ne vende in somma e chontanto a levare la pietra in tanto tempo, parte se ne afitta l'anno a cotanto l'anno, cioè: due chave vendute e una a Mattio di Manno e l'altra a Marcho di Sandro Ferrucci a levare il masso in 4 anni . . . e passato detto tempo non le levando, el masso resti alla chasa, poste dette chave nel popolo di Sancto Romolo e Canonica di Fiesole et luogho detto Palagio di Fiesole" (fol. 86r).

294. More information on the quarries is given in the *Decima Repubblicana* 28 (1498), fol. 455r.

295. ASF, *Catasto* 1016, fol. 476v: "Posso fare fede per iscrittura di terza persona, le limosine sopradette essere cresciute molto magiore somma per mio chonto proprio, et oltre a questo monna Lucretia, mia madre, per sé distribuiscie per l'amore di Dio buona soma di danari, e in espezialità tutte le rendite [delle proprietà] di Fiesole, perchè mio padre, alla morte sua, a pparole lasciò che ll'entrate di Fiesole si distribuissero per Dio." The document was written in 1480. Cited by Elio Conti et al., *La civiltà fiorentina del Quattrocento* (Florence: Vallecchi Editore, 1993), 223.

296. See the letter from Jacopo d'Orsino Lanfredini to Lorenzo dated June 12, 1475 (MAP 32, fol. 283), in which Lanfredini asks Lorenzo permission for Polo Morosino to visit Fiesole. Cited and partly transcribed by Foster, "A Study of Lorenzo de' Medici's Villa at Poggio a Caiano," 1:31, 334 n. 95.

297. Modena MS fol. 6r. The citation is from Alison Brown, *Bartolomeo Scala, 1430–1497, Chancellor of Florence: The Humanist as Bureaucrat* (Princeton: Princeton University Press, 1979), 17–18. Brown does not cite the document in the original.

298. The primary sources show that Lorenzo began the construction of his new villa at Poggio as late as 1485, whereas he had started to buy land on both sides of the Ombrone in the 1470s, when he began to form a large estate and his pursuits on the land were largely agricultural. In the winter of 1477 he had a hundred cattle brought to Poggio a Caiano from Lombardy, in conjunction with the construction of a dairy farm, called *La Cascina*, on his new estate. This does not mean that Poggio was not a place for leisure, however. Just as Fiesole incorporated the idea of a place used for the recreation of the mind where the Medici also exploited the functional aspects of country life, there are records showing that Lorenzo used to go to the farm at Poggio also to engage in falconry and fishing. See Foster, "A Study of Lorenzo de' Medici's Villa at Poggio a Caiano," 1:63, 105.

CHAPTER TWO. FROM WORK OF NATURE TO WORK OF ART

1. I have consulted the following editions at the BNCF: *Ruralia commoda*, Latin *editio princeps* (Augsburg: Johann Schüssler, 1471); *Ruralia commoda* (Florence: Nicolò di Lorenzo,

1478); *Ruralia commoda*, Italian *editio princeps* (Florence: Nicholaum Vratislaviensis, 1478; a copy of this incunable is at the Biblioteca Universitaria of Bologna; another copy is at the Biblioteca Civica of Siena); *De agricultura vulgare* (Venice, Albertino da Lessona e fratelli, 1511); *De agricoltura, omnibusque plantarum, et animalium generibus, libri XII* (Basel: Per Henricum Petrum, 1538); *Trattato dell'agricoltura*, 2 vols. (Naples: Felice Mosca, 1724).

2. Of the surviving manuscripts of the *Liber*, 133 copies are in Latin, Italian, French, or German, many of which were produced in the fourteenth century. The total number of printed editions is approximately sixty. See Tommaso Alfonsi et al., *Pier de' Crescenzi (1233–1321): Studi e documenti* (Bologna: Cappelli, 1933). Also Robert G. Calkins, "Piero de' Crescenzi and the Medieval Garden," in *Medieval Gardens*, ed. Elisabeth Blair MacDougall (Washington, D.C.: Dumbarton Oaks Research Library and Collection, 1986), 157–169. Among the most recent studies see Jean Louis Gaulin, "Pietro de' Crescenzi et l'agronomie en Italie (XIIe-XIVe siècles)," doctoral dissertation, Université de Paris I: Panthéon-Sorbonne (Lille: ANRT Université de Lille III, 1990). Also Johanna Bauman, "Tradition and Transformation: The Pleasure Garden in Piero de' Crescenzi's *Liber ruralium commodorum*," *Studies in the History of Gardens and Designed Landscapes* 22, no. 2 (2002), 99–141.

3. "E molti libri d'antichi e di novelli savi lessi e studiai, e diverse e varie operazioni dei coltivatori delle terre vidi e conobbi." Crescenzi, *De agricultura vulgare*, "proemio." Idem, *Trattato dell'agricoltura*, vol. 1, "proemio." Translations into English are mine.

4. Crescenzi's property, called Villa Olmo, was located near the monastery of S. Stefano, outside the city walls.

5. Among Crescenzi's other sources are the pseudo-Aristotle's *De plantis*; Isidore of Seville's *Etymologiae*; and Palladius's *De re rustica*.

6. "Sottili erbe, e minute, le quali massimamente dilettano il vedere." Crescenzi, *Trattato dell'agricoltura*, 2:93.

7. "De[v]e essere il luogo del verziere quadrato di tanta misura, che basti a coloro, che in esso dovranno dimorare." Ibid.

8. "Non solamente dilettino per lo loro odore, ma daranno eziandio diletto e recreazione alla vista." Ibid., 94.

9. "In questi cotali arbori si ricerca più l'ombra che 'l frutto." Ibid., 93.

10. "Le quali daranno diletto e utilitade." Ibid., 95.

11. Ibid., 96.

12. "Di quelle cose che a dilectatione fare si possono." Crescenzi, *Ruralia commoda* (Florence: Niccolò di Lorenzo, 1478).

13. "Riguardando sempre l'utilità de' campi, imperocchè 'l diletto non dee andare innanzi all'utilità, avvegnachè ne' giardini si dee il contrario osservare." Crescenzi, *Trattato dell'agricoltura*, 2:99.

14. Calkins, "Piero de' Crescenzi and the Medieval Garden," 165. Johanna Bauman has also written on the supposedly aesthetic connotations of Crescenzi's gardens in "Tradition and Transformation: The Pleasure Garden in Piero de' Crescenzi's *Liber ruralium commodorum*," 137. In the section entitled "Aesthetics and Representation," she analyzes an illustration from Crescenzi's book on the garden included in the Venice edition of 1495.

The woodcut is analyzed with modern language borrowed from the *Critique of Judgment*, but it is unlikely that an image may have revealed a place's aesthetic quality, in the modern sense, to a fourteenth-century observer. At most, the presence of a couple, and a rabbit—symbol of fertility—may suggest that the illuminator's intention was that of representing a garden of love. Therefore, the anonymous illustrator felt free to give his own interpretation, likely molded by his fifteenth-century Venetian culture, to a text written almost two centuries earlier and in which its medieval author does not make any reference either to the art of courtly love or to the beauty of the garden.

15. The earliest manuscripts of Crescenzi's work were not illustrated, and only a few fourteenth-century manuscript copies of the *Liber* contain decorated initials or small miniatures that introduce each of the twelve books. Eighteen of the ninety manuscripts in Latin contain such illustrations, many of which were prepared by Bolognese monks. One example is housed in the Vatican Library (Vat. Lat. 1529) and dates to the 1330s. See Bauman, "Tradition and Transformation: The Pleasure Garden in Piero de' Crescenzi's *Liber ruralium commodorum*," 114; also Perrine Mane, "L'iconographie des manuscrits du *Traité d'agriculture* de Pier de' Crescenzi," *Mélange de l'École Française de Rome* 97 (1985), 727–818. Eight of the manuscripts written in French in the fifteenth century were illuminated. One of the most famous examples, which shows full-page illuminations, was produced in Bruges around 1470 and is now conserved at the Pierpont Morgan Library in New York (MS. M.232). Another manuscript copy made in Bruges is now at the Bibliothèque de l'Arsenal in Paris; see Pietro de' Crescenzi, *Les profits champêtres de Pierre de Crescens*, preface by Maurice Genevoix (Paris: Editions Chavane, 1965). The most detailed illustrations are those made for a manuscript written in French in Flanders late in the fifteenth century. This copy is now at the British Library (MS. Add. 19720; Calkins, "Piero de' Crescenzi and the Medieval Garden," 163). The printed copies that are illustrated are more numerous. A French edition of 1486 has a set of four illustrations introducing nine of the twelve books; another edition with illustrations was produced in Venice in 1495, and a copy is at Dumbarton Oaks (Washington, D.C.); the Strasbourg and Spires editions used several single-column woodcuts, usually more than once.

16. Calkins, "Piero de' Crescenzi and the Medieval Garden," 168.

17. Ibid.

18. Ibid., 166.

19. Paul Oskar Kristeller has explained that the central view of modern aesthetics implies that beauty is "neatly or consistently distinguished from the moral good." Kristeller, "The Modern System of the Arts: A Study in the History of Aesthetics. Part I," *Journal of the History of Ideas* 12, no. 4 (October 1951), 499.

20. "Conciosia cosa che per la virtù della prudenza, la quale tra 'l bene e 'l male cautamente discerne, l'animo dell'uomo sia informato alla conoscenza delle cose utili e dilettevoli: e conciossiecosa che nelle terrene si trovi lo stato pacifico . . . il predetto è da ricercare a podere, e quello trovato, è siccome tesoro inestimabile, con molta umiltà e pacienza da essere conservato: imperciocchè per esso, agevolmente il benigno amor divino si provoca, e s'acquista, e la vita dell'huomo, senza lesion, si conserva, e l'abbondante copia

delle cose utilmente si procaccia. Questo non desiderano, nè domandano, i malvagi . . . sicome orbati, per superbia o per altro abominevole vizio." (If by virtue of prudence, which cautiously distinguishes between good and evil, man's soul learns the knowledge of good and delightful things, and if peace is found in earthly matters . . . this is to be sought in the farm, and once this is found, since it is an invaluable treasure, it must be preserved with great humility and patience: for the love of God is easily stimulated and obtained by means of it [the farm] and the life of man is preserved without pain, and abundance of things is usefully obtained. This the wicked do not wish, nor do they ask for it . . . since they are blind by their pride or other abominable vice.) Crescenzi, *De agricultura vulgare*, "proemio." Also *Trattato dell'agricoltura*, "proemio."

21. "L'esquisita dottrina del coltivamento, per la quale più agevolmente e abbondantemente si riceve utilità e s'acquista diletto . . . meritevolmente è da desiderare da uomini buoni, che sanza danno d'alcuno vogliono vivere giustamente delle rendite delle loro possessioni e però al coltivamento della villa la mente e l'animo ho rivolto." Crescenzi, *Trattato dell'agricoltura*, "proemio."

22. "Che all'animo danno diletto, e poi appresso conservare la sanità del corpo, perocchè la complessione del corpo sempre s'accosta e conforma al desiderio dell'animo." Ibid., 2:93.

23. "Ed in cotale giardino non si dee sempre il re dilettare, ma alcuna fiata rinnovare, cioè, quando avrà soddisfatto alle necessarie cose del suo reggimento, glorificando Iddio, il qual di tutti i buoni e leciti diletti è principio e fattore e cagione. Imperocchè, siccome scrisse Tullio, noi non semo nati a sollazzo, ma innanzi a servitude, e più gravi ufici. Vero è, che alcuna volta è lecito cioè, quando alle necessarie, e utili cose avrem soddisfatto, alcuna volta diportarsi." Ibid., 97.

24. "Nei campi diletta molto il lor bello, e adorno sito, che non sieno piccioli e rustichi campicelli, ma gran quantità in uno." Ibid., 99.

25. "Conciossiecosachè molto diletto sia averli belli, e adorni vignai . . . che facciano diverse generazioni di buone uve." Ibid., 100.

26. "Si faccia discender nel mezzo di detto verziere, una fontana chiarissima, la cui bellezza adduca diletto, e giocondità." Ibid., 94.

27. Crescenzi, *De agricoltura, omnibusque plantarum, et animalium generibus, libri XII*, 378.

28. Kristeller, "The Modern System of the Arts," 496.

29. If on the one hand it is true that Crescenzi's way of thinking was steeped in medieval ethics, on the other the pursuit of the good was more a way of life than the result of philosophical speculation.

30. Alberti's *De re aedificatoria* was published for the first time in 1485, with a dedicatory letter written by Angelo Poliziano to Lorenzo il Magnifico.

31. In the Middle Ages the liberal arts were seven and included the *Trivium* (grammar, rhetoric, dialectic) and the *Quadrivium* (arithmetic, geometry, astronomy, and music). Hugh of St. Victor was probably the first to formulate a scheme of seven mechanical arts corresponding to the seven liberal arts. These were: *lanificium, armatura, navigatio,*

agricultura, venatio, medicina, and *theatrica.* However, the fine arts were not grouped together or singled out but scattered among various sciences, or crafts. Kristeller, "The Modern System of the Arts," 507.

32. This opinion was expressed for the first time by Giovanni Boccaccio in the *Decameron* (VI.5). In this novella Boccaccio says that the art of painting before Giotto had been subjected for many centuries to the "error d'alcuni, che più a dilettar gli occhi degl'ignoranti che a compiacere allo 'ntelletto de' savi dipignendo." Boccaccio, *Decameron,* vol. 4 of *Tutte le opere di Giovanni Boccaccio,* ed. Vittore Branca (Milan: Mondadori, 1976), 551.

33. Vitruvius's *De architectura* was discovered around 1410 and published only in 1514. Alberti lamented, though, that Vitruvius's text was not refined, for it was neither Greek nor good Latin. Alberti's sources on garden making include not his recent predecessors—such as Crescenzi—but rather Cicero and Pliny the Younger. *De officiis* and *De senectute* are among the most cited (although implicitly) of Cicero's works. On Pliny's influence on Alberti see Lise Bek, "Ut ars natura, ut natura ars: Le ville di Plinio e il concetto del giardino nel Rinascimento," *Analecta Romana Instituti Danici* 7 (1974), 109–156.

34. Ibid., 134.

35. Although Alberti formulated a theory of architectural design, his recommendations about architecture often include practical advice and detailed technical instruction.

36. Francesco di Giorgio Martini, "Giardini e barco (1485–1492)," in *L'arte dei giardini: Scritti teorici e pratici dal XIV al XIX secolo,* ed. Margherita Azzi Visentini (Milan: Il Polifilo, 1999), 81–89. Also Francesco di Giorgio Martini, *Trattati di architettura, ingegneria e arte militare,* ed. Corrado Maltese (Milan: Il Polifilo, 1967), 1:70–72, 245–246, 348, 107–109; 2:348.

37. "Pure si debba il compositore ingegnare di redurla a qualche spezie di figure perfetta, come circulare, quadra o triangulare; dopo queste più apparenti la pentagona, esagona, ortogonia etcetera si ponno applicare." Martini, "Giardini e barco (1485–1492)," 86.

38. Lucia Tongiorgi Tomasi, "Projects for Botanical and Other Gardens: A 16th-Century Manual," *Journal of Garden History* 3, no. 1 (1983), 7.

39. Filarete [Antonio Averlino], "Il Giardino di Plusiapolis e la riserva di caccia della Sforzinda (1461–1464)," in *L'arte dei giardini: Scritti teorici e pratici dal XIV al XIX secolo,* ed. Margherita Azzi Visentini (Milan: Il Polifilo, 1999), 65–79. Also Filarete, *Trattato di architettura,* ed. Anna Maria Finoli and Liliana Grassi (Milan: Il Polifilo, 1972), bks. 15 and 20; 450–456, 602–607.

40. "Cum hortorum amoenitas ad aedificiorum ornatum haud parum certe conducant, id circo nos quatuor subscriptis hisce designationibus nunc proposuimus, etsi earum usus ad alia quoque transferri perquam commode posset. Quinetiam Labyrinthos duos tamquam proposito huic mirifice accomodatos, in postremis subiunximus atque delineavimus." Sebastiano Serlio, *De architectura* (Venice: De Franciscis, 1569), 355–356.

41. James Ackerman made this point in his "Architectural Practice in the Italian Renaissance," *Journal of the Society of Architectural Historians* 13, no. 3 (October 1954), 4.

42. Surprisingly, Alberti does not mention gardens in his writings on agriculture, such as the *De familia.* See *I libri della famiglia,* ed. Ruggiero Romano and Alberto Tenenti (Turin: Einaudi, 1969), esp. 236–239; 246–248. Also idem, "Villa," 359–363, 456–458. In

both texts the villa is discussed from a strictly utilitarian point of view. Moreover, living in the country is considered a model of virtue. On this topic see Michel Paoli, *L'idée de Nature chez Leon Battista Alberti* (Paris: Editions Honoré Champion, 1999). When Alberti speaks of the beauty of nature, he usually refers to a *locus amoenus* more than a man-made garden.

43. Margherita Azzi Visentini, ed., *L'arte dei giardini: Scritti teorici e pratici dal XIV al XIX secolo*, 9–10.

44. For a general overview of the scholarship on Italian gardens see Mirka Benes, "Recent Developments and Perspectives in the Historiography of Italian Gardens," in *Perspectives on Garden Histories*, ed. Michel Conan (Washington, D.C.: Dumbarton Oaks Research Library and Collection, 1999), 37–76.

45. Wright, "Some Medici Gardens of the Florentine Renaissance," 34–59.

46. Ibid., 59.

47. Ibid.

48. Ibid.

49. Claudia Lazzaro, *The Italian Renaissance Garden: From the Conventions of Planting, Design, and Ornament to the Grand Gardens of Sixteenth-Century Central Italy* (New Haven: Yale University Press, 1990), 3–4.

50. Lazzaro, *The Italian Renaissance Garden*, 10.

51. Ibid., 44.

52. The *Hypnerotomachia Poliphili*, literally Polifilo's love struggle in a dream, is often described as a treatise, but it is, in fact, a hermetic novel that has been attributed to the Venetian monk Francesco Colonna.

53. Lazzaro, *The Italian Renaissance Garden*, 34, 37.

54. Ibid., 69-70.

55. Ibid., 34.

56. I borrow this expression from Michel de Certeau, *The Practice of Everyday Life* (Berkeley: University of California Press, 1984).

CHAPTER THREE. WRITING THE GARDEN IN THE AGE OF HUMANISM

1. Petrarch's annotations regarding his plantings are on fols. 156r–156v. For Petrarch's annotations on the entire codex see Caterina Tristano, "Le postille del Petrarca nel Vaticano Lat. 2193 (Apuleio, Frontino, Vegezio, Palladio)," *Italia Medioevale e Umanistica* 17 (1974), 365–468.

2. Pierre de Nolhac, "Pétrarque et son jardin d'après ses notes inédites," *Giornale Storico della Letteratura Italiana* 9 (1887), 404–414. A more reliable transcription than de Nolhac's is that by Marco Vattasso, "Brevi note del Petrarca sull'orticoltura," in *I codici petrarcheschi della biblioteca vaticana* (Rome: Tipografia Poliglotta Vaticana, 1908), 229–234. For a description of the codex see 161–162. An Italian translation of Petrarch's annotations and a summary of his horticultural experiments have been published by Franco Cardini

and Massimo Miglio, *Nostalgia del paradiso: Il giardino medievale* (Rome: Laterza, 2002), 101–114.

3. "Itaque se quod fortuna obtulit in rationem et consuetudinem transtulisse perpetuam, et ex illo sic usum semperque feliciter. Unde et michi libitum experiri." Vattasso, "Brevi note del Petrarca sull'orticoltura," 230.

4. Crescenzi, *Trattato dell'agricoltura* (Naples: Felice Mosca, 1724). Book 8 also includes a chapter on *agri*: it is possible that the name refers simply to an entire property of cultivated fields, which includes several kitchen gardens or *horti*.

5. Ibid., 2:93, "Ma ora è da dire delle predette cose, secondo che all'animo danno diletto, e poi appresso, conservan la sanità del corpo, perocchè la complessione del corpo sempre s'accosta e conforma al disiderio dell'animo."

6. Ibid., 94, "E ancora non si richiede il frutto degli alberi nel verziere, ma solamente il diletto."

7. Ibid., 99, "Riguardando sempre l'utilità dei campi, imperocchè 'l diletto non de[v]e andare innanzi all'utilità, avvegnachè nei giardini si de[v]e il contrario osservare."

8. Ibid., 104, "E quivi nudrisca tutte generazioni di buone erbe, così da mangiare, come medicinali, ciascuna, secondo che la sua natura richiede."

9. Boccaccio alone mentioned the presence of flowers, in a letter he addressed to Petrarch. According to de Nolhac, the poet was allowed to cultivate the *hortulum* adjacent to the common dwelling of the canons at Padua. Boccaccio must have seen this place during his visit to Petrarch in March 1351: "Ego compositionum tuaram avidus ex illis scribens sumebam copiam; die autem in vesperum declinante a laboribus surgebamus unanimes et in hortulum ibamus tuum, iam ob novum ver frondibus atque floribus ornatum." Cited by Pierre de Nolhac, "Pétrarque jardinier," in *Pétrarque et l'humanisme* (Paris: Librairie Honoré Champion, 1965), 2:263 n. 1. Boccaccio's words, however, are not sufficient to give an idea of the kind of place (whether kitchen garden or garden, or both). And Petrarch himself does not mention it in his *Palladius*. See also Ernest Wilkins, *Life of Petrarch* (Chicago: University of Chicago Press, 1961), 101.

10. See chap. 2, note 7.

11. See the letter *Familiares* XIII.8 in Petrarch, *Petrarch at Vaucluse: Letters in Verse and Prose,* ed. and trans. Ernest Hatch Wilkins (Chicago: University of Chicago Press, 1958), 123.

12. Ibid.

13. Petrarch bought his house at Vaucluse in 1337, while the codex including his *postille* was written for him around 1340 (Armando Petrucci, *La scrittura di Francesco Petrarca* [Vatican City: Biblioteca Apostolica Vaticana, 1967], 117), and in those years he traveled to Rome, Naples, and Parma. However, Petrarch returned to Vaucluse in 1345–1346 and 1351–1352, and at that time he already possessed the *Palladius*. Therefore, if his property in Provence included gardens, and if he was also engaged in the practice of horticulture, he must have chosen, surprisingly, not to make any record of it. In fact, his annotations, related to the years 1348–1350, 1353, 1357, 1359, and 1369, only refer to Milan, Padua, and Arquà. In his article "Non chiare acque," Eugenio Battisti says that the gardens at Vaucluse were actually *pomaria* that Petrarch cultivated with vines, pear and apple trees, peach and

fig trees, and walnut and almond trees. But Battisti does not say from what source he derives the latter information. See *Francis Petrarch: Six Centuries Later. A Symposium*, ed. Aldo Scaglione (Portland, Ore.: International Scholarly Book Service, 1975), 318.

14. Petrarch, *Petrarch's Remedies for Fortune Fair and Foul: A Modern English Translation of De remediis utriusque fortunae*, trans. Conrad H. Rawski (Bloomington: Indiana University Press, 1991), 1:174–175.

15. In his *De vera religione* III.4, Saint Augustine quotes from the first letter of John (2, 15–16): "Nolite diligere mundum, quoniam ea, quae in mundo sunt, concupiscientia carnis est et concupiscientia oculorum et ambitio saeculi." Saint Augustine, *La vera religione*, ed. and trans. Onorato Grassi (Milan: Rusconi, 1997), 34.

16. Although some critics, such as Giuseppe Billanovich in *Petrarca letterato: Lo scrittoio del Petrarca* (Rome: Edizioni di Storia e Letteratura, 1947), 195, do not believe that the ascent ever took place, I think it is more important to point out what Petrarch wanted his readers to think, that is, that the ascent had truly taken place, as the presence of his brother as the companion of the trip seems to guarantee.

17. "Sola videndi insignem loci altitudinem cupiditate ductus." Francesco Petrarca, *Le familiari (libri I–XI)*, vol. 1, pt. 1, trans. Ugo Dotti (Urbino: Argaglía Editore, 1974), 363–365.

18. Manlio Pastore Stocchi, "La cultura geografica dell'umanesimo," in *Optima Hereditas: Sapienza giuridica romana e conoscenza dell'ecumene* (Milan: Libri Scheiwiller, 1992), 566.

19. Petrarch, *Petrarch's Remedies for Fortune Fair and Foul*, 3:224–225.

20. Incidentally, Augustine's quotation from the *De vera religione* cited above (note 15) sounds ambiguous, especially if we consider the unconditional love for nature the saint expresses elsewhere. An answer may be found in the third book, entitled "The Religion of Our Times." Here Augustine remarks that truth cannot be reached through sense perception, for the latter is deceptive, but rather through contemplation, which is the only path to God. Only then will man know that real beauty is immutable, and he will no longer suffer from the consideration that anything that exists on this earth is only temporary, for it is destined to continuing change and eventual death.

21. The quotation is from Petrarch, *Petrarch's Remedies for Fortune Fair and Foul*, 4:376–377.

22. Ibid., 1:176.

23. Ibid., 174.

24. Ibid., 172.

25. Petrarca, *Le familiari (libri I–XI)*, 2:1207.

26. Enrico Carrara, "Aridulum rus," in *Scritti varii di erudizione e di critica in onore di Rodolfo Renier* (Turin: Fratelli Bocca, 1912), 271–288.

27. Francesco Petrarca, *Laurea occidens: Bucolicum Carmen X*, ed. and trans. Guido Martellotti (Rome: Edizioni di Storia e Letteratura, 1968), 17–19; 35–37.

28. "Le nuove ricchezze sono le soddisfazioni interiori che il culto degli studi letterari gli procurava." Carrara, "Aridulum rus," 273.

29. Enrico Castelnuovo, *Un pittore italiano alla corte di Avignone: Matteo Giovannetti e la pittura in Provenza nel secolo XIV* (Turin: Giulio Einaudi Editore, 1962), 40–42.

Castelnuovo points out that Petrarch may have drawn inspiration from the frescoes of the papal palace for the description of Vaucluse in the *Familiares* XVII.5 that he wrote to Guido Sette in 1353: "Ludunt argentei pisces in gurgite vitreo, rari procul in pratis mugiunt boves, sibilant aure salubres leviter percussis arboribus, volucres canunt varie in ramis." See Petrarca, *Epistole di Francesco Petrarca*, ed. Ugo Dotti (Turin: Unione Tipografico-Editrice Torinese, 1978), 400.

30. Petrarca, "Invectiva contra eum qui maledixit Italie," in *Opere latine*, ed. Antonietta Bufano (Turin: Unione Tipografico-Editrice Torinese, 1975), 2:1158. The relationship between Petrarch and Avignon has been described by Roberto Mercuri, "Avignone e Napoli in Dante, Petrarca e Boccaccio," *Analecta Romana Studi Danici*, supplement 25 (1998), 117–129.

31. A more explicit condemnation of Avignon, and of the time he spent there, occurs in the letters *Sine nomine*, which reflect, like most of Petrarch's works written in Latin, a moral and polemical viewpoint.

32. Of the Greek poets, however, Petrarch only read Homer, in the Latin translation and late in life. The references he makes to Greek poets are usually to those about whom he had read.

33. See letter XIII.8 in Petrarch, *Petrarch at Vaucluse*, 119.

34. Ibid., 120–121.

35. Ibid., 121.

36. H. David Brumble, *Classical Myths and Legends in the Middle Ages and Renaissance: A Dictionary of Allegorical Meanings* (Westport: Greenwood Press, 1998), 28–32; 48–52.

37. Petrarca, *Rime, trionfi e poesie latine*, ed. F. Neri et al. (Milan: Riccardo Ricciardi, 1951), 766–773.

38. Fred J. Nichols, "Petrarch Transplants the Muses," *Analecta Romana Studi Danici*, supplement 25 (1998), 61–68.

39. Francesco Petrarca, *Lettere di Francesco Petrarca: Delle cose familiari libri ventiquattro*, trans. G. Fracassetti (Florence: Felice Le Monnier, 1865), 3:261.

40. Boccaccio makes an explicit reference to Petrach's property at Vaucluse in the *Genealogie deorum gentilium*, where he describes it as "parva domus et hortulus," thus confirming the presence of at least one *hortulus*. See Giovanni Boccaccio, *Genealogie deorum gentilium*, ed. Vittorio Zaccaria, vols. 7–8, pt. 2 of *Tutte le opere di Giovanni Boccaccio*, ed. Vittore Branca (Milan: Mondadori, 1998), 1484.

41. The link between Petrarch and the gardens of the mature Italian Renaissance seems to run—according to present-day scholars—along a double path: on the one hand, the poet's horticultural activity, and the fact that he writes about it, shows a first interest in gardens; on the other, his perception of the beauty of nature makes garden historians speak of an early "aesthetic feeling." Allen Weiss in his *Unnatural Horizons: Paradox and Contradiction in Landscape Architecture* (New York: Princeton Architectural Press, 1998), 13, considers Petrarch and the early humanist sensibility that informed his gardens a precondition "to localize and systematize such apperceptions in the creation of the Italian Renaissance garden." Also, in *The Idea of the Garden in the Renaissance* (New Brunswick: Rutgers University Press, 1978), 64, Terry Comito argues that "the aesthetic possession of physical space" that takes place in

Petrarch's gardens anticipates the peculiar aspirations of Renaissance gardens. In "Picta poesis: Ricerche sulla poesia e il giardino dalle origini al Seicento," in *Il paesaggio*, ed. Cesare De Seta, vol. 5 of *Storia d'Italia: Annali*, ed. Ruggiero Romano and Corrado Vivanti (Turin: Einaudi, 1982), 684, Gianni Venturi says that the garden for Petrarch symbolizes a return to classical times, especially those of Theocritus and Virgil, when the laws of an ideal time and place were laid out, characterized by the belief in an ideal nature, in an eternal spring and everlasting happiness. Petrarch is conscious of this symbolism, and his gardens at Vaucluse carry out—according to Venturi—the same function that will be assigned to the gardens at Careggi or to those of Lorenzo the Magnificent and Poliziano. In "Non chiare acque," 313, Battisti says that Petrarch describes Vaucluse as both *locus amoenus* and *locus asper*: "Come vedremo, questi due caratteri sono congiunti nel duplice giardino, differentemente usato dal poeta, e la loro associazione rimarrà un tratto tipico del giardino rinascimentale italiano." And he continues, 325: "Il Petrarca, con le sue impressionanti testimonianze, dovette contribuire non poco, d'altronde, alla creazione del giardino rinascimentale, quando, addirittura, i suoi interventi non costituiscano esempi direttamente e largamente imitati. Se Cosimo de' Medici o Pio II hanno letto le sue pagine (o Alberti le lesse e commentò per loro), l'idea, ad esempio, di un hortus citerior e di un hortus ulterior (come sono definiti i giardini petrarcheschi di Parma, e come potrebbero benissimo essere definiti quelli di Arquà), potè sembrare una perfetta anticipazione del nuovo concetto di villa come luogo esteticamente qualificato."

42. Paris: Bibliothèque Nationale, ms. Lat. 6802, fol. 143v.

43. It has been ascertained that the sketch could not have been drawn at Vaucluse, for Petrarch bought the manuscript containing Pliny's *Naturalis historia* in 1350 at Mantua—after he had left Provence—and the manuscript was in Verona at the time of Petrarch's last sojourn in France. See Florence Callu and François Avril, *Boccace en France: De l'humanisme à l'érotisme* (Paris: Bibliothèque Nationale, 1975), 14. According to Avril the sketch, traditionally attributed to Petrarch, was actually drawn by Boccaccio during one of his visits to the poet, for the style is very similar to Boccaccio's drawings in the *Zibaldone magliabechiano*. See also Vittore Branca, *Boccaccio visualizzato: Narrare per parole e per immagini fra Medioevo e Rinascimento* (Turin: Giulio Einaudi Editore, 1999), 1:5. Since the words *Sorgie fons* that appear on the upper margin of the same page resemble Boccaccio's handwriting, while the note "transalpina solitudo mea iocundissima" seems to have been written by Petrarch, it is possible that Boccaccio drew the sketch in the presence of his friend and following the latter's indications.

44. For a detailed study of Petrarch's illuminated manuscripts and their location see Joseph B. Trapp, "The Iconography of Petrarch in the Age of Humanism," *Quaderni Petrarcheschi* 9–10 (1992–1993), 11–73. Cf. Millard Meiss, "The First Fully Illustrated Decameron," in *Essays in the History of Art Presented to Rudolf Wittkower*, ed. D. Fraser, H. Hibbard, and M. Lewine (London: Phaidon, 1967), 56–61.

45. The codex is located in Milan: Ambrosiana Library, Ms. Petrarcae Codex, A. 79 inf.

46. For the literary key to the meaning of the painted allegory see Joel Brink, "Simone Martini, Francesco Petrarca and the Humanistic Program of the Virgil Frontispiece," *Mediaevalia: A Journal of Medieval Studies* 3 (1977), 83–117.

47. See especially Purgatorio XXVIII, in Dante Alighieri, *The Divine Comedy*, trans. Charles Singleton, vol. 2, pt. 1 (Princeton: Princeton University Press, 1973), 302–313.

48. Boccaccio, *Genealogie deorum gentilium*, 1426.

49. Ibid., 1426, 1428.

50. Giovanni Boccaccio, *Comedia delle ninfe fiorentine*, ed. Antonio Enzo Quaglio, vol. 2 of *Tutte le opere di Giovanni Boccaccio*, ed. Vittore Branca (Milan: Mondadori, 1964).

51. "Graceful voice." Ibid., 685. Translations into English are mine.

52. Vittore Branca, "Interespressività narrativo-figurativa e rinnovamenti topologici e iconografici," in *Boccaccio visualizzato*, 1:39–74 (esp. 62).

53. "D'animale bruto, uomo divenuto." Boccaccio, *Comedia delle ninfe fiorentine*, 829.

54. Edward Panofsky, *Studies in Iconology: Humanist Themes in the Art of the Renaissance*, 2nd ed. (New York: Harper and Row, 1962), 142.

55. "Singular bellezza . . . dilettevole di graziose ville e di campi fruttiferi copiosa." Boccaccio, *Comedia delle ninfe fiorentine*, 683.

56. Ibid., 684.

57. Ibid.

58. Tommaseo, *Dizionario della lingua italiana*. s.v. *seno*.

59. "E questo loco, / al mio piacere assai più ch'altro degno, / io signoreggio." Boccaccio, *Comedia delle ninfe fiorentine*, 688.

60. Ibid., 696.

61. "In questo loco." Ibid., 698.

62. Marshall Brown, "In the Valley of the Ladies," *Italian Quarterly* 18, no. 72 (1975), 33–52.

63. Ibid., 49.

64. "Una bellissima giovane con un vestimento indosso tanto sottile . . . dalla cintura in giù coperta d'una coltre bianchissima." Boccaccio, *Decameron*, 443.

65. "Sopra il verde prato." Ibid.

66. "La divina foresta spessa e viva . . . / tal qual di ramo in ramo si raccoglie / per la pineta in su 'l lito di Chiassi." Purgatorio XXVIII, 2:19–20, in Dante Alighieri, *The Divine Comedy*, vol. 2, pt. 1, 302–304. Boccaccio hints at the courtly life that Nastagio leads at Chiassi, and this again reminds the reader of Dante's nostalgic description of the courtly lifestyle in Purgatorio XIV. Moreover, just as Dante slowly enters the forest of Paradise with *lenti passi* on an early spring morning (304), Nastagio—"foot after foot" ("piede innanzi piè," Boccaccio, *Decameron*, 504)—enters the grove of pines absorbed in his own thoughts on a May morning.

67. "Più le parole pesan che' fatti." Boccaccio, *Decameron*, 960.

68. Ibid., 960.

69. According to Edith Kern and Millicent Marcus the gardens of the frame settings are linked only by the journey of the *novellatori* through them. Marcus, following Kern, suggested that "the frame story be read as a movement to three studiedly *different* garden sites, and not as one homogeneous setting." (Emphasis in original.) Edith G. Kern, "The

Gardens in the Decameron Cornice," *PMLA* 66 (1951), 505. Also Millicent Marcus, "An Allegory of Two Gardens: The Tale of Madonna Dianora (Decameron X, 5)," *Forum Italicum* 14 (1980), 166.

70. To consider the gardens as independent from the architecture of the first setting can only make commentators say that "what the first setting lacks is precision" (Marcus, "An Allegory of two Gardens," 166) and "the first garden has no distinct character and therefore deserves . . . no special mention" (Kern, "The Gardens in the Decameron Cornice," 511–512).

71. "Era il detto luogo sopra una piccola montagnetta . . . di varii albuscelli e piante tutte di verdi fronde ripiene piacevoli a riguardare; in sul colmo della quale era un palagio con bello e gran cortile nel mezzo, e con logge e con sale e con camere . . . con pratelli da torno e con giardini maravigliosi e con pozzi d'acque freschissime e con volte di preziosi vini." Boccaccio, *Decameron*, 26.

72. "Il quale tutto spazzato, e nelle camere i letti fatti, e ogni cosa di fiori quali nella stagione si potevano avere piena e di giunchi giuncata." Ibid., 26–27.

73. Ibid., 27.

74. "Ma per ciò che le cose che sono senza modo non possono lungamente durare, io, che cominciatrice fui de' ragionamenti da' quali questa così bella compagnia è stata fatta, pensando al continuar della nostra letizia, estimo che di necessità sia convenire esser tra noi alcuno principale, il quale noi e onoriamo e ubidiamo come maggiore." Ibid.

75. "Esso avea dintorno da sé e per lo mezzo in assai parti vie ampissime, tutte diritte come strale e coperte di pergolati di viti." Ibid., 236.

76. "Lungo sarebbe a raccontare." Ibid.

77. Marcus, "An Allegory of Two Gardens," 167.

78. "Artificiosamente." Boccaccio, *Decameron*, 237.

79. "Quasi dimestichi." Ibid., 237–238.

80. "Quantunque artificio della natura e non manual paresse." Ibid., 577.

81. "Successivamente ordinati." Ibid., 578.

82. "Sì ben composti e sì bene ordinati, come se qualunque è di ciò il migliore artefice gli avesse piantati." Ibid.

83. Marcus, "An Allegory of Two Gardens," 167–168.

84. Ibid., 168.

85. As Boccaccio was well aware, deciduous trees do not make an ordered grid visible at all times—especially when they lose their leaves and also because they do not have an "architectural" outline, such as that of the conifers covering the lower part of the valley. In fact, whereas the evergreen trees of the valley's lower slopes are planted in a grid, the cherries, figs, and almonds of the upper tiers are planted at random, although they form a thick bosquet that does not lessen the visible order of the third setting.

86. The journey of the *novellatori* back to the city, from the valley of the ladies, through the second and first gardens, suggests precisely the possibility of an inverse reading of the garden sites.

87. Kern, "The Gardens in the Decameron Cornice," 514–515.

88. Boccaccio also tells the story of the enchanted garden in the *Filocolo*, when he introduces the fourth question about love. Here too the morphology of the garden is not addressed, although the operations that the necromancer carries out in order to fulfill his magic are described in detail. But these operations are not included in the *Decameron* story. See Boccaccio, *Filocolo*, ed. Antonio Enzo Quaglio, vol. 1 of *Tutte le opere di Giovanni Boccaccio*, ed. Vittore Branca (Milan: Mondadori, 1964), 398–403.

89. "Il veder questo giardino, il suo bello ordine, le piante e la fontana co' ruscelletti procedenti da quella tanto piacque a ciascuna donna e a' tre giovani, che tutti cominciarono a affermare che, se Paradiso si potesse in terra fare, non sapevano conoscere che altra forma che quella di quel giardino gli si potesse dare, né pensare, oltre a questo, qual bellezza gli si potesse agiugnere." Boccaccio, *Decameron*, 237.

90. The first illustrations of Petrarch at Vaucluse appear in the miniatures of only a few manuscripts of the late fifteenth century. One of these, the Florentine ms. Strozzi 172 of the BML, shows the poet sitting on a chair in an open landscape. Laura is represented offering him a bay leaf that he promptly accepts (fol. 1r). See Trapp, "The Iconography of Petrarch in the Age of Humanism," 21.

91. The *Decameron* was accepted among higher literary circles only later, that is, when the vulgar tongue started to be considered worthy of literary expression. Moreover, in the fourteenth century only those literary works that expressed monumental and heroic ideals were considered worthy of the major liberal arts.

92. This codex is in Paris: Bibliothèque Nationale, ms. It. 482. The first illustrated codex is a holograph of the *Decameron* (Berlin: Staatsbibliothek Preussischer Kulturbesitz, Hamilton 90, circa 1370), which is only decorated with half busts of the main characters drawn by Boccaccio himself in the margins of the text. It was Degenhart and Schmitt who attributed these figures to Boccaccio in 1968, on the basis of a comparison with a copy of the *Divine Comedy* transcribed and illustrated by Boccaccio (Florence, BR, ms. 1035). Bernhard Degenhart and Annegrit Schmitt, *Corpus der Italienischen Zeichnungen 1300–1450*. vol. 1, pt. 1 (Berlin: Mann, 1968), 129–131, 134–138. The latter drawings have also been compared to other sketches found in the *Zibaldone laurenziano* (Florence, BML, ms. Pluteo 38.17), and in the *Zibaldone magliabechiano* (Florence, BNCF, ms. B. R. 50), with the result that they all seem to have been drawn by the same hand, that of Boccaccio.

93. Maria Grazia Ciardi Dupré dal Poggetto, "L'iconografia nei codici miniati boccacciani dell'Italia centrale e meridionale," in *Boccaccio visualizzato*, 2:3–52 (esp. 13).

94. Thus, for example, in the illustration of Filippo Balducci's story (Capponi manuscript) the illustrator used the famous scene of the Lamentation over the dead Christ in order to represent a group of people lamenting the death of Filippo's wife. Meiss, "The First Fully Illustrated Decameron," 57.

95. This codex is in Paris: Bibliothèque Nationale, ms. It. 63. It is only by the first half of the fifteenth century that the production of illustrated copies of the *Decameron* starts to flourish in Florence. The revival of the Gothic taste with its aristocratic descent, its typical delicacy and richness, attracted patrons of mercantile origins but with aristocratic ambitions, who commissioned the most costly, and of course illustrated, copies of

the *Decameron*. However, the Ceffini manuscript was executed not by a professional scribe but probably by Ceffini himself, an amateur who transcribed the book "per me proprio," for himself alone. Because the illuminator did not employ continuous illustrations, the parts to be illustrated were chosen carefully, according to a personal interpretation of the text.

96. Ibid., fol. 150.

97. The matrix used for the preface, for example, was copied from the Venetian model, although with some differences: the characters appear amid a few blades of grass and look rather clumsy under the fragile trellised latticework. The tales narrating a typical Florentine subject, such as those about Florentine painters, also did not inspire an adequate figurative reaction. Even the second edition published in Florence in 1573 did not represent a great innovation in the history of Florentine book illustration, for it was diligently expurgated according to the rules of the Council of Trent (1545–1563).

98. However, after the almost absolute silence of the most important artists of the late fourteenth century, it is Renaissance painting, so distant from medieval times, that will draw again inspiration from Boccaccio, especially after the solicitations of writers like Lorenzo, Poliziano, and Bembo. Branca, "Introduzione: Il narrar boccacciano per immagini," in *Boccaccio visualizzato*, 1:3–34.

99. In 1597 the last *Decameron* of the sixteenth century was published, which specified in its introduction that the illustrations for each novella were morally appropriate.

100. See note 41.

101. "Alla configurazione del giardino presiedono la suggestione del petrarchismo insieme all'influenza determinante del progressivo affermarsi a Firenze delle teorie connesse con l'ideologia dell'Accademia neoplatonica." Mastrorocco, *Le mutazioni di Proteo: I giardini medicei del Cinquecento* (Florence: Sansoni, 1981), 6–17.

102. Ficino argues that man as a species is able to appreciate the quality of objects, i.e., the alignment of lines and angles, the proportion of the human body, and the harmony present in song and dance. However, man is not aware of the reasons of his appreciation, and in fact he approves without deliberation (Marsilio Ficino, *Platonic Theology*, trans. Michael J. B. Allen and John Warden, ed. James Hankins and William Bowen [Cambridge: Harvard University Press, 2001–2006], 3:283). This, continues Ficino, is because man's soul receives from the eternal Ideas the seals of every object without their matter. Further, the mind of man imposes these seals on his sense perception, or else forms his perceptions, which allow him to create for himself "the concord, the proportions, the satisfying shapes that constitute beauty." On the other hand, since form, in the general Platonic sense, actually abides in things, because of a universal harmony we are able to justify, or fit the perceptions of material forms to, the prints or images of the purely Ideal Forms. See Michael J. B. Allen, *Icastes: Marsilio Ficino's Interpretation of Plato's Sophist* (Berkeley: University of California Press, 1989), 130, 132.

103. Marsilio Ficino, *Three Books on Life*, ed. and trans. Carol V. Kaske and John R. Clark (Binghamton, N.Y.: Medieval & Renaissance Texts & Studies in conjunction with the Renaissance Society of America, 1989; reprint, Tempe: Arizona Center for Medieval

and Renaissance Studies in conjunction with the Renaissance Society of America, 1998), 205. All translations are from this edition.

104. Ibid., 289.

105. Ficino, *Platonic Theology*, 1:203.

106. Ibid.

107. Ficino, *Three Books on Life*, 289. As Kristeller has pointed out, the analogy between macrocosm and microcosm holds sway from the Middle Ages to the Renaissance because of the creative principle that characterizes both. Paul Oskar Kristeller, *Il pensiero filosofico di Marsilio Ficino* (Florence: Sansoni Editore, 1953), 52–65.

108. Love itself, as Ficino points out more than once in his commentary on Plato's *Symposium*, is a form of analogy, for it is a mutual attraction moved by likeness. Kaske and Clark maintain, however, that in the *De vita* Ficino's concept of cosmic love has evolved into an attraction that also unites opposites. Ficino, *Three Books on Life*, 29.

109. Ibid., 135.

110. Ibid., 205.

111. Ibid., 291.

112. Ibid. 225: "The spirit indeed is what lives in us first. . . . Do not life, sense, and motion often in a certain sudden accident or passion suddenly desert the bodily parts, the spirit having retreated suddenly to the chambers of the heart; and often do they not return right away to the bodily parts through rubbings and odors when the spirit returns to them, as if life indeed inhered rather in that volatile spirit than in the humors or the bodily parts?"

113. According to some critics, the Hebrew words *adam* (man) and *dama* (earth), and their respective phonemes, represent the bond of life existing between man and earth. Gerhard von Rad, *Genesis: A Commentary*, trans. John H. Marks (Philadelphia: Westminster Press, 1961), 75.

114. Ibid. In the Old Testament the body is not yet distinguished from the soul, only from life.

115. Ficino, *Three Books on Life*, 221. The most nourishing odors are those coming from things that are themselves nourishing, as for example the aromatic pear, the peach, and similar kinds of fruits.

116. Ibid., 293. Having a variety of plants is dictated not only by the "spiritual" necessity of breathing different odors. In fact, bearing in mind the analogy between the cosmos, whose structure is shared by any pleasance, and the human body, it is obvious that a variety of species is as indispensable to a green place as different kinds of food and nutrients are to the body. See bk. 2, chap. 18.

117. Ibid., 135.

118. Ibid., 201.

119. Ibid., 221.

120. Ibid., 379.

121. Marsilio Ficino, *The Letters*, 1:53.

122. For the intellectuals, the quality of the animal spirit is of the highest concern because they mostly work by means of this spirit; and so they, more than anyone, have to select pure and luminous air, scents, and music.

123. Plato, *Timaeus*, 88–90, in *Plato: Complete Works*, ed. John Cooper (Indianapolis: Hackett, 1997), 1287–1289.

124. Ficino, *Three Books on Life*, 293.

125. Plato, *Phaedo*, 110b–111c, in *Plato: Complete Works*, 94–95.

126. Although these words are being pronounced by a god, and not by Ficino himself, they still retain their credibility. That Liber, or Bacchus, represents an authorial figure, amid the other gods, is proven by the association that often occurs in *De vita* between the god of wine and the god of the sun, Phoebus. In the concluding chapter of book 2, Ficino says that "Phoebus indeed is the very soul of that sphere [the sun], Bacchus assuredly is the sphere itself . . . they are always brothers and comrades and practically always second selves." What this implies is that Bacchus would be the visible sun, Phoebus the fostering light. As Kaske and Clark have remarked, "Phoebus and Bacchus may be explainable as a personal compliment, since they are the nicknames of Ficino and of his 'alter idem,' Pico della Mirandola." Ficino, *Three Books on Life*, 426 n. 7.

127. "Liber ipse semper odit servos et, quam vino promittit vitam, solis liberis implet longam. . . . Risum ex meis hortis legite, negligite ficum." Ficino, *Three Books on Life*, 205. Although in the Middle Ages the Latin term *risus* acquires the meaning "rice," in addition to the earlier "laughter," I think that Ficino is using it here as a pun. In fact, rice is not cultivated in a "garden," and "gaiety" better reflects the association with Bacchus. Although I agree with Kaske's translation of *risum* as "rice," I have reservations about his rendering of the word *hortus* as garden.

128. As John Freccero has pointed out in "The Fig Tree and the Laurel: Petrarch's Poetics," *Diacritics* 5 (Spring 1975), 34–40, in the eighth book of Augustine's *Confessions* the fig tree in the garden of Milan represents "the revelation of God's Word to the Saint at a particular time and place, recapitulating the Christ event in an individual soul," but it is also meant to represent "the broader pattern of salvation history," after the Fall, "for all Christians" (esp. 36). The allegory of the fig tree thus seems to take on, during the Middle Ages, the positive meaning of the conversion, after a life of sin. Moreover, for Petrarch the fig tree represents the beginning of a new life, when, in the first book of the *Secretum,* he says to Augustine, his interlocutor: "Nor can I ever forget that life-giving fig tree, under whose shadow this miracle (the conversion) happened to you." But if the fig tree stands for the righteous life, why does Ficino exclude it from his *hortus?* We know that Petrarch was obsessed with the deceptive allure of sensual pleasure—the worst of the sins—to which he opposed a higher spiritual desire, that of God. Thus, the fig tree represents the achievement of a complete separation of the mind from the body, which is ultimately abandoned. But for Ficino a sinful life is not a matter of devoting oneself to sensual satisfaction instead of living a life of pure contemplation: to take joy from a beautiful sight by appreciating the beauty of a human body, or to please the ear with melodious sounds, is not something to be condemned (the only neglected senses seem to be, in the commentary on Plato's *Symposium*, those of touch and taste), for body, spirit, and soul are, to Ficino, parts of a harmonious ensemble. Thus, by rejecting the allegorical medieval meaning of the fig tree, based on the Gospels and the Apocalypse of the New Testament, Ficino goes back to Genesis, where the tree represents the first loss of that primordial harmony, or the effect of the original sin.

129. Ficino, *Three Books on Life*, 205.

130. In the tradition of secular literature—especially in thirteenth-century France—the figure of the garden is often used to stage love enterprises of young characters aiming for sexual intercourse, and thus old age—usually its personification—is banned from the paradisal place. The fact that Ficino's pleasance invites both youth and old age may indicate that we are dealing with a *locus amoenus*, rather than a garden.

131. Ficino, *Three Books on Life*, 201.

132. Ficino does not at all deny the importance of the senses. Knowledge itself, or at least part of it, begins with the senses, and people should learn how to make good use of them, for, according to the logic of the philosopher, if we are born with them, there must be a reason and they must serve a function. As Ficino says in a letter to Cavalcanti, God himself assigns men's souls to a corporeal service, so that at an earlier stage, when distracted by the agitation of the body, the soul is engaged in inferior activities "more attentively and more often than in higher ones." Ficino, *The Letters*, 1:52. What Ficino deprecates is the indulgence in the satisfaction of immediate and sensual desires for more than is necessary, without attempting to train the mind toward the appreciation of God, the divine and invisible sun.

133. Ficino says more than once in the *De vita* that his treatise is dedicated to an elite of intellectuals, and, more precisely, he advises those who favor sexual intercourse to consult another doctor. Ficino, *Three Books on Life*, 217.

134. Ibid., 291.

135. "Nothing more than light resembles the nature of the good. First of all, according to our senses, light is the purest and highest thing; secondly, light diffuses itself instantaneously and more easily and broadly than anything else; thirdly, it spreads itself over anything without doing any harm and penetrates everything very dimly. Further, light bears a vital heat that warms anything up. . . . Similarly, good is that which masters the order of reality, it diffuses itself everywhere and softens anything . . . it is accompanied by love, almost heat, with which it variously attracts any things, which are delighted to receive it." Ficino, "De Sole," in *Prosatori latini del Quattrocento*, ed. Eugenio Garin (Milan: Riccardo Ricciardi Editore, 1952), 970. My translation.

136. It seems that for Ficino, knowledge, like anything else, has gradients of exactitude, starting from the sensible perception of that which surrounds us, which is still an incomplete knowledge, to a final apotheosis, during which men achieve the true understanding of God. The latter step of knowledge is still linked to experience, but it is called contemplative experience and usually pertains to philosophers.

137. Ficino explains that triple hues of light derive from the single light of the sun: the totally white light, the reddish light, and the mixed light, and three sensual capacities correspond to each of them: the corporeal senses of touch and taste to the red light; the incorporeal senses of imagination and sight to the white light; and the medium senses of olfaction and hearing to the mixed light, which, for the temperateness that it reflects, is Ficino's favorite one.

138. *Atto*, which Plato also calls "science," implies the performance of an action that does not result in any material product, in that the one who makes and that which is made

are undistinguishable. Thus—and this is true for Aristotle too—action may be equated with "use."

139. Ficino, "De Sole," 992.

140. On the relationship between the human spirit and the world spirit see Cesare Vasoli, *Tra "maestri" umanisti e teologi: Studi quattrocenteschi* (Florence: Le Lettere, 1991), 120–141.

141. Ficino, *Three Books on Life*, 353.

142. Ibid, 307.

143. Allen, *Icastes*, 119. As Allen explains: "We may refer to the natural world as 'created' if we mean loosely that it was made, not out of preexistent matter, but rather out of the potentiality of 'chaos' to receive form; but even then, strictly speaking, we should refer to it as being 'formed' or 'generated.' . . . All art is . . . a making, not a creating." (Ibid.)

144. Ficino, *Platonic Theology*, 4:173.

145. Ibid.

146. Ibid., 175.

147. Ibid., 169.

148. Giovanni Rucellai, *Giovanni Rucellai ed il suo Zibaldone*, ed. Alessandro Perosa (London: Warburg Institute, University of London, 1960–1981), 1:20–23.

149. Ficino, *Platonic Theology*, 4:169–171.

150. Ibid., 171.

151. Ibid., 3:285.

152. Ibid.

153. Ibid., 289.

154. In his article "The *Decameron*: The Literal and the Allegorical," *Italian Quarterly* 18, no. 72, (Spring 1975), 53–73, Giuseppe Mazzotta writes that in the story collection "the allegory and the letter function each as a critical perspective on the other" (68). The apology that Boccaccio writes in the conclusion of the *Decameron* "implies that all writings, sacred and profane alike, are morally neutral allegories and openly claims that the responsibility in interpreting the stories lies with the reader" (62).

155. Ficino arranged the entities capable of attracting celestial powers on a scale of seven. From the top to the bottom he lists: acts of contemplation; acts of reason; acts of imagination; sounds, words, and song; powders, vapors, and scents; organic matter; stones and metals. Although he places stones and metals at the bottom, thus following the typical Neoplatonic contempt for matter, he is only singling out the most opaque materials, which, nevertheless, still retain a minimum capacity for attracting celestial influence. See Brian P. Copenhaver, "Scholastic Philosophy and Renaissance Magic in the De vita of Marsilio Ficino," *Renaissance Quarterly* 37, no. 4, (1984), 523–554.

156. *Marsilii Ficini Opera*, with an introduction by Stéphane Toussaint (Paris: Phénix Éditions, 2000), 1: fols. 893–894.

157. "An forte qualem mente machinabamur formam, talem imaginationis potentia fecimus." Ibid., fol. 894.

158. Ibid.

159. Ficino, *Opera*, vol. 2, fol. 1969. On the meaning of Platonic allegory see André Chastel, *Marsile Ficin et l'art*, 3rd ed. (Geneva: Droz, 1996), 160.

CHAPTER FOUR. PRACTICE AND THEORY

1. Grazia Gobbi Sica, *La villa fiorentina: Elementi storici e critici per una lettura* (Florence: Alinea Editrice, 1998), 72. It is arguable whether or not the garden at Quaracchi was the product of design. In fact, the description by Rucellai portrays a garden that lacks unity and symmetry, and that appears made of an episodic sequence of discrete parts, whose organization did not necessarily require an overall design scheme. In this regard the description recalls the familiar accounts of villa gardens by Pliny the Younger, which historians have tried to reconstruct in a number of different ways. See Giovanni Rucellai, *Giovanni Rucellai ed il suo Zibaldone*, ed. Alessandro Perosa (London: Warburg Institute, University of London, 1960–1981), 1:20–23.

2. Gobbi Sica, *La villa fiorentina*, 78.

3. Ibid., 73.

4. Ibid. Gobbi Sica argues that Florentine gardens, unlike Roman ones, ignore the third dimension, insofar as their layout is rarely structured on the articulation of terraces, which in Tuscany will be adopted only later, in the seventeenth century. Of course, the very existence of the Medici villa at Fiesole shows that her statement is not completely accurate.

5. GDSU, 4016r A. "Questo è il disegnio del modo del tutto fatto brevemente p[e]rch[è] più facilmente V[ostra[S[anti]tà si possa resolvere; et e' giardinj si faran[n]o più larghi ch[e] no[n] sono in disegnio el doppio et quello più o mancho [come] parrà a V[ostra] S[anti]tà S[egnato] D." This drawing was first catalogued by Pasquale Nerino Ferri as being by Bernardo Buontalenti (c. 1536–1608); see Real Galleria di Firenze, *Indice geografico-analitico dei disegni di architettura civile e militare esistenti nella Reale Galleria degli Uffizi in Firenze* (Rome, 1885), 3:73, s.v. Poggio a Caiano. Foster, however, suggested that the drawing may be attributed to the Sangallo workshop. See his "A Study of Lorenzo de' Medici's Villa at Poggio a Caiano" (Ph.D. diss., Yale University, 1974), 1:440 n. 378. Foster also called attention to the annotation on this drawing, which indicates that it was presented to the pope. Thus, it seems likely that the drawing dates from the reign of either one of the two early Medici popes, Leo X (1513–1521) or Clement VII (1523–1534).

6. "Volle Sua Eccellenza che il Tribolo cominciasse a mettere in opera per ornamento di quel luogo i disegni ed i modelli, che già gli aveva fatto vedere." Vasari, *Le vite de' più eccellenti pittori, scultori e architettori*, ed. Gaetano Milanesi (Florence: G. C. Sansoni, 1878–1885), 6:72.

7. "E' nel mezzo di questo giardino un salvatico d'altissimi e folti cipressi, lauri e mortelle, i quali girando in tondo fanno la forma d'un laberinto circondato di bossoli alti due braccia e mezzo, e tanto pari e con bell'ordine condotti, che paiono fatti col pennello." Ibid., 74.

8. This is especially true in regard to the Florentine painting tradition, which, unlike the Venetian, emphasized drawing before the application of color on canvas.

9. It is useful to remember that for the earlier Medici villas such a figure as the garden designer is never acknowledged, and the composition of the gardens is more often only attributed to Michelozzo by garden historians, on the basis of Vasari's testimony, which is not always dependable, rather than proved with the aid of archival sources.

10. "Il Tribolo fu quelli che mise innanzi che detta pianta si facesse, acciò meglio si potesse considerar l'altezza de' monti, la bassezza de' piani, e gli altri particolari di rilievo." Vasari, *Le vite.* The citation is from Filippo Camerota, "Tribolo e Benvenuto della Volpaia: Il modello ligneo per l'assedio di Firenze," in *Niccolò detto il Tribolo tra arte, architettura e paesaggio*, ed. Elisabetta Pieri and Luigi Zangheri (Poggio a Caiano: Comune di Poggio a Caiano, 2001), 87.

11. Luigi Zangheri, "Le 'piante de' condotti' dei giardini di Castello e Petraia," *Bollettino degli Ingegneri* 19, nos. 2–3 (1971), 19–26.

12. "I viali verticali appaiono tutti in pendio dolce et agevole, e quelli trasversali tutti dritti e piani." Michel de Montaigne, *Journal de voyage en Italie par la Suisse et l'Allemagne en 1580 et 1581.* Cf. the Italian edition by Ettore Camesasca (Milan: Rizzoli, 1956). Citation is from Aurora Scotti, "Giardini fiorentini e torinesi fra '500 e '600. Loro struttura e significato," *L'Arte* 6 (1969), 40, 53 n. 7. Among the first testimonies on the oldest ducal garden, after the long discussion by Vasari in his life of Tribolo, is a letter written by Niccolò Martelli in 1543. See Niccolò Martelli, *Dal primo e dal secondo libro delle lettere di Niccolò Martelli*, ed. Cartesio Marconcini (Lanciano: Carabba, 1916), 20–23. See also the letter that Anton Francesco Doni wrote to Alberto Lollio on August 17, 1549, in which he mentions the garden (in *Il disegno del Doni* [Venice: Gabriele Giolito, 1549], fol. 49). In 1558 Pierre Belon published a detailed description of the garden, which he visited in 1549.

13. Castello is located a few kilometers to the northwest of Florence, on a tract of land at the foot of Mount Morello, gently declining toward the Arno. Its name derives from the Latin *castellum*, a word that both Vitruvius in his *De architectura* (8, 6) and Pliny in the *Naturalis historia* (36, 15, 24, §121) use to mean something other than castle, namely, a structure in which the water of an aqueduct is collected for distribution by pipes or channels in different directions. The site of the Medici villa was, in fact, named after a Roman aqueduct created to bring water from the Val di Marina to Florence. Charlton T. Lewis and Charles Short, *A Latin Dictionary* (New York: Oxford University Press, 1998), s.v. *castellum.* The construction of water conduits at Castello is mentioned in a letter from Pier Francesco Riccio to Cosimo de' Medici, December 31, 1546. ASF, *Mediceo del Principato*, 613, ins. 2, fol. 64.

14. GDSU, 1640v A. Foster, "A Study of Lorenzo de' Medici's Villa at Poggio a Caiano," 1:442 n. 384. Foster analyzed the façade of Poggio a Caiano represented on the verso of the folio, and indicated the presence of a watermark datable to the years 1520–1536. Cf. Edward Wright, "The Medici Villa at Olmo a Castello: Its History and Iconography," (Ph.D. diss., Princeton University, 1976). Wright implicitly attributes the drawing to Tribolo: "Vasari indicates Tribolo made his grotto 'con bel disegno d'architettura,' and the Uffizi plan has a more architectonic character, with its various recesses and projections, than the rough irregular walls of the present grotto," 1:162. Pasquale Nerino Ferri attributed the drawing to Giovan Battista da Sangallo. See Real Galleria di Firenze, *Indice*

geografico-analitico dei disegni di architettura civile e militare, 3:70, s.v. Poggio a Caiano. Bernhard Degenhart attributed the drawing to Francesco da Sangallo. See his "Dante, Leonardo und Sangallo: Dante-Illustrationen Giuliano da Sangallo in ihrem Verhältnis zu Leonardo da Vinci und zu den Figureneichungen der Sangallo," *Römischen Jahrbuch für Kunstgeschichte* 7 (1955), 101–288. Other drawings by Tribolo are located at the John Soane Museum in London; at the Kupferstichkabinett of Berlin; and at the Biblioteca Nacional of Madrid. See, in particular, B 16–49, fol. 41, in Carmen Añón Feliú et al., *Felipe II el rey íntimo: Jardín y naturaleza en el siglo XVI* (Madrid: Sociedad Estatal para la Conmemoración de los Centenarios de Felipe II y Carlos V, 1998), 38.

15. Giorgio Galletti, "Tribolo maestro delle acque dei giardini," in *Niccolò detto il Tribolo tra arte, architettura e paesaggio,* ed. Elisabetta Pieri and Luigi Zangheri (Poggio a Caiano: Comune di Poggio a Caiano, 2001), 155–156. According to Galletti, the drawing at the Uffizi, which he attributes to a collaborator of Tribolo, resembles one of the drawings included in manuscript 464 of the Biblioteca Universitaria of Pisa, described by Tongiorgi Tomasi, "Projects for Botanical and Other Gardens: A 16th-century Manual," *Journal of Garden History* 3, no. 1 (1983), 1–34. See in particular fol. 1588 on p. 21.

16. ASF, *Mediceo del Principato* 1171, ins. 6, fol. 292r: "Reverendo S.o maiodomo. Stamatina Sua Ecellezia mi chomese io dovesi fare pia[n]tare quelo bosch[o] e sa piantare nel g[i]a[r]dino che va inverso la strada. E che io lo dovesi disegnare ali detti operatti. E si desi mano subito. E chosi si desi mano a la fo[s]sa do[ve vanno [i] melara[n]ci. E io visto qua[n]to si disidera tali chosa ogi [h]o fat[t]o e disegno in sur uno foglio. E stasera ave[n]do ichomodo ne ve mostrerò. E . . . domatina di buonora si meterà mano i[n]ta[n]to a spianare e chosì a fare la fos[s]a dove vanno e melara[n]ci che sareno a dì primo di febbraio perché chosì sichorera sua Ecelezia. Sarano i[n] tut[t]o opere sei per ora. E subito fia fata la fo[s]sa de melara[n]ci o come so qui a capo mi schriva alora. Vostra signoria darà comesione a Bernardo Delavachio ma[n]di pia[n]te 60 di detti melara[n]ci. La[l]tre pia[n]te de boscho sarano 400 e di questo vostra Signoria sia informata. Di poi ma chomeso io faci fare una porta in chamera sua che v'escha sopra al poz[z]o di verso Fire[n]ze per potere u[s]cire in su' choridoi del palazo sa[n]za avere a u[s]cire pel mezo de palazo choruponte a levatoio. E chosi michomete e mi dice queste parole proprio ['] tribolo io le vorei a mia dì pe[r]chè le vorei godere ['] io li rispose che da me no ma[n]cherebe. E che mi pareva che Sua Ecelezia avesi rag[i]one. So che vostra signoria di questo no bisogna. Li dicha atro pe[r]che saza vostra Signoria no[n] poso operare. E a[n]chora mi dise de la rette de la piatera [?] si maravigliava non era fata. Li disi s'era dato l'o[r]dine a prete Jachopo e che io no potevo fare a[l]tro che non era ufizio mio che dare l'o[r]dine a qua[n]to mi chomete. E chosi de cha[n]celi me li solecita forte i[n] modo penso[..]ire i[n]fino a Pistoia. A[n]chora darò aviso a vostra signoria chome Sua Ecelezia è ito vege[n]do le sta[n]ze de[l] palazo si sono as[s]et[t]ate e li piacano [piacciono] asai. Si chotetta [contenta] e ane auto gra[n]de piacere e pe[n]so vor[r]à seguire la muraglia. Altro non è i[n]fastidirò vostra signoria se non e pregho che la mivogi bene che no disidero atro. Fatta di 30 di gennaio 1548. Vostro servidore tribolo al poggio." Fol. 292v: "A R.o S.o maiodomo di sua Ecellezia mesere Pierfacescho Ricci. In Firenze. 1548 Del Tribolo Alli[ni]z[i]o di Gennaio al Poggio."

17. ASF, *Mediceo del Principato* filza 1170a, ins. 4, "Varie lettere di diversi senza serie a Pier Francesco Riccio nel 1546," fol. 67: "Per trovarci qui in sulli neghozi di sua Ex tia [Eccellenza] e avere lui volontà di fare de postimi asai gli [Cosimo I] è parso disegniare uno giardino a piè del palazzo verso Firenze et per quello si vede sarà braccia 180 in circha per ogni verso benché non s'è risoluto a dirlo che M[aestr]o Tribolo lo disegna. E ssi [è] fatto la tagliata de' frutti. Appresso s'è disegniato e liberato in subito porre e diverre una ucelaria da todi [ucellaia da tordi] fatto [sotto] il paretaio verso Pistoia. E questa ma[t]tina si mette mano ad essa che penso avendo a condurre tutte queste opere e disegni Vostra Signoria ci darà l'ordine. Di questa setimana ho tenuti quattro chavatori alle chave a sassi e farossi munizione per le stalle." Letter from Niccolò Sermanni to Pier Francesco Riccio, October 29, 1545. The letter was partially transcribed by Wiebke Aschoff, "Studien zu Niccolò Tribolo" (D.Phil. diss., Frankfurt, Johann Wolfgang Goethe University, 1967), 136.

18. GDSU, 3246r A. Foster, "A Study of Lorenzo de' Medici's Villa at Poggio a Caiano," 1:442 n. 385. Ferri attributes this drawing (c. 1550) to Bernardo Buontalenti. See Real Galleria di Firenze, *Indice geografico-analitico dei disegni di architettura civile e militare*, s.v. Poggio a Caiano. Reference to payment made to Tribolo for the execution of garden drawings for Poggio a Caiano is found at ASF, *Guardaroba Medicea*, 11, fol. 114: "E a dì 13 di maggio lire 6 [e soldi] 3 per spese a maestro Tribolo e Andrea fattore a Chastello e loro gharzoni lire 3 e mezzo per postimi e disegni al giardino." The title of the volume, "1548 Libro di fabrica del Poggio," erroneously refers to the villa at Poggio Imperiale, whereas the documents include a series of accounts and payments for the works of restoration and extension of the villa at Poggio a Caiano in 1546.

19. ASF, *Mediceo del Principato*, 613, ins. 6, fol. 119: "Tucti li disegni del orto de Pitti e tucti li indirizzi che 'l povero Tribolo havveva perchè diamo l'ordine a finir la piantata." The quote is a rescript by Cosimo I written on a letter that Pier Francesco Riccio sent to him on September 27, 1550. The document was first published by Wright, "The Medici Villa at Olmo a Castello: Its History and Iconography," 2:573 n. 72.

20. Eduard Vodoz, "Studien zum architektonischen Werk des Bartolomeo Amannati," *Mitteilungen des Kunsthistorischen Instituts in Florenz* 7 (July–December 1941), 43.

21. ASF, *Fabbriche Medicee*, 20, fol. 6v: "Da murare nell'orto de' pitti di dentro a di fuori dove sono le due niccie come mostra il disegno di mr giorgio vasari e da fare le lastre di pietra forte che vanno nel piano dove è posta la niccia del vivaio nella banda di fuori come mostra detto disegno larga b. 5 in circa alta b. 10 1/4." See Luigi Zangheri, "Vasari e la grotta grande," in *Boboli 90: Atti del Convegno Internazionale di Studi per la salvaguardia e valorizzazione del Giardino*, ed. Cristina Acidini Luchinat and Elvira Garbero Zorzi (Florence: Edifir, 1991), 2:399.

22. ASF, *Fabbriche Medicee*, 21, fol. 123r. See Zangheri, "Vasari e la grotta grande," 398.

23. Wright, "The Medici Villa at Olmo a Castello." Also Claudia Conforti, "L'invenzione delle allegorie territoriali e dinastiche nel giardino di Castello a Firenze," in *Il giardino come labirinto della storia: Convegno internazionale, Palermo 14–17 aprile 1984*, ed. Jette Abel and Eliana Mauro (Palermo: Centro studi di storia e arte dei giardini, 1984), 190–197.

24. Neither grottoes nor fountains were contemplated in the earlier gardens, such as Fiesole. As for the role of sculpture, we know that Giovanni de' Medici had ordered a group of ancient statues from Rome and also commissioned a group of twelve marble heads (probably the Caesars), but these were not meant to be placed in the garden. See chap. I, note 280.

25. Gloria Fossi, *Uffizi Gallery: Art, History, Collections* (Florence: Giunti, 2001), 128–129. For an interpretation of Botticelli's *Primavera* see Gloria Fossi, *Botticelli: La Primavera* (Florence: Giunti, 1998). Also Claudia Villa, "Per una lettura della 'Primavera': Mercurio 'retrogrado' e la Retorica nella Bottega di Botticelli," *Strumenti critici* 13, no. I (January 1998), 1–28.

26. "La grandezza e la bontà della casa de' Medici, e tutte le virtù si truovono nel duca Cosimo: e queste erano la Iustizia, la Pietà, il Valore, la Nobiltà, la Sapienza e la Liberalità." Vasari, *Le vite*, 6:83.

27. Indicative of Varchi's intention is his *Storia fiorentina*, which, in spite of its title, deals only with the history of the Medici.

28. Gianluca Belli, "Alcune osservazioni sulla carriera architettonica del Tribolo," in *Niccolò detto il Tribolo tra arte, architettura e paesaggio*, ed. Elisabetta Pieri and Luigi Zangheri (Poggio a Caiano: Comune di Poggio a Caiano, 2001), 65.

29. When Lorenzo and Giovanni di Pierfrancesco de' Medici bought the villa at Castello from Andrea della Stufa in 1477, the property consisted of a rural building and a small kitchen garden. The description of the property is contained in the notarial deed signed on May 17. ASF, *Notarile Antecosimiano*, B 735 (1476–1482), fols. 57r–62r. There was a medieval castellated palace, with rooms, loggia, courtyard, cellars, stables, granary, and other service buildings. Moreover, the document describes a "pratello" with "melaranti," or orange trees, to the north side of the building, and a "pratello dallato di sotto," with a "vivaio murato con ponte in mezzo" to the south. This pond collected the water from the old Roman aqueduct. There was also a walled garden, adjacent to the west side of the building, which included vineyards, fruit trees, a threshing floor, a well, and a "pratello." This area was also surrounded by olive trees, more vineyards and fruit trees, and two farmhouses with an oil press and a dovecote. The document has been partially transcribed by Wright, "The Medici Villa at Olmo a Castello," 2:465–466 n. 7. Also Cristina Acidini Luchinat, "Il giardino della villa dell'Olmo a Castello," in *Giardini Medicei: Giardini di palazzo e di villa nella Firenze del Quattrocento*, ed. Cristina Acidini Luchinat (Florence: Federico Motta Editore, 1996), 201–203.

30. Scotti, "Giardini fiorentini e torinesi fra '500 e '600," 42, 54 n. 11. Also Henry W. Kaufmann, "Art for the Wedding of Cosimo de' Medici and Eleonora of Toledo (1539)," *Paragone* 21, 243 (1970), 52–67.

31. Elio Conti et al., *La civiltà fiorentina del Quattrocento* (Florence: Vallecchi Editore, 1993), 111.

32. Ibid., 149.

33. "Usa parentevolmente con ogni tuo cittadino, amagli tutti e porta loro amore; e se puoi, usa verso di loro delle cortesie. Vogliti ritrovare ispesso con loro: dà loro mangiare e

bere alcuna volta, e nondimeno abbi riguardo a chi, e più spesso a' buoni che a' cattivi."
Ibid., 164. My translation.

34. "A' dì 8 di giugno del 1466 facemmo la festa delle Nozze di Bernardo mio figliuolo
e della Nannina figliuola di Piero di Cosimo de' Medici sua donna, la quale ne venne a
marito accompagnata da quattro cavalieri. . . . La quale festa fu fuori di casa in su un
palchetto alto da terra braccia 11/2 di grandezza di braccia 1600 quadre circa, che teneva
tutta la piazzuola che è dirimpetto alla casa nostra, ritratto a modo di triangolo con bellissimo apparato di panni, d'arazzi, di pancali e spalliere e con un cielo di sopra per difesa del
sole di panni turchini, adornato tutto con ghirlande e con rose e con scudi la metà col-
l'arme de' Medici e la metà coll'arme de' Rucellai. . . . E là, su quel palco, i convitati dan-
zarono, mangiarono, bevettero, mentre in Via della Vigna giovani cavalieri facevano ogni
sorta d'armeggerie, e le musiche mandavano fino al cielo le note, in modo che se ne ralle-
grò non solo il parentado, ma tutto il popolo fiorentino." Cited by Pietro Gori, *Le feste
fiorentine attraverso i secoli: Le feste per San Giovanni* (Florence: R. Bemporad & Figlio Editori, 1926), 48. Also Guido Pampaloni, "Le nozze," in Piero Bargellini et al., *Vita privata a
Firenze nei secoli XIV e XV* (Florence: Olschki, 1966), 50–52.

35. Pampaloni, "Le nozze," 47.

36. Gori, *Le feste fiorentine attraverso i secoli,* 46–47. The panel from the *cassone* is located at the Galleria dell'Accademia in Florence.

37. One of the last *feste* was celebrated in 1491, a year before the death of Lorenzo il
Magnifico.

38. "Nel cortile grande del palazzo de' Medici, dove è la fonte." See "Vita di Bastiano
detto Aristotile da San Gallo," in Vasari, *Le vite,* 6:441.

39. The lack of an iconographical documentation for the reconstruction of the scenes is
compensated for by their literary description written by Pier Francesco Giambullari,
*Apparato et feste nelle noze dello illustrissimo Signor Duca di Firenze, et della Duchessa sua Con-
sorte, con le sue Stanze, Madriali, Comedia et Intermedij, in quelle recitati. MDXXXIX. Impressa in Fiorenza per Benedetto Giunta, nell'anno MDXXXIX di XXIX d'Agosto.* See Piero
Marchi, "Il giardino come 'luogo teatrale,'" in *Il giardino storico italiano: Problemi di
indagine, fonti letterarie e storiche,* ed. Giovanna Ragionieri (Florence: Olschki, 1981), 211–219.

40. Ibid., 212–213. Marchi points to some useful literary and iconographical sources,
such as a description of the celebrations written by Michelangelo Buonarroti il Giovane,
*Descrizione delle felicissime nozze della Cristianissima Maestà di Madama Maria Medici
Regina di Francia e di Navarra* (Florence: Giorgio Marescotti, 1600). Also, filza 88, fol. 231,
of the Fondo Buonarroti at the BML includes a *Scrittura del Riccardi sul festino,* which was
probably written by the host for Michelangelo. More information on the event is included
in a diary written by Francesco Settimanni, *Memorie fiorentine Regnante Don Ferdinando
Medici Granduca di Toscana 3°,* IV (1596–1608), ASF, *Manoscritti* 131. The iconographical
source is a series of lunettes attributed to Bernardino Poccetti, representing the celebrations taking place in the garden (today at the Palazzo Giuntini, Florence). See also E.
Costa, "Le nozze di Enrico IV re di Francia con Maria de' Medici, documenti inediti,"
Rassegna emiliana di storia, letteratura e arte 1, no. 2 (1888).

41. Malcolm Campbell, "Hard Times in Baroque Florence: The Boboli Garden and the Grand Ducal Public Works Administration," in *The Italian Garden: Art, Design and Culture*, ed. John Dixon Hunt (Cambridge: Cambridge University Press, 1996), 162.

42. ASF, SFF, M, 40, fol. 42v. See Fiorella Facchinetti Bottai, "L'Anfiteatro, pernio scenico fra reggia urbana e giardino di delizie: riflessioni sul significato e sulle origini di un 'teatro in cerca di autore,'" in *Boboli 90: Atti del Convegno Internazionale di Studi per la salvaguardia e valorizzazione del Giardino*, ed. Cristina Acidini Luchinat and Elvira Garbero Zorzi (Florence: Edifir, 1991), 2:435.

43. Edward Wright, "The Boboli Garden in the Evolution of European Garden Design: A Study in Practical Function and Organizing Structure," in *Boboli 90: Atti del Convegno Internazionale di Studi per la salvaguardia e valorizzazione del Giardino*, ed. Cristina Acidini Luchinat and Elvira Garbero Zorzi (Florence: Edifir, 1991), 1:316. It is also possible that Tribolo's plan for the amphitheater already included the first perspectival axis of the garden, namely, the northwest-southeast axis, which, starting ideally from the main entrance of the building, through the sloping hill, reaches Fort Belvedere.

44. Facchinetti Bottai, "L'Anfiteatro, pernio scenico fra reggia urbana e giardino di delizie," 436 n. 18.

45. "Desidero che Vostra Signoria Illustratissima mi facci gratia di servire a Sua Altezza che quando ella determinasse di far qualche cosa di cavalleria nelle nozze del Serenissimo Signor Principe, che l'Altezza Sua si compiaccia di mandarmi il disegno del Suo Giardino con la peschiera, et con quelle montuosità che le sono dentro verso la muraglia della città, con la scala dà poter misurarlo, accio che anchio potessi affaticarmi in trovar qualche inventione bizarra dà fare una Bariera ò uno torneo à cavallo. . . . Si come desidererei di sapere se detta peschiera si può asciugare ò tutta ò parte, et quant'acqua vi si può alzare dentro, scorrendomi per . . . un gran pensiero di fare una Barriera d'inventione grandissima et piena di molte cose meravigliose, et un Amphiteatro magnificentissimo." Archivio di Stato di Modena, Archivio per Materie, Ingegneri, b. I. The citation is from Riccardo Pacciani, "Nuovi rilievi dell'Anfiteatro di Boboli," in *Boboli 90: Atti del Convegno Internazionale di Studi per la salvaguardia e valorizzazione del Giardino*, ed. Cristina Acidini Luchinat and Elvira Garbero Zorzi (Florence: Edifir, 1991), 2:426 n. 21. My translation.

46. On the meaning of "tradition" see Jaroslav Pelikan, *The Vindication of Tradition* (New Haven: Yale University Press, 1984).

47. Bartolomeo Taegio, *La villa* (Milan: Moscheni, 1559), 155.

48. This section does not aspire to be an exhaustive survey of garden writings from the sixteenth century onward. I plan on expanding on the topic of this chapter, including the use of drawings for the design of gardens, in a future project.

49. Giovan Battista Ferrari, *Flora overo cultura di fiori* (Florence: Olschki, 2001), 14.

50. The first edition of *La coltivazione*, which is a vernacular poem on agriculture in imitation of Virgil's *Georgics*, was printed in Paris by Ruberto Stefano Regio Stampatore, and it seems that it was revised by the author. The work was also published by Bernardo Giunti in Florence in 1546, 1549, 1569, and 1590. The *Api di Giovanni Rucellai* was added to the latter edition. Another edition was printed in Padua in 1718 by Giuseppe Comino.

The edition that I use here is Luigi Alamanni, *La coltivazione di Luigi Alamanni e le api di Giovanni Rucellai con annotazioni del dottor Giuseppe Bianchini da Prato sopra La coltivazione e di Roberto Titi sopra Le api* (Milan: Società Tipografica de' Classici Italiani, 1804).

51. Together with the botanical garden at Padua, the Giardino dei Semplici at Pisa is the oldest in Europe. Luca Ghini, physician and botanist, founded it in 1543. See Lucia Tongiorgi Tomasi, "Il giardino, l'orto e il frutteto: Le scienze orticole in Toscana nei disegni, tempere e incisioni dal XVI al XVIII secolo," in *"Flora e Pomona": L'orticoltura nei disegni e nelle incisioni dei secoli XVI–XIX*, ed. Lucia Tongiorgi Tomasi and Alessandro Tosi (Florence: Olschki, 1990), 11.

52. "Natura / Cede insomma all'industria, e per lungo uso / Continovando ogn'or rimuta e tempre" (vv. 354–356). Alamanni, *La coltivazione*, 173. On Alamanni see Tagliolini, *Storia del giardino italiano: Gli artisti, l'invenzione, le forme dall'antichità al XIX secolo* (1988; reprint, Florence: La Casa Usher, 1994), 217–219.

53. "Ma il saggio Giardinier, che ben comprenda / Di ciascuna il desir, può con bell'arte / Accomodarsi tal, ch'a poco a poco / Faccia porle in oblio l'antiche usanze, / E rinnovar per lui costumi, e voglie" (vv. 341–345). Alamanni, *La coltivazione*, 172–173.

54. "Tal che l'occhio al mirar non senta offesa" (v. 197). Ibid., 166.

55. For instance, when Alamanni describes how to choose a site, what its qualities should be, or how to build a beehive, he draws both from the *Georgics* and from Columella's *De cultu hortorum*. See *La coltivazione* (vv. 66ff.), 160.

56. The treatise is conserved in manuscript form at the BML in Florence, *Fondo Ashburnham*, n. 538.

57. Ibid., fol. 1r: "Io adunque ho messo *in nota* certe esperienze, le quali mi son dilettato di fare circa all'annestare et porre diversi frutti, et vite et altre fantasie, tutte appartenenti alla . . . grande arte della Agricultura, per passarmi talvolta tempo alla villa . . . cosi come v.s. m'impose che io facessi, quando alli giorni passati di cotali cose seco ragionando, et . . . l'esperienze sopra di cio fatte, *discorrendo conferimo*, le quali scrivendo, benche io non le giudichi degne di esser messe in luce" (emphasis added). We do not have precise information on the occupation of Firenzuola; we only know that he wrote his treatise while he was in prison at the "carcere secreta delle Stinche" (fol. 1r), and it is likely that he was involved in the production and distribution of wood. See Alessandro Tagliolini, "Firenzuola e il giardino nelle fonti della metà del '500," in *Il giardino storico italiano: Problemi di indagine, fonti letterarie e storiche*, ed. Giovanna Ragionieri (Florence: Olschki, 1981), 295–308.

58. In 1871 Bernardi edited a version of Firenzuola's treatise found at the Biblioteca of Siena. This manuscript version, together with another found at the Biblioteca Ambrosiana in Milan, is but an excerpt of the entire work. One thousand copies were published from Bernardi's edition.

59. "Alla nostra moderna, e co' nostri vocaboli, onde a noi è più utile che non sono gli antichi, o forestieri autori: et anco è buona e sicura, come quella che fu scritta da uno, che la intendeva; ma con molta lunghezza." Bernardo Davanzati, "Toscana coltivazione delle viti e delli arbori," in *Le opere di Bernardo Davanzati*, ed. Enrico Bindi (Florence: Le Monnier, 1852–1853), 2:487 n. 2. According to Bindi, Davanzati wrote this text around

1574. The dedication letter to Giulio del Caccia was written by the author in 1579. The work was published for the first time by Giunti in 1600, and again in 1610 and 1622. The original manuscript is included in the Magliabecchiana collection (BNCF), classe XIV, n. 48, and it used to be part of Carlo di Tommaso Strozzi's library. The latest edition is *Coltivazione toscana*, with a preface by Sergio Ricossa (Turin: Fogola, 1978).

60. Davanzati, however, omits the book on gardens and does not address the architecture of the villa in the last chapter as Firenzuola does.

61. "Far porre vite variate et di bella sorte, cominciandosj da principio del giardino, su l'entrata andare scompartendo i vizzatj in questo modo . . . tenute di poi le vite delle viottole . . . con ordine et modo, et cosi per tutte l'altre viottole mettendovi di tutte l'altre sorti di vite che si puo ritrovare che buone, varie, nuove et belle siano, et di poi ne i quadri del detto giardino, scompartiti in croce, creare certi viottoletti fatti per corre gl'erbaggi, scompartendo ancora questi in croce." Firenzuola, "Trattato di agricoltura," fol. 98v.

62. "Pratello aovato a proporzione." Ibid., fol. 98r.

63. "Selvatico et bosco, fatto con misura." Ibid.

64. "Ben fatte, ben tenute, et gastigate, nelle quali si entrassi per una porta sola, la quale fussi in su la viottola verso la spalliera dell'ellera . . . con certe buche fatte alla spalliera che riesce sul pratello, a sommo studio per posser porgere le vivande alla tavola per quando vi si cenassi." Ibid.

65. "Et cosi fatto il selvatico, comporre le viottole scompartite in croce del giardino." Ibid., fol. 98v.

66. "Componimento vario, piacevole et riguardevole." Ibid., fols. 99r–99v.

67. "Che ritiene in se bonissimo odore, et un bellissimo colore di verde." Ibid., fol. 97r.

68. "Sono molto più belle assaj et più dilettevolj all'occhio." Ibid.

69. "E' necessario ancora fare et creare gl'orticinj intorno al giardino murati con buona distanzia." Ibid., fol. 99r.

70. Tagliolini, *Storia del giardino italiano*, 223.

71. "Et sopra tutto io stimo per una delle più importanti cose, che si possa desiderare da questo nostro autore, ch'egli faccia nota chiara e palese in tutte le cose, ch'egli tratterà la esperientia propria, alla quale ognuno crede più facilmente, et acqueta senz'altro. Il qual testimonio della isperienza non si è ancor veduto da nessuno de moderni dimostrato, e fatto palese al mondo." The letter from Giovan Battista da Romano, written in Venice on February 23, 1560, is included in Agostino Gallo, *Le vinti giornate dell'agricoltura et de' piaceri della villa* (Venice: Appresso Ghirardo Imberti, 1629), 413.

72. The author probably refers to Bartolomeo Cavalcanti (b. Florence 1503, d. Padua 1562), who wrote *La retorica*, the first treatise on the art of oratory written in Italian. The text was published in Venice by Gabriele Giolito de' Ferrari in 1559.

73. "Hora io credo, che se verrà in luce un libro di Agricoltura con tutti questi avvertimenti, la nostra lingua potrà arrichirsi di un bello et utilissimo volume et che la stampa dell'arrivabene potrà andare altresì gloriosa di questo, come quella dell'honorato Giolito va tanto altiera della non mai abbastanza lodata Retorica del famosissimo e celebratissimo Cavalcanti. . . . Et se voi M. Agostino . . . sarete degno al mondo di così rara, et perfetta

opera, riportarete egual premio d'immortal gloria." Gallo, *Le vinti giornate dell'agricoltura et de' piaceri della villa*, 413.

74. "Et però non aspettate da me che vi dichiari i nomi, i numeri, le misure, le Calende, None, Idi, Solstitij, Equinotij, Stelle, et venti, de i quali gli Autori celeberrimi han trattato abbastanza, et dotamente. Percioche non pure io fui sempre poco intendente di simili cose, per convenirsi solamente agli scienziati, ma anco quando ben le sapessi, non perderei tempo altramette, nella opera mia perchè non reputo tal sottigliezze esser così necessarie agli Agricoltori. . . . Parimente non aspettate che mi ponga a sciogliere il fiore delle tante opere diversamente scritte o tradutte: perche dubitarei che una gran parte non giovarebbe alla coltivazione moderna di questi paesi, per essere molto lontana da i famosi Autori di quei tempi." Ibid., 414–415.

75. The first seven *giornate* were written around 1552; the other three were added in 1553. A new expanded edition called *Le tredici giornate della vera agricoltura* was published in Venice by Bevilacqua in 1566. The final and most complete version of the treatise, entitled *Le venti giornate della vera agricoltura*, was printed in Venice in 1569. See Sergio Zaninelli, ed., *Scritti teorici e tecnici di agricoltura* (Milan: Il Polifilo, 1995), 1:129–147.

76. Agostino Gallo, *Le dieci giornate della vera agricoltura e piaceri della villa* (Venice: Domenico Farri, 1565), 88v. All quotations (except for the letter written by Giovan Battista and Agostino's response) are from this edition.

77. "I miei discorsi (che già otto anni vo adunando) sono molto lontani delle cose che voi cercate percioche ho sempre atteso alla pura prattica de' riti utili dell'Agricoltura: lasciando la Theorica ad altri piu sublimi, ed eccellenti ingegni di quello, che conosco essere il mio." Gallo, *Le vinti giornate dell'agricoltura et de' piaceri della villa*, 414.

78. "Horti . . . che si fanno per ricreatione." Gallo, *Le dieci giornate della vera agricoltura e piaceri della villa*, 112v.

79. "Si debbe fare d'ogni horti, massimamente essendo possibile, che sia da Settentrione all'habitatione del patrone; accioche dalle finestre si possa commodamente godere per modo di prospettiva, e specialmente quando è fatto piutosto per allegria, che per utilità." Ibid., 113v.

80. Agostino's ideas are expressed in form of a dialogue between two fictitious characters, Messer Avogadro and Messer Maggio.

81. Taegio, *La villa*. Also Thomas Edward Beck, "A Critical Edition of Bartolomeo Taegio's La Villa" (Ph.D. diss., University of Pennsylvania, 2001).

82. Taegio derives this sentence from Alamanni's *La coltivazione*. See n. 53.

83. "Esso ha d'intorno da se, et per lo mezzo in molte parti vie con dritta ragione si ben misurate; et a dritto occhio tirate, che essendo pari i cantoni, et le faccie uguali, l'occhio al mirar non ne sente offesa alcuna, ne sono le strade troppo ampie, ne strettissime; ma tali, che ben confanno al delicato giardino. L'altre parti poi di questo piacevol loco, ove deono albergare i fiori, et l'herbe surgono quadrate con vago aspetto, et tra lor distinte, et pari. . . . Le piante poi sono con meraviglioso ordine poste, et di quelle, che sono tanto lodevoli, che l'aer nostro patiscono quivi n'è grandissima copia; quivi sono senza fine gl'ingegnosi innesti, che con sì gran meraviglia al mondo mostrano, quanto sia l'industria

d'un accorto giardiniero, che incorporando l'arte con la natura fà, che d'amendue ne riesce una terza natura, la qual causa, che i frutti siano quivi più saporiti, che altrove." Taegio, *La villa*, 57–58. Also Beck, "A Critical Edition of Bartolomeo Taegio's La Villa," 255–257.

84. I do not agree with the translation of the same passage by Peter Armour in Tongiorgi Tomasi, "Projects for Botanical and Other Gardens: A 16th-Century Manual," 9 n. 1: "Surrounding and running through it in several places, [the garden] has paths so carefully measured out with reasoned linear proportions that, since the outlines and aspects are all equal, the eye is not offended by looking at them; nor are the avenues too wide or too narrow, but they are all so *designed* that the exquisiteness of the whole delightful garden is perfectly matched in its various parts" (emphasis added). Taegio, in fact, does not use the word *design*, nor does he hint at a process of design in the making of gardens.

85. On the other hand, the use of the dialogue may be due to the imitation of a conventional form of writing. As Beck has demonstrated, however, Taegio's *La villa* "is an exception among sixteenth-century dialogues written in the Italian language because it is not documentary," in that its interlocutors are not named after existing individuals, "and because it is not based on a Ciceronian model." Beck, "A Critical Edition of Bartolomeo Taegio's La Villa," 95. Other sources on the use of the dialogic form in Italian literature, and more generally in philosophy, are Virginia Cox, *The Renaissance Dialogue: Literary Dialogue in Its Social and Political Contexts, from Castiglione to Galileo* (Cambridge: Cambridge University Press, 1992), and Hans-Georg Gadamer, *Dialogue and Dialectic: Eight Hermeneutical Studies on Plato*, trans. Christopher Smith (New Haven: Yale University Press, 1980).

86. None of the treatises written by Agostino del Riccio was published; in fact, they all remained in manuscript form until recently. A manuscript of the treatise "Agricultura sperimentale" in three volumes—which the author probably left unfinished—is at the BNCF (Targioni Tozzetti 56, vols. 1–3). This manuscript includes a section called "Agricultura sperimentale ridotta a teorica" that is attached to the third volume (fols. 104r–234v) and contains a list of all the agricultural activities to be done every month. These volumes do not include illustrations. A copy of the "Agricultura sperimentale–libro II" can be found at the Biblioteca Estense at Modena (ms. a. H.3.5. It. 400). Another copy of the treatise can be found at the Biblioteca Medica at Careggi. Detlef Heikamp has edited the chapter called "Del giardino di un re," which is included in the third volume of the "Agricultura sperimentale" (Targioni Tozzetti 56, vol. 3, fols. 42r–93r). See Heikamp, "Agostino del Riccio: Del giardino di un re," in *Il giardino storico italiano: Problemi di indagine, fonti letterarie e storiche*, ed. Giovanna Ragionieri (Florence: Olschki, 1981), 59–123. A reduced version of the same chapter is included in Margherita Azzi Visentini, ed., *L'arte dei giardini: Scritti teorici e pratici dal XIV al XIX secolo* (Milan: Il Polifilo, 1999), 1:419–445. Other treatises written by Agostino del Riccio are: *Libro dei fiori che vengono nei vari mesi dell'anno*, of which there exist several editions; the "Arte della Memoria," written in 1595 (BNCF, Magl. II, I, 13), and *Istoria delle pietre*, written in 1597, which was edited by Paola Barocchi (Florence: S.P.E.S., 1979).

87. "Ma la piazza poi dee essere quadra come s'è detto di sopra, maggiore due volte che non è quella di Santa Croce di Firenze ove si fanno quasi tutte le feste e spettacoli comuni in

guisa di dar contento a tutti, come facevano i romani nostri padri." Heikamp, "Agostino del Riccio: Del giardino di un re," 122.

88. This does not mean that jousts and other games no longer took place within the city walls, it means that now gardens were mentioned as alternative venues for such events. The chronicler Benedetto Dei writes that jousts used to be organized yearly at Santa Croce in the fifteenth century. In 1479 Luigi Pulci wrote a poem in octaves to celebrate Lorenzo's victory of the joust that took place on February 7 (BNCF, Cod. Magl. II. I. 394, fol. 27r). On that particular joust see Cesare Carocci, *La giostra di Lorenzo de' Medici messa in rima da Luigi Pulci* (Bologna: Zanichelli, 1899). Between 1475 and 1478 Angelo Poliziano composed a vernacular poem in ottava rima, *Stanze cominciate per la giostra del Magnifico Giuliano de' Medici*, to celebrate another Medici victory, that of Giuliano in the joust of January 1475. On the *gioco del calcio* see Luciano Artusi and Silvano Gabrielli, *L'antico gioco del calcio in Firenze* (Florence: Sansoni, 1971). Soccer continued to be played at Santa Croce as late as 1739.

89. Scholars point to the existence of a late sixteenth-century plan of the botanical garden of Florence, alternatively attributed to Tribolo and Buontalenti, published by Targioni Tozzetti in his preface to Pietro Antonio Micheli's *Catalogus Plantarum Horti Caesarei Florentini* (1748). Upon examination of the catalogue I did not find the late sixteenth-century plan. There is a later plan (after Tozzetti's preface) that was apparently drawn by Antonio Falleri. (At the bottom of the drawing we read: "Antonius Falleri fecit" and "Marcus Ant. Corsi Sculpt. flor." In a footnote to the sentence "Architecton quisquis horti ornatur praefuit, follers certe fuit" we read: "Num fuit Nicolaus Tribolo noncupatus, quo Cosmus in ornando viridario regiae villae Castelli usus est V. Vasari in eius vita et Baldinucci Decen. I. della P. . . . num vero Bernardus Bontalentius, qui paulo post Regium Boboleum Viridarium instruxit? V. Baldinuc. In eius vita.")

90. "Ma io che vi sono stato molte volte in detto giardino per mio diporto et salvezza, ho considerato . . . che havendo fatto mettere in uno scompartimento tutti i muschi greci, in un altro i tulipani o anemoni, come hanno fatto i lor fiori, non si vede bellezza veruna in tali quadretti; però non sarebbe se non bene, che in ogni quadro che ha garbo di quore [*sic*] o di stella et altri garbi che tu facessi porre intorno intorno altre piante che sempre stessino fiorite, et tal cosa bisogna che faccia un giardiniere ben pratico . . . in questa guisa, sempre il gran giardino del Re sarebbe sempre vago o bello di tutti i mesi dell'anno." Heikamp, "Agostino del Riccio: Del giardino di un re," 75–76.

91. "Sebbene non ho gran disegno tuttavolta ho in me qualche principio, et mi pare di essere pittore, scultore et architettore per havere tanto soventemente grande amista pratica con simili huomini virtuosi." Ibid., 72.

92. "Scompartito con mirabil ordine." Ibid., 66.

93. "Altrimenti se il sito del giardino non è quadro, ma à [*sic*] altra forma, i f[r]utti e piante non si diranno mai per tutte le vedute . . . et tutto si fa per godere tutto il giardino in una occhiata." Ibid., 83.

94. "Laonde la bellezza d'un corpo si dice essere in tal guisa bello in quanto tutte le parti che ha in sè son proporzionate insieme et tutto ciò si veggono tutti quei che attendono

al disegno sempre hanno questo per regola generalissima, come sono i seguaci e aveduti pittori, scultori e architettori." Ibid., 72.

95. Ibid., 61.

96. Giorgio Vasari il Giovane, *La città ideale: Piante di chiese [palazzi e ville] di Toscana e d'Italia*, ed. Virginia Stefanelli (Rome: Officina Edizioni, 1970), 109, 117, 125. Also Bartolomeo Ammannati, *La città: Appunti per un trattato*, ed. Mazzino Fossi (Rome: Officina, 1970).

97. Agostino himself hints at the oral transmission of tradition when he says that without spoken words it would not be possible to teach any know-how: "Et senza queste [words, songs, and voices] non si potrebbono insegnare l'arti infine che sono ne' regni, et saremo a guisa di bestie." Heikamp, "Agostino del Riccio: Del giardino di un re," 104.

98. "Hor metto il disegno, perchè puoi torre quel disegno del laberinto che è dipinto nel giardino di Bagnaia, o quel giardino di Tivoli che è bello e bene inteso, se potrò dar fine a quest'opera, ma ci saranno nell'ultimo disegnati più sorte di laberinti." Ibid., 94.

99. Agostino del Riccio, "Agricultura sperimentale ridotta a teorica," Targioni Tozzetti 56, vol. 3, fol. 105v. Also Tongiorgi Tomasi and Tosi, eds., *"Flora e Pomona": L'orticoltura nei disegni e nelle incisioni dei secoli XVI–XIX*, 14.

100. The autograph manuscript in two volumes is housed at the BNCF, Magl. 2, 4, 74, and 75. The *Trattato della coltivazione delle viti* was published in 1600, and numerous other parts of Soderini's work were published in the nineteenth century. The section called *Della cultura degli orti e dei giardini* was published for the first time in Florence by Stamperia del Giglio (1814). See BNCF, Magl. 19.1.44. The first integral edition is Giovanvettorio Soderini, *Le opere di Giovanni Vettorio Soderini*, 4 vols., ed. Alberto Bacchi della Lega (Bologna: Romagnoli Dall'Acqua, 1902–1907).

101. "E primieramente si squadri e si disamini ciascheduna parte della pianta ove sopra s'ha a rilevare l'edificio: il quale, perchè riesca bene e sia commendato, dee essere fatto comodo utile e bello e perpetuo." Soderini, *I due trattati dell'Agricoltura e della coltivazione delle viti*, vol. 1 of *Le opere di Giovanni Vettorio Soderini*, 139. Firenzuola adds a chapter about the architecture of the villa at the end of his treatise, but his comments are mostly practical advice on the location of the house, which he describes as a building with a square courtyard and walled garden. See Firenzuola, "Trattato di agricoltura," bk. 7, chap. 16, fols. 116v–117r: "Come et dove vorrebbe esser situata la possessione et il casamento et che parte se li richiederebbe."

102. "La bellezza procederà dalla forma graziosa e dalla corrispondenza del tutto alle parti e delle parti fra loro e di quelle al tutto, sendo che gli edifizii han da parere e essere un ben finito et inteso corpo, nel quale l'un membro con l'altro corrisponda, e tutte le membra sien necessarie a quello che si vuol fare. Considerate queste cose nel disegno di carta e modello di legname che si vuol fare in opera, con la ragione delle sue misure tutte." Soderini, *I due trattati dell'Agricoltura e della coltivazione delle viti*, 143. On the meaning of *grazia* see Carlo Del Bravo, "Quella quiete, e quella libertà," *Annali della Scuola Normale Superiore di Pisa: Classe di Lettere e Filosofia* 8, 3rd series, no. 4 (1978), 1455–1490.

103. "Il modello dee essere grande, non pur delli edifizii, ma d'ogni altra cosa d'invenzione e d'ingegno, perchè si possi da questa ragionevole e moderata grandezza giudicar meglio l'opera intera." Soderini, *I due trattati dell'Agricoltura e della coltivazione delle viti*, 140.

104. "Che egli sia di rilievo o di disegno." Ibid., 141.

105. "Per relazionarmi come stia in quelle parti." Ibid.

106. "Secondo che s'appartenghi all'uso et alla degnità del luogo et alla qualità dell'essere della persona che l'ha a fare, avendo sempre a mente che la villa non superi l'edifizio nè l'edifizio la villa; e per dir meglio, che la casa non paia che desideri più terreno di quello che l'abbi, e così la terra che vi è d'attorno casa maggiore, ma sia l'uno corrispondente all'altra." Ibid., 142. This view is also indebted to Alberti's architectural theory as expressed in his *De re aedificatoria*.

107. "L'edifizio poi della villa e la fabbrica di tutto il circuito d'esso sia sempre posto in luogo che e vegga e sia visto, lontano da ogni profondità di valli chiuse fra i monti. . . . Sia la casa della villa tuttavia comoda alla possessione et in tutta vista d'essa nel mezzo di quella, affinchè il padrone con non molta fatica possi scoprire e vedere i suoi luoghi d'intorno." Ibid., 216–217.

108. "Si godrà meglio lo scompartimento et acconcio dei viali e delle strade, che, dividendoli con debita ragione, corrispondino insieme ai campi et alla casa addirizzati." Ibid., 217.

109. "Abbi posto quasi che sotto gli occhi la delicatezza dei giardini, degli orti e de' campi fruttiferi, nei quali e negli orti, in diversi quadri partiti l'un dall'altro ugualmente da diverse strade larghe e spaziose, appariscano quadro per quadro, facendosi alle finestre e risguardando dalle loggie, tutti gli arbori, o domestichi o salvatichi che sieno, all'intorno, tenuti tutti a un paro; e mentre creschino, scemare con le forbici, falce o pennato, sì che non ecceda d'altezza e disagguaglianza l'un l'altro; e sia a vedere un prato come di verdi erbe uguale, et i quadri siano a corrispondenza e grandezza degli angoli e facciate della casa." Ibid., 222–223.

110. "Faccinsi oltre a questo cerchi, secondo quelli disegni che dalla pianta degli edifizii son lodati, d'allori, di cedro e di ginepro, intrecciati, avviluppati e rimessi l'uno nell'altro. I vasi ancora nei viali, pieni di frutti nani d'ogni sorte, sono di grandissimo ornamento e gustevole piacevolezza. . . . Oggi si veggono nei giardini principali i viali rinvestiti di viti a mezza botte impergolandole, scoperte nel mezzo e sfogate all'aere, ritte sopra colonne di quà e di là. . . . Gli alberi, o per me' dire i frutti, s'hanno a porre con l'ordine quincunce, alla foggia che si segna il cinque nei dadi." Ibid., 251–252.

111. "Ma per uscire di questa usitata trivialità e non mai abbastanza frequentata consuetudine di fabbricare in angoli e quadrato, si può condecentissimamente e con pari compariscenza di vista, bellezza e comodità, utilità et agiatezza . . . mutar foggia . . . murare in forma aovata . . . corte e cortile, piazze, pratelli e giardino . . ordinando nondimeno tutto secondo le regole della buona architettura quanto all'altezze, lunghezze e larghezze e graziosa proporzione e vani delle stanze, sì che tutto il componimento stia di modo che corrisponda unitamente alle parti e le parti a quello, nè più nè meno bene e attamente dicendosi insieme, che si facci la fattura del corpo umano." Ibid., 262–263.

112. "E si potrà ancora all'ultimo, dove per altro si potria adattare il tetto, farvi un fermo lastricato . . . et ordinandovi orticini quadri o con altra forma, et attorno attorti come più paia, mettendovi ancora dei vasi pieni di agrumi e di arbori nani; et insomma un giardino pensile vi starà bene." Ibid., 274.

113. Soderini does mention the preparation of drawings with regard to the design of buildings: "I divisamenti delle piante e le piante istesse siano secondo i disegni che più aggradischino, soddisfaccino e contentino coloro che gli hanno a fare che sieno intendenti, o secondo la volontà del padrone che anch'esso ne sappi; e tutto sempre con disegno di buona architettura e di saggio maestro." Ibid., 275. Before this passage, however, Soderini, described the making of a roof garden, thus, the phrase "divisamenti delle piante e le piante istesse" may also refer to a planimetric drawing of the garden. Further on, when he mentions the presence of stones sculpted in the shape of animals to be found especially on the meadows of Indian properties, he advises: "Volentieri vi si affaticherà buono e giudizioso scultore a cavarne quelle figure che egli giudichi piú atte a poterne uscire, sbozzandole prima come si fa con buon disegno." Ibid., 277.

114. Morolli, however, attributes the drawing to Giovanni Antonio Dosio. Gabriele Morolli, "I progetti di architettura," in *Roma antica e i disegni di architettura agli Uffizi: Giovanni Antonio Dosio*, ed. Franco Borsi et al. (Rome: Officina Edizioni, 1976), 275. The drawing is located at the GDSU 3888r A. For the attribution of Dosio's drawings to Soderini see Andrew Morrogh, *Disegni di architetti fiorentini, 1540–1640* (Florence: Olschki, 1985), 73–76. Morrogh claims that the handwriting of the annotations made on the drawings corresponds to that of Soderini's manuscripts. However, I compared the annotations on the Uffizi drawing with the autograph manuscript housed at the BNCF, Magl. 2.4.74, and the handwriting does not appear to be the same. Bacchi, who edited *I due trattati dell'Agricoltura e della coltivazione delle viti*, says that Soderini started writing the manuscript from fol. 5r onward. The previous folios, apparently, were written by a scribe (see esp. 7). Claudia Lazzaro does not seem to doubt Soderini's authorship of the drawing. See her *The Italian Renaissance Garden: From the Conventions of Planting, Design, and Ornament to the Grand Gardens of Sixteenth-Century Central Italy* (New Haven: Yale University Press, 1990), 79. At any rate, it is known that Dosio worked for Soderini as a draftsman in the 1560s.

115. Soderini, *I due trattati dell'Agricoltura e della coltivazione delle viti*, 140.

116. Io. Bapt. Ferrari senensis et societate Iesus, *De Florum cultura*, libri IV (Rome: Excudebat S. Paulinus, 1633). This first Latin edition was dedicated to Cardinal Barberini. Five years later the treatise was translated into Italian by Lodovico Aureli of Perugia and published with the title *Flora overo cultura di fiori* (Rome: Faciotti, 1638). Of this translation there exist two anastatic reprints (Rome: Vivarelli, 1975, and Florence: Olschki, 2001). Ferrari is also the author of *Hesperides sive de malorum aureorum cultura et usu*, a study of citrus fruits, with their classification, rules for their planting, and the myths and legends about them, published in 1646. See Azzi Visentini, ed., *L'arte dei giardini: Scritti teorici e pratici dal XIV al XIX secolo*, 2:553–566.

117. Isa Belli Barsali, "Una fonte per i giardini del Seicento: Il trattato di Giovan Battista Ferrari," in *Il giardino storico italiano: Problemi di indagine, fonti letterarie e storiche*, ed. Giovanna Ragionieri (Florence: Olschki, 1981) 221–234.

118. "O pure io sia quegli, che la cultura soavemente faticosa de' fioriti giardini, dianzi nata, e da molti già posta in uso, ma da niuno ancora particolareggiata in iscritto, prima di ogni altro insegni." Giovan Battista Ferrari, *Flora, overo cultura di fiori* (Florence: Olschki, 2001), 2. Translations from Ferrari are mine.

119. "Due cose io sconfido, ed ingenuamente nego potersi da me attenere. L'una è di abbracciare i precetti tutti di quest'arte: però che chi farà egli mai, che essendo il primo ad imprendere una cotal'opera, tutto habbia antiveduto, e n[on] una cosa lasciata in dietro per coloro, che dopo se trattar ne volessero? Stimo io dunque a me bastevole le più e le principali mostrarne. L'altra è di aggradire a tutti: però che qual'huomo, che stolto non sia, cotanto oserà di sperare, che in numero e diversità infinita di huomini, per lo più contrari e discordanti, una istessa composizione possa a tutti essere gradevole. . . .? Si che io mi appagherò, se a pochi, purche saggi, non sarò dispiacevole." Ibid., 8.

120. "In pruova di ciò produrrei il catalogo degli scrittori tutti di questa materia con gli stessi argomenti de' loro copiosi trattati, se non sapessi esser ciò stato già fatto." Ibid., 11.

121. "Saggio architetto di questa ingenua amenità." Ibid., 20.

122. "Oltre a ciò eleggasi figura tale per l'Horto, che del sito, che si havrà, poco, o nulla si perda." Ibid., 16.

123. "Eleggasi pure a voglia di ciascuno qual si sia figura, o quadra, o che habbia del lungo, o tonda, o di molti angoli." Ibid.

124. "Dovrà adunque il Giardino quasi militare alloggiamento delle fiorite schiere, se per altro non sarà assicurato, et impenetrabile, circondarsi di muro, o di siepe . . . il Giardino, che, quasi Città di fiori, havrai preso a cingere di riparo, secondo l'uso antico nell'edificar Città." Ibid., 17.

125. Ferrari's comparison of gardens with military camps does not seem to have been further explored by other georgic writers. This is probably due to the fact that already in the mid sixteenth century military design was no longer a concern of architects, but rather became the subject matter of military engineering. Among the treatises on military architecture see Girolamo Maggi's *Della fortificatione delle città*, which was an edition of a work by Giacomo Castriotto, published posthumously (Venice: Appresso Camillo Borgomiano, 1583).

126. "Comparta diligentemente e misuri, formandone prima in carta uno schizzo, con cui poscia il giardino si conformi e confronti." Ferrari, *Flora overo cultura di fiori*, 20.

127. "Di cotali spartimenti molti disegni ed elegga il più vago." Ibid.

128. "Diverse forme di giardini, acciò che l'architettura di quelli, meglio che dalle parole istesse, dal disegno venga additata." Ibid., 22.

129. "Ciascun'aiuola riempie di due, o di tre sorti di fiori, sì come diversi tra loro di natura, e di colore, così di luogo separati, e fa sì, che i medesimi, o somiglianti, posti dirimpetto, o a traverso, vagamente si guardino, e si corrispondano." Ibid., 217.

130. "Suole ancora esprimere i colori stessi de' fiori di due o tre sorti, di cui detto habbiamo, nello schizzo, o ritratto in carta, dipingendo e distinguendo ciascun'aietta con gli colori stessi de' fiori che dee contenere." Ibid.

131. "Laonde veracemente da noi potrà dirsi, che questi nostri Elisij senza fiori ancora fioriscano, ed habbiano le loro stelle, che la bellissima progenie de' fiori producono con evidenza maggiore, che i rimotissimi influssi celestiali co' loro influssi non fanno." Ibid., 12.

132. "In sito quadro o, per lungo, di angoli retti, formane il disegno in carta, e in quello tira linee per ogni verso a foggia di cancello o di rete, misurando gli spatij in maniera che a proportione corrispondano a mattoni interi." Ibid., 40.

CONCLUSION

1. In addition to his suburban villa, Soderini owned two gardens, one located near the Ponte della Carraia and the other at his urban residence on via del Palagio. See Pompeo Litta and Luigi Passerini, *Famiglie celebri italiane*, vol. 9, pt. 3, no. 141 (Milan: Tip. delle Famiglie celebri italiane, 1868).

2. "Coloro ch'amano la villa, e l'agricoltura, accioche più facilmente intendano le cose che convengono a questa così lodevol professione." Gallo, "Protesti dell'auttore," in *Le dieci giornate della vera agricoltura e piaceri della villa* (Venice: Domenico Farri, 1565).

3. "Il nostro Gallo non fu versato negli studi delle lingue e delle scienze e non si applicò giammai nè a poesie, nè a discorsi filosofici." See "Breve notizia istorica intorno alla persona dell'autore," in Gallo, *Le venti giornate dell'agricoltura e de' piaceri della villa* (Brescia: Nella stamperia di G. Bossini, 1775), viii.

4. Isa Belli Barsali, "Una fonte per i giardini del Seicento: Il trattato di Giovan Battista Ferrari," in *Il giardino storico italiano: Problemi di indagine, fonti letterarie e storiche*, ed. Giovanna Ragionieri (Florence: Olschki, 1981), 222.

5. "Que omnia sunt contra doctrinam Maronis. Sed placet experiri." Marco Vattasso, "Brevi note del Petrarca sull'orticoltura," in *I codici petrarcheschi della biblioteca vaticana* (Rome: Tipografia Poliglotta Vaticana, 1908), 230.

6. This point has been made by Nicholas Mann, "From Laurel to Fig: Petrarch and the Structures of the Self," in *1999 Lectures and Memoirs*, ed. F. M. L. Thompson, Proceedings of the British Academy, vol. 105 (Oxford: Oxford University Press, 2000), 41.

7. "Ipsis amicissimus." Vattasso, "Brevi note del Petrarca sull'orticoltura," 233.

8. Mann, "From Laurel to Fig: Petrarch and the Structures of the Self," 17–42.

9. "Concedo fabulosos, id est fabularum compositores, esse poetas." Boccaccio defines the figure of the poet in his work on the mythology of antiquity. See Boccaccio, *Genealogie deorum gentilium*, ed. Vittorio Zaccaria, vols. 7–8 of *Tutte le opere di Giovanni Boccaccio*, ed. Vittore Branca (Milan: Mondadori, 1998), 1410–1412.

10. Ibid., 1398.

11. "Ciascuna cosa in se medesima è buona a alcuna cosa, e male adoperata può essere nociva di molte; e così dico delle mie novelle. Chi vorrà da quelle malvagio consiglio e malvagia operazion trarre, elle nol vieteranno a alcuno, se forse in sé l'hanno, e torte e tirate fieno a averlo: e chi utilità e frutto ne vorrà, elle nol negheranno." See Boccaccio, *Decameron*, vol. 4 of *Tutte le opere di Giovanni Boccaccio*, ed. Vittore Branca (Milan: Mondadori, 1976), 961.

12. Ficino, *Platonic Theology*, tran. Michael J. B. Allen and John Warden, Latin text ed. James Hankins and William Bowen (Cambridge, Mass.: Harvard University Press, 2001–2006), 1:204–205.

13. According to Scholastic philosophy "species," or *forma*, is a medium of knowledge. The shapes and proportions of all objects abide in things but they are also present, without their matter, in man's soul. The mind of man imposes the seals of things on his sense perceptions, that is, it forms his perceptions. The process of knowledge entails in part the fitting, or justification, of the forms existing in the mind of man with the species, or forms, of material things.

14. Ficino, *Platonic Theology*, 3:287.

15. Michael J. B. Allen, *Icastes: Marsilio Ficino's Interpretation of Plato's Sophist* (Berkeley: University of California Press, 1989), 132.

BIBLIOGRAPHY

Acidini Luchinat, Cristina. "Il giardino della villa dell'Olmo a Castello." In *Giardini Medicei: Giardini di palazzo e di villa nella Firenze del Quattrocento*. Edited by Cristina Acidini Luchinat. Florence: Federico Motta Editore, 1996.

Ackerman, James S. "Architectural Practice in the Italian Renaissance." *Journal of the Society of Architectural Historians* 13, no. 3 (October 1954): 3–11.

———. "The Medici Villa in Fiesole." In *"Il se rendit en Italie": Etudes offertes à André Chastel*. Rome: Edizioni dell'Elefante. Paris: Flammarion, 1987.

———. "Sources of the Renaissance Villa." In *Distance Points: Essays in Theory and Renaissance Art and Architecture*. Cambridge, Mass.: MIT Press, 1991. First published in *Studies in Western Art: Acts of the Twentieth International Congress of the History of Art*. Edited by Millard Meiss. Vol. 2. Princeton: Princeton University Press, 1963.

———. *The Villa: Form and Ideology of Country Houses*. Princeton: Princeton University Press, 1990.

Agnoletti, Bice. *Alessandro Braccesi: Contributo alla Storia dell'Umanesimo e della Poesia Volgare*. Florence: B. Seeber, 1901.

Alamanni, Luigi. *La coltivazione di Luigi Alamanni e le api di Giovanni Rucellai con annotazioni del dottor Giuseppe Bianchini da Prato sopra La coltivazione e di Roberto Titi sopra Le api*. Milan: Società Tipografica de' Classici Italiani, 1804.

Alberti, Leon Battista. *On the Art of Building in Ten Books*. Translated by J. Rykwert, N. Leach, and R. Tavernor. Cambridge, Mass.: MIT Press, 1997.

———. *I libri della famiglia*. Edited by Ruggiero Romano and Alberto Tenenti. Turin: Einaudi, 1969.

———. "Villa." In *Opere volgari*. Edited by Cecil Grayson. Vol. 1. Bari: Laterza, 1960.

Aleardi, Andrea, et al. *Fiesole: Alle origini della città. La costruzione della carta archeologica*. Fiesole: Comune di Fiesole, Museo Civico, 1990.

Alfonsi, Tommaso, et al. *Pier de' Crescenzi (1233–1321): Studi e documenti*. Bologna: L. Cappelli, 1933.

Alighieri, Dante. *The Divine Comedy*. 3 vols. Translated by Charles Singleton. Princeton: Princeton University Press, 1973.

Allen, Michael J. B. *Icastes: Marsilio Ficino's Interpretation of Plato's Sophist*. Berkeley: University of California Press, 1989.

Ames-Lewis, Francis. *The Library and Manuscripts of Piero di Cosimo de' Medici.* New York: Garland, 1984.

Angelis, Laura de. "Tecniche di coltura agraria e attrezzi agricoli alla fine del Medioevo." In *Civiltà ed economia agricola in Toscana nei secc. XIII–XV: Problemi della vita delle campagne nel tardo medioevo.* Pistoia: Centro Italiano di Studi di Storia e d'Arte, 1981.

Añón Feliz, Carmen, et al. *Felipe II el rey íntimo: Jardín y naturaleza en el siglo XVI.* Madrid: Sociedad Estatal para la Conmemoración de los Centenarios de Felipe II y Carlos V, 1998.

Artusi, Luciano, and Silvano Gabrielli. *L'antico gioco del calcio in Firenze.* Florence: Sansoni, 1971.

Aschoff, Wiebke. "Studien zu Niccolò Tribolo." D.Phil. diss., Frankfurt, Johann Wolfgang Goethe University, 1967.

Augustine. *La vera religione.* Edited and translated by Onorato Grassi. Milan: Rusconi, 1997.

Azzi Visentini, Margherita, ed. *L'arte dei giardini: Scritti teorici e pratici dal XIV al XIX secolo.* 2 vols. Milan: Il Polifilo, 1999.

Baccini, Giuseppe. *Le ville medicee di Cafaggiolo e Trebbio in Mugello oggi proprietà Borghese di Roma.* Florence: Baroni e Lastrucci, 1897.

Bandini, Angelo Maria. *Catalogus codicum latinorum bibliothecae Mediceae Laurentianae.* 3 vols. Florence, 1776.

———. *Lettere XII nelle quali si ricerca, e s'illustra l'antica e moderna situazione della città di Fiesole e suoi contorni.* Siena: Bindi, 1800.

Bargellini, Clara, and P. Ruffinière du Prey. "Sources for a Reconstruction of the Villa Medici, Fiesole." *Burlington Magazine* III (1969) : 597–605.

Baron, Hans. "Cicero and the Roman Civic Spirit in the Middle Ages and Early Renaissance." *Bulletin of the John Rylands Library* 22 (Manchester, 1938): 72–97.

Bartoli, Roberta. *Biagio d'Antonio.* Milan: Federico Motta Editore, 1999.

Battisti, Eugenio. "Non chiare acque." In *Francis Petrarch, Six Centuries Later: A Symposium.* Edited by Aldo Scaglione. Portland, Ore.: International Scholarly Book Service, 1975.

Bauman, Johanna. "Tradition and Transformation: The Pleasure Garden in Piero de' Crescenzi's Liber ruralium commodorum." *Studies in the History of Gardens and Designed Landscapes* 22, no. 2 (2002): 99–141.

Beck, Thomas E. "A Critical Edition of Bartolomeo Taegio's La Villa." Ph.D. diss., University of Pennsylvania, 2001.

———. "Gardens as a 'Third Nature': The Ancient Roots of a Renaissance Idea." *Studies in the History of Gardens and Designed Landscapes* 22, no. 4 (Winter 2002): 327–334.

Bek, Lise. "Ut ars natura, ut natura ars: Le ville di Plinio e il concetto del giardino nel Rinascimento." *Analecta Romana Instituti Danici* 7 (1974): 109–156.

Belli, Gianluca. "Alcune osservazioni sulla carriera architettonica del Tribolo." In *Niccolò detto il Tribolo tra arte, architettura e paesaggio.* Edited by Elisabetta Pieri and Luigi Zangheri. Poggio a Caiano: Comune di Poggio a Caiano, 2001.

Belli Barsali, Isa. "Una fonte per i giardini del Seicento: Il trattato di Giovan Battista Ferrari." In *Il giardino storico italiano: Problemi di indagine, fonti letterarie e storiche.* Edited by Giovanna Ragionieri. Florence: Olschki, 1981.

Beltramini, Guido, and Howard Burns, eds. *Andrea Palladio e la Villa Veneta da Petrarca a Carlo Scarpa*. Venice: Marsilio, 2005.

Beneš, Mirka. "Recent Developments and Perspectives in the Historiography of Italian Gardens." In *Perspectives on Garden Histories*. Edited by Michel Conan. Washington, D.C.: Dumbarton Oaks Research Library and Collection, 1999.

Berque, Augustine. "Beyond the Modern Landscape." *AA Files* 25 (Summer 1993): 33–37.

Billanovich, Giuseppe. *Petrarca letterato: Lo scrittoio del Petrarca*. Rome: Edizioni di Storia e Letteratura, 1947.

Boccaccio, Giovanni. *Comedia delle ninfe fiorentine*. Edited by Antonio Enzo Quaglio. Vol. 2 of *Tutte le opere di Giovanni Boccaccio*, edited by Vittore Branca. Milan: Mondadori, 1964.

———. *Decameron*. Vol. 4 of *Tutte le opere di Giovanni Boccaccio*, edited by Vittore Branca. Milan: Mondadori, 1976.

———. *Genealogie deorum gentilium*. Edited by Vittorio Zaccaria. Vols. 7–8 of *Tutte le opere di Giovanni Boccaccio*, edited by Vittore Branca. Milan: Mondadori, 1998.

Bonaiuti, Telemaco. *Una giornata d'istruzione a Fiesole*. Florence: Nella Tipografia di Luigi Pezzati, 1824.

Borsi, Franco, et al. *La Badia Fiesolana*. Florence: Le Monnier, 1976.

Bosworth, Richard J. B. *Italy and the Wider World, 1860–1960*. London: Routledge, 1996.

Braccesi, Alessandro. *Alexandri Braccii Carmina*. Edited by Alessandro Perosa. Florence: Libreria Editrice Bibliopolis, 1943.

Branca, Vittore, ed. *Boccaccio visualizzato: Narrare per parole e per immagini fra Medioevo e Rinascimento*. 3 vols. Turin: Einaudi, 1999.

———. *Mercanti scrittori: Ricordi nella Firenze tra Medioevo e Rinascimento*. Milan: Rusconi, 1986.

Brink, Joel. "Simone Martini, Francesco Petrarca and the Humanistic Program of the Virgil Frontispiece." *Mediaevalia: A Journal of Medieval Studies* 3 (1977): 83–117.

Brown, Alison. *Bartolomeo Scala, 1430–1497, Chancellor of Florence: The Humanist as Bureaucrat*. Princeton: Princeton University Press, 1979.

———. "Perfrancesco de' Medici, 1430–1476: A Radical Alternative to Elder Medicean Supremacy?" In *The Medici in Florence: The Exercise of Language and Power*. Florence: L. S. Olschki; Perth: University of Western Australia Press, 1992.

Brown, Marshall. "In the Valley of the Ladies." *Italian Quarterly* 18, no. 72 (1975): 33–52.

Brucker, Gene A. "The Medici in the Fourteenth Century." *Speculum: A Journal of Medieval Studies* 32, no. 1 (January 1957): 1–26.

Brumble, H. David. *Classical Myths and Legends in the Middle Ages and Renaissance: A Dictionary of Allegorical Meanings*. Westport: Greenwood Press, 1998.

Buser, Benjamin von. *Die Beziehungen der Mediceer zu Frankreich während der Jahre 1434–1494 in ihrem Zusammenhang mit den allgemeinen Verhältnissen Italiens*. Leipzig: Duncker & Humblot, 1879.

Calkins, Robert G. "Piero de' Crescenzi and the Medieval Garden." In *Medieval Gardens*. Edited by Elisabeth Blair MacDougall. Washington, D.C.: Dumbarton Oaks Research Library and Collection, 1986.

Callu, Florence, and François Avril. *Boccace en France: De l'humanisme à l'érotisme.* Paris: Bibliotèque Nationale, 1975.

Camerota, Filippo. "Tribolo e Benvenuto della Volpaia: il modello ligneo per l'assedio di Firenze." In *Niccolò detto il Tribolo tra arte, architettura e paesaggio.* Edited by Elisabetta Pieri and Luigi Zangheri. Poggio a Caiano: Comune di Poggio a Caiano, 2001.

Campbell, Malcolm. "Hard Times in Baroque Florence: The Boboli Garden and the Grand Ducal Public Works Administration." In *The Italian Garden: Art, Design and Culture.* Edited by John Dixon Hunt. Cambridge: Cambridge University Press, 1996.

Cardini, Franco, and Massimo Miglio. *Nostalgia del paradiso: Il giardino medievale.* Rome: Laterza, 2002.

Carocci, Cesare. *La giostra di Lorenzo de' Medici messa in rima da Luigi Pulci.* Bologna: Zanichelli, 1899.

Carocci, Guido. *Fiesole: Breve illustrazione dei suoi monumenti pubblicata nella circostanza dell'inaugurazione del museo e degli scavi fiesolani.* Florence, 1874.

———. *I dintorni di Firenze.* 2 vols. 1906–1907. Reprint, Rome: Multigrafica, 1968.

———. *La villa Medicea di Careggi: Memorie e ricordi.* Florence, 1888.

Carrara, Enrico. "Aridulum rus." In *Scritti varii di erudizione e di critica in onore di Rodolfo Renier.* Turin: Fratelli Bocca, 1912.

Cartwright, Julia. *Italian Gardens of the Renaissance.* London: Smith, Elder, 1914.

Casali, Giovanna. "Le proprietà medicee nel Mugello." In *Il Mugello, un territorio, una presenza culturale.* Florence: Edizioni all'Insegna del Giglio, 1983.

Castelnuovo, Enrico. *Un pittore italiano alla corte di Avignone: Matteo Giovannetti e la pittura in Provenza nel secolo XIV.* Turin: Giulio Einaudi Editore, 1962.

Cazzato, Vincenzo. "Firenze 1931: La consacrazione del 'primato' italiano nell'arte dei giardini." In *Il giardino: Idea, natura, realtà.* Edited by Alessandro Tagliolini and Massimo Venturi Ferriolo. Milan: Guerini, 1987.

———. *Ville e Giardini Italiani: I disegni di architetti e paesaggisti dell'American Academy in Rome.* Rome: Istituto Poligrafico e Zecca dello Stato, 2004.

Centro Italiano di Studi di Storia e d'Arte. *Civiltà ed economia agricola in Toscana nei secc. XIII–XV: Problemi della vita delle campagne nel tardo medioevo.* Pistoia: Centro Italiano di Studi di Storia e d'Arte, 1981.

Chastel, André. *Arte e umanesimo a Firenze al tempo di Lorenzo il Magnifico: Studi sul Rinascimento e sull'umanesimo platonico.* Turin: Einaudi, 1964.

———. *Marsile Ficin et l'art.* 3rd ed. Geneva: Droz, 1996.

Chini, P. Lino. *La storia antica e moderna del Mugello.* 2 vols. Florence, 1875. Anastatic reprint, Rome: Multigrafica Editrice, 1969.

Ciacci, Margherita. "Non tutti i giardini di delizie sono uguali." In *I giardini delle regine: Il mito di Firenze nell'ambiente preraffaellita e nella cultura Americana fra Ottocento e Novecento.* Edited by Margherita Ciacci and Grazia Gobbi Sica. Florence: Sillabe, 2004.

Ciardi Dupré dal Poggetto, Maria Grazia. "L'iconografia nei codici miniati boccacciani dell'Italia centrale e meridionale." In *Boccaccio visualizzato: Narrare per parole e per immagini fra Medioevo e Rinascimento.* Edited by Vittore Branca. Vol. 2. Turin: Einaudi, 1999.

Cicero Marcus Tullius. *De senectute*. In *De senectute, de amicitia, de divinatione*. Loeb Classical Library. London: W. Heinemann, 1923.

———. *Letters to Atticus*. 4 vols. Loeb Classical Library. Cambridge, Mass.: Harvard University Press, 1999.

Colucci, Benedetto. *Scritti inediti di Benedetto Colucci da Pistoia*. Edited by Arsenio Frugoni. Florence: Olschki, 1939.

Comito, Terry. *The Idea of the Garden in the Renaissace*. New Brunswick: Rutgers University Press, 1978.

Comune di Firenze. *Mostra del Giardino Italiano: Catalogo*. 2nd ed. Florence: Comune di Firenze, 1931.

Comune di Roma. *Mostra del Giardino Romano al Valentino nella esposizione di Torino MCMXXVIII*. Rome: Bestetti e Tumminelli, 1928.

Conforti, Claudia. "L'invenzione delle allegorie territoriali e dinastiche del giardino di Castello a Firenze." In *Il giardino come labirinto della storia: Convegno internazionale, Palermo 14–17 aprile 1984*. Edited by Jette Abel and Eliana Mauro. Palermo: Centro Studi di Storia e Arte dei Giardini, 1984.

Conti, Alessandro. "Niccolò Tribolo nel giardino di Castello." *Antichità viva* 28, nos. 5–6 (1989): 51–61.

Conti, Elio. *I catasti agrari della Repubblica fiorentina e il catasto particellare toscano*. Rome: Istituto Storico Italiano per il Medio Evo, 1966.

Conti, Elio, et al. *La civiltà fiorentina del Quattrocento*. Florence: Vallecchi Editore, 1993.

Contorni, Gabriella. "'Felici ville, campi, e voi, silvestri boschi . . . ': La villa di Careggi da Cosimo il Vecchio a Lorenzo il Magnifico." In *L'arte al potere: Universi simbolici e reali nelle terre di Firenze al tempo di Lorenzo il Magnifico*. Edited by Domenico Conci, Vittorio Dini, and Francesco Magnelli. Bologna: Editrice Compositori, 1992.

———. "La villa di Careggi al tempo di Lorenzo il Magnifico." *QUA.S.A.R.: Quaderni di storia dell'architettura e restauro* 6–7 (1991–1992): 9–18.

———. *La villa medicea di Careggi*. Florence: Lo Studiolo, 1992.

Copenhaver, Brian P. "Scholastic Philosophy and Renaissance Magic in the De vita of Marsilio Ficino." *Renaissance Quarterly* 37, no. 4 (1984): 523–554.

Corti, Gino, and Frederick Hartt. "New Documents Concerning Donatello, Luca and Andrea della Robbia, Desiderio, Mino, Uccello, Pollaiuolo, Filippo Lippi, Baldovinetti and Others." *Art Bulletin* 44, no. 1 (1962): 155–167.

Crescenzi, Piero de'. *De agricultura vulgare*. Venice, 1511.

———. *Ruralia commoda*. Florence: Niccolò di Lorenzo, 1478.

———. *Trattato dell'agricoltura*. 2 vols. Naples: Felice Mosca, 1724.

Curtius, Ernst Robert. *European Literature and the Latin Middle Ages*. Translated by Willard R. Trask. 1953. Reprint, with an epilogue by Peter Godman. Princeton: Princeton University Press, 1990.

Dami, Luigi. "Il giardino inglese." *La vita britannica* (September–October 1919): 372–375.

———. *Il giardino italiano*. Milan: Bestetti and Tumminelli, 1924.

————. *Il nostro giardino.* Florence: Felice Le Monnier, 1923.

Davanzati, Bernardo. "Toscana coltivazione delle viti e delli arbori." In *Le opere di Bernardo Davanzati.* Edited by Enrico Bindi. Vol. 2. Florence: Le Monnier, 1852–1853.

De Certeau, Michel. *The Practice of Everyday Life.* Berkeley: University of California Press, 1984.

Del Bravo, Carlo. "Quella quiete, e quella libertà." *Annali della Scuola Normale Superiore di Pisa: Classe di Lettere e Filosofia* 8, 3rd series, no. 4 (1978): 1455–1490.

Degenhart, Bernhard. "Dante, Leonardo und Sangallo: Dante-Illustrationen Giuliano da Sangallo in ihrem Verhältnis zu Leonardo da Vinci und zu den Figureneichungen der Sangallo." *Römischen Jahrbuch für Kunstgeschichte* 7 (1955): 101–288.

Degenhart, Bernhard, and Annegrit Schmitt. *Corpus der Italienischen Zeichnungen 1300–1450.* 3 vols. Berlin: Mann, 1968.

De la Mare, Albinia. "Cosimo and His Books." In *Cosimo "il Vecchio" de' Medici, 1389–1464.* Edited by Francis Ames-Lewis. Oxford: Clarendon Press, 1992.

De Roover, Raymond Adrien. Ficino, *Platonic Theology, 1397–1494.* Cambridge, Mass.: Harvard University Press, 1963.

Doni, Anton Francesco. *Il Disegno del Doni.* Venice: Gabriele Giolito, 1549.

Dunn, Richard M. "An Architectural Partnership: Cecil Pinsent and Geoffrey Scott." In *Cecil Pinsent and His Gardens in Tuscany.* Edited by Marcello Fantoni, Heidi Flores, and John Pfordresher. Florence: Edifir, 1996.

Durand, André, *La Toscane: Album Monumental et Pittoresque exécuté sous la direction de M. le Prince Anatole Démidoff, dessiné d'après nature par André Durand.* Paris: Lemercier, 1863.

Fabriczy, Cornelius von. "Michelozzo di Bartolomeo." *Jahrbuch der Königlich Preuszischen Kunstsammlungen* 25 (1904): 34-110.

Fabroni, Angelo. *Laurentii Medicis Magnifici vita.* 2 vols. Pisa: J. Gratiolius, 1784.

Facchinetti Bottai, Fiorella. "L'Anfiteatro, pernio scenico fra reggia urbana e giardino di delizie: riflessioni sul significato e sulle origini di un 'teatro in cerca di autore.'" In *Boboli 90: Atti del Convegno Internazionale di Studi per la salvaguardia e valorizzazione del Giardino.* Edited by Cristina Acidini Luchinat and Elvira Garbero Zorzi. Vol. 2. Florence: Edifir, 1991.

Fantoni, Marcello, Heidi Flores, and John Pfordresher, eds. *Cecil Pinsent and His Gardens in Tuscany.* Florence: Edifir, 1996.

Ferrara, Miranda, and Francesco Quinterio. *Michelozzo di Bartolomeo.* Florence: Libreria Salimbeni, 1984.

Ferrari, Giovan Battista. *Flora overo cultura di fiori.* Rome: Faciotti, 1638. Anastatic reprint, with an introduction by Lucia Tongiorgi Tomasi, Florence: Olschki, 2001.

Ficino, Marsilio. "De Sole." In *Prosatori latini del Quattrocento.* Edited by Eugenio Garin. Milan: Riccardo Ricciardi Editore, 1952.

————. *The Letters of Marsilio Ficino.* 3 vols. With a preface by Paul Oskar Kristeller. 2nd ed. New York: Gingko Press, 1985.

————. *Marsilii Ficini Opera.* 2 vols. With an introduction by Stéphane Toussaint. Paris: Phénix Éditions, 2000.

————. *Platonic Theology*. 6 vols. Translated by Michael J. B. Allen and John Warden, with Latin text edited by James Hankins and William Bowen. Cambridge, Mass.: Harvard University Press, 2001–2006.

————. *Three Books on Life*. Translated by Carol V. Kaske and John R. Clark. Binghamton, N.Y.: Medieval & Renaissance Texts & Studies in conjunction with the Renaissance Society of America, 1989. Reprint, Tempe: Arizona Center for Medieval and Renaissance Studies in conjunction with the Renaissance Society of America, 1998.

Filarete [Antonio Averlino]. "Il Giardino di Plusiapolis e La riserva di caccia della Sforzinda (1461–1464)." In *L'arte dei giardini: Scritti teorici e pratici dal XIV al XIX secolo*. Vol. 1. Edited by Margherita Azzi Visentini. Milan: Il Polifilo, 1999.

————. *Trattato di Architettura*. 2 vols. Edited by Anna Maria Finoli and Liliana Grassi. Milan: Il Polifilo, 1972.

Fiorani, Camillo. *Giardini d'Italia: Arte, carattere e storia del giardino italiano*. Rome: Edizioni Mediterranee, 1960.

Firenzuola [Giacomo Gatteschi]. "Trattato di agricoltura." Fondo Ashburnham, n. 538. Biblioteca Medicea Laurenziana, Florence, c. 1552.

Fossi, Gloria. *Uffizi Gallery: Art, History, Collections*. Florence: Giunti, 2001.

Foster, Philip Ellis. "Donatello Notices in Medici Letters." *Art Bulletin* 62, no. 1 (March 1980): 148–149.

————. "A Study of Lorenzo de' Medici's Villa at Poggio a Caiano." 2 vols. Ph.D. diss., Yale University, 1974.

Franchetti Pardo, Vittorio. "Le ville medicee nel contado fiorentino (sec. XV–XVI): Ideologia di un investimento patrimoniale." *Storia della città* 6 (1978): 42–57.

Franchetti Pardo, Vittorio, and Giovanna Casali. *I Medici nel contado fiorentino: Ville e possedimenti agricoli fra quattrocento e cinquecento*. Florence: CLUSF, 1978.

Freccero, John. "The Fig Tree and the Laurel: Petrarch's Poetics." *Diacritics* 5 (Spring 1975): 34–40.

Frommel, Christoph Luitpold. *Die Farnesina und Peruzzis Architektonisches Frühwerk*. Berlin: De Gruyter, 1961.

Galletti, Giorgio. "Una committenza medicea poco nota: Giovanni di Cosimo e il giardino di villa Medici at Fiesole." In *Giardini Medicei: Giardini di palazzo e di villa nella Firenze del Quattrocento*. Edited by Cristina Acidini Luchinat. Florence: Federico Motta Editore, 1996.

————. "A Record of the Works of Cecil Pinsent in Tuscany." In *Cecil Pinsent and His Gardens in Tuscany*. Edited by Marcello Fantoni, Heidi Flores, and John Pfordresher. Florence: Edifir, 1996.

————. "Tribolo maestro delle acque dei giardini." In *Niccolò detto il Tribolo tra arte, architettura e paesaggio*. Edited by Elisabetta Pieri and Luigi Zangheri. Poggio a Caiano: Comune di Poggio a Caiano, 2001.

Gallo, Agostino. *Le dieci giornate della vera agricoltura e piaceri della villa*. Venice: Domenico Farri, 1565.

————. *Le vinti giornate dell'agricoltura et de' piaceri della villa*. Venice: Appresso Ghirardo Imberti, 1629.

————. *Le venti giornate dell'agricoltura e de' piaceri della villa.* Brescia: Nella Stamperia di G. Bossini, 1775.

Garin, Eugenio. *La cultura filosofica del rinascimento italiano: Ricerche e documenti.* Florence: Sansoni, 1961.

Gathercole, Patricia M. *Tension in Boccaccio: Boccaccio and the Fine Arts.* University, Miss.: Romance Monographs, 1975.

Ginex, Giovanna, ed. *L'Italia liberale (1870–1900).* Rome: Editori Riuniti, 1998.

Gobbi Sica, Grazia. "Nell'occhio anglo-americano: Firenze fra Ottocento e Novecento." In *I giardini delle regine: Il mito di Firenze nell'ambiente preraffaellita e nella cultura Americana fra Ottocento e Novecento.* Edited by Margherita Ciacci and Grazia Gobbi Sica. Florence: Sillabe, 2004.

————. *La villa fiorentina: Elementi storici e critici per una lettura.* Florence: Alinea Editrice, 1998.

Gombrich, Ernst Hans. "Alberto Avogadro's Description of the Badia of Fiesole and of the Villa of Careggi." *Italia medioevale e umanistica* 5 (1962): 217–229.

Gori, Pietro. *Le feste fiorentine attraverso i secoli.* Florence: Bemporad & Figlio, 1926.

Gori Sassoli, Mario. "Michelozzo e l'architettura di villa nel primo Rinascimento." *Storia dell'arte* 23 (1975): 5–51.

Gradi, Adriano. "Il paesaggio agrario-forestale toscano nel XV secolo e sue trasformazioni." In *L'Arte al potere: Universi simbolici e reali nelle terre di Firenze al tempo di Lorenzo il Magnifico.* Edited by Domenico Conci, Vittorio Dini, and Francesco Magnelli. Bologna: Editrice Compositori, 1992.

Grafton, Anthony. *Leon Battista Alberti: Master Builder of the Italian Renaissance.* New York: Hill and Wang, 2000.

Graves, Robert. *The Greek Myths.* 2 vols. Harmondsworth: Penguin Books, 1960.

Guidotti, Alessandro. "Agricoltura e vita agricola nell'arte Toscana del Tre e Quattrocento (di alcune miniature fiorentine e senesi del XV secolo)." In *Civiltà ed economia agricola in Toscana nei secc. XIII–XV: Problemi della vita delle campagne nel tardo medioevo.* Pistoia: Centro Italiano di Studi di Storia e d'Arte, 1981.

Gutkind, Curt. *Cosimo de' Medici il Vecchio.* Florence: Marzocco, 1940.

Hankins, James. "Cosimo de' Medici and the 'Platonic Academy.'" *Journal of the Warburg and Courtauld Institutes* 53 (1990): 144–162.

————. "The Myth of the Platonic Academy of Florence." *Renaissance Quarterly* 44, no. 3 (Autumn 1991): 429–475.

————. *Plato in the Italian Renaissance.* 2 vols. Leiden: E. J. Brill, 1990.

Heikamp, Detlef. "Agostino del Riccio: Del giardino di un re." In *Il giardino storico italiano: Problemi di indagine, fonti letterarie e storiche.* Edited by Giovanna Ragionieri. Florence: Olschki, 1981.

Hook, Judith. *Lorenzo de' Medici: An Historical Biography.* London: H. Hamilton, 1984.

Hunt, John Dixon. "Cecil Pinsent and the Making of La Foce: 'A Pattern of the World as He Would Have It.'" In *La Foce: A Garden and Landscape in Tuscany.* Philadelphia: University of Pennsylvania Press, 2001.

———. *Garden and Grove: The Italian Renaissance Garden in the English Imagination, 1600–1750*. 2nd ed. Philadelphia: University of Pennsylvania Press, 1996.

———. *Greater Perfections: The Practice of Garden Theory*. Philadelphia: University of Pennsylvania Press, 2000.

Isidore of Seville. *Etimologías*. 2 vols. Edited by José Oroz Reta and Manuel A. Marcos Casquero. Madrid: Biblioteca de Autores Cristianos, 1994.

Jahn-Rusconi, Arturo. *Le ville medicee: Boboli, Castello, Petraia e Poggio a Caiano*. Rome: Istituto Poligrafico dello Stato, 1938.

Kaufmann, Henry W. "Art for the Wedding of Cosimo de' Medici and Eleonora of Toledo (1539)." *Paragone* 21, no. 243 (1970): 52–67.

Kent, Dale. *Cosimo de' Medici and the Florentine Renaissance: The Patron's Oeuvre*. New Haven: Yale University Press, 2000.

Kent, Francis W. *Lorenzo de' Medici and the Art of Magnificence*. Baltimore: Johns Hopkins University Press, 2004.

Kern, Edith G. "The Gardens in the Decameron Cornice." *PMLA* 66 (1951): 505–523.

Kristeller, Paul Oskar. "Marsilio Ficino e Venezia." In *Umanesimo e Rinascimento a Firenze e Venezia*. Vol. 3, pt. 2, of *Miscellanea di studi in onore di Vittore Branca*. Florence: Olschki, 1983.

———. "The Modern System of the Arts: A Study in the History of Aesthetics. Part I." *Journal of the History of Ideas* 12, no. 4 (October 1951): 496–527.

———. *Il pensiero filosofico di Marsilio Ficino*. Florence: Sansoni Editore, 1953.

———. *Supplementum Ficinianum*. 2 vols. Florence: Olschki, 1937.

———. "An Unknown Correspondence of Alessandro Braccesi with Niccolò Michelozzi, Naldo Naldi, Bartolomeo Scala, and Other Humanists (1470–1472) in Ms. Bodl. Auct. F. 2.17." In *Classical, Mediaeval and Renaissance Studies in Honor of Berthold Louis Ullman*. Edited by Charles Henderson Jr. Vol. 2. Rome: Edizioni di Storia e Letteratura, 1964.

Lamarche-Vadel, Gaätane. *Jardin secrets de la Renaissance: Des astres, des simples, et des prodiges*. Paris: L'Harmattan, 1997.

Lamberini, Daniela. "Residenti anglo-americani e *genius loci*: Ricostruzioni e restauri delle dimore fiorentine." In *Gli anglo-americani a Firenze: Idea e costruzione del Rinascimento*. Edited by Marcello Fantoni. Rome: Bulzoni, 2000.

Lami, Giovanni. *Deliciae eruditorum*. 18 vols. Florence: Petr. Caiet. Viviani, 1736–1769.

Lasansky, D. Medina. *The Renaissance Perfected: Architecture, Spectacle, and Tourism in Fascist Italy*. University Park: Pennsylvania State University Press, 2004.

Latini, Brunetto. *Li livres dou Tresor*. Edited by Spurgeon Baldwin and Paul Barrette. Tempe: Arizona Center for Medieval and Renaissance Studies, Arizona State University, 2003.

Lazzaro, Claudia. *The Italian Renaissance Garden: From the Conventions of Planting, Design, and Ornament to the Grand Gardens of Sixteenth-Century Central Italy*. New Haven: Yale University Press, 1990.

———. "Italy Is a Garden: The Idea of Italy and the Italian Garden Tradition." In *Villas and Gardens in Early Modern Italy and France*. Edited by Mirka Beneš and Dianne Harris. Cambridge: Cambridge University Press, 2001.

Lee, Vernon. "Old Italian Gardens." In *In Praise of Old Gardens.* Portland, Me.: Thomas B. Mosher, 1912.

Lensi, Alfredo. "Ville fiorentine medievali." *Dedalo* 12 (1930–1931): 1319–34.

Lensi Orlandi Cardini, Giulio Cesare. *Le ville di Firenze.* 2 vols. Florence: Vallecchi, 1954.

Lewis, Charlton T., and Charles Short. *A Latin Dictionary.* New York: Oxford University Press, 1998.

Lillie, Amanda Rhoda. *Florentine Villas in the Fifteenth Century: An Architectural and Social History.* Cambridge: Cambridge University Press, 2005.

———. "Giovanni di Cosimo and the Medici Villa at Fiesole." In *Piero de' Medici, "il Gottoso" (1416–1469): Kunst im Dienste der Medicer.* Edited by Andreas Beyer and Bruce Boucher. Berlin: Akademie Verlag, 1993.

———. "The Humanist Villa Revisited." In *Language and Images of Renaissance Italy.* Edited by Alison Brown. Oxford: Clarendon Press, 1995.

———. "Lorenzo's Rural Investments and Territorial Expansion." *Rinascimento: Rivista dell'Istituto Nazionale di Studi sul Rinascimento* 33, 2nd series (1993): 53–67.

Litta, Pompeo, and Luigi Passerini. *Famiglie celebri italiane.* 11 vols. Milan: Giusti & Basadonna, 1819–1898.

Mane, Perrine. "L'iconographie des manuscrits du *Traité d'agriculture* de Pier de' Crescenzi." *Mélange de l'École Française de Rome* 97 (1985): 727–818.

Mann, Nicholas. "From Laurel to Fig: Petrarch and the Structures of the Self." In *1999 Lectures and Memoirs.* Edited by Francis Michael Longstreth Thompson. Proceedings of the British Academy, vol. 105. Oxford: Oxford University Press, 2000.

———. *Petrarch.* Oxford: Oxford University Press, 1984.

Marchi, Piero. "Il giardino come 'luogo teatrale.'" In *Il giardino storico italiano: Problemi di indagine, fonti letterarie e storiche.* Edited by Giovanna Ragionieri. Florence: Olschki, 1981.

Marchini, Giuseppe. *Giuliano da Sangallo.* Florence: Sansoni, 1942.

Marcus, Millicent. "An Allegory of Two Gardens: The Tale of Madonna Dianora (Decameron X, 5)." *Forum Italicum* 14 (1980): 162–174.

Martelli, Niccolò. *Dal primo e dal secondo libro delle lettere di Niccolò Martelli.* Edited by Cartesio Marconcini. Lanciano: Carabba, 1916.

Martinelli, Maurizio. *Al tempo di Lorenzo: Viaggio nella Firenze dei Medici dal Palazzo di Via Larga al Contado e nella Toscana del '400.* Florence: FMG, 1992.

Martini, Francesco di Giorgio. "Giardini e barco (1485–1492)." In *L'arte dei giardini: Scritti teorici e pratici dal XIV al XIX secolo.* Vol. 1. Edited by Margherita Azzi Visentini. Milan: Il Polifilo, 1999.

———. *Trattati di Architettura, ingegneria e arte militare.* 2 vols. Edited by Corrado Maltese. Milan: Il Polifilo, 1967.

Masson, Georgina [Barbara Johnson]. *Italian Gardens.* New York: Harry N. Abrams, 1961.

Mastrorocco, Mila. *Le mutazioni di Proteo: I giardini medicei del Cinquecento.* Florence: Sansoni, 1981.

Mazzini, Donata, ed. *Villa Medici a Fiesole: Leon Battista Alberti e il prototipo di villa rinascimentale.* Florence: Centro Di, 2004.

Mazzotta, Giuseppe. "The *Decameron*: The Literal and the Allegorical." *Italian Quarterly* 18, no. 72 (Spring 1975): 53–73.

McCracken, George. "Cicero's Tusculan Villa." *Classical Journal* 30, no. 5 (February 1935): 261–277.

McGrath, Elizabeth. "From Parnassus to Careggi: A Seventeenth-Century Celebration of Plato and Renaissance Florence." In *Sight and Insight: Essays on Art and Culture in Honour of E. H. Gombrich at 85*. Edited by John Onians. London: Phaidon, 1994.

McGuire, Frances Margaret. *Gardens of Italy*. London: Heinemann, 1965.

Medici, Filigno de'. *Libro di memorie di Filigno de' Medici*. Edited by Giovanni Biondi de' Medici Tornaquinci. Florence: Spes, 1981.

Medici, Lorenzo de'. *Lorenzo de' Medici: Tutte le opere*. 2 vols. Edited by Paolo Orvieto. Rome: Salerno Editrice, 1992.

Meiss, Millard. "The First Fully Illustrated Decameron." In *Essays in the History of Art Presented to Rudolf Wittkower*. Edited by D. Fraser, H. Hibbard, and M. Lewine. London: Phaidon, 1967.

Mercuri, Roberto. "Avignone e Napoli in Dante, Petrarca e Boccaccio." *Analecta Romana Studi Danici*, supplement 25 (1998): 117–129.

Mignani, Daniela. "I giardini della villa medicea di Careggi." In *Giardini medicei: Giardini di palazzo e di villa nella Firenze del Quattrocento*. Edited by Cristina Acidini Luchinat. Florence: Federico Motta Editore, 1996.

———. "I giardini di Careggi." In *L'architettura di Lorenzo il Magnifico: Firenze, Spedale degli Innocenti. 8 aprile–26 luglio 1992*. Edited by Gabriele Morolli, Cristina Acidini Luchinat, and Luciano Marchetti. Cinisello Balsamo: Silvana, 1992.

———. *Le ville medicee di Giusto Utens*. Florence: Arnaud, 1982.

Monaci Moran, Lucia, ed. *La Toscana di Joseph Pennel tra Otto e Novecento*. Florence: Olschki, 2004.

Moreni, Domenico. *Notizie istoriche dei contorni di Firenze dalla Porta al Prato fino alla Real villa di Castello*. 6 vols. Florence: Cambiagi, 1791–1795.

Morisani, Ottavio. *Michelozzo architetto*. Milan: Giulio Einaudi, 1951.

Morolli, Gabriele. "I progetti di architettura." In *Roma antica e i disegni di architettura agli Uffizi: Giovanni Antonio Dosio*. Edited by Franco Borsi et al. Rome: Officina Edizioni, 1976.

———. *"Vetus Etruria": Il mito degli Etruschi nella letteratura architettonica nell'arte e nella cultura da Vitruvio a Winckelmann*. Florence: Alinea Editrice, 1985.

Morrogh, Andrew. *Disegni di architetti fiorentini 1540–1640*. Florence: Olschki, 1985.

Mosco, Marilena. "Flora medicea in Florentia." In *Floralia: Florilegio dalle collezioni fiorentine del 600–700*. Edited by Marilena Mosco e Milena Rizzotto. Florence: Centro Di, 1988.

Natali, Antonio. "Cosimo il Vecchio, la campagna e due tracce michelozziane." *Antichità viva* 17, no. 6 (1978): 36–38.

Neubauer, Erika. "The Garden Architecture of Cecil Pinsent, 1884–1864." *Journal of Garden History* 3, no. 1 (1983): 35–48.

Newton, Norman T. "Villa Medici at Fiesole." *Landscape Architecture* 17, no. 3 (April 1927): 185–198.

Nichols, Fred J. "Petrarch Transplants the Muses." *Analecta Romana Studi Danici*, supplement 25 (1998): 61–68.

Nichols, Rose Standish. *Italian Pleasure Gardens*. New York: Dodd, Mead, 1931.

Nolhac, Pierre de. "Pétrarque et son jardin d'après ses notes **inédites**." *Giornale storico della letteratura italiana* 9 (1887): 404–414.

———. "Pétrarque jardinier." In *Pétrarque et l'humanisme*. Vol. 2. Paris: Librairie Honoré Champion, 1965.

Nuvolari, Francesco. *Il giardino storico all'italiana*. Milan: Electa, 1992.

Ojetti, Ugo, ed. *I palazzi e le ville che non sono più dei Re*. Milan: Fratelli Treves, 1921.

Osborne, Robin. "Classical Greek Gardens: Between Farm and Paradise." In *Garden History: Issues, Approaches, Methods*. Edited by John Dixon Hunt. Washington, D.C.: Dumbarton Oaks Research Library and Collection, 1992.

Ottewill, David. "Outdoor Rooms: Houses into Gardens in Britain at the Turn of the Century." In *Cecil Pinsent and His Gardens in Tuscany*. Edited by Marcello Fanton, Heidi Flores, and John Pfordresher. Florence: Edifir, 1996.

Pacciani, Riccardo. "Nuovi rilievi dell'Anfiteatro di Boboli." In *Boboli 90: Atti del Convegno Internazionale di Studi per la salvaguardia e valorizzazione del Giardino*. Edited by Cristina Acidini Luchinat and Elvira Garbero Zorzi. Vol. 2. Florence: Edifir, 1991.

Palagi, Giuseppe. *Della Prioria di San Pietro a Careggi e del sigillo del suo primo rettore: Notizie storiche*. Florence: Tipi dei Successori di Le Monnier, 1871.

Pampaloni, Guido. "Le nozze." In Piero Bargellini et al., *Vita privata a Firenze nei secoli XIV e XV*. Florence: Olschki, 1966.

Panofsky, Erwin. *Idea: A Concept in Art Theory*. 2nd ed. Translated by Joseph J. S. Peake. New York: Harper and Row, 1968.

———. *Studies in Iconology: Humanist Themes in the Art of the Renaissance*. 2nd ed. New York: Harper and Row, 1962.

Paoli, Michel. *L'idée de Nature chez Leon Battista Alberti*. Paris: Editions Honoré Champion, 1999.

Pasolini Ponti, Maria. *Il giardino italiano*. Rome: Ermanno Loescher, 1915.

Pastore Stocchi, Manlio. "La cultura geografica dell'umanesimo." In *Optima Hereditas: Sapienza giuridica romana e conoscenza dell'ecumene*. Milan: Libri Scheiwiller, 1992.

Pelikan, Jaroslav. *The Vindication of Tradition*. New Haven: Yale University Press, 1984.

Perosa, Alessandro. "Note e discussioni: Miscellanea di filologia umanistica." *Rinascita: Rivista del Centro Nazionale di Studi sul Rinascimento* 5 (1942): 323–331.

Petrarca, Francesco. *L'Ascension du Mont Ventoux*. Translated from the Latin by Denis Montebello. Preface by Pierre Dubrunquez. Rezé: Séquences, 1990.

———. *Epistole di Francesco Petrarca*. Edited by Ugo Dotti. Turin: Unione Tipografico-Editrice Torinese, 1978.

———. *Le familiari (libri I–XI)*. 2 vols. Translated by Ugo Dotti. Urbino: Argalia, 1974.

———. "Invectiva contra eum qui maledixit Italie." In *Opere latine*. Edited by Antonietta Bufano. Vol. 2. Turin: Unione Tipografico-Editrice Torinese, 1975.

———. *Laurea occidens: Bucolicum Carmen X*. Edited and translated by Guido Martellotti. Rome: Edizioni di Storia e Letteratura, 1968.

———. *Lettere di Francesco Petrarca: Delle cose familiari libri ventiquattro*. 5 vols. Translated by G. Fracassetti. Florence: Felice Le Monnier, 1865.

———. *Petrarch at Vaucluse: Letters in Verse and Prose*. Edited and translated by Ernst E. Wilkins. Chicago: University of Chicago Press, 1958.

———. *Petrarch's Remedies for Fortune Fair and Foul: A Modern English Translation of De remediis utriusque fortunae*. 5 vols. Translated by Conrad H. Rawski. Bloomington: Indiana University Press, 1991.

———. *Rime, Trionfi e poesie latine*. Edited by F. Neri, G. Martellotti, E. Bianchi, and N. Sapegno. Milan: Riccardo Ricciardi, 1951.

Petrucci, Armando. *La scrittura di Francesco Petrarca*. Vatican City: Biblioteca Apostolica Vaticana, 1967.

Piccolomini, Enea. *Intorno alle condizioni ed alle vicende della libreria medicea privata*. Florence: Cellini, 1875.

Pieraccini, Gaetano. *La stirpe dei Medici di Cafaggiolo*. 3 vols. 2nd ed. Florence: Vallecchi, 1947.

Pieri, Silvio. *Toponomastica della valle dell'Arno*. Rome, 1919. Anastatic reprint, Bologna: Forni, 1985.

Pinsent, Cecil. "Giardini moderni all'italiana, con i fiori che più vi si adattano." *Il giardino fiorito* I, no. 5 (June 1931): 69–73.

Pintor, Fortunato. *La libreria di Cosimo de' Medici nel 1418*. Florence, 1902. Reprint, "Per la storia della libreria medicea nel Rinascimento. Appunti d'archivio. I: La libreria di Cosimo de' Medici nel 1418." *Italia medioevale e umanistica* 3 (1960): 190–199.

Plato. *Plato: Complete Works*. Edited by John Cooper. Indianapolis: Hackett, 1997.

Platt, Charles A. *Italian Gardens*. Portland, Ore.: Sagapress/Timber Press, 1993.

Plesner, Johan F. *L'emigrazione dalle campagne alla città libera di Firenze nel XIII secolo*. Florence: Papafava, 1979.

Pliny the Elder. *Natural History*. 10 vols. Translated by H. Rackham. Loeb Classical Library. Cambridge: Harvard University Press, 1949–1962.

Poliziano, Angelo. *I detti piacevoli*. Edited by Mariano Fresta. Montepulciano, Siena: Editori del Grifo, 1985.

———. *Silvae*. Edited by Francesco Bausi. Florence: Olschki, 1996.

Pozzana, Mariachiara. "Il giardino del Trebbio." In *Giardini medicei: Giardini di palazzo e di villa nella Firenze del Quattrocento*. Edited by Cristina Acidini Luchinat. Florence: Federico Motta Editore, 1996.

Rad, Gerhard von. *Genesis: A Commentary*. Translated by John H. Marks. Philadelphia: Westminster Press, 1961.

Razzi, Silvano. *Vite di cinque uomini illustri*. Florence: Giusti, 1602.

Real Galleria di Firenze. *Indice geografico-analitico dei disegni di architettura civile e militare esistenti nella Reale Galleria degli Uffizi in Firenze*. Rome: Presso i principali librai, 1885.

Recchi, Mario. "La villa e il giardino nel concetto della Rinascenza italiana." *Critica d'arte* 2 (1937): 131–137.

Repetti, Emanuele. *Dizionario geografico, fisico, storico della Toscana.* 6 vols. Florence: Repetti, 1833–1846. Anastatic reprint. Rome: Multigrafica, 1972.

Riccio, Agostino del. "Agricultura sperimentale ridotta a teorica." Targioni Tozzetti 56, vol. 3, fols. 104r-234v. Biblioteca Nazionale Centrale, Florence.

Roscoe, William. *Life of Lorenzo de' Medici called the Magnificent.* 3 vols. Philadelphia: Bronson & Chauncey, 1803.

Ross, Janet. *Florentine Villas.* London: J. M. Dent; New York: Dutton, 1901.

Rossi, Vittorio. *L'indole e gli studi di Giovanni di Cosimo de' Medici.* Rendiconti dell'Accademia dei Lincei. Classe di scienze morali, storiche e filologiche, no. 5, vol. 2. Rome: L'Accademia, 1893.

Rosso, Giuseppe del. *Guida di Fiesole e suoi dintorni.* Florence: Luigi Pezzati, 1846.

Rucellai, Giovanni. *Giovanni Rucellai ed il suo Zibaldone.* 2 vols. Edited by Alessandro Perosa. London: Warburg Institute, University of London, 1960–1981.

Rupprecht, Bernhard. "Villa: Zur Geschichte eines Ideals." In *Wandlungen des Paradiesischen und Utopischen: Studien zum Bild Eines Ideals.* Edited by H. Bauer et al. Berlin: Walter de Gruyter, 1966.

Saalman, Howard. *Filippo Brunelleschi: The Cupola of Santa Maria del Fiore.* London: A. Zwemmer, 1980.

Said, Edward W. *Beginnings: Intention and Method.* New York: Columbia University Press, 1975.

Santoni, Luigi. *Raccolta di notizie storiche riguardanti le chiese dell'arci-diocesi di Firenze.* Florence: Mazzoni, 1847. Anastatic reprint, Bologna: Forni, 1974.

Scotti, Aurora. "Giardini fiorentini e torinesi fra '500 e '600: Loro struttura e significato." *L'Arte* 2, no. 6 (1969): 36–55.

Serlio, Sebastiano. *De architectura.* Venice: De Franciscis, 1569.

Shepherd, John C., and Geoffrey Jellicoe. *Italian Gardens of the Renaissance.* New York: Princeton Architectural Press, 1993.

Sitwell, George. *On the Making of Gardens.* 1909. Reprint, with a foreword by John Dixon Hunt. Boston: David R. Godine, 2003.

Soderini, Giovanvettorio. *I due trattati dell'Agricoltura e della coltivazione delle viti.* Vol. 1 of *Le opere di Giovanni Vettorio Soderini.* Edited by Alberto Bacchi della Lega. Bologna: Romagnoli Dall'Acqua, 1902.

Spallanzani, Marco, and Giovanni Gaeta Bertelai. *Libro d'inventario dei beni di Lorenzo il Magnifico.* Florence: Studio per Edizioni Scelte, 1992.

Steenbergen, Clemens, and Wouter Reh. *Architecture and Landscape: The Design Experiment of the Great European Gardens and Landscapes.* Bussum, Netherlands: Thoth, 1996.

Taegio, Bartolomeo. *La villa.* Milan: Moscheni, 1559.

Tagliolini, Alessandro. "Firenzuola e il giardino nelle fonti della metà del '500." In *Il giardino storico italiano: Problemi di indagine, fonti letterarie e storiche.* Edited by Giovanna Ragionieri. Florence: Olschki, 1981.

———. *Storia del giardino italiano: Gli artisti, l'invenzione, le forme, dall'antichità al XIX secolo.* 1988. Reprint, Florence: La Casa Usher, 1994.

Tagliolini, Alessandro, and Massimo Venturi Ferriolo, eds. *Il giardino: Idea, natura, realtà.* Milan: Guerini, 1987.

Tanzer, Helen H. *The Villas of Pliny the Younger.* New York: Columbia University Press, 1924.

Tarassi, Massimo. "Il committente: La famiglia Medici dalle origini al Quattrocento." In *Il palazzo Medici Riccardi di Firenze.* Edited by G. Cherubini and G. Fanelli. Florence: Giunti, 1990.

Tommaseo, Niccolò. *Dizionario della lingua italiana.* 4 vols. Turin: Unione Tipografico-Editrice Torinese, 1865–1879.

Tongiorgi Tomasi, Lucia. "Il giardino, l'orto e il frutteto. Le scienze orticole in Toscana nei disegni, tempere e incisioni dal XVI al XVIII secolo." In *"Flora e pomona": L'orticoltura nei disegni e nelle incisioni dei secoli XVI–XIX.* Edited by Lucia Tongiorgi Tomasi and Alessandro Tosi. Florence: Olschki, 1990.

———. "Projects for Botanical and Other Gardens: A 16th-Century Manual." *Journal of Garden History* 3, no. 1 (1983): 1–34.

Torre, Arnaldo della. "La prima ambasceria di Bernardo Bembo a Firenze." *Giornale storico della letteratura italiana* 35 (1900): 258–333.

———. *Storia dell'Accademia Platonica di Firenze.* Florence: Tipografia G. Carnesecchi, 1902.

Tosi, Alessandro. "Fruit and Flower Gardens from the Neoclassical and Romantic Periods in Tuscany." In *The Italian Garden: Art, Design and Culture.* Edited by John Dixon Hunt. Cambridge: Cambridge University Press, 1996.

Trapp, Joseph B. "The Iconography of Petrarch in the Age of Humanism." *Quaderni petrarcheschi* 9–10 (1992–1993): 11–73.

Triggs, Harry Inigo. *The Art of Garden Design in Italy.* London: Longmans, Green, 1906.

Tristano, Caterina. "Le postille del Petrarca nel Vaticano Lat. 2193 (Apuleio, Frontino, Vegezio, Palladio)." *Italia medioevale e umanistica* 17 (1974): 365–468.

Vasari, Giorgio. *Le vite de' più eccellenti pittori, scultori e architettori.* 9 vols. Edited by Gaetano Milanesi. Florence: G. C. Sansoni, 1878–1885.

Vasari il Giovane, Giorgio. *La città ideale: Piante di chiese [palazzi e ville] di Toscana e d'Italia.* Edited by Virginia Stefanelli. Rome: Officina Edizioni, 1970.

Vasoli, Cesare. "Michelozzo e la cultura fiorentina del suo tempo." In *Michelozzo: Scultore e architetto (1396–1472).* Edited by Gabriele Morolli. Florence: Centro Di, 1998.

———. *Tra "maestri" umanisti e teologi: Studi quattrocenteschi.* Florence: Le Lettere, 1991.

Vattasso, Marco. "Brevi note del Petrarca sull'orticoltura." In *I codici petrarcheschi della biblioteca vaticana.* Rome: Tipografia Poliglotta Vaticana, 1908.

Vegio, Maffeo. *Maphei Vegii Laudensis de educatione liberorum et eorum claris moribus libri sex: A Critical Text of Books IV–VI.* Edited by Sister Anne Stanislaus Sullivan. Washington, D.C.: Catholic University of America, 1936.

Venturi, Gianni. "Picta poesis: Ricerche sulla poesia e il giardino dalle origini al Seicento." In *Il paesaggio.* Edited by Cesare De Seta. Vol. 5 of *Storia d'Italia: Annali,* edited by Ruggiero Romano and Corrado Vivanti. Turin: Einaudi, 1982.

Vercelloni, Virgilio. "Attorno alla banalità dell'attenzione italiana al giardino negli anni trenta." In *Il giardino europeo del Novecento 1900–1940: Atti del III Colloquio Internazionale Pietrasanta, 27–28 settembre 1991.* Edited by Alessandro Tagliolini. Florence: Edifir, 1993.

Vespasiano da Bisticci. *Le vite.* 2 vols. Edited by Aulo Greco. Florence: Istituto Nazionale di Studi sul Rinascimento, 1976.

Villa, Claudia. "Per una lettura della 'Primavera': Mercurio 'retrogrado' e la Retorica nella Bottega di Botticelli." *Strumenti critici* 13, no. 1 (January 1998): 1–28.

Villani, Giovanni. *Cronica fiorentina.* Florence, 1537.

Virgil (Publius Vergilius Maro). *Le Georgiche.* Edited and translated by Egisto Gerunzi. Florence: Sansoni, 1921.

Viti, Vincenzo. *La Badia Fiesolana: Pagine di storia e d'arte.* Florence: Giuntina, 1926.

Vodoz, Eduard. "Studien zum architektonischen Werk des Bartolomeo Amannati." *Mitteilungen des Kunsthistorischen Instituts in Florenz* 7 (July–December 1941): 35-58.

Volpi, Guglielmo. *Le feste di Firenze: Notizia di un poemetto del secolo XV.* Pistoia: Libreria Pagnini, 1902.

Waldburg, Franz von. "Appunti sui giardini fiorentini del tardo Settecento e del primo Ottocento." In *Il giardino storico italiano: Problemi di indagine, fonti letterarie e storiche.* Edited by Giovanna Ragionieri. Florence: Olschki, 1981.

Watson, Paul F. *The Garden of Love in Tuscan Art of the Early Renaissance.* Philadelphia: Art Alliance Press, 1979.

Weiss, Allen. *Unnatural Horizons: Paradox and Contradiction in Landscape Architecture.* New York: Princeton Architectural Press, 1998.

Wharton, Edith. *Italian Villas and Their Gardens.* 1904. Reprint, with introductory notes by Arthur Ross, Henry Hope Reed, and Thomas S. Hayes. New York: Da Capo Press, 1988.

Wilkins, Ernest Hatch. *Life of Petrarch.* Chicago: University of Chicago Press, 1961.

———. *Petrarch at Vaucluse: Letters in Verse and Prose.* Chicago: University of Chicago Press, 1958.

Wright, D. R. Edward. "The Boboli Garden in the Evolution of European Garden Design: A Study in Practical Function and Organizing Structure." In *Boboli 90: Atti del Convegno Internazionale di Studi per la salvaguardia e valorizzazione del Giardino.* Edited by Cristina Acidini Luchinat and Elvira Garbero Zorzi. Vol 1. Florence: Edifir, 1991.

———. "The Medici Villa at Olmo a Castello: Its History and Iconography." 2 vols. Ph.D. diss., Princeton University, 1976.

———. "Some Medici Gardens of the Florentine Renaissance: An Essay in Post-Aesthetic Interpretation." In *The Italian Garden: Art, Design and Culture.* Edited by John Dixon Hunt. Cambridge: Cambridge University Press, 1996.

Zangheri, Luigi. "Le 'piante de' condotti' dei giardini di Castello e Petraia." *Bollettino degli ingegneri* 19, 2–3 (1971): 19–26.

————. "Vasari e la Grotta Grande." In *Boboli 90: Atti del Convegno Internazionale di Studi per la salvaguardia e valorizzazione del Giardino.* Edited by Cristina Acidini Luchinat and Elvira Garbero Zorzi. Vol. 2. Florence: Edifir, 1991.

————. *Ville della provincia di Firenze.* Milan: Rusconi, 1989.

Zaninelli, Sergio, ed. *Scritti teorici e tecnici di agricoltura.* 3 vols. Milan: Il Polifilo, 1995.

Zocchi, Giuseppe. *Vedute delle ville, e d'altri luoghi della Toscana.* Florence: G. Bouchard, 1744.

PHOTOGRAPHIC ACKNOWLEDGMENTS

For permission to publish illustrations in this book I wish to thank the following: American Academy in Rome: 36, 38; Archivio Storico Comunale in Florence: 2; Bibliothèque Nationale de France, Paris: 41, 44; British Library, London: 39; Fratelli Alinari: 7; Kunsthistorisches Institut in Florenz: 19; Donata Mazzini and Centro Di for illustrations from Donata Mazzini, ed., *Villa Medici a Fiesole: Leon Battista Alberti e il prototipo di villa rinascimentale* (Florence: Centro Di, 2004): 22, 35; Arnaud for an illustration from Daniela Mignani, *Le ville medicee di Giusto Utens* (Florence: Arnaud, 1993): 3; Ministero dei Beni e le Attività Culturali, Italy, and Direzione Cultura del Comune di Firenze: 4, 5, 8–11, 13–17, 34, 37, 43, 45, 47–50, 52–54; National Gallery of Victoria, Melbourne: 46; Scala Archives/Art Resource, New York: 6, 12, 20, 40, 42, 51; Servizio Musei Comunali, Florence: 18. Luigi Pezzati for Telemaco Bonaiuti, *Veduta della Villa Mozzi, già de' Medici*, in Giuseppe del Rosso, *Guida di Fiesole e suoi dintorni* (Florence: Luigi Pezzati, 1846): 21.

All photographs not otherwise acknowledged are by the author.

INDEX

Page references in italics refer to illustrations.

academia, 51
Accademici della Crusca, 20, 212n.65
Ackerman, James, 83, 224n.170, 233n.248
Acton, Arthur, 4
Adimari, Boccaccio, 157, *157*
aesthetics: and modern reading of Crescenzi, 90, 95, 239–40n.14; modern view of beauty vs. goodness, 91, 240n.19; origins of, 92; origins of aesthetic appreciation of gardens, 95, 246–47n.41; and pleasure, 90–91; Pre-Raphaelite aesthetic, 2
Agnoletti, Bice, 42, 222n.156
Agostino del Riccio: "Agricultura sperimentale," 168–70, 266n.86, 268n.97; "Agricultura teorica," 168, 266n.86; at Santa Maria Novella, 180
agriculture: Cicero on, 34–35; ethical values associated with, 34, 37, 91, 115; handbooks on, 98 (*see also* manuals on garden making); as a mechanical art, 241–42n.31; and religion, 91, 241n.20; specialization and diversification of products, 40; techniques for, 27–29; writings on, 88–95, 161
Alamanni, Luigi: *Coltivazione,* 162, 263n.55
Albergotti, Colonel, 233n.244
Alberti, Leon Battista, 97; and Braccesi, 222n.158; *De familia,* 242–43n.42; *De re aedificatoria,* 93–94, 171, 237n.276, 241n.30, 242n.33; *Villa,* 34, 40, 217n.110, 242–43n.42
Aleotti, Giovan Battista, 160–61
Alessandri, Maria Ginevra degli, 56, 70, 215n.100
Allen, Michael, 141, 255n.143
Ammannati, Bartolomeo, 159
amphitheaters, 158–61, 262n.43

amplificatio, 43
animal spirit, 136, 252n.122
Apollo, 110–11
architecture, 5, 88, 93
Argyropoulos, John, 226n.191
aridulum rus, 109–11
Aristotle, 226n.191
armatura, 93, 241–42n.31
Armour, Peter, 266n.84
Artimino, 11, *12*
art of gardens: Ferrari on, 161–62, 175–78, 271n.125; vs. garden as work of nature, 95–96, 143; geometric topiary, 3; in poetry and painting, 115–16; vs. practice, xi, 88 (*see also* design of gardens); vs. technique, 167
Augustine, Saint: *Confessions,* 105–6, 253n.128; *De civitate Dei,* 107; *De vera religione,* 105, 107, 245n.20
Augustus, 155
Avicenna: *Liber canonis,* 92
Avignon, 109–10
Avogadro da Vercelli, Alberto, 24, 31, 42–44, 80, 184, 215n.96, 222–23n.159
Avril, François, 247n.43

Bacchi della Lega, Alberto, 270n.114
Bacchus (Liber), 110–11, 137, 253n.126
Baccini, Giuseppe, 10
Badia Fiesolana (Fiesole), 79–82, 235–36nn.266–267, 236n.269
Bandini, Angelo Maria, 53–55
banquets, 156
Barberini, Francesco, 180
Bargellini, Clara, 64, 82, 232–33n.244
Battisti, Eugenio, 244–45n.13